W. B. YEATS

SELECTED CRITICISM AND PROSE

William Butler Yeats, son of the painter J. B. Yeats, was born near Dublin in 1865. In his twenties he became interested in occultism and theosophy, and began writing plays, ballads and poetry. He wrote many of his plays for the Abbey Theatre, the Irish national theatre he had helped to found. Though never abandoning symbolism, Yeats's later poetry became increasingly hard-edged and realistic. His later work also included *A Vision* — his philosophical treatise — and three volumes of autobiography. W. B. Yeats was awarded the Nobel Prize in 1923 and died in 1939 in the South of France. His grave is near Sligo, Ireland.

Also available in Pan Books

W. B. Yeats Selected Plays
W. B. Yeats Selected Poetry

W. B. YEATS

SELECTED CRITICISM AND PROSE

edited with an introduction and notes
by A. Norman Jeffares, Professor of English Literature,
University of Stirling

Pan Books
in association with
Macmillan London

This selection first published 1964 as two
separate volumes by Macmillan and Co. Ltd
and subsequently published 1976 in two volumes by Pan Books Ltd
This collected edition published 1980
by Pan Books Ltd, Cavaye Place, London SW10 9PG
in association with Macmillan London Ltd
Selection and editorial matter © A. Norman Jeffares 1980
Select bibliography © A. Norman Jeffares 1970
ISBN 0 330 26270 X
Printed and bound in Great Britain by
Richard Clay (The Chaucer Press) Ltd, Bungay, Suffolk

CONTENTS

ACKNOWLEDGEMENTS

THE editor and publishers wish to acknowledge their indebtedness to the following, who have kindly given permission for the use of copyright material: the Clarendon Press, Oxford, for the extract from the introduction to *The Oxford Book of Modern Verse*; Rupert Hart-Davis Ltd, for the letters from *The Letters of W. B. Yeats*, edited by Allan Wade; Harvard University Press, for 'The Irish National Literary Society', from *Letters to the New Island*; the Controller, the Stationery Office, Dublin, for 'What We Did or Tried to Do', from *Coinage of Saorstát Éireann;* and Faber and Faber Ltd, for 'Copyright Protection' and 'The Child and the State', from *The Senate Speeches of W. B. Yeats*, edited by Donald R. Pearce.

INTRODUCTION

When Yeats wrote in old age, in the poem 'What then?', that he had crammed his twenties with toil, he was in no way exaggerating. He was twenty in 1885, and in that year the *Dublin University Review* began to publish his poetry; his first prose, enthusiastic reactions to Sir Samuel Ferguson's poetry, appeared a year later. His long career as a writer was to last till his death in 1939 at the age of seventy-three. Though we think of him primarily as a poet, and following that as a playwright, his prose writing is extensive. Yeats wrote articles, reviews, introductions, prefaces, reports, criticism, stories, novels, philosophy, letters and autobiography. Within this wide range there is much diversity, for his prose altered in style, in subject matter, as he developed and so remarkably 'remade' himself.

He grew up in a milieu where discussion and criticism were a natural part of life. His father the artist John Butler Yeats (1839–1922) was a superb conversationalist, a man of ideas with strong views about literature. When the family lived at Howth, then a fishing village north of Dublin, father and son travelled to Dublin by train, walked through the city to the painter's studio in York Street and breakfasted there before the son went the short distance up Harcourt Street to the High School founded by Erasmus Smith. Over breakfast the painter read aloud passages from his favourite poets, seeking the most passionate moments in play or poem because he disliked overmuch reliance upon intellect, and thought contemplative men overrated their way of living. He challenged accepted ideas, enjoyed argument, and used exagger-

ation gaily. Pre-Raphaelite in taste, he disliked the Victorians'
poetry of ideas, and persuaded his son to admire Balzac and
Shakespeare. Spenser and Jonson, Shelley and Keats were, at
this stage, the main influence on the schoolboy, who had
become an art student as he wrote his pastoral play *The
Island of Statues*.

About the time of its publication Yeats came in touch with
John O'Leary, a former Fenian who had returned from exile
in Paris to Ireland in 1884, and it was O'Leary who introduced
the patriotic rhetoric of the young Ireland poets of the 1840s
to him. Yeats had found for himself Standish O'Grady's
treatment of Irish heroic legends. He was equipped now with
the making of a new mythology; he moved on from his
father's belief in Home Rule to a nationalism made more
intense by his falling in love with Maud Gonne in 1889.
Though he had veered from his father's views — John Butler
Yeats was a rationalist and a firm follower of John Stuart
Mill — and had begun to steep himself in psychical research
and mystical philosophy yet he was none the less deeply
impressed by his father's insistence on the need for the artist
to be true to himself and his vision, rejecting the practical
problems of getting on in life.

Money, however, had to be found, and the poet found it,
in pitiably small quantities, in occasional journalism. He wrote
on Irish topics, reviewing Irish literature and putting his views
on nationalism and literature strongly. The *Irish Fireside* and
the *Jael* took his pieces, and through O'Leary he began to
contribute to two American journals, the *Boston Pilot* and
Providence Sunday Journal. (These contributions have been
reprinted as *Letters to the New Island, 1934*, and are included in
Uncollected Prose by W. B. Yeats, Volume One, ed. John P.
Frayne, 1970.) After this came work for the *Scots Observer*,
edited by W. E. Henley, and then Yeats gradually found his

way on to the pages of the *Nation, National Observer, United Ireland, Bookman, Speaker* and *Academy*. In his first ten years of writing critical and journalistic articles he wrote about the following Irish writers: Sir Samuel Ferguson, R. D. Joyce, James Clarence Mangan, William Allingham, John Todhunter, William Carleton, the Banim brothers, Jeremiah Curtin, Lady Wilde, Douglas Hyde, Rose Kavanagh, Ellen O'Leary, Oscar Wilde, Standish O'Grady, William Larminie, AE (George Russell), Thomas Davis and John Eglinton. He also discussed the aims and activities of Irish writers in London, and explained the purposes of the London Irish Literary Society and the National Literary Society. His creative energy and vision were bringing the literary movement known as the Irish Literary Renaissance or the Celtic Revival into being. He was a controversialist, propagandist and educator. His early critical articles were at first fairly simply written, with a gentle, even wistful missionary zeal, but his style altered rather as his poetry did, moving from local subjects in Sligo to the material of the Irish legends, from folklore to symbolism. Thus by 1894 he was reviewing a performance in Paris of Villiers de l'Isle-Adam's *Axel*, and in the next two years was criticizing books by Arthur Symons and Maeterlinck, and writing on Verlaine and on Blake.

This literary journalism occupied a lot of time but it aided Yeats's self-education in Irish literature and it did not hinder his exploration of his own character in the novel *John Sherman and Dhoya* (1891) set in the West of Ireland. He selected and edited *Fairy and Folk Tales of the Irish Peasantry* (1888), *Stories from Carleton* (1889) and *Representative Irish Tales* (1891). *The Celtic Twilight* (1893) was an original work, which included some material from *Fairy and Folk Tales of the Irish Peasantry* as well as essays previously published in journals, and it gave a name to the literary movement. The book corresponded to

Yeats's early poetry in its aims of portraying the traditional
beliefs and scenery of the West of Ireland. In 1895 Yeats
selected poems for *A Book of Irish Verse*, having earlier contributed to *Poems and Ballads of Young Ireland* (1888). By 1897,
with the publication of the stories of *The Secret Rose*, Yeats's
prose style matched the complexity of the symbolic poems
that he collected together in the volume of *The Wind among
the Reeds* (1899). Yeats wrote the stories of *The Secret Rose*,
as he put it later, 'in that artificial elaborate English so many of
us played with in the nineties'. This prose, reminiscent of
Pater and Wilde, reached its most decorative, most mannered,
most elaborate expression in 'The Autumn of the Body', an
essay of 1898. Here there is virtually an incantatory quality
about the wistful writing: 'Man has wooed and won the
world, and has fallen weary, and not, I think, for a time but
with a weariness that will not end until the last autumn,
when the stars shall be blown away like withered leaves . . .'
There is an insistence upon the role of the arts, which were,
he believed, about to take upon their shoulders the burdens
that had fallen from the shoulders of priests, 'to lead us back
upon our journey by filling our thoughts with the essences of
things and not with things'.

In 'The Symbolism of Poetry' of 1900 he was still flowing,
almost ritualistic in his cadences:

> With this change of substance, this return to imagination,
> this understanding that the laws of art, which are the
> hidden laws of the world, can alone bind the imagination,
> would come a change of style, and we would cast out of
> serious poetry those energetic rhythms, as of a man run-
> ning, which are the invention of the will with its eyes
> always on something to be done or undone; and we would
> seek out those wavering, meditative organic rhythms,

which are the embodiment of the imagination, that neither desires nor hates, because it has done with time and only wishes to gaze upon some reality, some beauty; nor would it be any longer possible for anybody to deny the importance of form, in all its kinds, for although you can expound an opinion or describe a thing, when your words are not quite well chosen you cannot give a body to something that moves beyond the senses, unless your words are as subtle, as complex, as full of mysterious life, as the body of a flower or of a woman.

He preached a return to imagination; he sought 'wavering meditative organic rhythms that were the embodiment of the imagination'. The prose, however, was beginning to become more direct in his essay on 'The Philosophy of Shelley's Poetry' of 1900, in which he was exploring Shelley's continually repeated symbols. Yeats was very forthright indeed in his essay on magic, published in 1901, linking the conscious use made of symbols by the masters of magic with the half-conscious use employed by poets, musicians and artists. He believed, he wrote, in the practice and philosophy of magic:

in what I must call the evocation of spirits, though I do not know what they are, in the power of creating magical illusions, in the visions of truth in the depths of the mind when the eyes are closed; and I believe in three doctrines, which have, as I think, been handed down from early times, and been the foundations of nearly all magical practices. These doctrines are:

1) That the borders of our mind are ever shifting, and that many minds can flow into one another, as it were, and create or reveal a single mind, a single energy.

2) That the borders of our memories are as shifting, and

that our memories are a part of one great memory, the memory of Nature herself.

3) That this great mind and great memory can be evoked by symbols.

After the turn of the century Yeats's poetry was no longer restricted to subjects of beauty; indeed a bitter note had entered it after the shock of Maud Gonne's marriage in 1903. Yeats came back into contact with the speech of Irish country people during the summers he spent at Coole Park from 1897 onwards. His prose became stronger, simpler, much more direct, and his Introduction to an edition of Spenser of 1906 exhibits a greater ease and confidence. In his comments on Shakespeare in an essay on Stratford-on-Avon his prose takes on the quality of good lively talk, with wide ranging wit and anecdotal humour balancing his appreciation of Shakespeare and his place in English literary tradition. Yeats was, however, at his best when writing of Irish matter, and two essays in particular, 'The Galway Plains' and 'Dust hath closed Helen's Eye', show the effect of his friendship with Lady Gregory on his prose style and on his new Galway subject matter.

His prose writings in the nineties had centred upon the creation of an Irish literary movement. The next objective was the creation of an Irish national theatre. Out of the struggle to achieve this came some of Yeats's most original criticism, written less under the immediate pressures of journalism, more through a compulsion to set his own thoughts upon theatre into order, to test out the convictions he was forming as a result of seeing his characters in action on the stage. His 'First Principles' of 1904 has a buoyant feeling about it, a confidence that Ireland would remake its image of itself. The ideals Yeats puts forward, however, have to be defended. Our friends, he says, tell us that we have no right to name 'because we do not write in Irish, and others because we do not plead the National cause in our plays, as if we were writers for the newspapers'.

For ten years Yeats expressed his views on drama, and the essays written between 1899 and 1909 for *Beltaine*, *Samhain* and the *Arrow*, occasional publications issued by the Abbey Theatre, reveal him as more aware of the audience, more experienced as a result of his increasingly practical knowledge of 'theatre business, management of men'. As a result Yeats's criticism gains in assurance, indeed where his discerning praise of Synge's work was concerned (in prefaces to volumes of Synge's work, and the essay on 'J. M. Synge and the Ireland of his Time'), in authority.

In Synge and especially in Lady Gregory he had found friends who shared his beliefs and his experience in fighting for the kind of theatre they wanted; but the theatre did not follow the path he had hoped for it. He was able, however, to view this development of the Abbey with detachment in 'A People's Theatre' written in 1919, perhaps because he had begun to write, in *The Plays for Dancers*, a different kind of drama for a smaller audience. His lecture on 'The Irish Dramatic Movement' delivered in Sweden when he was awarded the Nobel Prize in 1923 has the benefit of distance. In it he celebrates what the theatre had achieved in the face of financial and political difficulties; and this is a theme to which he reverted later in the retrospective reveries prompted by a visit to the Dublin Municipal Art Gallery:

John Synge, I and Augusta Gregory, thought
All that we did, all that we said or sang
Must come from contact with the soil, from that
Contact everything Antaeus-like grew strong.
We three alone in modern times had brought

Everything down to that sole test again,
Dream of the noble and the beggar-man.

While fighting for the theatre and trying to educate an
audience worthy of its aims Yeats was also occupied in the
first decade of the century with fighting within the Order of
the Golden Dawn, the magical order which he had joined
some years previously, and with trying to piece together the
ideas he developed from his extensive reading in the occult
writers, producing *Per Amica Silentia Lunae* in 1918. Here,
too, are subjective meditations upon the nature of literary art,
given arresting expression in memorable phrases: 'We make
out of the quarrel with others, rhetoric, but of the quarrel
with ourselves, poetry', 'The poet finds and makes his mask
in disappointment, the hero in defeat', or 'A poet when he is
growing old will ask himself if he cannot keep his mask and
his vision without new bitterness, new disappointment.'
These essays contain ideas on the 'mask', on the self and anti-
self, the daimon. They are later given fuller utterance, sometimes more elegant, sometimes more gnomic, in *A Vision*
(1926). They can be supplemented by entries in the Journal he
began in 1908 (included in *Memoirs*, ed. Denis Donoghue,
1972), often germs of later writing, or ideas worked up later
in more polished form, but fascinating in their direct —
'quite frank', in his own words — recording of experiences
that went to the making of later prose and verse: 'Why is
life a perpetual preparation for something that never happens?'
Yeats was moving to more personal revelation. There is,
for instance, the moving description of happiness (echoed
much later in the poem 'Vacillation') contained in

At certain moments, always unforeseen, I became happy,
most commonly when at hazard I have opened some book
of verse. Sometimes it is my own verse when, instead of

discovering new technical flaws, I read with all the excitement of the first writing. Perhaps I am sitting in some crowded restaurant, the open book beside me, or closed, my excitement having overbrimmed the page. I look at the strangers near as if I had known them all my life, and it seems strange that I cannot speak to them: everything fills me with affection, I have no longer any fears or needs; I do not even remember that this happy mood must come to an end. It seems as if the vehicle had suddenly grown pure and far extended and so luminous that the images from *Anima Mundi*, embodied there and drunk with that sweetness, would, like a country drunkard who has thrown a wisp into his own thatch, burn up time.

The Cuala Press published the first volume of Yeats's *Autobiographies*, *Reveries over Childhood and Youth*, in 1916; he began to write it in January 1914 and finished it on Christmas Day that year. Yeats's turning to autobiography was in part prompted by George Moore's *Ave* (1911) and, after its initial appearance in the *English Review* in 1914, *Salve* (1912) — though Yeats's reply to Moore did not appear until 1935 with the publication of *Dramatis Personae*. What Yeats was doing in his autobiographical writing was selecting, defining, shaping and interpreting events; making them match his mythologizing needs and instincts; selecting crucial moments in the lives of men and women where the meaning of those lives is clear against the backdrop of history — and his own life. This autobiographical writing, richly patterned and evocative in its details, conveys a sense of the uniqueness of Yeats's experience, of his family's diversity and originality. He does not want to be labelled; and so he emphasizes the dramatic nature of childhood in Sligo, his sense of alienation from his English school fellows, his divided attitude to the

Anglo-Irish from whom he came, his discovery of the Irish nationalists, his development among followers of Pre-Raphaelite traditions, decadent poets of the nineties and eccentric members of heterodox religious, magical or occult groups. Always he chooses the moment, the image which illuminates, and presents what seems the essential; a method deriving from his earlier symbolist's searching for essences.

In the 1920s, under the stimulus of writing *A Vision*, of 'getting it all in order', he read history and philosophy with an excitement which is clearly conveyed in his letters. Yeats was a prolific letter-writer; his letters record his preoccupations, above all the energetic quality of his mind. Early letters written to Katharine Tynan, for instance, convey his enthusiasm; his hopes and his ideas flowed when he felt his audience was sympathetic. Yeats's letters to Maud Gonne have not survived, but those he wrote to Mrs Shakespear provide an unreserved running-commentary on his life. These are written out of a secure confidence in the recipient's interest in his thoughts and reflections, his reading and writing, his preoccupations and plans, his doings and the drama of others' lives as well. As a young man Yeats preferred talking to women, and he wrote better, livelier, less inhibited letters to women than to men, though his letters to his father (himself an often brilliant and original correspondent) were conversational rather than confidential, and reveal his readiness to exchange views, to explain, to argue — and to persuade, as in the letter urging his father to write *his* autobiography.

A Vision, first published in 1926 and in revised form in 1937, contained his 'system', a means of seeing history in terms of 'gyres', two-thousand-year periods ushered in by some revelation, only to be reversed in the succeeding gyre, itself announced by another revelation. The prose is complementary to the great poems Yeats wrote in his fifties and sixties, 'The

Second Coming' for instance, 'Sailing to Byzantium' and
'Byzantium'. But many of his finest poems are constructed
from the scaffolding of *A Vision*, which is itself of interest
for its rich synthesis of Yeats's speculation and his searching
among the mystical writers, Swedenborg, Boehme, Blake
and the neo-Platonists, among the writings of occultists,
magicians and spiritualists, of the Cabbala, of Rosicrucianism
and of Theosophy. To this reading in the occult and heterodox
traditions dating back to his schooldays Yeats added in the
twenties the exploration of his own literary inheritance: the
Anglo-Irish writers whom he now began to read with excitement: Swift and Goldsmith, the philosophy of Bishop
Berkeley and the political wisdom of Edmund Burke.

His delight in the direct speech of his Anglo-Irish literary
forbears now blended effectively with the Paterian involution
of his nineteenth-century prose and the pungency which
public controversy had sharpened over the years. His experience of public life, crowned by his becoming a Senator of the
Irish Free State, demanded strength and simplicity, but he
could — as in, say, *The Bounty of Sweden* (1925) — use richness
of imagery freely. His speeches in the Senate — carefully
rehearsed — were intended as dignified representations of the
role of the arts in the nascent Free State; they are full of
common sense, shot through with some trenchant irony. His
speeches, occasional articles and such essays as the Introduction
to his play *The Words upon the Window-Pane*, included in
Wheels and Butterflies (1934), are part of a continuous process
of self-explanation. Yeats had the confidence as he grew older
to rely less upon the citing of authorities, to avoid an earlier
need for mystery in order to seem wise. Still grandiloquent,
still given to rhetorical flourishes, he wrote emotively, his
prose full of vigour and his ideas intended, at times, to shock
his readers. He could indulge himself in malice, for instance in

his long delayed reply to George Moore in *Dramatis Personae*. His broadcast talks blended a conversational tone with a touch of the authority he had achieved by long meditation upon the nature of literary creativity, an authority which informs his General Introduction to his work.

Yeats's treatment of other writers who had stimulated him was warmly appreciative; his admiration appears in his Introductions to the work of his friends, Lady Gregory, Douglas Hyde, J. M. Synge and Oliver St John Gogarty, of Tagore and Shri Purohit Swami, of J. M. Hone and Mario Rossi, of Arland Ussher, of Dorothy Wellesley and Margot Ruddock. He could at times be over-mannered in style; he could also be over-generous in praising the work of his friends, annoying many by his Introduction to and selection of *The Oxford Book of Modern Verse* (1936). Yeats obviously enjoyed himself in the often prejudiced, often provocative essays of *On the Boiler* (1939), with an obvious touch of the 'wild old man' about them. No need now for allusive, decorative effects; clarity and strength make his prose arresting, an apt means of putting his ideas forward with panache.

W. B. YEATS
SELECTED CRITICISM

THE IRISH NATIONAL LITERARY SOCIETY

YOUR Celt has written the greater bulk of his letters from the capitol of the enemy, but he is now among his own people again, and no longer The Celt in London, but The Celt in Ireland. At this moment he is sitting writing, or trying to write, in the big, florid new National Library with its stone balcony, where nobody is allowed to walk, and its numberless stone niches, in which there will never be any statues. He is sitting dreaming much, and writing a little from time to time, watching the people come and go, and wondering what shall be born of the new generation that is now so very busy reading endless scholasticisms along the five rows of oak tables. An old fairy tale which exists in many forms in many countries tells of a giant whose life was hidden away in an egg, which was in its turn hid in the mouth of a fish, or some such unlikely place. The library is just such an egg, for it hides under its white curved ceiling a good portion of the scholastic life of student Dublin. Here they come to read for examinations, and to work up their various subjects. At my left hand is a man reading some registers of civil service or other examinations; opposite me an ungainly young man with a puzzled face is turning over the pages of a trigonometry work; and a little beyond him a medical student is deep in anatomical diagrams. On all sides men are studying the things that are to get them bodily food, but no man among them is searching for the imaginative and spiritual food to be got out of great literature. Nobody, with the exception of a few ladies, perhaps, ever seems to do any disinterested reading in this library, or indeed anywhere else in

Ireland. Every man here is grinding at the mill wherein he grinds all things into pounds and shillings, and but few of them will he get when all is done. Ireland, half through her own fault and half through circumstances over which she has no control, is not a reading nation, nor has she been so for many a long day. A single town in Scotland is said to buy more books than all Ireland put together, and surely nowhere out of Ireland will you find a great library like this given over completely to the student cramming for examinations.

Can we find a remedy? Can we not unite literature to the great passion of patriotism and ennoble both thereby? This question has occupied a good many of us this spring. We think that a national literary society and a series of national books like Duffy's Library of Ireland may do something, and have accordingly founded such a society and planned out, with the help of a number of well known men of letters, such a national series. Our task should not, after all, be so difficult. These very students will do for the love of Ireland what they would not do for the love of literature. When literature comes to them, telling of their own country and of its history and of its legends, they will listen gladly enough. The people of Ireland have ever honoured intellect, although they have no intellectual life themselves. I have heard a drunken fisherman tell a man that he was no gentleman 'because nobody is a gentleman who has not been educated at Trinity College Dublin'. The people of Ireland have created perhaps the most beautiful folk-lore in the world, and have made a wild music that is the wonder of all men, and yet to-day they have turned aside from imaginative arts. Can we bring them to care once more for the things of the mind? Well, we are going to do our best to bring books to their doors and music, too, perhaps. Thomas of Erceldoune foretold the day when the gray goose quill would rule the world; and may not we men of the pen hope to move some Irish hearts and make them beat true to manhood and to Ireland? Will not the day come when we shall have again in Ireland men who will not lie for any party advantage, or traffic away eternal principles for any expediency however urgent — men like the men of '48, who lived by the light of noble books and the great traditions of the past? Amidst the clash of party against party we have tried to put forward a nationality that is above party, and amid the oncoming roar of a general election we have tried to assert those everlasting principles of love of truth and love of country that speak to men in solitude and in the silence of the night. So far all has gone well with us, for men who are saddened and disgusted with the turn public affairs have taken have sought in our society occasion to do work for Ireland that will bring about assured good, whether that good be great or small. We have met more support than we ventured to hope for, and there is no sign of its falling off.

The committee represents all parties and opinions which have any claim to be considered national. The Reverend T. A. Finlay of the Catholic University, Mr. John O'Leary, Sir Charles Gavan Duffy, Dr. Douglas Hyde, Dr Sigerson, Count Plunkett, Miss Katharine Tynan, Miss Maud Gonne, so well known for her oratory and her beauty, and Mr. Richard Ashe King, the novelist, are among the best known. Books have been offered upon all manner of national epochs and events from the Ossianic days to our own time.

Apart from the literary society altogether, things are not looking so badly for the future of our literature. Mr. Standish O'Grady, for instance, is doing better and better work. He has on hand an historical romance dealing with the invasions of Strongbow, and is contributing also from time to time singularly moving and picturesque little stories on events in Irish history to the Dublin papers. He will doubtless collect them into a volume before long. He has also written for Fisher Unwin's Children's Library a book called *Finn and His Companions*, which gives the most vivid pictures of the Ossianic age I ever hope to see. Caoilte, having survived to the time of St. Patrick by enchantment, describes to the saint the life of the Fenians, and tells numbers of the old tales out of the bardic poems in English both powerful and beautiful.

Dr. Douglas Hyde has also a book on the legendary age in progress. It will give translations of bardic stories, and will be, I believe, but the first of a series if Dr. Hyde meets with proper support. It is impossible to overrate the importance of such books, for in them the Irish poets of the future will in all likelihood find a good portion of their subject matter. From that great candle of the past we must all light our little tapers.

In England I sometimes hear men complain that the old themes of verse and prose are used up. Here in Ireland the marble block is waiting for us almost untouched, and the statues will come as soon as we have learned to use the chisel. Our history is full of incidents well worthy of drama, story and song. And they are incidents involving types of character of which this world has not yet heard. If we can but put those tumultuous centuries into tale or drama, the whole world will listen to us and sit at our feet like children who hear a new story. Nor is this new thing we have to say in our past alone. The very people who come and go in this library where I write are themes full of new wisdom and new mystery, for in them is that yet uncultured thing — Irish character. And if history and the living present fail us, do there not lie hid among those spear heads and golden collars over the way in the New Museum, suggestions of that age before history when the art legends and wild mythology of earliest Ireland rose out of the void? There alone is enough of the stuff that dreams are made on to keep us busy a thousand years.

November 19, 1892

WILLIAM BLAKE AND HIS ILLUSTRATIONS
TO THE DIVINE COMEDY

I. HIS OPINIONS UPON ART

WILLIAM BLAKE was the first writer of modern times to preach
the indissoluble marriage of all great art with symbol. There
had been allegorists and teachers of allegory in plenty, but the
symbolic imagination, or, as Blake preferred to call it,
'vision', is not allegory, being 'a representation of what
actually exists really and unchangeably'. A symbol is indeed
the only possible expression of some invisible essence, a
transparent lamp about a spiritual flame; while allegory is one
of many possible representations of an embodied thing, or
familiar principle, and belongs to fancy and not to imagination: the one is a revelation, the other an amusement. It is
happily no part of my purpose to expound in detail the relations he believed to exist between symbol and mind, for in
doing so I should come upon not a few doctrines which,
though they have not been difficult to many simple persons,
ascetics wrapped in skins, women who had cast away all
common knowledge, peasants dreaming by their sheepfolds
upon the hills, are full of obscurity to the man of modern
culture; but it is necessary to just touch upon these relations,
because in them was the fountain of much of the practice and
of all the precept of his artistic life.

If a man would enter into 'Noah's rainbow', he has
written, and 'make a friend' of one of 'the images of wonder'
which dwell there, and which always entreat him 'to leave
mortal things', 'then would he arise from the grave and

meet the Lord in the air'; and by this rainbow, this sign of a covenant granted to him who is with Shem and Japhet, 'painting, poetry and music', 'the three powers in man of conversing with Paradise which the flood "of time and space" did not sweep away', Blake represented the shapes of beauty haunting our moments of inspiration: shapes held by most for the frailest of ephemera, but by him for a people older than the world, citizens of eternity, appearing and reappearing in the minds of artists and of poets, creating all we touch and see by casting distorted images of themselves upon 'the vegetable glass of nature'; and because beings, none the less symbols, blossoms, as it were, growing from invisible immortal roots, hands, as it were, pointing the way into some divine labyrinth. If 'the world of imagination' was 'the world of eternity', as this doctrine implied, it was of less importance to know men and nature than to distinguish the beings and substances of imagination from those of a more perishable kind, created by the fantasy, in uninspired moments, out of memory and whim; and this could best be done by purifying one's mind, as with a flame, in study of the works of the great masters, who were great because they had been granted by divine favour a vision of the unfallen world from which others are kept apart by the flaming sword that turns every way; and by flying from the painters who studied 'the vegetable glass' for its own sake, and not to discover there the shadows of imperishable beings and substances, and who entered into their own minds, not to make the unfallen world a test of all they heard and saw and felt with the senses, but to cover the naked spirit with 'the rotten rags of memory' of older sensations. The struggle of the first part of his life had been to distinguish between these two schools, and to cleave always to the Florentine, and so to escape the fascination of those who seemed to him to offer the sleep of nature to a spirit weary with the labours of inspiration; but it was only after his return to London from Felpham in 1804 that he finally escaped from 'temptations and perturbations' which sought to destroy 'the imaginative power' at 'the hands of Venetian and Flemish Demons'. 'The spirit of Titian' — and one must always remember that he had only seen poor engravings, and what his disciple, Palmer, has called 'picture-dealers' Titians' — 'was particularly active in raising doubts concerning the possibility of executing without a model; and when once he had raised the doubt it became easy for him to snatch away the vision time after time'; and Blake's imagination 'weakened' and 'darkened' until a 'memory of nature and of pictures of various schools possessed his mind, instead of appropriate execution' flowing from the vision itself. But now he wrote, 'O glory, and O delight! I have entirely reduced that spectrous fiend to his station' — he had overcome the merely reasoning and sensual portion of the mind — 'whose annoyance has been the ruin of my labours for the last passed twenty years of my life. . . . I speak with perfect confidence and certainty of the fact which has passed upon me. Nebuchadnezzar had seven times passed over him, I have had twenty; thank God I was not altogether a beast as he was. . . . Suddenly, on the day after vising the Truchsessian Gallery of pictures' — this was a gallery containing pictures by Albert Dürer and by the great Florentines — 'I was again enlightened with the light I enjoyed in my youth, and which has for exactly twenty years been closed from me, as by a door and by window-shutters. . . . Excuse my enthusiasm, or rather madness, for I am really drunk with intellectual vision whenever I take a pencil or graver into my hand, even as I used to be in my youth.'

This letter may have been the expression of a moment's enthusiasm, but was more probably rooted in one of those intuitions of coming technical power which every creator feels, and learns to rely upon; for all his greatest work was done, and the principles of his art were formulated, after this date. Except a word here and there, his writings hitherto had not dealt with the principles of art except remotely and by implication; but now he wrote much upon them, and not in obscure symbolic verse, but in emphatic prose, and explicit if not very poetical rhyme. He explained spiritual art, and praised the painters of Florence and their influence and cursed all that has come of Venice and Holland in his *Descriptive Catalogue*, in the *Address to the Public*, in the notes on Sir Joshua Reynolds, in *The Book of Moonlight* — of which some not very dignified rhymes alone remain — in beautiful detached passages of his *MS. Book*. The limitation of his view was from the very intensity of his vision; he was a too literal realist of imagination, as others are of nature; and because he believed that the figures seen by the mind's eye, when exalted by inspiration, were 'external existences', symbols of divine essences, he hated every grace of style that might obscure their lineaments. To wrap them about in reflected lights was to do this, and to dwell over-fondly upon any softness of hair or flesh was to dwell upon that which was least permanent and least characteristic, for 'The great and golden rule of art, as well as of life, is this: that the more distinct, sharp and wiry the bounding line, the more perfect the work of art; and the less keen and sharp, the greater is the evidence of weak imitation, plagiarism and bungling'. Inspiration was to see the permanent and characteristic in all forms, and if you had it not, you must needs imitate with a languid mind the things you saw or remembered, and so sink into the sleep of nature where all is soft and melting. 'Great inventors in all ages knew this. Protogenes and Apelles knew each other by this line. Raphael and Michelangelo and Albert Dürer are known by this and this alone. . . . How do we distinguish the oak from the beech, the horse from the ox, but by the bounding outline? How do we distinguish one face or countenance from another, but by the bounding outline and its infinite inflections and movements? What is it that builds a house and plants a garden, but the definite and determinate? What is it that distinguishes honesty from knavery, but the hard and wiry line of rectitude and certainty in the actions and intentions? Leave out this line and you leave out life itself; all is chaos again, and the line of the Almighty must be drawn out upon it before man or beast can exist.' He even insisted that 'colouring does not depend upon where the colours are put, but upon where the lights and darks are put, and all depends on form or outline' — meaning, I suppose, that a colour gets its brilliance or its depth from being in light or in shadow. He does not mean by outline the bounding line dividing a form from its background, as one of his commentators has thought, but the line that divides it from surrounding space, and unless you have an overmastering sense of this you cannot draw true beauty at all, but only 'the beauty that is appended to folly', a beauty of mere voluptuous softness, 'a lamentable accident of the mortal and perishing life', for 'the beauty proper for sublime art is lineaments, or forms and features that are capable of being the receptacles of intellect', and 'the face or limbs that alter least from infancy to old age are the face and limbs of greatest beauty and perfection'. His praise of a severe art had been beyond price had his age rested a moment to listen, in the midst of its enthusiasm for Correggio and the later Renaissance, for Bartolozzi and for Stothard. What matter if in his visionary realism, in his enthusiasm for what, after all, is perhaps the greatest art, he refused to admit that he who wraps the vision in lights and shadows, in irridescent or glowing colour, until form be half lost in pattern, may, as did Titian in his *Bacchus and Ariadne*, create a talisman as powerfully charged with intellectual virtue as though it were a jewel-studded door of the city seen on Patmos?

To cover the imperishable lineaments of beauty with shadows and reflected lights was to fall into the power of his 'Vala', the indolent fascination of Nature, the woman divinity who is so often described in the 'Prophetic Books' as 'sweet pestilence', and whose children weave webs to take the souls of men; but there was a yet more lamentable chance, for Nature has also a 'masculine portion' or 'spectre' which kills instead of taking prisoner, and is continually at war with inspiration. To 'generalise' forms and shadows, to 'smooth out' spaces and lines in obedience to 'laws of composition', and of painting; founded not upon imagination, which always thirsts for variety and delights in freedom, but upon reasoning from sensation, which is always seeking to reduce everything to a lifeless and slavish uniformity; as the popular art of Blake's day had done, and as he understood Sir Joshua Reynolds to advise, was to fall into 'Entuthon Benithon', or 'the Lake of Udan Adan', or some other of those regions where the imagination and the flesh are alike dead, that he names by so many resonant fantastical names. 'General knowledge is remote knowledge,' he wrote; 'it is in particulars that wisdom consists, and happiness too. Both in art and life general masses are as much art as a pasteboard man is human. Every man has eyes, nose and mouth; this every idiot knows. But he who enters into and discriminates most minutely the manners and intentions, the characters in all their branches, is the alone wise or sensible man, and on this discrimination all art is founded. . . . As poetry admits not a letter that is insignificant, so painting admits not a grain of sand or a blade of grass insignificant, much less an insignificant blot or blur.'

Against another desire of his time, derivative also from what

he has called 'corporeal reason', the desire for 'a tepid modera-
tion', for a lifeless 'sanity in both art and life', he had protested years before with a paradoxical violence. 'The road-
way of excess leads to the palace of wisdom', and we must
only 'bring out weight and measure in time of dearth'. This
protest, carried, in the notes on Sir Joshua Reynolds, to the
point of dwelling with pleasure on the thought that 'The
Lives of the Painters say that Raphael died of dissipation',
because dissipation is better than emotional penury, seemed
as important to his old age as to his youth. He taught it to his
disciples, and one finds it in its purely artistic shape in a diary
written by Samuel Palmer, in 1824: 'Excess is the essential
vivifying spirit, vital spark, embalming spice of the finest art.
There are many mediums in the *means* — none, oh, not a jot,
not a shadow of a jot, in the *end* of great art. In a picture
whose merit is to be excessively brilliant, it can't be too
brilliant, but individual tints may be too brilliant. . . . We
must not begin with medium, but think always on excess and
only use medium to make excess more abundantly excessive.'

These three primary commands, to seek a determinate outline, to avoid a generalised treatment, and to desire always
abundance and exuberance, were insisted upon with vehe-
ment anger, and their opponents called again and again
'demons' and 'villains', 'hired' by the wealthy and the idle;
but in private, Palmer has told us, he could find 'sources of
delight throughout the whole range of art', and was ever
ready to praise excellence in any school, finding, doubtless,
among friends, no need for the emphasis of exaggeration.
There is a beautiful passage in *Jerusalem* in which the merely
mortal part of the mind, 'the spectre', created 'pyramids of
pride', and 'pillars in the deepest hell to reach the heavenly
arches', and seeks to discover wisdom in 'the spaces between
the stars', not 'in the stars', where it is, but the immortal

part makes all his labours vain, and turns his pyramids to 'grains of sand', his 'pillars' to 'dust on the fly's wing', and makes of 'his starry heavens a moth of gold and silver mocking his anxious grasp'. So when man's desire to rest from spiritual labour, and his thirst to fill his art with mere sensation and memory, seem upon the point of triumph, some miracle transforms them to a new inspiration; and here and there among the pictures born of sensation and memory is the murmuring of a new ritual, the glimmering of new talismans and symbols.

It was during and after the writing of these opinions that Blake did the various series of pictures which have brought him the bulk of his fame. He had already completed the illustrations to Young's *Night Thoughts* — in which the great sprawling figures, a little wearisome even with the luminous colours of the original water-colour, became nearly intolerable in plain black and white — and almost all the illustrations to the 'Prophetic Books', which have an energy like that of the elements, but are rather rapid sketches taken while some phantasmic procession swept over him, than elaborate compositions, and in whose shadowy adventures one finds not merely, as did Dr. Garth Wilkinson, 'the hells of the ancient people, the Anakim, the Nephalim, and the Rephaim . . . gigantic petrifications from which the fires of lust and intense selfish passion have long dissipated what was animal and vital'; not merely the shadows cast by the powers who had closed the light from him as 'with a door and window-shutters', but the shadows of those who gave them battle. He did now, however, the many designs to Milton, of which I have only seen those to *Paradise Regained*; the reproductions of those to *Comus*, published, I think, by Mr. Quaritch; and the three or four to *Paradise Lost*, engraved by Bell Scott — a series of designs which one good judge considers his greatest work; the illustrations to Blair's *Grave*, whose gravity and passion struggled with the mechanical softness and trivial smoothness of Schiavonetti's engraving; the illustrations to Thornton's *Virgil*, whose influence is manifest in the work of the little group of landscape-painters who gathered about him in his old age and delighted to call him master. The member of the group whom I have already so often quoted has alone praised worthily these illustrations to the first Eclogue: 'There is in all such a misty and dreamy glimmer as penetrates and kindles the inmost soul and gives complete and unreserved delight, unlike the gaudy daylight of this world. They are like all this wonderful artist's work, the drawing aside of the fleshly curtain, and the glimpse which all the most holy, studious saints and sages have enjoyed, of the rest which remains to the people of God.' Now, too, he did the great series, the crowning work of his life, the illustrations to *The Book of Job* and the illustrations to the *Divine Comedy*. Hitherto he had protested against the mechanical 'dots and lozenges' and 'blots and blurs' of Woollett and Strange,[1] but had himself used both 'dot and lozenge', 'blot and blur', though always in subordination 'to a firm and determinate outline'; but in Marc Antonio, certain of whose engravings he was shown by Linnell, he found a style full of delicate lines, a style where all was living and energetic, strong and subtle. And almost his last words, a letter written upon his death-bed, attack the 'dots and lozenges' with even more than usually quaint symbolism, and praise expressive lines. 'I know too well that the majority of Englishmen are fond of the infinite . . . a line is a line in its minutest subdivisions,

---

[1] Woollett and Strange had established names when Blake began to draw, and must have seemed to Blake in certain moods the types of all triumphant iniquity. Woollett used to fire a cannon from the roof of his house whenever he finished an important plate.

straight or crooked. It is itself, not intermeasurable by anything else . . . but since the French Revolution' — since the reign of reason began, that is —'Englishmen are all intermeasurable by one another; certainly a happy state of agreement, in which I for one do not agree.' The Dante series occupied the last years of his life; even when too weak to get out of bed he worked on, propped up with the great drawing-book before him. He sketched a hundred designs, but left nearly all incomplete, some greatly so, and partly engraved seven plates, of which the 'Francesca and Paolo' is the most finished. It is not, I think, inferior to any but the finest in *Job*, if indeed to them, and shows in its perfection Blake's mastery over elemental things, the swirl in which the lost spirits are hurried, 'a watery flame' he would have called it, the haunted waters and the huddling shapes. In the illustrations of Purgatory there is a serene beauty, and one finds his Dante and Virgil climbing among the rough rocks under a cloudy sun, and in their sleep upon the smooth steps towards the summit, a placid, marmoreal, tender, starry rapture.

All in this great series are in some measure powerful and moving, and not, as it is customary to say of the work of Blake, because a flaming imagination pierces through a cloudy and indecisive technique, but because they have the only excellence possible in any art, a mastery over artistic expression. The technique of Blake was imperfect, incomplete, as is the technique of wellnigh all artists who have striven to bring fires from remote summits; but where his imagination is perfect and complete, his technique has a like perfection, a like completeness. He strove to embody more subtle raptures, more elaborate intuitions than any before him; his imagination and technique are more broken and strained under a great burden than the imagination and technique of any other master. 'I am,' wrote Blake, 'like others, just equal in invention and execution.' And again, 'No man can improve an original invention; nor can an original invention exist without execution, organised, delineated and articulated either by God or man . . . I have heard people say, "Give me the ideas; it is no matter what words you put them into"; and others say, "Give me the design; it is no matter for the execution". . . . Ideas cannot be given but in their minutely appropriate words, nor can a design be made without its minutely appropriate execution.' Living in a time when technique and imagination are continually perfect and complete, because they no longer strive to bring fire from heaven, we forget how imperfect and incomplete they were in even the greatest masters, in Botticelli, in Orcagna, and in Giotto.

The errors in the handiwork of exalted spirits are as the more fantastical errors in their lives; as Coleridge's opium cloud; as Villiers de l'Isle-Adam's candidature for the throne of Greece; as Blake's anger against causes and purposes he but half understood; as that veritable madness an Eastern scripture thinks permissible among the saints; for he who half lives in eternity endures a rending of the structures of the mind, a crucifixion of the intellectual body.

[1896]

A SYMBOLIC ARTIST AND THE COMING
OF SYMBOLIC ART

The only two powers that trouble the deeps are religion and love, the others make a little trouble upon the surface. When I have written of literature in Ireland, I have had to write again and again about a company of Irish mystics, who have taught for some years a religious philosophy which has changed many ordinary people into ecstatics and visionaries. Young men, who were, I think, apprentices or clerks, have told me how they lay awake at night hearing miraculous music, or seeing forms that made the most beautiful painted or marble forms seem dead and shadowy. This philosophy has changed its symbolism from time to time, being now a little Christian, now very Indian, now altogether Celtic and mythological; but it has never ceased to take a great part of its colour and character from one lofty imagination. I do not believe I could easily exaggerate the direct and indirect influences which 'A. E.' (Mr. George Russell), the most subtle and spiritual poet of his generation, and a visionary who may find room beside Swedenborg and Blake, has had in shaping to a definite conviction the vague spirituality of young Irish men and women of letters. I know that Miss Althea Gyles, in whose work I find so visionary a beauty, does not mind my saying that she lived long with this little company, who had once a kind of conventual house; and that she will not think I am taking from her originality when I say that the beautiful lithe figures of her art, quivering with a life half mortal tragedy, half immortal ecstasy, owe something of their inspiration to this little company. I indeed believe that I see in them a beginning of what may become a new manner in the arts of the modern world; for there are tides in the imagination of the world, and a motion in one or two minds may show a change of tide.

Pattern and rhythm are the road to open symbolism, and the arts have already become full of pattern and rhythm. Subject pictures no longer interest us, while pictures with patterns and rhythms of colour, like Mr. Whistler's, and drawings with patterns and rhythms of line, like Mr. Beardsley's in his middle period, interest us extremely. Mr. Whistler and Mr. Beardsley have sometimes thought so greatly of these patterns and rhythms, that the images of human life have faded almost perfectly; and yet we have not lost our interest. The arts have learned the denials, though they have not learned the fervours of the cloister. Men like Sir Edward Burne-Jones and Mr. Ricketts have been too full of the emotion and the pathos of life to let its images fade out of their work, but they have so little interest in the common thoughts and emotions of life, that their images of life have delicate and languid limbs that could lift no burdens, and souls vaguer than a sigh; while men like Mr. Degas, who are still interested in life, and life at its most vivid and vigorous, picture it with a cynicism that remind one of what ecclesiastics have written in old Latin about women and about the world.

Once or twice an artist has been touched by a visionary energy amid his weariness and bitterness, but it has passed away. Mr. Beardsley created a visionary beauty in *Salome with the Head of John the Baptist*, but because, as he told me, 'beauty is the most difficult of things', he chose in its stead the satirical grotesques of his later period. If one imagine a flame burning in the air, and try to make one's mind dwell on it, that it may continue to burn, one's mind strays immediately to other images; but perhaps, if one believed that it was a divine flame, one's mind would not stray. I think that I would find this visionary beauty also in the work of some of the younger French artists, for I have a dim memory of a little statue in ebony and ivory. Certain recent French writers, like Villiers de l'Isle Adam, have it, and I cannot separate art and literature in this, for they have gone through the same change, though in different forms. I have certainly found it in the poetry of a young Irish Catholic who was meant for the priesthood, but broke down under the strain of what was to him a visionary ecstasy; in some plays by a new Irish writer; in the poetry of 'A. E.'; in some stories of Miss Macleod's; and in the drawings of Miss Gyles; and in almost all these a passion for symbol has taken the place of the old interest in life. These persons are of very different degrees and qualities of power, but their work is always energetic, always the contrary of what is called 'decadent'. One feels that they have not only left the smoke of human hearths and come to The Dry Tree, but that they have drunk from The Well at the World's End.

Miss Gyles' images are so full of abundant and passionate life that they remind one of William Blake's cry, 'Exuberance is Beauty', and Samuel Palmer's command to the artist 'Always seek to make excess more abundantly excessive'. One finds in them what a friend, whose work has no other passion, calls 'the passion for the impossible beauty'; for the beauty which cannot be seen with the bodily eyes, or pictured otherwise than by symbols. Her own favourite drawing, which unfortunately cannot be printed here, is *The Rose of God*, a personification of this beauty as a naked woman, whose hands are stretched against the clouds, as upon a cross, in the traditional attitude of the Bride, the symbol of the microcosm in the Kabala; while two winds, two destinies, the one full of white and the other full of red rose petals, personifying all purities and all passions, whirl about her and descend upon a fleet of ships and

a walled city, personifying the wavering and the fixed powers,
the masters of the world in the alchemical symbolism. Some
imperfect but beautiful verses accompany the drawing, and
describe her as for 'living man's delight and his eternal rever-
ing when dead'.

I have described this drawing because one must understand
Miss Gyles' central symbol, the Rose, before one can understand her dreamy and intricate *Noah's Raven*. The ark floats
upon a grey sea under a grey sky, and the raven flutters above
the sea. A sea nymph, whose slender swaying body drifting
among the grey waters is a perfect symbol of a soul untouched
by God or by passion, coils the fingers of one hand about his
feet and offers him a ring, while her other hand holds a shining
rose under the sea. Grotesque shapes of little fishes flit about
the rose, and grotesque shapes of larger fishes swim hither and
thither. Sea nymphs swim through the windows of a sunken
town and reach towards the rose hands covered with rings;
and a vague twilight hangs over all. The story is woven out of
as many old symbols as if it were a mystical story in 'The
Prophetic Books'. The raven, who is, as I understand him, the
desire and will of man, has come out of the ark, the personality
of man, to find if the Rose is anywhere above the flood, which
is here, as always, the flesh, 'the flood of the five senses'. He
has found it and is returning with it to the ark, that the soul
of man may sink into the ideal and pass away; but the sea
nymphs, the spirits of the senses, have bribed him with a ring
taken from the treasures of the kings of the world, a ring that
gives the mastery of the world, and he has given them the
Rose. Henceforth man will seek for the ideal in the flesh, and
the flesh will be full of illusive beauty, and the spiritual beauty
will be far away.

The Knight upon the Grave of his Lady tells much of its meaning to the first glance; but when one has studied for a time,

one discovers that there is a heart in the bulb of every hyacinth, to personify the awakening of the soul and of love out of the grave. It is now winter, and beyond the knight, who lies in the abandonment of his sorrow, the trees spread their leafless boughs against a grey winter sky; but spring will come, and the boughs will be covered with leaves, and the hyacinths will cover the ground with their blossoms, for the moral is not the moral of the Persian poet: 'Here is a secret, do not tell it to anybody. The hyacinth that blossomed yesterday is dead.' The very richness of the pattern of the armour, and of the boughs, and of the woven roots, and of the dry bones, seems to announce that beauty gathers the sorrows of man into her breast and gives them eternal peace.

It is some time since I saw the original drawing of *Lilith*, and it has been decided to reproduce it in this number of *The Dome* too late for me to have a proof of the engraving; but I remember that Lilith, the ever-changing phantasy of passion, rooted neither in good nor evil, half crawls upon the ground, like a serpent before the great serpent of the world, her guardian and her shadow; and Miss Gyles reminds me that Adam, and things to come, are reflected on the wings of the serpent; and that beyond, a place shaped like a heart is full of thorns and roses. I remember thinking that the serpent was a little confused, and that the composition was a little lacking in rhythm, and upon the whole caring less for this drawing than for others, but it has an energy and a beauty of its own. I believe that the best of these drawings will live, and that if Miss Gyles were to draw nothing better, she would still have won a place among the few artists in black and white whose work is of the highest intensity. I believe, too, that her inspiration is a wave of a hidden tide that is flowing through many minds in many places, creating a new religious art and poetry.

[December, 1898]

THE AUTUMN OF THE BODY

OUR thoughts and emotions are often but spray flung up from hidden tides that follow a moon no eye can see. I remember that when I first began to write I desired to describe outward things as vividly as possible, and took pleasure, in which there was, perhaps, a little discontent, in picturesque and declamatory books. And then quite suddenly I lost the desire of describing outward things, and found that I took little pleasure in a book unless it was spiritual and unemphatic. I did not then understand that the change was from beyond my own mind, but I understand now that writers are struggling all over Europe, though not often with a philosophic understanding of their struggle, against that picturesque and declamatory way of writing, against that 'externality' which a time of scientific and political thought has brought into literature. This struggle has been going on for some years, but it has only just become strong enough to draw within itself the little sinner world which alone seeks more than amusement in the arts. In France, where movements are more marked, because the people are pre-eminently logical, *The Temptation of Saint Anthony*, the last great dramatic invention of the old romanticism, contrasts very plainly with *Axël*, the first great dramatic invention of the new; and Maeterlinck has followed Count Villiers de l'Isle-Adam. Flaubert wrote unforgettable descriptions of grotesque, bizarre, and beautiful scenes and persons, as they show to the ear and to the eye, and crowded them with historical and ethnographical details; but Count Villiers de l'Isle-Adam swept together, by what seemed a sudden energy, words behind which glimmered a spiritual and passionate mood, as the flame glimmers behind the dusky blue and red glass in an Eastern lamp; and created persons from whom has fallen all even of personal characteristic except a thirst for that hour when all things shall pass away like a cloud, and a pride like that of the Magi following their star over many mountains; while Maeterlinck has plucked away even this thirst and this pride and set before us faint souls, naked and pathetic shadows already half vapour and sighing to one another upon the border of the last abyss. There has been, as I think, a like change in French painting, for one sees everywhere, instead of the dramatic stories and picturesque moments of an older school, frail and tremulous bodies unfitted for the labour of life, and landscape where subtle rhythms of colour and of form have overcome the clear outline of things as we see them in the labour of life.

There has been a like change in England, but it has come more gradually and is more mixed with lesser changes than in France. The poetry which found its expression in the poems of writers like Browning and Tennyson, and even of writers who are seldom classed with them, like Swinburne, and like Shelley in his earlier years, pushed its limits as far as possible, and tried to absorb into itself the science and politics, the philosophy and morality of its time; but a new poetry, which is always contracting its limits, has grown up under the shadow of the old. Rossetti began it, but was too much of a painter in his poetry to follow it with a perfect devotion; and it became a movement when Mr. Lang and Mr. Gosse and Mr. Dobson devoted themselves to the most condensed of lyric poems, and when Mr. Bridges, a more considerable poet, elaborated a rhythm too delicate for any but an almost bodiless emotion, and repeated over and over the most ancient notes of poetry, and none but these. The poets who followed have either, like Mr. Kipling, turned from serious poetry altogether, and so passed out of the processional order, or speak out of some personal or spiritual passion in words and types and metaphors that draw one's imagination as far as possible from the complexities of modern life and thought. The change has been more marked in English painting, which, when intense enough to belong to the processional order, began to cast out things, as they are seen by minds plunged in the labour of life, so much before French painting that ideal art is sometimes called English art upon the Continent.

I see, indeed, in the arts of every country those faint lights and faint colours and faint outlines and faint energies which many call 'the decadence', and which I, because I believe that the arts lie dreaming of things to come, prefer to call the autumn of the body. An Irish poet whose rhythms are like the cry of a sea-bird in autumn twilight has told its meaning in the line, 'The very sunlight's weary, and it's time to quit the plough'. Its importance is the greater because it comes to us at the moment when we are beginning to be interested in many things which positive science, the interpreter of exterior law, has always denied: communion of mind with mind in thought and without words, foreknowledge in dreams and in visions, and the coming among us of the dead, and of much else. We are, it may be, at a crowning crisis of the world, at the moment when man is about to ascend, with the wealth he has been so long gathering upon his shoulders, the stairway he has been descending from the first days. The first poets, if one may find their images in the *Kalevala*, had not Homer's preoccupation with things, and he was not so full of their excitement as Virgil. Dante added to poetry a dialectic which, although he made it serve his laborious ecstasy, was the invention of minds strained by the labour of life, by a traffic among many things, and not a spontaneous expression of an interior life; while Shakespeare shattered the symmetry of verse and of drama that he might fill them with things and their accidental relations to one another.

Each of these writers had come further down the stairway than those who had lived before him, but it was only with the modern poets, with Goethe and Wordsworth and Browning, that poetry gave up the right to consider all things in the world as a dictionary of types and symbols and began to call itself a critic of life and an interpreter of things as they are. Painting, music, science, politics, and even religion, because they have felt a growing belief that we know nothing but the fading and flowering of the world, have changed in numberless elaborate ways. Man has wooed and won the world, and has fallen weary, and not, I think, for a time, but with a weariness that will not end until the last autumn, when the stars shall be blown away like withered leaves. He grew weary when he said, 'These things that I touch and see and hear are alone real', for he saw them without illusion at last, and found them but air and dust and moisture. And now he must be philosophical above everything, even about the arts, for he can only return the way he came, and so escape from weariness, by philosophy. The arts are, I believe, about to take upon their shoulders the burdens that have fallen from the shoulders of priests, and to lead us back upon our journey by filling our thoughts with the essences of things, and not with things. We are about to substitute once more the distillation of alchemy for the analyses of chemistry and for some other sciences; and certain of us are looking everywhere for the perfect alembic that no silver or golden drop may escape. Mr. Symons has written lately on Mallarmé's method, and has quoted him as saying that we should 'abolish the pretension, aesthetically an error, despite its dominion over almost all the masterpieces, to enclose within the subtle paper other than — for example — the horror of the forest or the silent thunder in the leaves, not the intense dense wood of the trees', and as desiring to substitute for 'the old lyric afflatus or the enthusiastic personal direction of the phrase' words 'that take light from mutual reflection, like an actual trail of fire over precious stones', and 'to make an entire word hitherto unknown to the language' 'out of many vocables'. Mr. Symons understands these and other sentences to mean that poetry will henceforth be a poetry of essences, separated one from another in little and intense poems. I think there will be much poetry of this kind, because of an ever more arduous search for an almost disembodied ecstasy, but I think we will not cease to write long poems, but rather that we will write them more and more as our new belief makes the world plastic under our hands again. I think that we will learn again how to describe at great length an old man wandering among enchanted islands, his return home at last, his slow-gathering vengeance, a flitting shape of a goddess, and a flight of arrows, and yet to make all of these so different things 'take light from mutual reflection, like an actual trail of fire over precious stones', and become 'an entire word', the signature or symbol of a mood of the divine imagination as imponderable as 'the horror of the forest or the silent thunder in the leaves'.

1898

THE SYMBOLISM OF POETRY

I

SYMBOLISM, as seen in the writers of our day, would have no value if it were not seen also, under one 'disguise or another, in every great imaginative writer', writes Mr. Arthur Symons in *The Symbolist Movement in Literature*, a subtle book which I cannot praise as I would, because it has been dedicated to me; and he goes on to show how many profound writers have in the last few years sought for a philosophy of poetry in the doctrine of symbolism, and how even in countries where it is almost scandalous to seek for any philosophy of poetry, new writers are following them in their search. We do not know what the writers of ancient times talked of among themselves, and one bull is all that remains of Shakespeare's talk, who was on the edge of modern times; and the journalist is convinced, it seems, that they talked of wine and women and politics, but never about their art, or never quite seriously about their art. He is certain that no one who had a philosophy of his art, or a theory of how he should write, has ever made a work of art, that people have no imagination who do not write without forethought and afterthought as he writes his own articles. He says this with enthusiasm, because he has heard it at so many comfortable dinner-tables, where someone had mentioned through carelessness, or foolish zeal, a book whose difficulty had offended indolence, or a man who had not forgotten that beauty is an accusation. Those formulas and generalisations, in which a hidden sergeant has drilled the ideas of journalists and through them the ideas of all but all the modern world, have

43

created in their turn a forgetfulness like that of soldiers in battle, so that journalists and their readers have forgotten, among many like events, that Wagner spent seven years arranging and explaining his ideas before he began his most characteristic music; that opera, and with it modern music, arose from certain talks at the house of one Giovanni Bardi of Florence; and that the Pléiade laid the foundations of modern French literature with a pamphlet. Goethe has said, 'a poet needs all philosophy, but he must keep it out of his work', though that is not always necessary; and almost certainly no great art, outside England, where journalists are more powerful and ideas less plentiful than elsewhere, has arisen without a great criticism, for its herald or its interpreter and protector, and it may be for this reason that great art, now that vulgarity has armed itself and multiplied itself, is perhaps dead in England.

All writers, all artists of any kind, in so far as they have had any philosophical or critical power, perhaps just in so far as they have been delicate artists at all, have had some philosophy, some criticism of their art; and it has often been this philosophy, or this criticism, that has evoked their most startling inspiration, calling into outer life some portion of the divine life, or of the buried reality, which could alone extinguish in the emotions what their philosophy or their criticism would extinguish in the intellect. They had sought for no new thing it may be, but only to understand and to copy the pure inspiration of early times, but because the divine life wars upon our outer life, and must needs change its weapons and its movements as we change ours, inspiration has come to them in beautiful startling shapes. The scientific movement brought with it a literature which was always tending to lose itself in externalities of all kinds, in opinion, in declamation, in picturesque writing, in word-painting, or in what Mr. Symons has called an attempt 'to build in brick and mortar inside the covers of a book'; and now writers have begun to dwell upon the element of evocation, of suggestion, upon what we call the symbolism in great writers.

II

In 'Symbolism in Painting', I tried to describe the element of symbolism that is in pictures and sculpture, and described a little the symbolism in poetry, but did not describe at all the continuous indefinable symbolism which is the substance of all style.

There are no lines with more melancholy beauty than these by Burns:

> The white moon is setting behind the white wave,[1]
> And Time is setting with me, O!

and these lines are perfectly symbolical. Take from them the whiteness of the moon and of the wave, whose relation to the setting of Time is too subtle for the intellect, and you take from them their beauty. But, when all are together, moon and wave and whiteness and setting Time and the last melancholy cry, they evoke an emotion which cannot be evoked by any other arrangement of colours and sounds and forms. We may call this metaphorical writing, but it is better to call it symbolical writing, because metaphors are not profound enough to be moving, when they are not symbols, and when they are symbols they are the most perfect of all, because the most subtle, outside of pure sound, and through them one can best find out what symbols are. If one begins the reverie with any beautiful lines that one can remember, one finds they are like those by Burns. Begin with this line by Blake:

[1] [Burns actually wrote:
      'The wan moon is setting ayont the white wave,'
but Yeats's version has been retained for the sake of his comments.]

The gay fishes on the wave when the moon sucks up the dew;
or these lines by Nash:

> Brightness falls from the air,
> Queens have died young and fair,
> Dust hath closed Helen's eye;

or these lines by Shakespeare:

> Timon hath made his everlasting mansion
> Upon the beached verge of the salt flood;
> Who once a day with his embossed froth
> The turbulent surge shall cover;

or take some line that is quite simple, that gets its beauty
from its place in a story, and see how it flickers with the light
of the many symbols that have given the story its beauty, as a
sword-blade may flicker with the light of burning towers.

All sounds, all colours, all forms, either because of their
preordained energies or because of long association, evoke
indefinable and yet precise emotions, or, as I prefer to think,
call down among us certain disembodied powers, whose footsteps over our hearts we call emotions; and when sound, and
colour, and form are in a musical relation, a beautiful relation to one another, they become, as it were, one sound, one
colour, one form, and evoke an emotion that is made out of
their distinct evocations and yet is one emotion. The same
relation exists between all portions of every work of art,
whether it be an epic or a song, and the more perfect it is,
and the more various and numerous the elements that have
flowed into its perfection, the more powerful will be the
emotion, the power, the god it calls among us. Because an
emotion does not exist, or does not become perceptible and
active among us, till it has found its expression, in colour or
in sound or in form, or in all of these, and because no two

modulations or arrangements of these evoke the same emotion, poets and painters and musicians, and in a less degree
because their effects are momentary, day and night and cloud
and shadow, are continually making and unmaking mankind. It is indeed only those things which seem useless or very
feeble that have any power, and all those things that seem
useful or strong, armies, moving wheels, modes of architecture, modes of government, speculations of the reason,
would have been a little different if some mind long ago had
not given itself to some emotion, as a woman gives herself to
her lover, and shaped sounds or colours or forms, or all of
these, into a musical relation, that their emotion might live
in other minds. A little lyric evokes an emotion, and this
emotion gathers others about it and melts into their being in
the making of some great epic; and at last, needing an always
less delicate body, or symbol, as it grows more powerful, it
flows out, with all it has gathered, among the blind instincts
of daily life, where it moves a power within powers, as one
sees ring within ring in the stem of an old tree. This is maybe
what Arthur O'Shaughnessy meant when he made his poets
say they had built Nineveh with their sighing; and I am certainly never sure, when I hear of some war, or of some
religious excitement, or of some new manufacture, or of
anything else that fills the ear of the world, that it has not all
happened because of something that a boy piped in Thessaly.
I remember once telling a seeress to ask one among the gods
who, as she believed, were standing about her in their symbolic bodies, what would come of a charming but seeming
trivial labour of a friend, and the form answering, 'the deva-
station of peoples and the overwhelming of cities'. I doubt
indeed if the crude circumstance of the world, which seems
to create all our emotions, does more than reflect, as in multiplying mirrors, the emotions that have come to solitary men

in moments of poetical contemplation; or that love itself would be more than an animal hunger but for the poet and his shadow the priest, for unless we believe that outer things are the reality, we must believe that the gross is the shadow of the subtle, that things are wise before they become foolish, and secret before they cry out in the market-place. Solitary men in moments of contemplation receive, as I think, the creative impulse from the lowest of the Nine Hierarchies, and so make and unmake mankind, and even the world itself, for does not 'the eye altering alter all'?

> Our towns are copied fragments from our breast;
> And all man's Babylons strive but to impart
> The grandeurs of his Babylonian heart.

III

The purpose of rhythm, it has always seemed to me, is to prolong the moment of contemplation, the moment when we are both asleep and awake, which is the one moment of creation, by hushing us with an alluring monotony, while it holds us waking by variety, to keep us in that state of perhaps real trance, in which the mind liberated from the pressure of the will is unfolded in symbols. If certain sensitive persons listen persistently to the ticking of a watch, or gaze persistently on the monotonous flashing of a light, they fall into the hypnotic trance; and rhythm is but the ticking of a watch made softer, that one must needs listen, and various, that one may not be swept beyond memory or grow weary of listening; while the patterns of the artist are but the monotonous flash woven to take the eyes in a subtler enchantment. I have heard in meditation voices that were forgotten the moment they had spoken; and I have been swept, when in more profound meditation, beyond all memory but of those things that came from beyond the threshold of waking life. I was writing once at a very symbolical and abstract poem, when my pen fell on the ground; and as I stooped to pick it up, I remembered some fantastic adventure that yet did not seem fantastic, and then another like adventure, and when I asked myself when these things had happened, I found that I was remembering my dreams for many nights. I tried to remember what I had done the day before, and then what I had done that morning; but all my waking life had perished from me, and it was only after a struggle that I came to remember it again, and as I did so that more powerful and startling life perished in its turn. Had my pen not fallen on the ground and so made me turn from the images that I was weaving into verse, I would never have known that meditation had become trance, for I would have been like one who does not know that he is passing through a wood because his eyes are on the pathway. So I think that in the making and in the understanding of a work of art, and the more easily if it is full of patterns and symbols and music, we are lured to the threshold of sleep, and it may be far beyond it, without knowing that we have ever set our feet upon the steps of horn or of ivory.

IV

Besides emotional symbols, symbols that evoke emotions alone, — and in this sense all alluring or hateful things are symbols, although their relations with one another are too subtle to delight us fully, away from rhythm and pattern, — there are intellectual symbols, symbols that evoke ideas alone, or ideas mingled with emotions; and outside the very definite traditions of mysticism and the less definite criticism of certain modern poets, these alone are called symbols. Most things belong to one or another kind, according to the way we speak of them and the companions we give them, for symbols, associated with ideas that are more than fragments of the shadows thrown upon the intellect by the emotions they evoke, are the playthings of the allegorist or the pedant, and soon pass away. If I say 'white' or 'purple' in an ordinary line of poetry, they evoke emotions so exclusively that I cannot say why they move me; but if I bring them into the same sentence with such obvious intellectual symbols as a cross or a crown of thorns, I think of purity and sovereignty. Furthermore, innumerable meanings, which are held to 'white' or to 'purple' by bonds of subtle suggestion, and alike in the emotions and in the intellect, move visibly through my mind, and move invisibly beyond the threshold of sleep, casting lights and shadows of an indefinable wisdom on what had seemed before, it may be, but sterility and noisy violence. It is the intellect that decides where the reader shall ponder over the procession of the symbols, and if the symbols are merely emotional, he gazes from amid the accidents and destinies of the world; but if the symbols are intellectual too, he becomes himself a part of pure intellect, and he is himself mingled with the procession. If I watch a rushy pool in the moonlight, my emotion at its beauty is mixed with memories of the man that I have seen ploughing by its margin, or of the lovers I saw there a night ago; but if I look at the moon herself and remember any of her ancient names and meanings, I move among divine people, and things that have shaken off our mortality, the tower of ivory, the queen of waters, the shining stag among enchanted woods, the white hare sitting upon the hilltop, the fool of Faery with his shining cup full of dreams, and it may be 'make a friend of one of these images of wonder', and 'meet the Lord in the air'. So, too, if one is moved by Shakespeare, who is content with emotional symbols that he may come the nearer to our sympathy, one is mixed with the whole spectacle of the world; while if one is moved by Dante, or by the myth of Demeter, one is mixed into the shadow of God or of a goddess. So, too, one is furthest from symbols when one is busy doing this or that, but the soul moves among symbols and unfolds in symbols when trance, or madness, or deep meditation has withdrawn it from every impulse but its own. 'I then saw,' wrote Gérard de Nerval of his madness, 'vaguely drifting into form, plastic images of antiquity, which outlined themselves, became definite, and seemed to represent symbols of which I only seized the idea with difficulty.' In an earlier time he would have been of that multitude whose souls austerity withdrew, even more perfectly than madness could withdraw his soul, from hope and memory, from desire and regret, that they might reveal those processions of symbols that men bow to before altars, and woo with incense and offerings. But being of our time, he has been like Maeterlinck, like Villiers de l'Isle-Adam in *Axël*, like all who are preoccupied with intellectual symbols in our time, a foreshadower of the new sacred book, of which all the arts, as somebody has said, are beginning to dream. How can the arts overcome the slow dying of men's hearts that we call the progress of the world, and lay their hands upon men's heartstrings again, without becoming the garment of religion as in old times?

V

If people were to accept the theory that poetry moves us because of its symbolism, what change should one look for in the manner of our poetry? A return to the way of our fathers, a casting out of descriptions of nature for the sake of nature, of the moral law for the sake of the moral law, a casting out of all anecdotes and of that brooding over scientific opinion that so often extinguished the central flame in Tennyson, and of that vehemence that would make us do or not do certain things; or, in other words, we should come to understand that the beryl stone was enchanted by our fathers that it might unfold the pictures in its heart, and not to mirror our own excited faces, or the boughs waving outside the window. With this change of substance, this return to imagination, this understanding that the laws of art, which are the hidden laws of the world, can alone bind the imagination, would come a change of style, and we would cast out of serious poetry those energetic rhythms, as of a man running, which are the invention of the will with its eyes always on something to be done or undone; and we would seek out those wavering, meditative, organic rhythms, which are the embodiment of the imagination, that neither desires nor hates, because it has done with time, and only wishes to gaze upon some reality, some beauty; nor would it be any longer possible for anybody to deny the importance of form, in all its kinds, for although you can expound an opinion, or describe a thing, when your words are not quite well chosen, you cannot give a body to something that moves beyond the senses, unless your words are as subtle, as complex, as full of mysterious life, as the body of a flower or of a woman. The form of sincere poetry, unlike the form of the 'popular poetry', may indeed be sometimes obscure, or ungrammatical as in some of the best of the *Songs of Innocence and Experience*, but it must have the perfections that escape analysis, the subtleties that have a new meaning every day, and it must have all this whether it be but a little song made out of a moment of dreamy indolence, or some great epic made out of the dreams of one poet and of a hundred generations whose hands were never weary of the sword.

1900

THE PHILOSOPHY OF SHELLEY'S POETRY

I. HIS RULING IDEAS

WHEN I was a boy in Dublin I was one of a group who rented a room in a mean street to discuss philosophy. My fellow-students got more and more interested in certain modern schools of mystical belief, and I never found anybody to share my one unshakable belief. I thought that whatever of philosophy has been made poetry is alone permanent, and that one should begin to arrange it in some regular order, rejecting nothing as the make-believe of the poets. I thought, so far as I can recollect my thoughts after so many years, that if a powerful and benevolent spirit has shaped the destiny of this world, we can better discover that destiny from the words that have gathered up the heart's desire of the world, than from historical records, or from speculation, wherein the heart withers. Since then I have observed dreams and visions very carefully, and am now certain that the imagination has some way of lighting on the truth that the reason has not, and that its commandments, delivered when the body is still and the reason silent, are the most binding we can ever know. I have re-read *Prometheus Unbound*, which I had hoped my fellow-students would have studied as a sacred book, and it seems to me to have an even more certain place than I had thought among the sacred books of the world. I remember going to a learned scholar to ask about its deep meanings, which I felt more than understood, and his telling me that it was Godwin's *Political Justice* put into rhyme, and that Shelley was a crude revolutionist, and believed that the overturning

of kings and priests would regenerate mankind. I quoted the
lines which tell how the halcyons ceased to prey on fish, and
how poisonous leaves became good for food, to show that he
foresaw more than any political regeneration, but was too
timid to push the argument. I still believe that one cannot help
believing him, as this scholar I know believes him, a vague
thinker, who mixed occasional great poetry with a fantastic
rhetoric, unless one compares such passages, and above all
such passages as describe the liberty he praised, till one has discovered the system of belief that lay behind them. It should
seem natural to find his thought full of subtlety, for Mrs.
Shelley has told how he hesitated whether he should be a
metaphysician or a poet, and has spoken of his 'huntings after
the obscure' with regret, and said of that *Prometheus Unbound*,
which so many for three generations have thought *Political
Justice* put into rhyme, 'It requires a mind as subtle and pene-
rating as his own to understand the mystic meanings scattered
throughout the poem. They elude the ordinary reader by
their abstraction and delicacy of distinction, but they are far
from vague. It was his design to write prose metaphysical
essays on the nature of Man, which would have served to
explain much of what is obscure in his poetry; a few scattered
fragments of observations and remarks alone remain. He
considered these philosophical views of Mind and Nature to
be instinct with the intensest spirit of poetry.' From these
scattered fragments and observations, and from many passages
read in their light, one soon comes to understand that his
liberty was so much more than the liberty of *Political Justice*
that it was one with Intellectual Beauty, and that the regeneration he foresaw was so much more than the regeneration
many political dreamers have foreseen, that it could not come
in its perfection till the Hours bore 'Time to his tomb in
eternity'. In *A Defence of Poetry*, he will have it that the poet

and the lawgiver hold their station by the right of the same faculty, the one uttering in words and the other in the forms of society his vision of the divine order, the Intellectual Beauty. 'Poets, according to the circumstances of the age and nation in which they appeared, were called in the earliest epoch of the world legislators or prophets, and a poet essentially comprises and unites both these characters. For he not only beholds intensely the present as it is, and discovers those laws according to which present things are to be ordained, but he beholds the future in the present, and his thoughts are the germs of the flowers and the fruit of latest time.' 'Language, colour, form, and religious and civil habits of action are all the instruments and materials of poetry.' Poetry is 'the creation of actions according to the unchangeable process of human nature as existing in the mind of the creator, which is itself the image of all other minds'. 'Poets have been challenged to resign the civic crown to reasoners and merchants. . . . It is admitted that the exercise of the imagination is the most delightful, but it is alleged that that of reason is the more useful. . . . Whilst the mechanist abridges and the political economist combines labour, let them be sure that their speculations, for want of correspondence with those first principles which belong to the imagination, do not tend, as they have in modern England, to exasperate at once the extremes of luxury and want. . . . The rich have become richer, the poor have become poorer, . . . such are the effects which must ever flow from an unmitigated exercise of the calculating faculty.' The speaker of these things might almost be Blake, who held that the Reason not only created Ugliness, but all other evils. The books of all wisdom are hidden in the cave of the Witch of Atlas, who is one of his personifications of beauty, and when she moves over the enchanted river that is an image of all life, the priests cast aside their deceits, and the king crowns an ape to mock his own sovereignty, and the soldiers gather about the anvils to beat their swords to ploughshares, and lovers cast away their timidity, and friends are united; while the power which, in *Laon and Cythna*, awakens the mind of the reformer to contend, and itself contends, against the tyrannies of the world, is first seen as the star of love or beauty. And at the end of the *Ode to Naples*, he cries out to 'the spirit of beauty' to overturn the tyrannies of the world, or to fill them with its 'harmonising ardours'. He calls the spirit of beauty liberty, because despotism, and perhaps, as 'the man of virtuous soul commands not, nor obeys', all authority, pluck virtue from her path towards beauty, and because it leads us by that love whose service is perfect freedom. It leads all things by love, for he cries again and again that love is the perception of beauty in thought and things, and it orders all things by love, for it is love that impels the soul to its expressions in thought and in action, by making us 'seek to awaken in all things that are, a community with what we experience within ourselves'. 'We are born into the world, and there is something within us which, from the instant that we live, more and more thirsts after its likeness.' We have 'a soul within our soul that describes a circle around its proper paradise which pain and sorrow and evil dare not overleap', and we labour to see this soul in many mirrors, that we may possess it the more abundantly. He would hardly seek the progress of the world by any less gentle labour, and would hardly have us resist evil itself. He bids the reformers in the *Philosophical Review of Reform* receive 'the onset of the cavalry', if it be sent to disperse their meetings, 'with folded arms', and 'not because active resistance is not justifiable, but because temperance and courage would produce greater advantages than the most decisive victory'; and he gives them like advice in *The Masque of Anarchy*, for liberty, the poem cries, 'is love', and can make the rich man kiss its feet, and, like those who followed Christ, give away his goods and follow it throughout the world.

He does not believe that the reformation of society can bring this beauty, this divine order, among men without the regeneration of the hearts of men. Even in *Queen Mab*, which was written before he had found his deepest thought, or rather perhaps before he had found words to utter it, for I do not think men change much in their deepest thought, he is less anxious to change men's beliefs, as I think, than to cry out against that serpent more subtle than any beast of the field, 'the cause and the effect of tyranny'. He affirms again and again that the virtuous, those who have 'pure desire and universal love', are happy in the midst of tyranny, and he foresees a day when the 'Spirit of Nature', the Spirit of Beauty of his later poems, who has her 'throne of power unappealable' in every human heart, shall have made men so virtuous that 'kingly glare will lose its power to dazzle', and 'silently pass by', and, as it seems, commerce, 'the venal interchange of all that human art or nature yield; which wealth should purchase not', come as silently to an end.

He was always, indeed in chief, a witness for that 'power unappealable'. Maddalo, in *Julian and Maddalo*, says that the soul is powerless, and can only, like a 'dreary bell hung in a heaven-illumined tower, toll our thoughts and our desires to meet below round the rent heart and pray'; but Julian, who is Shelley himself, replies, as the makers of all religions have replied:

> Where is the love, beauty, and truth we seek
> But in our mind? And if we were not weak,
> Should we be less in deed than in desire?

while *Mont Blanc* is an intricate analogy to affirm that the soul has its sources in 'the secret strength of things which governs thought, and to the infinite dome of heaven is as a law'. He even thought that men might be immortal were they sinless, and his Cythna bids the sailors be without remorse, for all that live are stained as they are. It is thus, she says, that time marks men and their thoughts for the tomb. And the 'Red Comet', the image of evil in *Laon and Cythna*, when it began its war with the star of beauty, brought not only 'Fear, Hatred, Fraud and Tyranny', but 'Death, Decay, Earthquake, and Blight and Madness pale'.

When the Red Comet is conquered, when Jupiter is overthrown by Demogorgon, when the prophecy of Queen Mab is fulfilled, visible Nature will put on perfection again. Shelley declares, in one of the notes to *Queen Mab*, that 'there is no great extravagance in presuming . . . that there should be a perfect identity between the moral and physical improvement of the human species', and thinks it 'certain that wisdom is not compatible with disease, and that, in the present state of the climates of the earth, health, in the true and comprehensive sense of the word, is out of the reach of civilised man'. In *Prometheus Unbound* he sees, as in the ecstasy of a saint, the ships moving among the seas of the world without fear of danger —

> by the light
> Of wave-reflected flowers, and floating odours,
> And music soft,

and poison dying out of the green things, and cruelty out of all living things, and even the toads and efts becoming beautiful, and at last Time being borne 'to his tomb in eternity'.

This beauty, this divine order, whereof all things shall become a part in a kind of resurrection of the body, is already visible to the dead and to souls in ecstasy, for ecstasy is a kind of death. The dying Lionel hears the song of the nightingale, and cries:

> Heardst thou not sweet words among
> That heaven-resounding minstrelsy?
> Heardst thou not, that those who die
> Awake in a world of ecstasy?
> That love, when limbs are interwoven,
> And sleep, when the night of life is cloven,
> And thought, to the world's dim boundaries clinging,
> And music, when one beloved is singing,
> Is death? Let us drain right joyously
> The cup which the sweet bird fills for me.

And in the most famous passage in all his poetry he sings of Death as of a mistress. 'Life, like a dome of many-coloured glass, stains the white radiance of Eternity.' 'Die, if thou wouldst be with that which thou dost seek'; and he sees his own soon-coming death in a rapture of prophecy, for 'the fire for which all thirst' beams upon him, 'consuming the last clouds of cold mortality'. When he is dead he will still influence the living, for though Adonais has fled 'to the burning fountain whence he came', and 'is a portion of the Eternal which must glow through time and change, unquenchably the same', and has 'awakened from the dream of life', he has not gone from the 'young Dawn', or the caverns and the forests, or the 'faint flowers and fountains'. He has been 'made one with Nature', and his voice is 'heard in all her music', and his presence is felt wherever 'that Power may move which has withdrawn his being to its own', and he bears 'his part' when it is compelling mortal things to their appointed forms, and he overshadows men's minds at their supreme moments, for —

when lofty thought
Lifts a young heart above its mortal lair,
And love and life contend in it for what
Shall be its earthly doom, the dead live there,
And move like winds of light on dark and stormy air.

'Of his speculations as to what will befall this inestimable
spirit when we appear to die,' Mrs. Shelley has written, 'a
mystic ideality tinged these speculations in Shelley's mind;
certain stanzas in the poem of *The Sensitive Plant* express, in
some degree, the almost inexpressible idea, not that we die
into another state, when this state is no longer, from some
reason, unapparent as well as apparent, accordant with our
being — but that those who rise above the ordinary nature of
man, fade from before our imperfect organs; they remain in
their "love, beauty, and delight", in a world congenial to
them, and we, clogged by "error, ignorance, and strife", see
them not till we are fitted by purification and improvement
to their higher state.' Not merely happy souls, but all beautiful
places and movements and gestures and events, when we
think they have ceased to be, have become portions of the
Eternal.

In this life
Of error, ignorance and strive,
Where nothing is, but all things seem,
And we the shadows of the dream,

It is a modest creed, and yet
Pleasant, if one considers it,
To own that death itself must be,
Like all the rest, a mockery.

That garden sweet, that lady fair,
And all sweet shapes and odours there,

THE PHILOSOPHY OF SHELLEY'S POETRY 61

> In truth have never past away;
> 'Tis we, 'tis ours, are changed, not they.
>
> For love, and beauty, and delight
> There is no death nor change; their might
> Exceeds our organs, which endure
> No light, being themselves obscure.

He seems in his speculations to have lit on that memory of Nature the visionaries claim for the foundation of their knowledge; but I do not know whether he thought, as they do, that all things good and evil remain for ever, 'thinking the thought and doing the deed', though not, it may be, self-conscious; or only thought that 'love and beauty and delight' remain for ever. The passage where Queen Mab awakes 'all knowledge of the past', and the good and evil 'events of old and wondrous times', was no more doubtless than a part of the machinery of the poem, but all the machineries of poetry are parts of the convictions of antiquity, and readily become again convictions in minds that brood over them with visionary intensity.

Intellectual Beauty has not only the happy dead to do her will, but ministering spirits who correspond to the Devas of the East, and the Elemental Spirits of mediaeval Europe, and the Sidhe of ancient Ireland, and whose too constant presence, and perhaps Shelley's ignorance of their more traditional forms, give some of his poetry an air of rootless fantasy. They change continually in his poetry, as they do in the visions of the mystics everywhere and of the common people in Ireland, and the forms of these changes display, in an especial sense, the flowing forms of his mind when freed from all impulse not out of itself or out of supersensual power. These are 'gleams of a remoter world which visit us in sleep', spiritual essences whose shadows are the delights of all the senses, sounds 'folded in cells of crystal silence', 'visions swift, and sweet, and quaint', which lie waiting their moment 'each in its thin sheath, like a chrysalis', 'odours' among 'ever-blooming Eden-trees', 'liquors' that can give 'happy sleep', or can make tears 'all wonder and delight'; 'the golden genii who spoke to the poets of Greece in dreams'; 'the phantoms' which become the forms of the arts when 'the mind, arising bright from the embrace of beauty', 'casts on them the gathered rays which are reality'; 'the guardians' who move in 'the atmosphere of human thought', as 'the birds within the wind, or the fish within the wave', or man's thought itself through all things; and who join the throng of the happy Hours when Time is passing away —

> As the flying-fish leap
> From the Indian deep,
> And mix with sea-birds half asleep.

It is these powers which lead Asia and Panthea, as they would lead all the affections of humanity, by words written upon leaves, by faint songs, by eddies of echoes that draw 'all spirits on that secret way', by the 'dying odours' of flowers and by 'the sunlight of the spherèd dew', beyond the gates of birth and death to awake Demogorgon, eternity, that 'the painted veil called life' may be 'torn aside'.

There are also ministers of ugliness and all evil, like those that came to Prometheus:

> As from the rose which the pale priestess kneels
> To gather for her festal crown of flowers
> The aërial crimson falls, flushing her cheek,
> So from our victim's destined agony
> The shade which is our form invests us round;
> Else we are shapeless as our mother Night.

Or like those whose shapes the poet sees in *The Triumph of Life*, coming from the procession that follows the car of life, as 'hope' changes to 'desire', shadows 'numerous as the dead leaves blow in autumn evening from a poplar-tree'; and resembling those they come from, until, if I understand an obscure phrase aright, they are 'wrapt' round 'all the busy phantoms that were there as the sun shapes the clouds'. Some to sit 'chattering like restless apes', and some like 'old anatomies' 'hatching their bare broods under the shade of demon wings', laughing 'to reassume the delegated power' they had given to the tyrants of the earth, and some 'like small gnats and flies' to throng 'about the brow of lawyers, statesmen, priest and theorist', and some 'like discoloured flakes of snow' to fall 'on fairest bosoms and the sunniest hair', to be 'melted by the youthful glow which they extinguished', and many to 'fling shadows of shadows, yet unlike themselves', shadows that are shaped into new forms by that 'creative ray' in which all move like motes.

These ministers of beauty and ugliness were certainly more than metaphors or picturesque phrases to one who believed the 'thoughts which are called real or external objects' differed but in regularity of recurrence from 'hallucinations, dreams, and the ideas of madness', and lessened this difference by telling how he had dreamed 'three several times, between intervals of two or more years, the same precise dream', and who had seen images with the mind's eye that left his nerves shaken for days together. Shadows that were —

> as when there hovers
> A flock of vampire-bats before the glare
> Of the tropic sun, bringing, ere evening,
> Strange night upon some Indian isle,

could not but have had more than a metaphorical and

picturesque being to one who had spoken in terror with an image of himself, and who had fainted at the apparition of a woman with eyes in her breasts, and who had tried to burn down a wood, if we can trust Mrs. Williams' account, because he believed a devil, who had first tried to kill him, had sought refuge there.

It seems to me, indeed, that Shelley had reawakened in himself the age of faith, though there were times when he would doubt, as even the saints have doubted, and that he was a revolutionist, because he had heard the commandment, 'If ye know these things, happy are ye if ye do them'. I have re-read his *Prometheus Unbound* for the first time for many years, in the woods of Drim-na-Rod, among the Echtge hills, and sometimes I have looked towards Slieve ná nOg where the country people say the last battle of the world shall be fought till the third day, when a priest shall lift a chalice, and the thousand years of peace begin. And I think this mysterious song utters a faith as simple and as ancient as the faith of those country people, in a form suited to a new age, that will understand with Blake that the Holy Spirit is 'an intellectual fountain', and that the kinds and degrees of beauty are the images of its authority.

II. HIS RULING SYMBOLS

At a comparatively early time Shelley made his imprisoned Cythna become wise in all human wisdom through the contemplation of her own mind, and write out this wisdom upon the sands in 'signs' that were 'clear elemental shapes, whose smallest change' made 'a subtler language within language', and were 'the key of truths which once were dimly taught in old Crotona'. His early romances and much throughout his poetry show how strong a fascination the traditions of magic and of the magical philosophy had cast over his mind, and one can hardly suppose that he had not brooded over their doctrine of symbols or signatures, though I do not find anything to show that he gave it any deep study. One finds in his poetry, besides innumerable images that have not the definiteness of symbols, many images that are certainly symbols, and as the years went by he began to use these with a more and more deliberately symbolic purpose. I imagine that when he wrote his earlier poems he allowed the subconscious life to lay its hands so firmly upon the rudder of his imagination that he was little conscious of the abstract meaning of the images that rose in what seemed the idleness of his mind. Anyone who has any experience of any mystical state of the soul knows how there float up in the mind profound symbols,[1] whose meaning, if indeed they do not delude one into the dream that they are meaningless, one does not perhaps understand for years. Nor I think has any one, who has known that experience with any constancy, failed to find some day, in some old book or on some old monument, a strange or intricate image that had floated up before him, and to grow perhaps dizzy with the sudden conviction that our little memories are but a part of some great Memory that renews the world and men's thoughts age after age, and that our thoughts are not, as we suppose, the deep, but a little foam upon the deep. Shelley understood this, as is proved by what he says of the eternity of beautiful things and of the influence of the dead, but whether he understood that the great Memory is also a dwelling-house of symbols, of images that are living souls, I cannot tell. He had certainly experience of all but the most profound of the mystical states, and had known that union with created things

---

[1] *Marianne's Dream* was certainly copied from a real dream of somebody's, but like images come to the mystic in his waking state.

which assuredly must precede the soul's union with the un-created spirit. He says, in his fragment of an essay 'On Life', mistaking a unique experience for the common experience of all: 'Let us recollect our sensations as children . . . we less habitually distinguished all that we saw and felt from our-selves. They seemed as it were to constitute one mass. There are some persons who in this respect are always children. Those who are subject to the state called reverie, feel as if their nature were resolved into the surrounding universe or as if the surrounding universe were resolved into their being', and he must have expected to receive thoughts and images from beyond his own mind, just in so far as that mind trans-cended its preoccupation with particular time and place, for he believed inspiration a kind of death; and he could hardly have helped perceiving that an image that has transcended par-ticular time and place becomes a symbol, passes beyond death, as it were, and becomes a living soul.

When Shelley went to the Continent with Godwin's daughter in 1814 they sailed down certain great rivers in an open boat, and when he summed up in his preface to *Laon and Cythna* the things that helped to make him a poet, he spoke of these voyages: 'I have sailed down mighty rivers, and seen the sun rise and set, and the stars come forth, whilst I have sailed night and day down a rapid stream among mountains.'

He may have seen some cave that was the bed of a rivulet by some river-side, or have followed some mountain stream to its source in a cave, for from his return to England rivers and streams and wells, flowing through caves or rising in them, came into every poem of his that was of any length, and always with the precision of symbols. Alastor passed in his boat along a river in a cave; and when for the last time he felt the presence of the spirit he loved and followed, it was when he watched his image in a silent well; and when he died

it was where a river fell into 'an abysmal chasm'; and the
Witch of Atlas in her gladness, as he in his sadness, passed in
her boat along a river in a cave, and it was where it bubbled
out of a cave that she was born; and when Rousseau, the
typical poet of *The Triumph of Life*, awoke to the vision that
was life, it was where a rivulet bubbled out of a cave; and the
poet of *Epipsychidion* met the evil beauty 'by a well, under
blue nightshade bowers'; and Cythna bore her child imprisoned in a great cave beside 'a fountain round and vast, in
which the wave, imprisoned, boiled and leaped perpetually';
and her lover Laon was brought to his prison in a high column
through a cave where there was 'a putrid pool', and when he
went to see the conquered city he dismounted beside a polluted fountain in the market-place, foreshadowing thereby
that spirit who at the end of *Prometheus Unbound* gazes at a re-
generated city from 'within a fountain in the public square';
and when Laon and Cythna are dead they awake beside a
fountain and drift into Paradise along a river; and at the end
of things Prometheus and Asia are to live amid a happy world
in a cave where a fountain 'leaps with an awakening sound';
and it was by a fountain, the meeting-place of certain unhappy lovers, that Rosalind and Helen told their unhappiness
to one another; and it was under a willow by a fountain that
the enchantress and her lover began their unhappy love;
while his lesser poems and his prose fragments use caves and
rivers and wells and fountains continually as metaphors. It
may be that his subconscious life seized upon some passing
scene, and moulded it into an ancient symbol without help
from anything but that great Memory; but so good a
Platonist as Shelley could hardly have thought of any cave as
a symbol, without thinking of Plato's cave that was the world;
and so good a scholar may well have had Porphyry on 'the
Cave of the Nymphs' in his mind. When I compare

Porphyry's description of the cave where the Phaeacian boat left Odysseus, with Shelley's description of the cave of the Witch of Atlas, to name but one of many, I find it hard to think otherwise. I quote Taylor's translation, only putting Mr. Lang's prose for Taylor's bad verse. 'What does Homer obscurely signify by the cave in Ithaca which he describes in the following verses? "Now at the harbour's head is a long-leaved olive-tree, and hard by is a pleasant cave and shadowy, sacred to the nymphs, that are called Naiads. And therein are mixing-bowls and jars of stone, and there moreover do bees hide. And there are great looms of stone, whereon the nymphs weave raiment of purple stain, a marvel to behold; and there are waters welling evermore. Two gates there are to the cave, the one set towards the North wind, whereby men may go down, but the portals towards the South pertain rather to the gods, whereby men may not enter: it is the way of the immortals."' He goes on to argue that the cave was a temple before Homer wrote, and that 'the ancients did not establish temples without fabulous symbols', and then begins to inter-pret Homer's description in all its detail. The ancients, he says, 'consecrated a cave to the world' and held 'the flowing waters' and the 'obscurity of the cavern' 'apt symbols of what the world contains', and he calls to witness Zoroaster's cave with fountains; and often caves are, he says, symbols of 'all invisible power; because as caves are obscure and dark, so the essence of all these powers is occult', and quotes a lost hymn to Apollo to prove that nymphs living in caves fed men 'from intellectual fountains'; and he contends that fountains and rivers symbolise generation, and that the word nymph 'is commonly applied to all souls descending into generation', and that the two gates of Homer's cave are the gate of generation and the gate of ascent through death to the gods, the gate of cold and moisture, and the gate of heat and fire.

Cold, he says, causes life in the world, and heat causes life among the gods, and the constellation of the Cup is set in the heavens near the sign Cancer, because it is there that the souls descending from the Milky Way receive their draught of the intoxicating cold drink of generation 'The mixing-bowls and jars of stone' are consecrated to the Naiads, and are also, as it seems, symbolical of Bacchus, and are of stone because of the rocky beds of the rivers. And 'the looms of stone' are the symbols of the 'souls that descend into generation'. 'For the formation of the flesh is on or about the bones, which in the bodies of animals resemble stones,' and also because 'the body is a garment' not only about the soul, but about all essences that become visible, for 'the heavens are called by the ancients a veil, in consequence of being as it were the vestments of the celestial gods'. The bees hive in the mixing-bowls and jars of stone, for so Porphyry understands the passage, because honey was the symbol adopted by the ancients for 'pleasure arising from generation'. The ancients, he says, called souls not only Naiads but bees, 'as the efficient cause of sweetness'; but not all souls 'proceeding into generation' are called bees, 'but those who will live in it justly and who after having performed such things as are acceptable to the gods will again return (to their kindred stars). For this insect loves to return to the place from whence it came and is eminently just and sober.' I find all these details in the cave of the Witch of Atlas, the most elaborately described of Shelley's caves, except the two gates, and these have a far-off echo in her summer journeys on her cavern river and in her winter sleep in 'an inextinguishable well of crimson fire'. We have for the mixing-bowls, and jars of stone full of honey, those delights of the senses, 'sounds of air' 'folded in cells of crystal silence', 'liquors clear and sweet' 'in crystal vials', and for the bees, visions 'each in its thin sheath like a chrysalis', and for

'the looms of stone' and 'raiment of purple stain' the Witch's
spinning and embroidering; and the Witch herself is a Naiad,
and was born from one of the Atlantides, who lay in a
'chamber of grey rock' until she was changed by the sun's
embrace into a cloud.

When one turns to Shelley for an explanation of the cave
and fountain one finds how close his thought was to Porphyry's. He looked upon thought as a condition of life in
generation and believed that the reality beyond was something other than thought. He wrote in his fragment *On Life*:
'That the basis of all things cannot be, as the popular philosophy alleges, mind, is sufficiently evident. Mind, as far as
we have any experience of its properties, and beyond that
experience how vain is argument, cannot create, it can only
perceive'; and in another passage he defines mind as existence. Water is his great symbol of existence, and he continually meditates over its mysterious source. In his prose he tells
how 'thought can with difficulty visit the intricate and winding chambers which it inhabits. It is like a river, whose rapid
and perpetual stream flows outward. . . . The caverns of the
mind are obscure and shadowy; or pervaded with a lustre,
beautiful and bright indeed, but shining not beyond their
portals.' When the Witch has passed in her boat from the
caverned river, that is doubtless her own destiny, she passes
along the Nile 'by Moeris and the Mareotid lakes', and sees
all human life shadowed upon its waters in shadows that
'never are erased but tremble ever'; and in 'many a dark and
subterranean street under the Nile' — new caverns — and
along the bank of the Nile; and as she bends over the unhappy, she compares unhappiness to the strife that 'stirs the
liquid surface of man's life'; and because she can see the
reality of things she is described as journeying 'in the calm
depths' of 'the wide lake' we journey over unpiloted.

Alastor calls the river that he follows an image of his mind, and thinks that it will be as hard to say where his thought will be when he is dead as where its waters will be in ocean or cloud in a little while. In *Mont Blanc*, a poem so overladen with descriptions in parentheses that one loses sight of its logic, Shelley compares the flowing through our mind of 'the universe of things', which are, he has explained elsewhere, but thoughts, to the flowing of the Arve through the ravine, and compares the unknown sources of our thoughts, in some 'remoter world' whose 'gleams' 'visit the soul in sleep', to Arve's sources among the glaciers on the mountain heights. Cythna, in the passage where she speaks of making signs 'a subtler language within language' on the sand by the 'fountain' of sea water in the cave where she is imprisoned, speaks of the 'cave' of her mind which gave its secrets to her, and of 'one mind, the type of all' which is a 'moveless wave' reflecting 'all moving things that are'; and then passing more completely under the power of the symbol, she speaks of growing wise through contemplation of the images that rise out of the fountain at the call of her will. Again and again one finds some passing allusion to the cave of man's mind, or to the caves of his youth, or to the cave of mysteries we enter at death, for to Shelley as to Porphyry it is more than an image of life in the world. It may mean any enclosed life, as when it is the dwelling-place of Asia and Prometheus, or when it is 'the still cave of poetry', and it may have all meanings at once, or it may have as little meaning as some ancient religious symbol enwoven from the habit of centuries with the patterns of a carpet or a tapestry.

As Shelley sailed along those great rivers and saw or imagined the cave that associated itself with rivers in his mind, he saw half-ruined towers upon the hilltops, and once at any rate a tower is used to symbolise a meaning that is the contrary to the meaning symbolised by caves. Cythna's lover is brought through the cave where there is a polluted fountain to a high tower, for being man's far-seeing mind, when the world has cast him out he must to the 'towers of thought's crowned powers'; nor is it possible for Shelley to have forgotten this first imprisonment when he made men imprison Lionel in a tower for a like offence; and because I know how hard it is to forget a symbolical meaning, once one has found it, I believe Shelley had more than a romantic scene in his mind when he made Prince Athanase follow his mysterious studies in a lighted tower above the sea, and when he made the old hermit watch over Laon in his sickness in a half-ruined tower, wherein the sea, here doubtless, as to Cythna, 'the one mind', threw 'spangled sands' and 'rarest sea shells'. The tower, important in Maeterlinck, as in Shelley, is, like the sea, and rivers, and caves with fountains, a very ancient symbol, and would perhaps, as years went by, have grown more important in his poetry. The contrast between it and the cave in *Laon and Cythna* suggests a contrast between the mind looking outward upon men and things and the mind looking inward upon itself, which may or may not have been in Shelley's mind, but certainly helps, with one knows not how many other dim meanings, to give the poem mystery and shadow. It is only by ancient symbols, by symbols that have numberless meanings besides the one or two the writer lays an emphasis upon, or the half-score he knows of, that any highly subjective art can escape from the barrenness and shallowness of a too conscious arrangement, into the abundance and depth of Nature. The poet of essences and pure ideas must seek in the half-lights that glimmer from symbol to symbol as if to the ends of the earth, all that the epic and dramatic poet finds of mystery and shadow in the accidental circumstances of life.

The most important, the most precise of all Shelley's symbols, the one he uses with the fullest knowledge of its meaning, is the Morning and Evening Star. It rises and sets for ever over the towers and rivers, and is the throne of his genius. Personified as a woman it leads Rousseau, the typical poet of *The Triumph of Life*, under the power of the destroying hunger of life, under the power of the sun that we shall find presently as a symbol of life, and it is the Morning Star that wars against the principle of evil in *Laon and Cythna*, at first as a star with a red comet, here a symbol of all evil as it is of disorder in *Epipsychidion*, and then as a serpent with an eagle — symbols in Blake too and in the Alchemists; and it is the Morning Star that appears as a winged youth to a woman, who typifies humanity amid its sorrows, in the first canto of *Laon and Cythna*; and it is invoked by the wailing women of *Hellas*, who call it 'lamp of the free' and 'beacon of love' and would go where it hides flying from the deepening night among those 'kingless continents sinless as Eden', and 'mountains and islands' 'prankt on the sapphire sea' that are but the opposing hemispheres to the senses, but, as I think, the ideal world, the world of the dead, to the imagination; and in the *Ode to Liberty*, Liberty is bid lead wisdom out of the inmost cave of man's mind as the Morning Star leads the sun out of the waves. We know too that had *Prince Athanase* been finished it would have described the finding of Pandemos, the Star's lower genius, and the growing weary of her, and the coming of its true genius Urania at the coming of death, as the day finds the Star at evening. There is hardly indeed a poem of any length in which one does not find it as a symbol of love, or liberty, or wisdom, or beauty, or of some other expression of that Intellectual Beauty which was to Shelley's mind the central power of the world; and to its faint and fleeting light he offers up all desires, that are as —

> The desire of the moth for the star,
>   Of the night for the morrow,
> The devotion to something afar
>   From the sphere of our sorrow.

When its genius comes to Rousseau, shedding dew with one hand, and treading out the stars with her feet, for she is also the genius of the dawn, she brings him a cup full of oblivion and love. He drinks and his mind becomes like sand 'on desert Labrador' marked by the feet of deer and a wolf. And then the new vision, life, the cold light of day moves before him, and the first vision becomes an invisible presence. The same image was in his mind too when he wrote:

> Hesperus flies from awakening night
> And pants in its beauty and speed with light,
> Fast fleeting, soft and bright.

Though I do not think that Shelley needed to go to Porphyry's account of the cold intoxicating cup, given to the souls in the constellation of the Cup near the constellation Cancer, for so obvious a symbol as the cup, or that he could not have found the wolf and the deer and the continual flight of his Star in his own mind, his poetry becomes the richer, the more emotional, and loses something of its appearance of idle fantasy when I remember that these are ancient symbols, and still come to visionaries in their dreams. Because the wolf is but a more violent symbol of longing and desire than the hound, his wolf and deer remind me of the hound and deer that Oisin saw in the Gaelic poem chasing one another on the water before he saw the young man following the woman with the golden apple; and of a Galway tale that tells how Niamh, whose name means brightness or beauty, came to Oisin as a deer; and of a vision that a friend of mine saw when

gazing at a dark-blue curtain. I was with a number of Hermetists, and one of them said to another, 'Do you see something in the curtain?' The other gazed at the curtain for a
while and saw presently a man led through a wood by a black
hound, and then the hound lay dead at a place the seer knew
was called, without knowing why, 'the Meeting of the
Suns', and the man followed a red hound, and then the red
hound was pierced by a spear. A white fawn watched the
man out of the wood, but he did not look at it, for a white
hound came and he followed it trembling, but the seer knew
that he would follow the fawn at last, and that it would lead
him among the gods. The most learned of the Hermetists
said, 'I cannot tell the meaning of the hounds or where the
Meeting of the Suns is, but I think the fawn is the Morning
and Evening Star'. I have little doubt that when the man saw
the white fawn he was coming out of the darkness and passion
of the world into some day of partial regeneration, and that it
was the Morning Star and would be the Evening Star at its
second coming. I have little doubt that it was but the story of
Prince Athanase and what may have been the story of
Rousseau in *The Triumph of Life*, thrown outward once again
from that great Memory, which is still the mother of the
Muses, though men no longer believe in it.

It may have been this memory, or it may have been some
impulse of his nature too subtle for his mind to follow, that
made Keats, with his love of embodied things, of precision of
form and colouring, of emotions made sleepy by the flesh, see
Intellectual Beauty in the Moon; and Blake, who lived in that
energy he called eternal delight, see it in the Sun, where his
personification of poetic genius labours at a furnace. I think
there was certainly some reason why these men took so deep
a pleasure in lights that Shelley thought of with weariness and
trouble. The Moon is the most changeable of symbols, and

not merely because it is the symbol of change. As mistress of
the waters she governs the life of instinct and the generation
of things, for, as Porphyry says, even 'the apparition of
images' in the 'imagination' is through 'an excess of moisture'; and, as a cold and changeable fire set in the bare
heavens, she governs alike chastity and the joyless idle drifting
hither and thither of generated things. She may give God a
body and have Gabriel to bear her messages, or she may come
to men in their happy moments as she came to Endymion, or
she may deny life and shoot her arrows; but because she only
becomes beautiful in giving herself, and is no flying ideal, she
is not loved by the children of desire.

Shelley could not help but see her with unfriendly eyes.
He is believed to have described Mary Shelley at a time when
she had come to seem cold in his eyes, in that passage of
Epipsychidion which tells how a woman like the Moon led
him to her cave and made 'frost' creep over the sea of his
mind, and so bewitched Life and Death with 'her silver voice'
that they ran from him crying, 'Away, he is not of our crew'.
When he describes the Moon as part of some beautiful scene
he can call her beautiful, but when he personifies, when his
words come under the influence of that great Memory or of
some mysterious tide in the depth of our being, he grows unfriendly or not truly friendly or at the most pitiful. The
Moon's lips 'are pale and waning', it is 'the cold Moon', or
'the frozen and inconstant Moon', or it is 'forgotten' and
'waning', or it 'wanders' and is 'weary', or it is 'pale and
grey', or it is 'pale for weariness', and 'wandering companionless' and 'ever changing', and finding 'no object
worth' its 'constancy', or it is like a 'dying lady' who
'totters' 'out of her chamber led by the insane and feeble
wanderings of her fading brain', and even when it is no more
than a star, it casts an evil influence that makes the lips of

lovers 'lurid' or pale. It only becomes a thing of delight when
Time is being borne to his tomb in eternity, for then the
spirit of the Earth, man's procreant mind, fills it with his own
joyousness. He describes the spirit of the Earth and of the
Moon, moving above the rivulet of their lives, in a passage
which reads like a half-understood vision. Man has become
'one harmonious soul of many a soul' and 'all things flow to
all' and 'familiar acts are beautiful through love', and an
'animation of delight' at this change flows from spirit to
spirit till the snow 'is loosened' from the Moon's 'lifeless
mountains'.

Some old magical writer, I forget who, says if you wish to
be melancholy hold in your left hand an image of the Moon
made out of silver, and if you wish to be happy hold in your
right hand an image of the Sun made out of gold.[1] The Sun
is the symbol of sensitive life, and of belief and joy and pride
and energy, of indeed the whole life of the will, and of that
beauty which neither lures from far off, nor becomes beautiful
in giving itself, but makes all glad because it is beauty. Taylor
quotes Proclus as calling it 'the Demiurgos of everything
sensible'. It was therefore natural that Blake, who was always
praising energy, and all exalted overflowing of oneself, and
who thought art an impassioned labour to keep men from
doubt and despondency, and woman's love an evil, when it
would trammel man's will, should see the poetic genius not
in a woman star but in the Sun, and should rejoice throughout
his poetry in 'the Sun in his strength'. Shelley, however,
except when he uses it to describe the peculiar beauty of
Emilia Viviani, who was like 'an incarnation of the Sun
when light is changed to love', saw it with less friendly eyes.
He seems to have seen it with perfect happiness only when

[1] Wilde told me that he had read this somewhere. He had suggested
it to Burne-Jones as a subject for a picture. 1924.

veiled in mist, or glimmering upon water, or when faint enough to do no more than veil the brightness of his own Star; and in *The Triumph of Life*, the one poem in which it is part of the avowed symbolism, its power is the being and the source of all tyrannies. When the woman personifying the Morning Star has faded from before his eyes, Rousseau sees a 'new vision' in 'a cold bright car' with a rainbow hovering over her, and as she comes the shadow passes from 'leaf and stone' and the souls she has enslaved seem 'in that light, like atomies to dance within a sunbeam', or they dance among the flowers that grow up newly in 'the grassy vesture of the desert', unmindful of the misery that is to come upon them. These are 'the great, the unforgotten', all who have worn 'mitres and helms and crowns, or wreaths of light', and yet have not known themselves. Even 'great Plato' is there, because he knew joy and sorrow, because life that could not subdue him by gold or pain, by 'age, or sloth, or slavery', subdued him by love. All who have ever lived are there except Christ and Socrates and the 'sacred few' who put away all life could give, being doubtless followers throughout their lives of the forms borne by the flying ideal, or who, 'as soon as they had touched the world with living flame, fled back like eagles to their native noon'.

In ancient times, it seems to me that Blake, who for all his protest was glad to be alive, and ever spoke of his gladness, would have worshipped in some chapel of the Sun, but that Shelley, who hated life because he sought 'more in life than any understood', would have wandered, lost in a ceaseless reverie, in some chapel of the Star of infinite desire.

I think too that as he knelt before an altar where a thin flame burnt in a lamp made of green agate, a single vision would have come to him again and again, a vision of a boat drifting down a broad river between high hills where there were caves and towers, and following the light of one Star; and that voices would have told him how there is for every man some one scene, some one adventure, some one picture that is the image of his secret life, for wisdom first speaks in images, and that this one image, if he would but brood over it his life long, would lead his soul, disentangled from unmeaning circumstance and the ebb and flow of the world, into that far household where the undying gods await all whose souls have become simple as flame, whose bodies have become quiet as an agate lamp.

But he was born in a day when the old wisdom had vanished and was content merely to write verses, and often with little thought of more than verses.

1900

MAGIC

I

I BELIEVE in the practice and philosophy of what we have agreed to call magic, in what I must call the evocation of spirits, though I do not know what they are, in the power of creating magical illusions, in the visions of truth in the depths of the mind when the eyes are closed; and I believe in three doctrines, which have, as I think, been handed down from early times, and been the foundations of nearly all magical practices. These doctrines are:

(1) That the borders of our mind are ever shifting, and that many minds can flow into one another, as it were, and create or reveal a single mind, a single energy.

(2) That the borders of our memories are as shifting, and that our memories are a part of one great memory, the memory of Nature herself.

(3) That this great mind and great memory can be evoked by symbols.

I often think I would put this belief in magic from me if I could, for I have come to see or to imagine, in men and women, in houses, in handicrafts, in nearly all sights and sounds, a certain evil, a certain ugliness, that comes from the slow perishing through the centuries of a quality of mind that made this belief and its evidences common over the world.

II

Some ten or twelve years ago, a man with whom I have since quarrelled for sound reasons, a very singular man who had given his life to studies other men despised, asked me and an acquaintance, who is now dead, to witness a magical work. He lived a little way from London, and on the way my acquaintance told me that he did not believe in magic, but that a novel of Bulwer Lytton's had taken such a hold upon his imagination that he was going to give much of his time and all his thought to magic. He longed to believe in it, and had studied, though not learnedly, geomancy, astrology, chiromancy, and much cabbalistic symbolism, and yet doubted if the soul outlived the body. He awaited the magical work full of scepticism. He expected nothing more than an air of romance, an illusion as of the stage, that might capture the consenting imagination for an hour. The evoker of spirits and his beautiful wife received us in a little house, on the edge of some kind of garden or park belonging to an eccentric rich man, whose curiosities he arranged and dusted, and he made his evocation in a long room that had a raised place on the floor at one end, a kind of dais, but was furnished meagrely and cheaply. I sat with my acquaintance in the middle of the room, and the evoker of spirits on the dais, and his wife between us and him. He held a wooden mace in his hand, and turning to a tablet of many-coloured squares, with a number on each of the squares, that stood near him on a chair, he repeated a form of words. Almost at once my imagination began to move of itself and to bring before me vivid images that, though never too vivid to be imagination, as I had always understood it, had yet a motion of their own, a life I could not change or shape. I remember seeing a number of white figures, and wondering whether their mitred heads had been suggested by the mitred head of the mace, and then, of a sudden, the image of my acquaintance in the midst of them. I told what I had seen, and the evoker of spirits cried in a deep voice, 'Let him be blotted out,' and as he said it the image of my acquaintance vanished, and the evoker of spirits or his wife saw a man dressed in black with a curious square cap standing among the white figures. It was my acquaintance, the seeress said, as he had been in a past life, the life that had moulded his present, and that life would now unfold before us. I too seemed to see the man with a strange vividness. The story unfolded itself chiefly before the mind's eye of the seeress, but sometimes I saw what she described before I heard her description. She thought the man in black was perhaps a Fleming of the sixteenth century, and I could see him pass along narrow streets till he came to a narrow door with some rusty ironwork above it. He went in, and wishing to find out how far we had one vision among us, I kept silent when I saw a dead body lying upon the table within the door. The seeress described him going down a long hall and up into what she called a pulpit, and beginning to speak. She said, 'He is a clergyman, I can hear his words. They sound like Low Dutch.' Then after a little silence, 'No, I am wrong. I can see the listeners; he is a doctor lecturing among his pupils.' I said, 'Do you see anything near the door?' and she said, 'Yes, I see a subject for dissection.' Then we saw him go out again into the narrow streets, I following the story of the seeress, sometimes merely following her words, but sometimes seeing for myself. My acquaintance saw nothing; I think he was forbidden to see, it being his own life, and I think could not in any case. His imagination had no will of its own. Presently the man in black went into a house with two gables facing the road, and up some stairs into a room where a hump-backed woman gave him a key; and then along a corridor, and down some stairs into a large cellar full of retorts and strange vessels of all kinds. Here he seemed to stay a long while, and one saw him eating bread that he took down from a shelf. The evoker of spirits and the seeress began to speculate about the man's character and habits, and decided, from a visionary impression, that his mind was absorbed in naturalism, but that his imagination had been excited by stories of the marvels wrought by magic in past times, and that he was trying to copy them by naturalistic means. Presently one of them saw him go to a vessel that stood over a slow fire, and take out of the vessel a thing wrapped up in numberless cloths, which he partly unwrapped, showing at length what looked like the image of a man made by somebody who could not model. The evoker of spirits said that the man in black was trying to make flesh by chemical means, and though he had not succeeded, his brooding had drawn so many evil spirits about him that the image was partly alive. He could see it moving a little where it lay upon a table. At that moment I heard something like little squeals, but kept silent, as when I saw the dead body. In a moment more the seeress said, 'I hear little squeals.' Then the evoker of spirits heard them, but said, 'They are not squeals; he is pouring a red liquid out of a retort through a slit in the cloth; the slit is over the mouth of the image and the liquid is gurgling in rather a curious way.' Weeks seemed to pass by hurriedly, and somebody saw the man still busy in his cellar. Then more weeks seemed to pass, and now we saw him lying sick in a room upstairs, and a man in a conical cap standing beside him. We could see the image too. It was in the cellar, but now it could move feebly about the floor. I saw fainter images of the image passing continually from where it crawled to the man in his bed, and I asked the evoker of spirits what they were. He said, 'They are the images of his terror'. Presently the man in the conical cap began to speak, but who heard him I cannot remember. He made the sick man get out of bed and walk, leaning upon him, and in much terror till they came to the cellar. There the man in the conical cap made some symbol over the image, which fell back as if asleep, and putting a knife into the other's hand he said, 'I have taken from it the magical life, but you must take from it the life you gave.' Somebody saw the sick man stoop and sever the head of the image from its body, and then fall as if he had given himself a mortal wound, for he had filled it with his own life. And then the vision changed and fluttered, and he was lying sick again in the room upstairs. He seemed to lie there a long time with the man in the conical cap watching beside him, then, I cannot remember how, the evoker of spirits discovered that though he would in part recover, he would never be well, and that the story had got abroad in the town and shattered his good name. His pupils had left him and men avoided him. He was accursed. He was a magician.

The story was finished, and I looked at my acquaintance. He was white and awestruck. He said, as nearly as I can remember, 'All my life I have seen myself in dreams making a man by some means like that. When I was a child I was always thinking out contrivances for galvanising a corpse into life.' Presently he said, 'Perhaps my bad health in this life comes from that experiment'. I asked if he had read *Frankenstein*, and he answered that he had. He was the only one of us who had, and he had taken no part in the vision.

III

Then I asked to have some past life of mine revealed, and a new evocation was made before the tablet full of little squares. I cannot remember so well who saw this or that detail, for now I was interested in little but the vision itself. I had come to a conclusion about the method. I knew that the vision may be in part common to several people.

A man in chain armour passed through a castle door, and the seeress noticed with surprise the bareness and rudeness of castle rooms. There was nothing of the magnificence or the pageantry she had expected. The man came to a large hall and to a little chapel opening out of it, where a ceremony was taking place. There were six girls dressed in white, who took from the altar some yellow object — I thought it was gold, for though, like my acquaintance, I was told not to see, I could not help seeing. Somebody else thought that it was yellow flowers, and I think the girls, though I cannot remember clearly, laid it between the man's hands. He went out for a time, and as he passed through the great hall one of us, I forget who, noticed that he passed over two gravestones. Then the vision became broken, but presently he stood in a monk's habit among men-at-arms in the middle of a village reading from a parchment. He was calling villagers about him, and presently he and they and the men-at-arms took ship for some long voyage. The vision became broken again, and when we could see clearly they had come to what seemed the Holy Land. They had begun some kind of sacred labour among palm-trees. The common men among them stood idle, but the gentlemen carried large stones, bringing them from certain directions, from the cardinal points, I think, with a ceremonious formality. The evoker of spirits said they must be making some Masonic house. His mind, like the minds of so many students of these hidden things, was always running on Masonry and discovering it in strange places.

We broke the vision that we might have supper, breaking it with some form of words which I forget. When supper had ended the seeress cried out that while we had been eating they had been building, and that they had built not a Masonic house but a great stone cross. And now they had all gone away but the man who had been in chain armour and two monks we had not noticed before. He was standing against the cross, his feet upon two stone rests a little above the ground, and his arms spread out. He seemed to stand there all day, but when night came he went to a little cell, that was beside two other cells. I think they were like the cells I have seen in the Aran Islands, but I cannot be certain. Many days seemed to pass, and all day every day he stood upon the cross, and we never saw anybody there but him and the two monks. Many years seemed to pass, making the vision flutter like a drift of leaves before our eyes, and he grew old and white-haired, and we saw the two monks, old and white-haired, holding him upon the cross. I asked the evoker of spirits why the man stood there, and before he had time to answer I saw two people, a man and a woman, rising like a dream within a dream before the eyes of the man upon the cross. The evoker of spirits saw them too, and said that one of them held up his arms and they were without hands. I thought of the two gravestones the man in chain mail had passed over in the great hall when he came out of the chapel, and asked the evoker of spirits if the knight was undergoing a penance for violence, and while I was asking him, and he was saying that it might be so but he did not know, the vision, having completed its circle, vanished.

It had not, so far as I could see, the personal significance of the other vision, but it was certainly strange and beautiful, though I alone seemed to see its beauty. Who was it that made the story, if it were but a story? I did not, and the seeress did not, and the evoker of spirits did not and could not. It arose in three minds, for I cannot remember my acquaintance taking any part, and it rose without confusion, and without labour, except the labour of keeping the mind's eye awake, and more swiftly than any pen could have written it out. It may be, as Blake said of one of his poems, that the author was in eternity. In coming years I was to see and hear of many such visions, and though I was not to be convinced, though half convinced once or twice, that they were old lives, in an ordinary sense of the word life, I was to learn that they have almost always some quite definite relation to dominant moods and moulding events in this life. They are, perhaps, in most cases, though the vision I have but just described was not, it seems, among the cases, symbolical histories of these moods and events, or rather symbolical shadows of the impulses that have made them, messages as it were out of the ancestral being of the questioner.

At the time these two visions meant little more to me, if I can remember my feeling at the time, than a proof of the supremacy of imagination, of the power of many minds to become one, overpowering one another by spoken words and by unspoken thought till they have become a single, intense, unhesitating energy. One mind was doubtless the master, I thought, but all the minds gave a little, creating or revealing for a moment what I must call a supernatural artist.

*　　*　　*

VI

I once saw a young Irishwoman, fresh from a convent school, cast into a profound trance, though not by a method known to any hypnotist. In her waking state she thought the apple of Eve was the kind of apple you can buy at the greengrocer's, but in her trance she saw the Tree of Life with eversighing souls moving in its branches instead of sap, and among its leaves all the fowls of the air, and on its highest bough one white fowl wearing a crown. When I went home I took from the shelf a translation of *The Book of Concealed Mystery*,[1] an old Jewish book, and cutting the pages came upon this

---

[1] Translated by Mathers in *The Kabbalah Unveiled*.

passage, which I cannot think I had ever read: 'The Tree, .
is the Tree of the Knowledge of Good and Evil . . . in its
branches the birds lodge and build their nests, the souls and
the angels have their place.'

I once saw a young Church of Ireland man, a bank-clerk
in the West of Ireland, thrown in a like trance. I have no
doubt that he, too, was quite certain that the apple of Eve
was a greengrocer's apple, and yet he saw the tree and heard
the souls sighing through its branches, and saw apples with
human faces, and laying his ear to an apple heard a sound as of
fighting hosts within. Presently he strayed from the tree and
came to the edge of Eden, and there he found himself not by
the wilderness he had learned of at the Sunday-school, but
upon the summit of a great mountain, of a mountain 'two
miles high'. The whole summit, in contradiction to all that
would have seemed probable to his waking mind, was a great
walled garden. Some years afterwards I found a mediaeval
diagram, which pictured Eden as a walled garden upon a high
mountain.

Where did these intricate symbols come from? Neither I
nor the one or two people present nor the seers had ever seen,
I am convinced, the description in *The Book of Concealed
Mystery*, or the mediaeval diagram. Remember that the
images appeared in a moment perfect in all their complexity.
If one can imagine that the seers or that I myself or another
had indeed read of these images and forgotten it, that the
supernatural artist's knowledge of what was in our buried
memories accounted for these visions, there are numberless
other visions to account for. One cannot go on believing in
improbable knowledge for ever. For instance, I find in my
diary that on December 27, 1897, a seer, to whom I had given
a certain old Irish symbol, saw Brigid, the goddess, holding
out 'a glittering and wriggling serpent', and yet I feel certain

that neither I nor he knew anything of her association with the serpent until *Carmina Gaedelica* was published a few months ago. And an old Irishwoman who can neither read nor write has described to me a woman dressed like Dian, with helmet, and short skirt and sandals, and what seemed to be buskins. Why, too, among all the countless stories of visions that I have gathered in Ireland, or that a friend has gathered for me, are there none that mix the dress of different periods? The seers when they are but speaking from tradition will mix everything together, and speak of Finn mac Cumhal going to the Assizes at Cork. Almost every one who has ever busied himself with such matters has come, in trance or dream, upon some new and strange symbol or event, which he has afterwards found in some work he had never read or heard of. Examples like this are as yet too little classified, too little analysed, to convince the stranger, but some of them are proof enough for those they have happened to, proof that there is a memory of Nature that reveals events and symbols of distant centuries. Mystics of many countries and many centuries have spoken of this memory; and the honest men and charlatans, who keep the magical traditions which will some day be studied as a part of folk-lore, base most that is of importance in their claims upon this memory. I have read of it in *Paracelsus* and in some Indian book that describes the people of past days as still living within it, 'thinking the thought and doing the deed'. And I have found it in the 'Prophetic Books' of William Blake, who calls its images 'the bright sculptures of Los's Hall'; and says that all events, 'all love stories', renew themselves from those images. It is perhaps well that so few believe in it, for if many did many would go out of parliaments and universities and libraries and run into the wilderness to so waste the body, and to so hush the unquiet mind that, still living, they might pass the doors the dead pass daily; for who among the wise would trouble himself with making laws or in writing history or in weighing the earth if the things of eternity seemed ready to hand?

VII

I find in my diary of magical events for 1899 that I awoke at 3 a.m. out of a nightmare, and imagined one symbol to prevent its recurrence, and imagined another, a simple geometrical form, which calls up dreams of luxuriant vegetable life, that I might have pleasant dreams. I imagined it faintly, being very sleepy, and went to sleep. I had confused dreams which seemed to have no relation with the symbol. I awoke about eight, having for the time forgotten both nightmare and symbol. Presently I dozed off again and began half to dream and half to see, as one does between sleep and waking, enormous flowers and grapes. I awoke and recognised that what I had dreamed or seen was the kind of thing appropriate to the symbol before I remembered having used it. I find another record, though made some time after the event, of having imagined over the head of a person, who was a little of a seer, a combined symbol of elemental air and elemental water. This person, who did not know what symbol I was using, saw a pigeon flying with a lobster in his bill. I find that on December 13, 1898, I used a certain star-shaped symbol with a seeress, getting her to look at it intently before she began seeing. She saw a rough stone house, and in the middle of the house the skull of a horse. I find that I had used the same symbol a few days before with a seer, and that he had seen a rough stone house, and in the middle of the house something under a cloth marked with the Hammer of Thor. He had lifted the cloth and discovered a skeleton of gold with teeth of diamonds, and eyes of some unknown dim precious stones. I had made a note to this last vision, pointing out that we had been using a Solar symbol a little earlier. Solar symbols often call up visions of gold and precious stones. I do not give these examples to prove my arguments, but to illustrate them. I know that my examples will awaken in all who have not met the like, or who are not on other grounds inclined towards my arguments, a most natural incredulity. It was long before I myself would admit an inherent power in symbols, for it long seemed to me that one could account for everything by the power of one imagination over another, or by telepathy, as the Society for Psychical Research would say. The symbol seemed powerful, I thought, merely because we thought it powerful, and we would do just as well without it. In those days I used symbols made with some ingenuity instead of merely imagining them. I used to give them to the person I was experimenting with, and tell him to hold them to his forehead without looking at them; and sometimes I made a mistake. I learned from these mistakes that if I did not myself imagine the symbol, in which case he would have a mixed vision, it was the symbol I gave by mistake that[1] produced the vision. Then I met with a seer who could say to me, 'I have a vision of a square pond, but I can see your thought, and you expect me to see an oblong pond', or, 'The symbol you are imagining has made me see a woman holding a crystal, but it was a moonlight sea I should have seen'. I discovered that the symbol hardly ever failed to call up its typical scene, its typical event, its typical person, but that I could practically never call up, no matter how vividly I imagined it, the particular scene, the particular event, the particular person I had

---

[1] I forgot that my 'subconsciousness' would know clairvoyantly what symbol I had really given and would respond to the associations of that symbol. I am, however, certain that the main symbols (symbolic roots, as it were) draw upon associations which are beyond the reach of the individual 'subconsciousness'.   1924

in my own mind, and that when I could, the two visions rose side by side.

I cannot now think symbols less than the greatest of all powers whether they are used consciously by the masters of magic, or half unconsciously by their successors, the poet, the musician and the artist. At first I tried to distinguish between symbols and symbols, between what I called inherent symbols and arbitrary symbols, but the distinction has come to mean little or nothing. Whether their power has arisen out of themselves, or whether it has an arbitrary origin, matters little, for they act, as I believe, because the Great Memory associates them with certain events and moods and persons. Whatever the passions of man have gathered about, becomes a symbol in the Great Memory, and in the hands of him who has the secret it is a worker of wonders, a caller-up of angels or of devils. The symbols are of all kinds, for everything in heaven or earth has its association, momentous or trivial, in the Great Memory, and one never knows what forgotten events may have plunged it, like the toadstool and the ragweed, into the great passions. Knowledgeable men and women in Ireland sometimes distinguish between the simples that work cures by some medical property in the herb, and those that do their work by magic. Such magical simples as the husk of the flax, water out of the fork of an elm-tree, do their work, as I think, by awaking in the depths of the mind where it mingles with the Great Mind, and is enlarged by the Great Memory, some curative energy, some hypnotic command. They are not what we call faith cures, for they have been much used and successfully, the traditions of all lands affirm, over children and over animals, and to me they seem the only medicine that could have been committed safely to ancient hands. To pluck the wrong leaf would have been to go uncured, but, if one had eaten it, one might have been poisoned.

VIII

I have now described that belief in magic which has set me all but unwilling among those lean and fierce minds who are at war with their time, who cannot accept the days as they pass, simply and gladly; and I look at what I have written with some alarm, for I have told more of the ancient secret than many among my fellow-students think it right to tell. I have come to believe so many strange things because of experience, that I see little reason to doubt the truth of many things that are beyond my experience; and it may be that there are beings who watch over that ancient secret, as all tradition affirms, and resent, and perhaps avenge, too fluent speech. They say in the Aran Islands that if you speak over-much of the things of Faery your tongue becomes like a stone, and it seems to me, though doubtless naturalistic reason would call it auto-suggestion or the like, that I have often felt my tongue become just so heavy and clumsy. More than once, too, as I wrote this very essay I have become uneasy, and have torn up some paragraph, not for any literary reason, but because some incident or some symbol that would perhaps have meant nothing to the reader, seemed, I know not why, to belong to hidden things. Yet I must write or be of no account to any cause, good or evil; I must commit what merchandise of wisdom I have to this ship of written speech, and after all, I have many a time watched it put out to sea with not less alarm when all the speech was rhyme. We who write, we who bear witness, must often hear our hearts cry out against us, complaining because of their hidden things, and I know not but he who speaks of wisdom may some-times, in the change that is coming upon the world, have to fear the anger of the people of Faery, whose country is the heart of the world — 'The Land of the Living Heart'. Who can keep always to the little pathway between speech and silence, where one meets none but discreet revelations? And surely, at whatever risk, we must cry out that imagination is always seeking to remake the world according to the impulses and the patterns in that Great Mind, and that Great Memory? Can there be anything so important as to cry out that what we call romance, poetry, intellectual beauty, is the only signal that the supreme Enchanter, or some one in His councils, is speaking of what has been, and shall be again, in the consummation of time?

1901

AT STRATFORD-ON-AVON

*   *   *

II

I do not think there is anything I disliked in Stratford, besides certain new houses, but the shape of the theatre; and as a larger theatre must be built sooner or later, that would be no great matter if one could put a wiser shape into somebody's head. I cannot think there is any excuse for a half-round theatre, where land is not expensive, or no very great audience to be seated within earshot of the stage; or that it was adopted for a better reason than because it has come down to us, though from a time when the art of the stage was a different art. The Elizabethan theatre was a half-round, because the players were content to speak their lines on a platform, as if they were speakers at a public meeting, and we go on building in the same shape, although our art of the stage is the art of making a succession of pictures. Were our theatres of the shape of a half-closed fan, like Wagner's theatre, where the audience sit on seats that rise towards the broad end while the play is played at the narrow end, their pictures could be composed for eyes at a small number of points of view, instead of for eyes at many points of view, above and below and at the sides, and what is no better than a trade might become an art. With the eyes watching from the sides of a half-round, on the floor and in the boxes and galleries, would go the solid-built houses and the flat trees that shake with every breath of air; and we could make our pictures with robes that contrasted with great masses of colour in the back-cloth and

such severe or decorative forms of hills and trees and houses
as would not overwhelm, as our naturalistic scenery does, the
idealistic art of the poet, and all at a little price. Naturalistic
scene-painting is not an art, but a trade, because it is, at best,
an attempt to copy the more obvious effects of Nature by the
methods of the ordinary landscape-painter, and by his
methods made coarse and summary. It is but flashy landscape-
painting and lowers the taste it appeals to, for the taste it
appeals to has been formed by a more delicate art. Decorative
scene-painting would be, on the other hand, as inseparable
from the movements as from the robes of the players and
from the falling of the light; and being in itself a grave and
quiet thing it would mingle with the tones of the voices and
with the sentiment of the play, without overwhelming them
under an alien interest. It would be a new and legitimate art
appealing to a taste formed by itself and copying but itself.
Mr. Gordon Craig used scenery of this kind at the Purcell
Society performance the other day, and despite some marring
of his effects by the half-round shape of the theatre, it was the
first beautiful scenery our stage has seen. He created an ideal
country where everything was possible, even speaking in
verse, or speaking to music, or the expression of the whole of
life in a dance, and I would like to see Stratford-on-Avon
decorate its Shakespeare with like scenery. As we cannot, it
seems, go back to the platform and the curtain, and the argument for doing so is not without weight, we can only get rid
of the sense of unreality, which most of us feel when we listen
to the conventional speech of Shakespeare, by making scenery
as conventional. Time after time his people use at some
moment of deep emotion an elaborate or deliberate metaphor,
or do some improbable thing which breaks an emotion of
reality we have imposed upon him by an art that is not his,
nor in the spirit of his. It also is an essential part of his method

to give slight or obscure motives of many actions that our attention may dwell on what is of chief importance, and we set these cloudy actions among solid-looking houses, and what we hope are solid-looking trees, and illusion comes to an end, slain by our desire to increase it. In his art, as in all the older art of the world, there was much make-believe, and our scenery, too, should remember the time when, as my nurse used to tell me, herons built their nests in old men's beards! Mr. Benson did not venture to play the scene in *Richard III* where the ghosts walk as Shakespeare wrote it, but had his scenery been as simple as Mr. Gordon Craig's purple back-cloth that made Dido and Aeneas seem wandering on the edge of eternity, he would have found nothing absurd in pitching the tents of Richard and Richmond side by side. Goethe has said, 'Art is art, because it is not nature!'

III

In *La Peau de chagrin* Balzac spends many pages in describing a coquette, who seems the image of heartlessness, and then invents an improbable incident that her chief victim may discover how beautifully she can sing. Nobody had ever heard her sing, and yet in her singing, and in her chatter with her maid, Balzac tells us, was her true self. He would have us understand that behind the momentary self, which acts and lives in the world, and is subject to the judgment of the world, there is that which cannot be called before any mortal judgment seat, even though a great poet, or novelist, or philosopher be sitting upon it. Great literature has always been written in a like spirit, and is, indeed, the Forgiveness of Sin, and when we find it becoming the Accusation of Sin, as in George Eliot, who plucks her Tito in pieces with as much assurance as if he had been clockwork, literature has begun to

change into something else. George Eliot had a fierceness
hardly to be found but in a woman turned argumentative, but
the habit of mind her fierceness gave its life to was characteristic of her century, and is the habit of mind of the Shakespearian critics. They and she grew up in a century of utili-
tarianism, when nothing about a man seemed important
except his utility to the State, and nothing so useful to the State
as the actions whose effect can be weighed by reason. The deeds
of Coriolanus, Hamlet, Timon, Richard III had no obvious
use, were, indeed, no more than the expression of their personalities, and so it was thought Shakespeare was accusing
them, and telling us to be careful lest we deserve the like
accusations. It did not occur to the critics that you cannot
know a man from his actions because you cannot watch him
in every kind of circumstance, and that men are made useless
to the State as often by abundance as by emptiness, and that
a man's business may at times be revelation, and not reformation. Fortinbras was, it is likely enough, a better king than
Hamlet would have been, Aufidius was a more reasonable
man than Coriolanus, Henry V was a better man-at-arms than
Richard II, but, after all, were not those others who changed
nothing for the better and many things for the worse greater
in the Divine Hierarchies? Blake has said that 'the roaring of
lions, the howling of wolves, the raging of the stormy sea, and
the destructive sword are portions of Eternity, too great for
the eye of man', but Blake belonged by right to the ages of
Faith, and thought the State of less moment than the Divine
Hierarchies. Because reason can only discover completely the
use of those obvious actions which everybody admires, and
because every character was to be judged by efficiency in
action, Shakespearian criticism became a vulgar worshipper
of success. I have turned over many books in the library at
Stratford-on-Avon, and I have found in nearly all an anti-

thesis, which grew in clearness and violence as the century grew older, between two types, whose representatives were Richard II, 'sentimental', 'weak', 'selfish', 'insincere', and Henry V, 'Shakespeare's only hero'. These books took the same delight in abasing Richard II that schoolboys do in persecuting some boy of fine temperament, who has weak muscles and a distaste for school games. And they had the admiration for Henry V that schoolboys have for the sailor or soldier hero of a romance in some boys' paper. I cannot claim any minute knowledge of these books, but I think that these emotions began among the German critics, who perhaps saw something French and Latin in Richard II, and I know that Professor Dowden, whose book I once read carefully, first made these emotions eloquent and plausible. He lived in Ireland, where everything has failed, and he meditated frequently upon the perfection of character which had, he thought, made England successful, for, as we say, 'cows beyond the water have long horns'. He forgot that England, as Gordon has said, was made by her adventurers, by her people of wildness and imagination and eccentricity; and thought that Henry V, who only seemed to be these things because he had some commonplace vices, was not only the typical Anglo-Saxon, but the model Shakespeare held up before England; and he even thought it worth while pointing out that Shakespeare himself was making a large fortune while he was writing about Henry's victories. In Professor Dowden's successors this apotheosis went further; and it reached its height at a moment of imperialistic enthusiasm, of ever-deepening conviction that the commonplace shall inherit the earth, when somebody of reputation, whose name I cannot remember, wrote that Shakespeare admired this one character alone out of all his characters. The Accusation of Sin produced its necessary fruit, hatred of all that was abundant, extravagant, exuberant, of all that sets a sail for shipwreck, and flattery of the commonplace emotions and conventional ideals of the mob, the chief Paymaster of accusation.

IV

I cannot believe that Shakespeare looked on his Richard II with any but sympathetic eyes, understanding indeed how ill-fitted he was to be king, at a certain moment of history, but understanding that he was lovable and full of capricious fancy, 'a wild creature' as Pater has called him. The man on whom Shakespeare modelled him had been full of French elegances as he knew from Holinshed, and had given life a new luxury, a new splendour, and been 'too friendly' to his friends, 'too favourable' to his enemies. And certainly Shakespeare had these things in his head when he made his king fail, a little because he lacked some qualities that were doubtless common among his scullions, but more because he had certain qualities that are uncommon in all ages. To suppose that Shakespeare preferred the men who deposed his king is to suppose that Shakespeare judged men with the eyes of a Municipal Coun-cillor weighing the merits of a Town Clerk; and that had he been by when Verlaine cried out from his bed, 'Sir, you have been made by the stroke of a pen, but I have been made by the breath of God', he would have thought the Hospital Superintendent the better man. He saw indeed, as I think, in Richard II the defeat that awaits all, whether they be artist or saint, who find themselves where men ask of them a rough energy and have nothing to give but some con-templative virtue, whether lyrical fantasy, or sweetness of temper, or dreamy dignity, or love of God, or love of His creatures. He saw that such a man through sheer bewilder-ment and impatience can become as unjust or as violent as any common man, any Bolingbroke or Prince John, and yet remain 'that sweet lovely rose'. The courtly and saintly ideals of the Middle Ages were fading, and the practical ideals of the modern age had begun to threaten the unuseful dome of the sky; Merry England was fading, and yet it was not so faded that the poets could not watch the procession of the world with that untroubled sympathy for men as they are, as apart from all they do and seem, which is the substance of tragic irony.

Shakespeare cared little for the State, the source of all our judgments, apart from its shows and splendours, its turmoils and battles, its flamings-out of the uncivilised heart. He did indeed think it wrong to overturn a king, and thereby to swamp peace in civil war, and the historical plays from *Henry IV* to *Richard III*, that monstrous birth and last sign of the wrath of Heaven, are a fulfilment of the prophecy of the Bishop of Carlisle, who was 'raised up by God' to make it; but he had no nice sense of utilities, no ready balance to measure deeds, like that fine instrument, with all the latest improvements, Gervinus and Professor Dowden handle so skilfully. He meditated as Solomon, not as Bentham meditated, upon blind ambitions, untoward accidents, and capricious passions, and the world was almost as empty in his eyes as it must be in the eyes of God.

> Tired with all these, for restful death I cry; –
>   As, to behold desert a beggar born,
> And needy nothing trimm'd in jollity,
>   And purest faith unhappily forsworn,
> And gilded honour shamefully misplaced,
>   And maiden virtue rudely strumpeted,
> And right perfection wrongfully disgraced,
>   And strength by limping sway disabled,

And art made tongue-tied by authority,
    And folly, doctor-like, controlling skill,
And simple truth miscall'd simplicity,
    And captive good attending captain ill:
Tired with all these, from these would I be gone,
Save that, to die, I leave my love alone.

V

The Greeks, a certain scholar has told me, considered that
myths are the activities of the Daimons, and that the Daimons
shape our characters and our lives. I have often had the fancy
that there is some one myth for every man, which, if we but
knew it, would make us understand all he did and thought.
Shakespeare's myth, it may be, describes a wise man who was
blind from very wisdom, and an empty man who thrust him
from his place, and saw all that could be seen from very
emptiness. It is in the story of Hamlet, who saw too great
issues everywhere to play the trivial game of life, and of
Fortinbras, who came from fighting battles about 'a little
patch of ground' so poor that one of his captains would not
give 'six ducats' to 'farm it', and who was yet acclaimed by
Hamlet and by all as the only befitting king. And it is in the
story of Richard II, that unripened Hamlet, and of Henry V,
that ripened Fortinbras. To pose character against character
was an element in Shakespeare's art, and scarcely a play is
lacking in characters that are the complement of one another,
and so, having made the vessel of porcelain, Richard II, he
had to make the vessel of clay, Henry V. He makes him the
reverse of all that Richard was. He has the gross vices, the
coarse nerves, of one who is to rule among violent people,
and he is so little 'too friendly' to his friends that he bundles
them out of doors when their time is over. He is as remorse-

less and undistinguished as some natural force, and the finest thing in his play is the way his old companions fall out of it broken-hearted or on their way to the gallows; and instead of that lyricism which rose out of Richard's mind like the jet of a fountain to fall again where it had risen, instead of that fantasy too enfolded in its own sincerity to make any thought the hour had need of, Shakespeare has given him a resounding rhetoric that moves men as a leading article does to-day. His purposes are so intelligible to everybody that everybody talks of him as if he succeeded, although he fails in the end, as all men great and little fail in Shakespeare. His conquests abroad are made nothing by a woman turned warrior. That boy he and Katharine were to 'compound', 'half French, half English', 'that' was to 'go to Constantinople and take the Turk by the beard', turns out a saint and loses all his father had built up at home and his own life.

Shakespeare watched Henry V not indeed as he watched the greater souls in the visionary procession, but cheerfully, as one watches some handsome spirited horse, and he spoke his tale, as he spoke all tales, with tragic irony.

VI

The six plays, that are but one play, have, when played one after another, something extravagant and superhuman, something almost mythological. These nobles with their indifference to death and their immense energy seem at times no nearer the common stature of men than do the gods and the heroes of Greek plays. Had there been no Renaissance and no Italian influence to bring in the stories of other lands, English history would, it may be, have become as important to the English imagination as the Greek myths to the Greek imagination; and many plays by many poets would have woven it into a single story whose contours, vast as those of Greek myth, would have made living men and women seem like swallows building their nests under the architrave of some Temple of the Giants. English literature, because it would have grown out of itself, might have had the simplicity and unity of Greek literature, for I can never get out of my head that no man, even though he be Shakespeare, can write perfectly when his web is woven of threads that have been spun in many lands. And yet, could those foreign tales have come in if the great famine, the sinking down of popular imagination, the dying out of traditional fantasy, the ebbing out of the energy of race, had not made them necessary? The metaphors and language of Euphuism, compounded of the natural history and mythology of the classics, were doubtless a necessity also that something might be poured into the emptiness. Yet how they injured the simplicity and unity of the speech! Shakespeare wrote at a time when solitary great men were gathering to themselves the fire that had once flowed hither and thither among all men, when individualism in work and thought and emotion was breaking up the old rhythms of life, when the common people, sustained no longer by the myths of Christianity and of still older faiths, were sinking into the earth.

The people of Stratford-on-Avon have remembered little about him, and invented no legend to his glory. They have remembered a drinking-bout of his, and invented some bad verses for him, and that is about all. Had he been some hard-drinking, hard-living, hard-riding, loud-blaspheming squire they would have enlarged his fame by a legend of his dealings with the Devil; but in his day the glory of a poet, like that of all other imaginative powers, had ceased, or almost ceased, outside a narrow class. The poor Gaelic rhymer leaves a nobler memory among his neighbours, who will talk of angels standing like flames about his death-bed, and of voices speaking out of bramble-bushes that he may have the wisdom of the world. The Puritanism that drove the theatres into Surrey was but part of an inexplicable movement that was trampling out the minds of all but some few thousands born to cultivated ease.

May 1901

EDMUND SPENSER

*   *   *

III

When Spenser was buried in Westminster Abbey many poets read verses in his praise, and then threw their verses and the pens that had written them into his tomb. Like him they belonged, for all the moral zeal that was gathering like a London fog, to that indolent, demonstrative Merry England that was about to pass away. Men still wept when they were moved, still dressed themselves in joyous colours, and spoke with many gestures. Thoughts and qualities sometimes come to their perfect expression when they are about to pass away, and Merry England was dying in plays, and in poems, and in strange adventurous men. If one of those poets who threw his copy of verses into the earth that was about to close over his master were to come alive again, he would find some shadow of the life he knew, though not the art he knew, among young men in Paris, and would think that his true country. If he came to England he would find nothing there but the triumph of the Puritan and the merchant — those enemies he had feared and hated — and he would weep perhaps, in that womanish way of his, to think that so much greatness had been, not, as he had hoped, the dawn, but the sunset of a people. He had lived in the last days of what we may call the Anglo-French nation, the old feudal nation that had been established when the Norman and the Angevin made French the language of court and market. In the time of Chaucer

English poets still wrote much in French, and even English labourers lilted French songs over their work; and I cannot read any Elizabethan poem or romance without feeling the pressure of habits of emotion, and of an order of life, which were conscious, for all their Latin gaiety, of a quarrel to the death with that new Anglo-Saxon nation that was arising amid Puritan sermons and Marprelate pamphlets. This nation had driven out the language of its conquerors, and now it was to overthrow their beautiful haughty imagination and their manners, full of abandon and wilfulness, and to set in their stead earnestness and logic and the timidity and reserve of a counting-house. It had been coming for a long while, for it had made the Lollards; and when Anglo-French Chaucer was at Westminster, its poet, Langland, sang the office at Saint Paul's. Shakespeare, with his delight in great persons, with his indifference to the State, with his scorn of the crowd, with his feudal passion, was of the old nation, and Spenser, though a joyless earnestness had cast shadows upon him, and darkened his intellect wholly at times, was of the old nation too. His *Faerie Queene* was written in Merry England, but when Bunyan wrote in prison the other great English allegory, Modern England had been born. Bunyan's men would do right that they might come some day to the Delectable Mountains, and not at all that they might live happily in a world whose beauty was but an entanglement about their feet. Religion had denied the sacredness of an earth that commerce was about to corrupt and ravish, but when Spenser lived the earth had still its sheltering sacredness. His religion, where the paganism that is natural to proud and happy people had been strengthened by the Platonism of the Renaissance, cherished the beauty of the soul and the beauty of the body with, as it seemed, an equal affection. He would have had men live well, not merely that they might win eternal happiness, but that they might live splendidly among men and be celebrated in many songs. How could one live well if one had not the joy of the Creator and of the Giver of gifts? He says in his *Hymne in Honour of Beautie* that a beautiful soul, unless for some stubbornness in the ground, makes for itself a beautiful body, and he even denies that beautiful persons ever lived who had not souls as beautiful. They may have been tempted until they seemed evil, but that was the fault of others. And in his *Hymne of Heavenly Beautie* he sets a woman little known to theology, one that he names Wisdom or Beauty, above Seraphim and Cherubim and in the very bosom of God, and in the *Faerie Queene* it is pagan Venus and her lover Adonis who create the forms of all living things and send them out into the world, calling them back again to the gardens of Adonis at their lives' end to rest there, as it seems, two thousand years between life and life. He began in English poetry, despite a temperament that delighted in sensuous beauty alone with perfect delight, that worship of Intellectual Beauty which Shelley carried to a greater subtlety and applied to the whole of life.

The qualities, to each of whom he had planned to give a Knight, he had borrowed from Aristotle and partly Christianised, but not to the forgetting of their heathen birth. The chief of the Knights, who would have combined in himself qualities of all the others, had Spenser lived to finish the *Faerie Queene*, was King Arthur, the representative of an ancient quality, Magnificence. Born at the moment of change, Spenser had indeed many Puritan thoughts. It has been recorded that he cut his hair short and half regretted his hymns to Love and Beauty. But he has himself told us that the many-headed beast overthrown and bound by Calidore, Knight of Courtesy, was Puritanism itself. Puritanism, its zeal and its narrowness, and the angry suspicion that it had in common with all movements of the ill-educated, seemed no other to him than a slanderer of all fine things. One doubts, indeed, if he could have persuaded himself that there could be any virtue at all without courtesy, perhaps without something of pageant and eloquence. He was, I think, by nature altogether a man of that old Catholic feudal nation, but, like Sidney, he wanted to justify himself to his new masters. He wrote of knights and ladies, wild creatures imagined by the aristocratic poets of the twelfth century, and perhaps chiefly by English poets who had still the French tongue; but he fastened them with allegorical nails to a big barn-door of common sense, of merely practical virtue. Allegory itself had risen into general importance with the rise of the merchant class in the thirteenth and fourteenth centuries; and it was natural when that class was about for the first time to shape an age in its image, that the last epic poet of the old order should mix its art with his own long-descended, irresponsible, happy art.

IV

Allegory and, to a much greater degree, symbolism are a natural language by which the soul when entranced, or even in ordinary sleep, communes with God and with angels. They can speak of things which cannot be spoken of in any other language, but one will always, I think, feel some sense of unreality when they are used to describe things which can be described as well in ordinary words. Dante used allegory to describe visionary things, and the first maker of *The Romance of the Rose*, for all his lighter spirits, pretends that his adventures came to him in a vision one May morning; while Bunyan, by his preoccupation with Heaven and the soul, gives his simple story a visionary strangeness and intensity: he believes so little in the world that he takes us away from all ordinary standards of probability and makes us believe even in allegory for a while. Spenser, on the other hand, to whom allegory was not, as I think, natural at all, makes us feel again and again that it disappoints and interrupts our preoccupation with the beautiful and sensuous life he has called up before our eyes. It interrupts us most when he copies Langland, and writes in what he believes to be a mood of edification, and the least when he is not quite serious, when he sets before us some procession like a Court pageant made to celebrate a wedding or a crowning. One cannot think that he should have occupied himself with moral and religious questions at all. He should have been content to be, as Emerson thought Shakespeare was, a Master of the Revels to mankind. I am certain that he never gets that visionary air which can alone make allegory real, except when he writes out of a feeling for glory and passion. He had no deep moral or religious life. He has never a line like Dante's 'His Will is our Peace', or like Thomas à Kempis's 'The Holy Spirit has liberated me from a multitude of opinions', or even like Hamlet's objection to the bare bodkin. He had been made a poet by what he had almost learnt to call his sins. If he had not felt it necessary to justify his art to some serious friend, or perhaps even to 'that rugged forehead', he would have written all his life long, one thinks, of the loves of shepherdesses and shepherds, among whom there would have been perhaps the morals of the dovecot. One is persuaded that his morality is official and impersonal — a system of life which it was his duty to support — and it is perhaps a half understanding of this that has made so many generations believe that he was the first Poet Laureate, the first salaried moralist among the poets. His processions of deadly sins, and his houses, where the very cornices are arbitrary images of virtue, are an unconscious hypocrisy, an undelighted obedience to the 'rugged forehead', for all the while he is thinking of

nothing but lovers whose bodies are quivering with the
memory or the hope of long embraces. When they are not
together, he will indeed embroider emblems and images
much as those great ladies of the courts of love embroidered
them in their castles; and when these are imagined out of a
thirst for magnificence and not thought out in a mood of
edification, they are beautiful enough; but they are always
tapestries for corridors that lead to lovers' meetings or for the
walls of marriage chambers. He was not passionate, for the
passionate feed their flame in wanderings and absences, when
the whole being of the beloved, every little charm of body
and of soul, is always present to the mind, filling it with
heroical subtleties of desire. He is a poet of the delighted
senses, and his song becomes most beautiful when he writes
of those islands of Phaedria and Acrasia, which angered 'that
rugged forehead', as it seems, but gave to Keats his *Belle
Dame sans merci* and his 'perilous seas in faery lands forlorn',
and to William Morris his 'Water of the Wondrous Isles'.

v

The dramatists lived in a disorderly world, reproached by
many, persecuted even, but following their imagination
wherever it led them. Their imagination, driven hither and
thither by beauty and sympathy, put on something of the
nature of eternity. Their subject was always the soul, the
whimsical, self-awakening, self-exciting, self-appeasing soul.
They celebrated its heroical, passionate will going by its own
path to immortal and invisible things. Spenser, on the other
hand, except among those smooth pastoral scenes and lovely
effeminate islands that have made him a great poet, tried to
be of his time, or rather of the time that was all but at hand.
Like Sidney, whose charm, it may be, led many into slavery,
he persuaded himself that we enjoy Virgil because of the

virtues of Aeneas, and so planned out his immense poem that it would set before the imagination of citizens, in whom there would soon be no great energy, innumerable blameless Aeneases. He had learned to put the State, which desires all the abundance for itself, in the place of the Church, and he found it possible to be moved by expedient emotions, merely because they were expedient, and to think serviceable thoughts with no self-contempt. He loved his Queen a little because she was the protectress of poets and an image of that old Anglo-French nation that lay a-dying, but a great deal because she was the image of the State which had taken possession of his conscience. She was over sixty years old, ugly and, historians will have it, selfish, but in his poetry she is 'fair Cynthia', 'a crown of lilies', 'the image of the heavens', 'without mortal blemish', and has 'an angelic face', where 'the red rose' has 'meddled with the white'; 'Phoebus thrusts out his golden head' but to look upon her, and blushes to find himself outshone. She is 'a fourth Grace', 'a queen of love', 'a sacred saint', and 'above all her sex that ever yet has been'. In the midst of his praise of his own sweetheart he stops to remember that Elizabeth is more beautiful, and an old man in *Daphnaïda*, although he has been brought to death's door by the death of a beautiful daughter, remembers that though his daughter 'seemed of angels' race', she was yet but the primrose to the rose beside Elizabeth. Spenser had learned to look to the State not only as the rewarder of virtue but as the maker of right and wrong, and had begun to love and hate as it bid him. The thoughts that we find for ourselves are timid and a little secret, but those modern thoughts that we share with large numbers are confident and very insolent. We have little else to-day, and when we read our newspaper and take up its cry, above all, its cry of hatred, we will not think very carefully, for we hear

the marching feet. When Spenser wrote of Ireland he wrote
as an official, and out of thoughts and emotions that had been
organised by the State. He was the first of many Englishmen
to see nothing but what he was desired to see. Could he have
gone there as a poet merely, he might have found among its
poets more wonderful imaginations than even those islands of
Phaedria and Acrasia. He would have found among wandering story-tellers, not indeed his own power of rich, sustained
description, for that belongs to lettered ease, but certainly all
the kingdom of Faery, still unfaded, of which his own poetry
was often but a troubled image. He would have found men
doing by swift strokes of the imagination much that he was
doing with painful intellect, with that imaginative reason that
soon was to drive out imagination altogether and for a long
time. He would have met with, at his own door, story-
tellers among whom the perfection of Greek art was indeed
as unknown as his own power of sustained description, but
who, none the less, imagined or remembered beautiful
incidents and strange, pathetic outcrying that made them of
Homer's lineage. Flaubert says somewhere: 'There are things
in Hugo, as in Rabelais, that I could have mended, things
badly built, but then what thrusts of power beyond the reach
of conscious art!' Is not all history but the coming of that
conscious art which first makes articulate and then destroys
the old wild energy? Spenser, the first poet struck with remorse, the first poet who gave his heart to the State, saw
nothing but disorder, where the mouths that have spoken all
the fables of the poets had not yet become silent. All about
him were shepherds and shepherdesses still living the life
that made Theocritus and Virgil think of shepherd and poet as
the one thing; but though he dreamed of Virgil's shepherds
he wrote a book to advise, among many like things, the
harrying of all that followed flocks upon the hills, and of all

the 'wandering companies that keep the wood'. His *View of the Present State of Ireland* commends indeed the beauty of the hills and woods where they did their shepherding, in that powerful and subtle language of his which I sometimes think more full of youthful energy than even the language of the great playwrights. He is 'sure it is yet a most beautiful and sweet country as any is under heaven', and that all would prosper but for those agitators, those 'wandering companies that keep the wood', and he would rid it of them by a certain expeditious way. There should be four great garrisons. 'And those fowre garrisons issuing foorthe, at such convenient times as they shall have intelligence or espiall upon the enemye, will so drive him from one side to another, and tennis him amongst them, that he shall finde nowhere safe to keepe his creete, or hide himselfe, but flying from the fire shall fall into the water, and out of one daunger into another, that in short space his creete, which is his moste sustenaunce, shall be wasted in preying, or killed in driving, or starved for wante of pasture in the woodes, and he himselfe brought soe lowe, that he shall have no harte nor abilitye to indure his wretchednesse, the which will surely come to passe in very short space; for one winters well following of him will soe plucke him on his knees that he will never be able to stand up agayne.'

He could commend this expeditious way from personal knowledge, and could assure the Queen that the people of the country would soon 'consume themselves and devoure one another. The proofs whereof I saw sufficiently en-sampled in these late warres in Mounster; for notwithstanding that the same was a most rich and plentifull countrey, full of corne and cattell, that you would have thought they would have bene able to stand long, yet ere one yeare and a halfe they were brought to such wretchednesse, as that any stonye harte would have rued the same. Out of every corner of the woodes and glynnes they came creeping forth upon theyr hands, for theyr legges could not beare them; they looked like anatomyes of death, they spake like ghostes crying out of theyr graves; they did eate of the dead carrions, happy were they if they could finde them, yea, and one another soone after, insoemuch as the very carcasses they spared not to scrape out of theyr graves; and if they found a plot of watercresses or shamrokes, there they flocked as to a feast for the time, yet not able long to continue therewithall; that in short space there were none allmost left, and a most populous and plentifull countrey suddaynely made voyde of man or beast; yet sure in all that warre, there perished not many by the sword, but all by the extremitye of famine.'

VI

In a few years the Four Masters were to write the history of that time, and they were to record the goodness or the badness of Irishman and Englishman with entire impartiality. They had seen friends and relatives persecuted, but they would write of that man's poisoning and this man's charities and of the fall of great houses, and hardly with any other emotion than a thought of the pitiableness of all life. Friend and enemy would be for them a part of the spectacle of the world. They remembered indeed those Anglo-French invaders who conquered for the sake of their own strong hand, and when they had conquered became a part of the life about them, singing its songs, when they grew weary of their own Iseult and Guinevere. But famines and exterminations had not made them understand, as I think, that new invaders were among them, who fought for an alien State, for an alien religion. Such ideas were difficult to them, for they belonged to the old individual, poetical life, and spoke a language even in which it was all but impossible to think an abstract thought. They understood Spain, possibly, which persecuted in the interests of religion, but I doubt if anybody in Ireland could have understood as yet that the Anglo-Saxon nation was beginning to persecute in the service of ideas it believed to be the foundation of the State. I doubt if anybody in Ireland saw that with certainty, till the Great Demagogue had come and turned the old house of the noble into 'the house of the Poor, the lonely house, the accursed house of Cromwell'. He came, another Cairbry Cat-Head, with that great rabble who had overthrown the pageantry of Church and Court, but who turned towards him faces full of the sadness and docility of their long servitude, and the old individual, poetical life went down, as it seems, for ever. He had studied Spenser's book and approved of it, as we know, finding, doubtless, his own head there, for Spenser, a king of the old race, carried a mirror which showed kings yet to come though but kings of the mob. Those Bohemian poets of the theatres were wiser, for the States that touched them nearly were the States where Helen and Dido had sorrowed, and so their mirrors showed none but beautiful heroical heads. They wandered in the places that pale passion loves, and were happy, as one thinks, and troubled little about those marching and hoarse-throated thoughts that the State has in its pay. They knew that those marchers, with the dust of so many roads upon them, are very robust and have great and well-paid generals to write expedient despatches in sound prose; and they could hear Mother Earth singing among her cornfields:

Weep not, my wanton! smile upon my knee;
When thou art old there's grief enough for thee.

VII

There are moments when one can read neither Milton nor Spenser, moments when one recollects nothing but that their flesh had partly been changed to stone, but there are other moments when one recollects nothing but those habits of emotion that made the lesser poet especially a man of an older, more imaginative time. One remembers that he delighted in smooth pastoral places, because men could be busy there or gather together there, after their work, that he could love handiwork and the hum of voices. One remembers that he could still rejoice in the trees, not because they were images of loneliness and meditation, but because of their serviceableness. He could praise 'the builder oake', 'the aspine, good for staves', 'the cypresse funerall', 'the eugh, obedient to the bender's will', 'the birch for shaftes', 'the sallow for the mill', 'the mirrhe sweete bleeding in the bitter wound', 'the fruitful olive', and 'the carver holme'. He was of a time before undelighted labour had made the business of men a desecration. He carries one's memory back to Virgil's and Chaucer's praise of trees, and to the sweet-sounding song made by the old Irish poet in their praise.

I got up from reading the *Faerie Queene* the other day and wandered into another room. It was in a friend's house, and I came of a sudden to the ancient poetry and to our poetry side by side — an engraving of Claude's *Mill* hung under an engraving of Turner's *Temple of Jupiter*. Those dancing countrypeople, those cowherds, resting after the day's work, and that quiet millrace made one think of Merry England with its glad Latin heart, of a time when men in every land found poetry and imagination in one another's company and in the day's labour. Those stately goddesses, moving in slow procession towards that marble architrave among mysterious

trees, belong to Shelley's thought, and to the religion of the
wilderness – the only religion possible to poetry to-day. Certainly Colin Clout, the companionable shepherd, and Calidore, the courtly man-at-arms, are gone, and Alastor is
wandering from lonely river to river finding happiness in
nothing but in that Star where Spenser too had imagined the
fountain of perfect things. This new beauty, in losing so
much, has indeed found a new loftiness, a something of
religious exaltation that the old had not. It may be that those
goddesses, moving with a majesty like a procession of the
stars, mean something to the soul of man that those kindly
women of the old poets did not mean, for all the fullness of
their breasts and the joyous gravity of their eyes. Has not the
wilderness been at all times a place of prophecy?

VIII

Our poetry, though it has been a deliberate bringing back of
the Latin joy and the Latin love of beauty, has had to put off
the old marching rhythms, that once could give delight to
more than expedient hearts, in separating itself from a life
where servile hands have become powerful. It has ceased to
have any burden for marching shoulders, since it learned
ecstasy from Smart in his mad cell, and from Blake, who
made joyous little songs out of almost unintelligible visions,
and from Keats, who sang of a beauty so wholly preoccupied
with itself that its contemplation is a kind of lingering trance.
The poet, if he would not carry burdens that are not his and
obey the orders of servile lips, must sit apart in contemplative
indolence playing with fragile things.

If one chooses at hazard a Spenserian stanza out of Shelley
and compares it with any stanza by Spenser, one sees the
change, though it would be still more clear if one had chosen
a lyrical passage. I will take a stanza out of *Laon and Cythna*,

for that is story-telling and runs nearer to Spenser than the
meditative *Adonais*:

> The meteor to its far morass returned:
> The beating of our veins one interval
> Made still; and then I felt the blood that burned
> Within her frame, mingle with mine, and fall
> Around my heart like fire; and over all
> A mist was spread, the sickness of a deep
> And speechless swoon of joy, as might befall
> Two disunited spirits when they leap
> In union from this earth's obscure and fading sleep.

The rhythm is varied and troubled, and the lines, which are
in Spenser like bars of gold thrown ringing one upon another,
are broken capriciously. Nor is the meaning the less an
inspiration of indolent Muses, for it wanders hither and
thither at the beckoning of fancy. It is now busy with a
meteor and now with throbbing blood that is fire, and with a
mist that is a swoon and a sleep that is life. It is bound
together by the vaguest suggestion, while Spenser's verse is
always rushing on to some preordained thought. A 'popular
poet' can still indeed write poetry of the will, just as factory
girls wear the fashion of hat or dress the moneyed classes wore
a year ago, but 'popular poetry' does not belong to the
living imagination of the world. Old writers gave men four
temperaments, and they gave the sanguineous temperament to
men of active life, and it is precisely the sanguineous temperament that is fading out of poetry and most obviously out of
what is most subtle and living in poetry — its pulse and breath,
its rhythm. Because poetry belongs to that element in every
race which is most strong, and therefore most individual, the
poet is not stirred to imaginative activity by a life which is
surrendering its freedom to ever new elaboration, organisation,

mechanism. He has no longer a poetical will, and must be content to write out of those parts of himself which are too delicate and fiery for any deadening exercise. Every generation has more and more loosened the rhythm, more and more broken up and disorganised, for the sake of subtlety of detail, those great rhythms which move, as it were, in masses of sound. Poetry has become more spiritual, for the soul is of all things the most delicately organised, but it has lost in weight and measure and in its power of telling long stories and of dealing with great and complicated events. *Laon and Cythna*, though I think it rises sometimes into loftier air than the *Faerie Queene* and *Endymion*, though its shepherds and wandering divinities have a stranger and more intense beauty than Spenser's, has need of too watchful and minute attention for such lengthy poems. In William Morris, indeed, one finds a music smooth and unexacting like that of the old storytellers, but not their energetic pleasure, their rhythmical wills. One too often misses in his *Earthly Paradise* the minute ecstasy of modern song without finding that old happy-go-lucky tune that had kept the story marching.

Spenser's contemporaries, writing lyrics or plays full of lyrical moments, write a verse more delicately organised than his and crowd more meaning into a phrase than he, but they could not have kept one's attention through so long a poem. A friend who has a fine ear told me the other day that she had read all Spenser with delight and yet could remember only four lines. When she repeated them they were from the poem by Matthew Roydon, which is bound up with Spenser because it is a commendation of Sir Philip Sidney:

> A sweet, attractive kind of grace,
> A full assurance given by looks,
> Continual comfort in a face,
> The lineaments of Gospel books.

Yet if one were to put even these lines beside a fine modern song one would notice that they had a stronger and rougher energy, a featherweight more, if eye and ear were fine enough to notice it, of the active will, of the happiness that comes out of life itself.

*   *   *

October 1902

THE HAPPIEST OF THE POETS

★   ★   ★

IV

When I was a child I often heard my elders talking of an old turreted house where an old great-uncle of mine lived, and of its gardens and its long pond where there was an island with tame eagles; and one day somebody read me some verses and said they made him think of that old house where he had been very happy. The verses ran in my head for years and became to me the best description of happiness in the world, and I am not certain that I know a better even now. They were those first dozen verses of *Golden Wings* that begin:

> Midways of a walled garden,
>   In the happy poplar land,
>   Did an ancient castle stand,
> With an old knight for a warden.
>
> Many scarlet bricks there were
>   In its walls, and old grey stone;
>   Over which red apples shone
> At the right time of the year.
>
> On the bricks the green moss grew,
>   Yellow lichen on the stone,
>   Over which red apples shone;
> Little war that castle knew.

When William Morris describes a house of any kind, and makes his description poetical, it is always, I think, some

122

house that he would have liked to have lived in, and I remember him saying about the time when he was writing of that great house of the Wolfings, 'I decorate modern houses for people, but the house that would please me would be some great room where one talked to one's friends in one corner and ate in another and slept in another and worked in another.' Indeed all he writes seems to me like the make-believe of a child who is remaking the world, not always in the same way, but always after its own heart; and so, unlike all other modern writers, he makes his poetry out of unending pictures of happiness that is often what a child might imagine, and always a happiness that sets mind and body at ease. Now it is a picture of some great room full of merriment, now of the wine-press, now of the golden threshing-floor, now of an old mill among apple-trees, now of cool water after the heat of the sun, now of some well-sheltered, well-tilled place among woods or mountains, where men and women live happily, knowing of nothing that is too far off or too great for the affections. He has but one story to tell us, how some man or woman lost and found again the happiness that is always half of the body; and even when they are wandering from it, leaves must fall over them, and flowers make fragrances about them, and warm winds fan them, and birds sing to them, for being of Habundia's kin they must not forget the shadow of her Green Tree even for a moment, and the waters of her Well must be always wet upon their sandals. His poetry often wearies us as the unbroken green of July wearies us, for there is something in us, some bitterness because of the Fall, it may be, that takes a little from the sweetness of Eve's apple after the first mouthful; but he who did all things gladly and easily, who never knew the curse of labour, found it always as sweet as it was in Eve's mouth. All kinds of associations have gathered about the pleasant things of the world and half taken the pleasure out of them for the greater number of men, but he saw them as when they came from the Divine Hand. I often see him in my mind as I saw him once at Hammersmith holding up a glass of claret towards the light and saying, 'Why do people say it is prosaic to get inspiration out of wine? Is it not the sunlight and the sap in the leaves? Are not grapes made by the sunlight and the sap?'

V

In one of his little Socialist pamphlets he tells how he sat under an elm-tree and watched the starlings and thought of an old horse and an old labourer that had passed him by, and of the men and women he had seen in towns; and he wondered how all these had come to be as they were. He saw that the starlings were beautiful and merry, and that men and the old horse they had subdued to their service were ugly and miserable, and yet the starlings, he thought, were of one kind whether there or in the South of England, and the ugly men and women were of one kind with those whose nobility and beauty had moved the ancient sculptors and poets to imagine the gods and the heroes after the images of men. Then, he began, he tells us, to meditate how this great difference might be ended and a new life, which would permit men to have beauty in common among them as the starlings have, be built on the wrecks of the old life. In other words, his mind was illuminated from within and lifted into prophecy in the full right sense of the word, and he saw the natural things he was alone gifted to see in their perfect form; and having that faith which is alone worth having, for it includes all others, a sure knowledge established in the constitution of his mind that perfect things are final things, he announced that all he had seen would come to pass. I do not think he troubled to understand books of economics, and Mr. Mackail says, I think, that they vexed him and wearied him. He found it enough to hold up, as it were, life as it is to-day beside his visions, and to show how faded its colours were and how sapless it was. And if we had not enough artistic feeling, enough feeling for the perfect, that is, to admit the authority of the vision; or enough faith to understand that all that is imperfect passes away, he would not, as I think, have argued with us in a serious spirit. Though I think that he never used the kinds of words I use in writing of him, though I think he would even have disliked a word like faith with its theological associations, I am certain that he understood thoroughly, as all artists understand a little, that the important things, the things we must believe in or perish, are beyond argument. We can no more reason about them than can the pigeon, come but lately from the egg, about the hawk whose shadow makes it cower among the grass. His vision is true because it is poetical, because we are a little happier when we are looking at it; and he knew as Shelley knew, by an act of faith, that the economists should take their measurements not from life as it is, but from the vision of men like him, from the vision of the world made perfect that is buried under all minds. The early Christians were of the kin of the Wilderness and of the Dry Tree, and they saw an unearthly Paradise, but he was of the kin of the Well and of the Green Tree and he saw an Earthly Paradise.

He obeyed his vision when he tried to make first his own house, for he was in this matter also like a child playing with the world, and then houses of other people, places where one could live happily; and he obeyed it when he wrote essays about the nature of happy work, and when he spoke at street-corners about the coming changes.

He knew clearly what he was doing towards the end, for he lived at a time when poets and artists have begun again to carry the burdens that priests and theologians took from them angrily some few hundred years ago. His art was not more essentially religious than Rossetti's art, but it was different, for Rossetti, drunken with natural beauty, saw the super-natural beauty, the impossible beauty, in his frenzy, while he being less intense and more tranquil would show us a beauty that would wither if it did not set us at peace with natural things, and if we did not believe that it existed always a little, and would some day exist in its fullness. He may not have been, indeed he was not, among the very greatest of the poets, but he was among the greatest of those who prepare the last reconciliation when the Cross shall blossom with roses.

1902

THE GALWAY PLAINS

LADY GREGORY has just given me her beautiful *Poets and Dreamers*, and it has brought to mind a day two or three years ago when I stood on the side of Slieve Echtge, looking out over Galway. The Burren Hills were to my left, and though I forget whether I could see the cairn over Bald Conan of the Fianna, I could certainly see many places there that are in poems and stories. In front of me, over many miles of level Galway plains, I saw a low blue hill flooded with evening light. I asked a countryman who was with me what hill that was, and he told me it was Cruachmaa of the Sidhe. I had often heard of Cruachmaa of the Sidhe even as far north as Sligo, for the countrypeople have told me a great many stories of the great host of the Sidhe who live there, still fighting and holding festivals.

I asked the old countryman about it, and he told me of strange women who had come from it, and who would come into a house having the appearance of countrywomen, but would know all that happened in that house; and how they would always pay back with increase, though not by their own hands, whatever was given to them. And he had heard, too, of people who had been carried away into the hill, and how one man went to look for his wife there, and dug into the hill and all but got his wife again, but at the very moment she was coming out to him, the pick he was digging with struck her upon the head and killed her. I asked him if he had himself seen any of its enchantments, and he said, 'Sometimes when I look over to the hill, I see a mist lying on the top of it, that goes away after a while'.

A great part of the poems and stories in Lady Gregory's book were made or gathered between Burren and Cruachmaa. It was here that Raftery, the wandering country poet of ninety years ago, praised and blamed, chanting fine verses, and playing badly on his fiddle. It is here the ballads of meeting and parting have been sung, and some whose lamentations for defeat are still remembered may have passed through this plain flying from the battle of Aughrim.

'I will go up on the mountain alone; and I will come hither from it again. It is there I saw the camp of the Gael, the poor troop thinned, not keeping with one another; Och Ochone!' And here, if one can believe many devout people whose stories are in the book, Christ has walked upon the roads, bringing the needy to some warm fireside, and sending one of His saints to anoint the dying.

I do not think these country imaginations have changed much for centuries, for they are still busy with those two themes of the ancient Irish poets, the sternness of battle and the sadness of parting and death. The emotion that in other countries has made many love-songs has here been given, in a long wooing, to danger, that ghostly bride. It is not a difference in the substance of things that the lamentations that were sung after battles are now sung for men who have died upon the gallows.

The emotion has become not less, but more noble, by the change, for the man who goes to death with the thought —

> It is with the people I was,
> It is not with the law I was,

has behind him generations of poetry and poetical life.

The poets of to-day speak with the voice of the unknown priest who wrote, some two hundred years ago, that *Sorrowful Lament for Ireland* Lady Gregory has put into passionate and rhythmical prose:

I do not know of anything under the sky
That is friendly or favourable to the Gael,
But only the sea that our need brings us to,
Or the wind that blows to the harbour
The ship that is bearing us away from Ireland;
And there is reason that these are reconciled with us,
For we increase the sea with our tears,
And the wandering wind with our sighs.

There is still in truth upon these great level plains a people, a community bound together by imaginative possessions, by stories and poems which have grown out of its own life, and by a past of great passions which can still waken the heart to imaginative action. One could still, if one had the genius, and had been born to Irish, write for these people plays and poems like those of Greece. Does not the greatest poetry always require a people to listen to it? England or any other country which takes its tunes from the great cities and gets its taste from schools and not from old custom may have a mob, but it cannot have a people. In England there are a few groups of men and women who have good taste, whether in cookery or in books; and the great multitudes but copy them or their copiers. The poet must always prefer the community where the perfected minds express the people, to a community that is vainly seeking to copy the perfected minds. To have even perfectly the thoughts that can be weighed, the knowledge that can be got from books, the precision that can be learned at school, to belong to any aristocracy, is to be a little pool that will soon dry up. A people alone are a great river; and that is why I am persuaded that where a people has died, a nation is about to die.

1903

FIRST PRINCIPLES

Two Irish writers had a controversy a month ago, and they accused one another of being unable to think, with entire sincerity, though it was obvious to uncommitted minds that neither had any lack of vigorous thought. But they had a different meaning when they spoke of thought, for the one, though in actual life he is the most practical man I know, meant thought as Pascal, as Montaigne, as Shakespeare, or as, let us say, Emerson, understood it — a reverie about the adventures of the soul, or of the personality, or some obstinate questioning of the riddle. Many who have to work hard always make time for this reverie, but it comes more easily to the leisured, and in this it is like a broken heart, which is, a Dublin newspaper assured us lately, impossible to a busy man. The other writer had in mind, when he spoke of thought, the shaping energy that keeps us busy, and the obstinate questionings he had most respect for were, how to change the method of government, how to change the language, how to revive our manufactures, and whether it is the Protestant or the Catholic that scowls at the other with the darker scowl. Ireland is so poor, so mis-governed, that a great portion of the imagination of the land must give itself to a very passionate consideration of questions like these, and yet it is precisely these loud questions that drive away the reveries that incline the imagination to the lasting work of literature and give, together with religion, sweetness, and nobility, and dignity to life. We should desire no more from these propagandist thinkers than that they carry out their work, as far as possible, without making it more difficult for those fitted by nature or by circumstance for another kind of thought to do their work also; and certainly it is not well that Martha chide at Mary, for they have the one Master over them.

When one all but despairs, as one does at times, of Ireland welcoming a National literature in this generation, it is because we do not leave ourselves enough of time, or of quiet, to be interested in men and women. A writer in *The Leader*, who is unknown to me, elaborates this argument in an article full of beauty and dignity. He is speaking of our injustice to one another, and he says that we are driven into injustice 'not wantonly but inevitably, and at call of the exacting qualities of the great things. Until this latter dawning, the genius of Ireland has been too preoccupied really to concern itself about men and women; in its drama they play a subordinate part, born tragic comedians though all the sons and daughters of the land are. A nation is the heroic theme we follow, a mourning, wasted land its moving spirit; the impersonal assumes personality for us.' When I wrote my *Countess Cathleen*, I thought, of course, chiefly of the actual picture that was forming before me, but there was a secondary meaning that came into my mind continually. 'It is the soul of one that loves Ireland', I thought, 'plunging into unrest, seeming to lose itself, to bargain itself away to the very wickedness of the world, and to surrender what is eternal for what is temporary', and I know that this meaning seemed natural to others, for that great orator, J. F. Taylor, who was not likely to have searched very deeply into any work of mine, for he cared little for mine, or, indeed, any modern work, turned the play into such a parable in one of his speeches.

There is no use being angry with necessary conditions, or failing to see that a man who is busy with some reform that can only be carried out in a flame of energetic feeling, will not only be indifferent to what seems to us the finer kind of thinking, but will support himself by generalisations that seem untrue to the man of letters. A little play, *The Rising of the Moon*, which is in the present number of *Samhain*, and is among those we are to produce during the winter, has, for instance, roused the suspicions of a very resolute leader of the people, who has a keen eye for rats behind the arras. A Fenian ballad-singer partly converts a policeman, and is it not unwise under any circumstances to show a policeman in so favourable a light? It is well known that many of the younger policemen were Fenians; but it is necessary that the Dublin crowds should be kept of so high a heart that they will fight the police at any moment. Are not morals greater than literature? Others have objected to Mr. Synge's *Shadow of the Glen* because Irish women, being more chaste than those of England and Scotland, are a valuable part of our National argument. Mr. Synge should not, it is said by some, have chosen an exception for the subject of his play, for who knows but the English may misunderstand him? Some even deny that such a thing could happen at all, while others that know the country better, or remember the statistics, say that it could, but should never, have been staged. All these arguments, by their methods, even more than by what they have tried to prove, misunderstand how literature does its work. Men of letters have sometimes said that the characters of a romance or of a play must be typical. They mean that the character must be typical of something which exists in all men because the writer has found it in his own mind. It is one of the most inexplicable things about human nature that a writer, with a strange temperament, an Edgar Allan Poe, let us say, made what he is by conditions that never existed before, can create personages and lyric emotions which startle us by being at once bizarre and an image of our own secret thoughts. Are we not face to face with the microcosm, mirroring everything in universal Nature? It is no more necessary for the characters created by a romance-writer, or a dramatist, to have existed before, than for his own personality to have done so; characters and personality alike, as is perhaps true in the instance of Poe, may draw half their life not from the solid earth but from some dreamy drug. This is true even of historical drama, for it was Goethe, the founder of the historical drama of Germany, who said, 'We do the people of history the honour of naming after them the creations of our own minds'. All that a dramatic writer need do is to persuade us, during the two hours' traffic of the stage, that the events of his play did really happen. He must know enough of the life of his country, or of history, to create this illusion, but no matter how much he knows, he will fail if his audience is not ready to give up something of the dead letter. If his mind is full of energy he will not be satisfied with little knowledge, but he will be far more likely to alter incidents and characters, wilfully even as it may seem, than to become a literal historian. It was one of the complaints against Shakespeare, in his own day, that he made Sir John Falstaff out of a praiseworthy old Lollard preacher. One day, as he sat over Holinshed's *History of England*, he persuaded himself that Richard II, with his French culture, 'his too great friendliness to his friends', his beauty of mind, and his fall before dry, repelling Bolingbroke, would be a good image for an accustomed mood of fanciful, impracticable lyricism in his own mind. The historical Richard has passed away for ever and the Richard of the play lives more intensely, it seems, than did ever living man. Yet Richard II, as Shakespeare made him, could never have been born before the Renaissance, before the Italian influence, or even one hour before the innumerable streams that flowed in upon Shakespeare's mind, the innumerable experiences we can never know, brought Shakespeare to the making of him. He is typical not because he ever existed, but because he has made us know of something in our own minds we had never known of had he never been imagined.

Our propagandists have twisted this theory of the men of letters into its direct contrary, and when they say that a writer should make typical characters they mean personifications of averages, of statistics, or even personified opinions, or men and women so faintly imagined that there is nothing about them to separate them from the crowd, as it appears to our hasty eyes. We must feel that we could engage a hundred others to wear the same livery as easily as we could engage a coachman. We must never forget that we are engaging them to be the ideal young peasant, or the true patriot, or the happy Irish wife, or the policeman of our prejudices, or to express some other of those invaluable generalisations without which our practical movements would lose their energy. Who is there that likes a coachman to be too full of human nature, when he has his livery on? No one man is like another, but one coachman should be as like another as possible, though he may assert himself a little when he meets the gardener. The patriots would impose on us heroes and heroines, like those young couples in the Gaelic plays, who might all change brides or bridegrooms in the dance and never find out the difference. The personifications need not be true even, if they are about our enemy, for it might be more difficult to fight out our necessary fight if we remembered his virtue at wrong moments; and might not Teigue and Bocach, that are light in the head, go over to his party?

Ireland is indeed poor, is indeed hunted by misfortune, and

has indeed to give up much that makes life desirable and lovely, but is she so very poor that she can afford no better literature than this? Perhaps so, but if it is a Spirit from beyond the world that decides when a nation shall awake into imaginative energy, and no philosopher has ever found what brings the moment, it cannot be for us to judge. It may be coming upon us now, for it is certain that we have more writers who are thinking, as men of letters understand thought, than we have had for a century, and he who wilfully makes their work harder may be setting himself against the purpose of that Spirit.

I would not be trying to form an Irish National Theatre if I did not believe that there existed in Ireland, whether in the minds of a few people or of a great number I do not know, an energy of thought about life itself, a vivid sensitiveness as to the reality of things, powerful enough to overcome all those phantoms of the night. Everything calls up its contrary, unreality calls up reality, and, besides, life here has been sufficiently perilous to make men think. I do not think it a national prejudice that makes me believe we are harder, a more masterful race than the comfortable English of our time, and that this comes from an essential nearness to reality of those few scattered people who have the right to call themselves the Irish race. It is only in the exceptions, in the few minds where the flame has burnt, as it were, pure, that one can see the permanent character of a race. If one re-members the men who have dominated Ireland for the last hundred and fifty years, one understands that it is strength of personality, the individualising quality in a man, that stirs Irish imagination most deeply in the end. There is scarcely a man who has led the Irish people, at any time, who may not give some day to a great writer precisely that symbol he may require for the expression of himself. The critical mind of

Ireland is far more subjugated than the critical mind of England by the phantoms and misapprehensions of politics and social necessity, but the life of Ireland has rejected them more resolutely. Indeed, it is in life itself in England that one finds the dominion of what is not human life.

We have no longer in any country a literature as great as the literature of the old world, and that is because the newspapers, all kinds of second-rate books, the preoccupation of men with all kinds of practical changes, have driven the living imagination out of the world. I have read hardly any books this summer but Cervantes and Boccaccio and some Greek plays. I have felt that these men, divided from one another by so many hundreds of years, had the same mind. It is we who are different; and then the thought would come to me, that has come to me so often before, that they lived in times when the imagination turned to life itself for excitement. The world was not changing quickly about them. There was nothing to draw their imagination from the ripening of the fields, from the birth and death of their children, from the destiny of their souls, from all that is the unchanging substance of literature. They had not to deal with the world in such great masses that it could only be represented to their minds by figures and by abstract generalisations. Everything that their minds ran on came on them vivid with the colour of the senses, and when they wrote it was out of their own rich experience, and they found their symbols of expression in things that they had known all their life long. Their very words were more vigorous than ours, for their phrases came from a common mint, from the market, or the tavern, or from the great poets of a still older time. It is the change that followed the Renaissance, and was completed by newspaper government and the scientific movement, that has brought upon us all these phrases and generalisations, made by minds that would grasp what they have never seen. Yesterday I went out to see the reddening apples in the garden, and they faded from my imagination sooner than they would have from the imagination of that old poet who made the songs of the seasons for the Fianna, or out of Chaucer's, that celebrated so many trees. Theories, opinions, these opinions among the rest, flowed in upon me and blotted them away. Even our greatest poets see the world with preoccupied minds. Great as Shelley is, those theories about the coming changes of the world, which he has built up with so much elaborate passion, hurry him from life continually. There is a phrase in some old Cabbalistic writer about man falling into his own circumference, and every generation we get further away from life itself, and come more and more under the influence which Blake had in his mind when he said, 'Kings and Parliament seem to me something other than human life'. We lose our freedom more and more as we get away from ourselves, and not merely because our minds are overthrown by abstract phrases and generalisations, reflections in a mirror that seem living, but because we have turned the table of values upside-down, and believe that the root of reality is not in the centre but somewhere in that whirling circumference. How can we create like the ancients, while innumerable considerations of external probability or social utility destroy the seeming irresponsible creative power that is life itself? Who to-day could set Richmond's and Richard's tents side by side on the battlefield, or make Don Quixote, mad as he was, mistake a windmill for a giant in broad daylight? And when I think of free-spoken Falstaff I know of no audience but the tinkers of the roadside that could encourage the artist to an equal comedy. The old writers were content if their inventions had but an emotional and moral consistency, and created out of themselves a fantastic, energetic, extravagant art. A civilisation is very like a man or a woman, for it comes in but a few years into its beauty, and its strength, and then, while many years go by, it gathers and makes order about it, the strength and beauty going out of it the while, until in the end it lies there with its limbs straightened out and a clean linen cloth folded upon it. That may well be, and yet we need not follow among the mourners, for, it may be, before they are at the tomb, a messenger will run out of the hills and touch the pale lips with a red ember, and wake the limbs to the disorder and the tumult that is life. Though he does not come, even so we will keep from among the mourners and hold some cheerful conversation among ourselves; for has not Virgil, a know-ledgeable man and a wizard, foretold that other Argonauts shall row between cliff and cliff, and other fair-haired Achaeans sack another Troy?

Every argument carries us backwards to some religious conception, and in the end the creative energy of men depends upon their believing that they have, within themselves, some-thing immortal and imperishable, and that all else is but as an image in a looking-glass. So long as that belief is not a formal thing, a man will create out of a joyful energy, seeking little for any external test of an impulse that may be sacred, and looking for no foundation outside life itself. If Ireland could escape from those phantoms of hers she might create, as did the old writers; for she has a faith that is as theirs, and keeps alive in the Gaelic traditions — and this has always seemed to me the chief intellectual value of Gaelic — a portion of the old imaginative life. When Dr. Hyde or Father Peter O'Leary is the writer, one's imagination goes straight to the century of Cervantes, and, having gone so far, one thinks at every moment that they will discover his energy. It is precisely because of this reason that one is indignant with those who would substitute for the ideas of the folk-life the rhetoric of the newspapers, who would muddy what had begun to seem a fountain of life with the feet of the mob. Is it impossible to revive Irish and yet to leave the finer intellects a sufficient mastery over the more gross, to prevent it from becoming, it may be, the language of a nation, and yet losing all that has made it worthy of a revival, all that has made it a new energy in the mind?

Before the modern movement, and while it was but new, the ordinary man, whether he could read and write or not, was ready to welcome great literature. When Ariosto found himself among the brigands, they repeated to him his own verses, and the audience in the Elizabethan theatres must have been all but as clever as an Athenian audience. But to-day we come to understand great literature by a long preparation, or by some accident of nature, for we only begin to understand life when our minds have been purified of temporary interests by study.

But if literature has no external test, how are we to know that it is indeed literature? The only test that Nature gives, to show when we obey her, is that she gives us happiness, and when we are no longer obedient she brings us to pain sooner or later. Is it not the same with the artist? The sign that she makes to him is that happiness we call delight in beauty. He can only convey this in its highest form after he has purified his mind with the great writers of the world; but their example can never be more than a preparation. If his art does not seem, when it comes, to be the creation of a new personality, in a few years it will not seem to be alive at all. If he is a dramatist his characters must have a like newness. If they could have existed before his day, or have been imagined before his day, we may be certain that the spirit of life is not in them in its fullness. This is because art, in its highest moments, is not a deliberate creation, but the creation of intense feeling, of pure life; and every feeling is the child of all past ages and would be different if even a moment had been left out. Indeed, is it not that delight in beauty which tells the artist that he has imagined what may never die, itself but a delight in the permanent yet ever-changing form of life, in her very limbs and lineaments? When life has given it, has she given anything but herself? Has she any other reward, even for the saints? If one flies to the wilderness, is not that clear light that falls about the soul when all irrelevant things have been taken away, but life that has been about one always, enjoyed in all its fullness at length? It is as though she had put her arms about one, crying, 'My beloved, you have given up everything for me'. If a man spend all his days in good works till there is no emotion in his heart that is not full of virtue, is not the reward he prays for eternal life? The artist, too, has prayers and a cloister, and if he do not turn away from temporary things, from the zeal of the reformer and the passion of revolution, that jealous mistress will give him but a scornful glance.

What attracts me to drama is that it is, in the most obvious way, what all the arts are upon a last analysis. A farce and a tragedy are alike in this, that they are a moment of intense life. An action is taken out of all other actions; it is reduced to its simplest form, or at any rate to as simple a form as it can be brought to without our losing the sense of its place in the world. The characters that are involved in it are freed from everything that is not a part of that action; and whether it is, as in the less important kinds of drama, a mere bodily activity, a hairbreadth escape or the like, or as it is in the more important kinds, an activity of the souls of the characters, it is an energy, an eddy of life purified from everything but itself. The dramatist must picture life in action, with an unpreoccupied mind, as the musician pictures it in sound and the sculptor in form.

But if this be true, has art nothing to do with moral judgments? Surely it has, and its judgments are those from which there is no appeal. The character whose fortune we have been called in to see, or the personality of the writer, must keep our sympathy, and whether it be farce or tragedy, we must laugh and weep with him and call down blessings on his head. This character who delights us may commit murder like Macbeth, or fly the battle for his sweetheart as did Antony, or betray his country like Coriolanus, and yet we will rejoice in every happiness that comes to him and sorrow at his death as if it were our own. It is no use telling us that the murderer and the betrayer do not deserve our sympathy. We thought so yesterday, and we still know what crime is, but everything has been changed of a sudden; we are caught up into another code, we are in the presence of a higher court. Complain of us if you will, but it will be useless, for before the curtain falls, a thousand ages, grown conscious in our sympathies, will have cried *Absolvo te*. Blame if you will the codes, the philosophies, the experiences of all past ages that have made us what we are, as the soil under our feet has been made out of unknown vegetations: quarrel with the acorns of Eden if you will, but what has that to do with us? We understand the verdict and not the law; and yet there is some law, some code, some judgment. If the poet's hand had slipped, if Antony had railed at Cleopatra in the monument, if Coriolanus had abated that high pride of his in the presence of death, we might have gone away muttering the Ten Commandments. Yet maybe we are wrong to speak of judgment, for we have but contemplated life, and what more is there to say when she that is all virtue, the gift and the giver, the fountain whither all flows again, has given all herself? If the subject of drama or any other art were a man himself, an eddy of momentary breath, we might desire the contemplation of perfect characters; but the subject of all art is passion, and a passion can only be contemplated when separated by itself, purified of all but itself, and aroused into a perfect intensity by opposition with some other passion, or it may be with the law, that is the expression of the whole whether of Church or Nation or external nature. Had Coriolanus not been a law-breaker, neither he nor we had ever discovered, it may be, that noble pride of his, and if we had not seen Cleopatra through the eyes of so many lovers, would we have known that soul of hers to be all flame, and wept at the quenching of it? If we were not certain of law we would not feel the struggle, the drama, but the subject of art is not law, which is a kind of death, but the praise of life, and it has no commandments that are not positive.

But if literature does not draw its substance from history, or anything about us in the world, what is a National literature? Our friends have already told us, writers for the Theatre in Abbey Street, that we have no right to the name, some because we do not write in Irish, and others because we do not plead the National cause in our plays, as if we were writers for the newspapers. I have not asked my fellow-workers what they mean by the words National literature, but though I have no great love for definitions, I would define it in some such way as this: It is the work of writers who are moulded by influences that are moulding their country, and who write out of so deep a life that they are accepted there in the end.

It leaves a good deal unsettled — was Rossetti an Englishman, or Swift an Irishman? — but it covers more kinds of National literature than any other I can think of. If you say a National literature must be in the language of the country, there are many difficulties. Should it be written in the language that your country does speak or the language that it ought to speak? Was Milton an Englishman when he wrote in Latin or Italian, and had we no part in Columbanus when he wrote in Latin the beautiful sermon comparing life to a highway and to a smoke? And then there is Beckford, who is in every history of English literature, and yet his one memorable book, a story of Persia, was written in French.

Our theatre is of no great size, for though we know that if we write well we shall find acceptance among our countrymen in the end, we would think our emotions were on the surface if we found a ready welcome. Edgar Allan Poe and Walt Whitman are National writers of America, although the one had his first true acceptance in France and the other in England and Ireland. When I was a boy, six persons, who, alone out of the whole world, it may be, believed Walt Whitman a great writer, sent him a message of admiration, and of those names four were English and two Irish, my father's and Prof. Dowden's. It is only in our own day that America has begun to prefer him to Lowell, who is not a poet at all.

I mean by deep life that men must put into their writing the emotions and experiences that have been most important to themselves. If they say, 'I will write of Irish countrypeople and make them charming and picturesque like those dear peasants my great-grandmother used to put in the foreground of her water-colour paintings', then they had better be satisfied with the word 'provincial'. If one condescends to one's material, if it is only what a popular novelist would call local colour, it is certain that one's real soul is somewhere else. Mr. Synge, upon the other hand, who is able to express his own finest emotions in those curious ironical plays of his, where, for all that, by the illusion of admirable art, every one seems to be thinking and feeling as only countrymen could think and feel, is truly a National writer, as Burns was when he wrote finely and as Burns was not when he wrote *Highland Mary* and *The Cotter's Saturday Night*.

A writer is not less National because he shows the influence of other countries and of the great writers of the world. No nation, since the beginning of history, has ever drawn all its life out of itself. Even The Well of English Undefiled, the Father of English Poetry himself, borrowed his metres, and much of his way of looking at the world, from French writers, and it is possible that the influence of Italy was more powerful among the Elizabethan poets than any literary influence out of England herself. Many years ago, when I was contending with Sir Charles Gavan Duffy over what seemed to me a too narrow definition of Irish interests, Professor York Powell either said or wrote to me that the creative power of England was always at its greatest when her receptive power was greatest. If Ireland is about to produce a literature that is important to her, it must be the result of the influences that flow in upon the mind of an educated Irishman to-day, and, in a greater degree, of what came into the world with himself. Gaelic can hardly fail to do a portion of the work, but one cannot say whether it may not be some French or German writer who will do most to make him an articulate man. If he really achieve the miracle, if he really make all that he has seen and felt and known a portion of his own intense nature, if he puts it all into the fire of his energy, he need not fear being a stranger among his own people in the end. There never have been men more unlike an Englishman's idea of himself than Keats and Shelley, while Campbell, whose emotion came out of a shallow well, was very like that idea. We call certain minds creative because they are among the moulders of their nation and are not made upon its mould, and they resemble one another in this only — they have never been foreknown or fulfilled an expectation.

It is sometimes necessary to follow in practical matters some definition which one knows to have but a passing use. We, for instance, have always confined ourselves to plays upon Irish subjects, as if no others could be National literature. Our Theatre inherits this limitation from previous movements, which found it necessary and fruitful. Goldsmith and Sheridan and Burke had become so much a part of English life, were so greatly moulded by the movements that were moulding England, that, despite certain Irish elements that clung about them, we could not think of them as more important to us than any English writer of equal rank. Men told us that we should keep our hold of them, as it were, for they were a part of our glory; but we did not consider our glory very important. We had no desire to turn braggarts, and we did suspect the motives of our advisers. Perhaps they had reasons, which were not altogether literary, for thinking it might be well if Irish men of letters, in our day also, would turn their faces to England. But what moved me always the most, and I had something to do with forcing this limitation upon our organisations, is that a new language of expression would help to awaken a new attitude in writers themselves, and that if our organisations were satisfied to interpret a writer to his own countrymen merely because he was of Irish birth, the organisations would become a kind of trade union for the helping of Irishmen to catch the ear of London publishers and managers, and for upholding writers who had been beaten by abler Englishmen. Let a man turn his face to us, accepting the commercial disadvantages that would bring upon him, and talk of what is near to our hearts, Irish Kings and Irish Legends and Irish Countrymen, and we would find it a joy to interpret him. Our one philosophical critic, Mr. John Eglinton, thinks we were very arbitrary, and yet I would not have us enlarge our practice. England and France, almost alone among nations, have great works of literature which have taken their subjects from foreign lands, and even in France and England this is more true in appearance than reality. Shakespeare observed his Roman crowds in London, and saw, one doubts not, somewhere in his own Stratford, the old man that gave Cleopatra the asp. Somebody I have been reading lately finds the Court of Louis XIV in *Phèdre* and *Andromaque*. Even in France and England almost the whole prose fiction professes to describe the life of the country, often of the districts where its writers have lived, for, unlike a poem, a novel requires so much minute observation of the surface of life that a novelist who cares for the illusion of reality will keep to familiar things. A writer will indeed take what is most creative out of himself, not from observation, but experience, yet he must master a definite language, a definite symbolism of incident and scene. Flaubert explains the comparative failure of his Salammbô by saying, 'One cannot frequent her'. He could create her soul, as it were, but he could not tell with certainty how it would express itself before Carthage fell to ruins. In the small nations which have to struggle for their national life, one finds that almost every creator, whether poet or novelist, sets all his stories in his own country. I do not recollect that Björnson ever wrote of any land but Norway, and Ibsen, though he lived in exile for many years, driven out by his countrymen, as he believed, carried the little seaboard towns of Norway everywhere in his imagination. So far as we can be certain of anything, we may be certain that Ireland with her long National struggle, her old literature, her unbounded folk-imagination, will, in so far as her literature is National at all, be more like Norway than England or France.

If literature is but praise of life, if our writers are not to plead the National cause, nor insist upon the Ten Commandments, nor upon the glory of their country, what part remains for it, in the common life of the country? It will influence the life of the country immeasurably more, though seemingly less, than have our propagandist poems and stories. It will leave to others the defence of all that can be codified for ready understanding, of whatever is the especial business of sermons, and of leading articles; but it will bring all the ways of men before that ancient tribunal of our sympathies. It will measure all things by the measure not of things visible but of things invisible. In a country like Ireland, where personifications have taken the place of life, men have more hate than love, for the unhuman is nearly the same as the inhuman, but literature, which is a part of that charity that is the forgiveness of sins, will make us understand men no matter how little they conform to our expectations. We will be more interested in heroic men than in heroic actions, and will have a little distrust for everything that can be called good or bad in itself with a very confident heart. Could we understand it so well, we will say, if it were not something other than human life? We will have a scale of virtues, and value most highly those that approach the indefinable. Men will be born among us of whom it is possible to say, not 'What a philanthropist', 'What a patriot', 'How practical a man', but, as we say of the men of the Renaissance, 'What a nature', 'How much abundant life'. Even at the beginning we will value qualities more than actions, for these may be habit or accident; and should we say to a friend, 'You have advertised for an English cook', or 'I hear that you have no clerks who are not of your own faith', or 'You have voted an address to the King', we will add to our complaint, 'You have been unpatriotic and I am ashamed of you, but if you cease from doing any of these things because you have been terrorised out of them, you will cease to be my friend'. We will not forget how to be stern, but we will remember always that the highest life unites, as in one fire, the greatest passion and the greatest courtesy.

A feeling for the form of life, for the graciousness of life, for the dignity of life, for the moving limbs of life, for the nobleness of life, for all that cannot be written in codes, has always been greatest among the gifts of literature to mankind. Indeed, the Muses being women, all literature is but their love-cries to the manhood of the world. It is now one and now another that cries, but the words are the same: 'Love of my heart, what matter to me that you have been quarrelsome in your cups, and have slain many, and have given your love here and there? It was because of the whiteness of your flesh and the mastery in your hands that I gave you my love, when all life came to me in your coming.' And then in a low voice that none may overhear — 'Alas! I am greatly afraid that the more they cry against you the more I love you'.

There are two kinds of poetry, and they are commingled in all the greatest works. When the tide of life sinks low there are pictures, as in the *Ode on a Grecian Urn* and in Virgil at the plucking of the Golden Bough. The pictures make us sorrowful. We share the poet's separation from what he describes. It is life in the mirror, and our desire for it is as the

desire of the lost souls for God; but when Lucifer stands
among his friends, when Villon sings his dead ladies to so
gallant a rhythm, when Timon makes his epitaph, we feel no
sorrow, for life herself has made one of her eternal gestures,
has called up into our hearts her energy that is eternal delight.
In Ireland, where the tide of life is rising, we turn, not to
picture-making, but to the imagination of personality — to
drama, gesture.

1904

DISCOVERIES

*　　*　　*

THE PLAY OF MODERN MANNERS

Of all artistic forms that have had a large share of the world's attention, the worst is the play about modern educated people. Except where it is superficial or deliberately argumentative it fills one's soul with a sense of commonness as with dust. It has one mortal ailment. It cannot become impassioned, that is to say, vital, without making somebody gushing and sentimental. Educated and well-bred people do not wear their hearts upon their sleeves, and they have no artistic and charming language except light persiflage and no powerful language at all, and when they are deeply moved they look silently into the fireplace. Again and again I have watched some play of this sort with growing curiosity through the opening scene. The minor people argue, chaff one another, hint sometimes at some deeper stream of life just as we do in our houses, and I am content. But all the time I have been wondering why the chief character, the man who is to bear the burden of fate, is gushing, sentimental and quite without ideas. Then the great scene comes and I understand that he cannot be well-bred or self-possessed or intellectual, for if he were he would draw a chair to the fire and there would be no duologue at the end of the third act. Ibsen understood the difficulty and made all his characters a little provincial that they might not put each other out of countenance, and made a leading-article sort of poetry—phrases about vine-leaves and harps in the air — it was possible to believe them using in their moments of excitement, and if the play needed more than that, they could always do something stupid. They could go out and hoist a flag as they do at the end of *Little Eyolf*. One only understands that this manner, deliberately adopted, one doubts not, had gone into his soul and filled it with dust, when one has noticed that he could no longer create a man of genius. The happiest writers are those that, knowing this form of play to be slight and passing, keep to the surface, never showing anything but the arguments and the persiflage of daily observation, or now and then, instead of the expression of passion, a stage picture, a man holding a woman's hand or sitting with his head in his hands in dim light by the red glow of a fire. It was certainly an understanding of the slightness of the form, of its incapacity for the expression of the deeper sorts of passion, that made the French invent the play with a thesis, for where there is a thesis people can grow hot in argument, almost the only kind of passion that displays itself in our daily life. The novel of contemporary educated life is upon the other hand a permanent form because, having the power of psychological description, it can follow the thought of a man who is looking into the grate.

HAS THE DRAMA OF CONTEMPORARY LIFE A ROOT OF ITS OWN?

In watching a play about modern educated people, with its meagre language and its action crushed into the narrow limits of possibility, I have found myself constantly saying: 'Maybe it has its power to move, slight as that is, from being able to suggest fundamental contrasts and passions which

romantic and poetical literature have shown to be beautiful.'
A man facing his enemies alone in a quarrel over the purity
of the water in a Norwegian Spa and using no language but
that of the newspapers can call up into our minds, let us say,
the passion of Coriolanus. The lovers and fighters of old
imaginative literature are more vivid experiences in the soul
than anything but one's own ruling passion that is itself riddled
by their thought as by lightning, and even two dumb figures
on the roads can call up all that glory. Put the man who has no
knowledge of literature before a play of this kind and he will
say, as he has said in some form or other in every age at the
first shock of naturalism, 'Why should I leave my home
to hear but the words I have used there when talking of the
rates?' And he will prefer to it any play where there is visible
beauty or mirth, where life is exciting, at high tide as it were.
It is not his fault that he will prefer in all likelihood a worse
play although its kind may be greater, for we have been
following the lure of science for generations and have forgotten him and his. I come always back to this thought.
There is something of an old wives' tale in fine literature.
The makers of it are like an old peasant telling stories of the
great famine or the hangings of '98 or from his own memories.
He has felt something in the depth of his mind and he wants
to make it as visible and powerful to our senses as possible.
He will use the most extravagant words or illustrations if they
suit his purpose. Or he will invent a wild parable, and the
more his mind is on fire or the more creative it is, the less
will he look at the outer world or value it for its own sake.
It gives him metaphors and examples, and that is all. He is
even a little scornful of it, for it seems to him while the fit is on
that the fire has gone out of it and left it but white ashes. I
cannot explain it, but I am certain that every high thing was
invented in this way, between sleeping and waking, as it

were, and that peering and peeping persons are but hawkers of stolen goods. How else could their noses have grown so ravenous or their eyes so sharp?

WHY THE BLIND MAN IN ANCIENT TIMES WAS MADE A POET

A description in the *Iliad* or the *Odyssey*, unlike one in the *Aeneid* or in most modern writers, is the swift and natural observation of a man as he is shaped by life. It is a refinement of the primary hungers and has the least possible of what is merely scholarly or exceptional. It is, above all, never too observant, too professional, and when the book is closed we have had our energies enriched, for we have been in the mid-current. We have never seen anything Odysseus could not have seen while his thought was of the Cyclops, or Achilles when Briseis moved him to desire. In the art of the greatest periods there is something careless and sudden in all habitual moods, though not in their expression, because these moods are a conflagration of all the energies of active life. In primitive times the blind man became a poet, as he became a fiddler in our villages, because he had to be driven out of activities all his nature cried for, before he could be contented with the praise of life. And often it is Villon or Verlaine, with impediments plain to all, who sings of life with the ancient simplicity. Poets of coming days, when once more it will be possible to write as in the great epochs, will recognise that their sacrifice shall be to refuse what blindness and evil name, or imprisonment at the outsetting, denied to men who missed thereby the sting of a deliberate refusal. The poets of the ages of silver need no refusal of life, the dome of many-coloured glass is already shattered while they live. They look at life deliberately and as if from beyond life, and the greatest of them need suffer nothing but the sadness that the saints have known. This is their aim, and their temptation is not a passionate activity, but the approval of their fellows, which comes to them in full abundance only when they delight in the general thoughts that hold together a cultivated middle-class, where irresponsibilities of position and poverty are lacking; the things that are more excellent among educated men who have political preoccupations, Augustus Caesar's affability, all that impersonal fecundity which muddies the intellectual passions. Ben Jonson says in *The Poetaster* that even the best of men without Promethean fire is but a hollow statue, and a studious man will commonly forget after some forty winters that of a certainty Promethean fire will burn somebody's fingers. It may happen that poets will be made more often by their sins than by their virtues, for general praise is unlucky, as the villages know, and not merely as I imagine — for I am superstitious about these things — because the praise of all but an equal enslaves and adds a pound to the ball at the ankle with every compliment.

All energy that comes from the whole man is as irregular as the lightning, for the communicable and forecastable and discoverable is a part only, a hungry chicken under the breast of the pelican, and the test of poetry is not in reason but in a delight not different from the delight that comes to a man at the first coming of love into the heart. I knew an old man who had spent his whole life cutting hazel and privet from the paths, and in some seventy years he had observed little but had many imaginations. He had never seen like a naturalist, never seen things as they are, for his habitual mood had been that of a man stirred in his affairs; and Shakespeare, Tintoretto, though the times were running out when Tintoretto painted, nearly all the great men of the Renaissance, looked at the world with eyes like his. Their minds were never quiescent, never, as it were, in a mood for scientific observations, always in exaltation, never — to use known words — founded upon an elimination of the personal factor; and their attention and the attention of those they worked for dwelt constantly with what is present to the mind in exaltation. I am too modern fully to enjoy Tintoretto's *Origin of the Milky Way*, I cannot fix my thoughts upon that glowing and palpitating flesh intently enough to forget, as I can the make-believe of a faery-tale, that heavy drapery hanging from a cloud, though I find my pleasure in *King Lear* heightened by the make-believe that comes upon it all when the Fool says, 'This prophecy Merlin shall make, for I live before his time'; — and I always find it quite natural, so little does logic in the mere circumstance matter in the finest art, that Richard's and Richmond's tents should be side by side. I saw with delight *The Knight of the Burning Pestle* when Mr. Carr revived it, and found it none the worse because the apprentice acted a whole play upon the spur of the moment and without committing a line to heart. When *The Silent Woman* rammed a century of laughter into the two hours' traffic, I found with amazement that almost every journalist had put logic on the seat where our Lady Imagination should pronounce that unjust and favouring sentence her woman's heart is ever plotting, and had felt bound to cherish none but reasonable sympathies and to resent the baiting of that grotesque old man. I have been looking over a book of engravings made in the eighteenth century from those wall-pictures of Herculaneum and Pompeii that were, it seems, the work of journeymen copying from finer paintings, for the composition is always too good for the execution. I find in great numbers an indifference to obvious logic, to all that the eye sees at common moments. Perseus shows Andromeda the death she lived by in a pool, and though the lovers are carefully drawn the reflection is shown reversed that the forms it reflects may be seen the right side up and our eyes be the more content. There is hardly an old master who has not made known to us in some like way how little he cares for what every fool can see and every knave can praise. The men who imagined the arts were not less superstitious in religion, understanding the spiritual relations, but not the mechanical, and finding nothing that need strain the throat in those gnats the floods of Noah and Deucalion.

CONCERNING SAINTS AND ARTISTS

I took the Indian hemp with certain followers of Saint-Martin on the ground floor of a house in the Latin Quarter. I had never taken it before, and was instructed by a boisterous young poet, whose English was no better than my French. He gave me a little pellet, if I am not forgetting, an hour before dinner, and another after we had dined together at some restaurant. As we were going through the streets to the meeting-place of the Martinists, I felt suddenly that a cloud I was looking at floated in an immense space, and for an instant my being rushed out, as it seemed, into that space with ecstasy. I was myself again immediately, but the poet was wholly above himself, and presently he pointed to one of the street-lamps now brightening in the fading twilight, and cried at the top of his voice, 'Why do you look at me with your great eye?' There were perhaps a dozen people already much excited when we arrived; and after I had drunk some cups of coffee and eaten a pellet or two more, I grew very anxious to dance, but did not, as I could not remember any steps. I sat down and closed my eyes; but no, I had no visions, nothing but a sensation of some dark shadow which seemed to be telling me that some day I would go into a trance and so out of my body for a while, but not yet. I opened my eyes and looked at some red ornament on the mantelpiece, and at once the room was full of harmonies of red, but when a blue china figure caught my eye the harmonies became blue upon the instant. I was puzzled, for the reds were all there, nothing had changed, but they were no longer important or harmonious; and why had the blues so unimportant but a moment ago become exciting and delightful? Thereupon it struck me that I was seeing like a painter, and that in the course of the evening every one there would change through every kind of artistic perception.

After a while a Martinist ran towards me with a piece of paper on which he had drawn a circle with a dot in it, and pointing at it with his finger he cried out, 'God, God!' Some immeasurable mystery had been revealed, and his eyes shone; and at some time or other a lean and shabby man, with rather a distinguished face, showed me his horoscope and pointed with an ecstasy of melancholy at its evil aspects. The boisterous poet, who was an old eater of the Indian hemp, had told me that it took one three months growing used to it, three months more enjoying it, and three months being cured of it. These men were in their second period; but I never forgot myself, never really rose above myself for more than a moment, and was even able to feel the absurdity of that gaiety, a Herr Nordau among the men of genius, but one that was abashed at his own sobriety. The sky outside was beginning to grey when there came a knocking at the window-shutters. Somebody opened the window, and a woman and two young girls in evening dress, who were not a little bewildered to find so many people, were helped down into the room. She and her husband's two sisters had been at a

students' ball unknown to her husband, who was asleep overhead, and had thought to have crept home unobserved, but
for a confederate at the window. All those talking or dancing
men laughed in a dreamy way; and she, understanding that
there was no judgment in the laughter of men that had no
thought but of the spectacle of the world, blushed, laughed,
and darted through the room and so upstairs. Alas that the
hangman's rope should be own brother to that Indian happiness that keeps alone, were it not for some stray cactus, mother
of as many dreams, immemorial impartiality.

THE SUBJECT-MATTER OF DRAMA

I read this sentence a few days ago, or one like it, in an
obituary of Ibsen: 'Let nobody again go back to the old ballad
material of Shakespeare, to murders, and ghosts, for what
interests us on the stage is modern experience and the discussion of our interests'; and in another part of the article
Ibsen was blamed because he had written of suicides and in
other ways made use of 'the morbid terror of death'. Dramatic literature has for a long time been left to the criticism of
journalists, and all these, the old stupid ones and the new clever
ones, have tried to impress upon it their absorption in the life
of the moment, their delight in obvious originality and in
obvious logic, their shrinking from the ancient and insoluble.
The writer I have quoted is much more than a journalist,
but he has lived their hurried life, and instinctively turns to
them for judgment. He is not thinking of the great poets and
painters, of the cloud of witnesses, who are there that we may
become, through our understanding of their minds, spectators
of the ages, but of this age. Drama is a means of expression,
not a special subject-matter, and the dramatist is as free to
choose where he has a mind to, as the poet of *Endymion*, or

as the painter of Mary Magdalene at the door of Simon the Pharisee. So far from the discussion of our interests and the immediate circumstance of our life being the most moving to the imagination, it is what is old and far off that stirs us the most deeply.

There is a sentence in *The Marriage of Heaven and Hell* that is meaningless until we understand Blake's system of corespondences. 'The best wine is the oldest, the best water the newest.' Water is experience, immediate sensation, and wine is emotion, and it is with the intellect, as distinguished from imagination, that we enlarge the bounds of experience and separate it from all but itself, from illusion, from memory, and create among other things science and good journalism. Emotion, on the other hand, grows intoxicating and delightful after it has been enriched with the memory of old emotions, with all the uncounted flavours of old experience; and it is necessarily some antiquity of thought, emotions that have been deepened by the experiences of many men of genius, that distinguishes the cultivated man. The subject-matter of his meditation and invention is old, and he will disdain a too conscious originality in the arts as in those matters of daily life where, is it not Balzac who says, 'we are all conservatives'? He is above all things well-bred, and whether he write or paint will not desire a technique that denies or obtrudes his long and noble descent.

*   *   *

1906

POETRY AND TRADITION

★　　★　　★

II

Him who trembles before the flame and the flood,
And the winds that blow through the starry ways,
Let the starry winds and the flame and the flood
Cover over and hide, for he has no part
With the proud, majestical multitude.

Three types of men have made all beautiful things. Aristocracies have made beautiful manners, because their place in
the world puts them above the fear of life, and the countrymen
have made beautiful stories and beliefs, because they have
nothing to lose and so do not fear, and the artists have made
all the rest, because Providence has filled them with recklessness. All these look backward to a long tradition, for, being
without fear, they have held to whatever pleased them. The
others, being always anxious, have come to possess little that
is good in itself, and are always changing from thing to thing,
for whatever they do or have must be a means to something
else, and they have so little belief that anything can be an end
in itself that they cannot understand you if you say, 'All the
most valuable things are useless'. They prefer the stalk to the
flower, and believe that painting and poetry exist that there
may be instruction, and love that there may be children, and
theatres that busy men may rest, and holidays that busy men
may go on being busy. At all times they fear and even hate
the things that have worth in themselves, for that worth may

suddenly, as it were a fire, consume their Book of Life, where the world is represented by ciphers and symbols; and before all else, they fear irreverent joy and unserviceable sorrow. It seems to them that those who have been freed by position, by poverty, or by the traditions of art, have something terrible about them, a light that is unendurable to eyesight. They complain much of that commandment that we can do almost what we will, if we do it gaily, and think that freedom is but a trifling with the world.

If we would find a company of our own way of thinking, we must go backward to turreted walls, to Courts, to high rocky places, to little walled towns, to jesters like that jester of Charles V who made mirth out of his own death; to the Duke Guidobaldo in his sickness, or Duke Frederick in his strength, to all those who understood that life is not lived, if not lived for contemplation or excitement.

Certainly we could not delight in that so courtly thing, the poetry of light love, if it were sad; for only when we are gay over a thing, and can play with it, do we show ourselves its master, and have minds clear enough for strength. The raging fire and the destructive sword are portions of eternity, too great for the eye of man, wrote Blake, and it is only before such things, before a love like that of Tristan and Iseult, before noble or ennobled death, that the free mind permits itself aught but brief sorrow. That we may be free from all the rest, sullen anger, solemn virtue, calculating anxiety, gloomy suspicion, prevaricating hope, we should be reborn in gaiety. Because there is submission in a pure sorrow, we should sorrow alone over what is greater than ourselves, nor too soon admit that greatness, but all that is less than we are should stir us to some joy, for pure joy masters and impregnates; and so to world end, strength shall laugh and wisdom mourn.

III

In life courtesy and self-possession, and in the arts style, are the sensible impressions of the free mind, for both arise out of a deliberate shaping of all things, and from never being swept away, whatever the emotion, into confusion or dullness. The Japanese have numbered with heroic things courtesy at all times whatsoever, and though a writer, who has to withdraw so much of his thought out of his life that he may learn his craft, may find many his betters in daily courtesy, he should never be without style, which is but high breeding in words and in argument. He is indeed the creator of the standards of manners in their subtlety, for he alone can know the ancient records and be like some mystic courtier who has stolen the keys from the girdle of Time, and can wander where it please him amid the splendours of ancient Courts.

Sometimes, it may be, he is permitted the licence of cap and bell, or even the madman's bunch of straws, but he never forgets or leaves at home the seal and the signature. He has at all times the freedom of the well-bred, and being bred to the tact of words can take what theme he pleases, unlike the linen-drapers, who are rightly compelled to be very strict in their conversation. Who should be free if he were not? for none other has a continual deliberate self-delighting happiness — style, 'the only thing that is immortal in literature', as Sainte-Beuve has said, a still unexpended energy, after all that the argument or the story needs, a still unbroken pleasure after the immediate end has been accomplished — and builds this up into a most personal and wilful fire, transfiguring words and sounds and events. It is the playing of strength when the day's work is done, a secret between a craftsman and his craft, and is so inseparate in his nature that he has it most of all amid overwhelming emotion, and in the face of death. Shakespeare's persons, when the last darkness has gathered about them, speak out of an ecstasy that is one-half the self-surrender of sorrow, and one-half the last playing and mockery of the victorious sword before the defeated world.

It is in the arrangement of events as in the words, and in that touch of extravagance, of irony, of surprise, which is set there after the desire of logic has been satisfied and all that is merely necessary established, and that leaves one, not in the circling necessity, but caught up into the freedom of self-delight; it is, as it were, the foam upon the cup, the long pheasant's feather on the horse's head, the spread peacock over the pasty. If it be very conscious, very deliberate, as it may be in comedy, for comedy is more personal than tragedy, we call it fantasy, perhaps even mischievous fantasy, recognising how disturbing it is to all that drag a ball at the ankle. This joy, because it must be always making and mastering, remains in the hands and in the tongue of the artist, but with his eyes he enters upon a submissive, sorrowful contemplation of the great irremediable things, and he is known from other men by making all he handles like himself, and yet by the unlikeness to himself of all that comes before him in a pure contemplation. It may have been his enemy or his love or his cause that set him dreaming, and certainly the phoenix can but open her young wings in a flaming nest; but all hate and hope vanishes in the dream, and if his mistress brag of the song or his enemy fear it, it is not that either has its praise or blame, but that the twigs of the holy nest are not easily set afire. The verses may make his mistress famous as Helen or give a victory to his cause, not because he has been either's servant, but because men delight to honour and to remember all that have served contemplation. It had been easier to fight, to die even, for Charles's house with Marvell's poem in the memory, but there is no zeal of service that had not been an impurity in the pure soil where the marvel grew. Timon of Athens contemplates his own end, and orders his tomb by the beached verge of the salt flood, and Cleopatra sets the asp to her bosom, and their words move us because their sorrow is not their own at tomb or asp, but for all men's fate. That shaping joy has kept the sorrow pure, as it had kept it were the emotion love or hate, for the nobleness of the arts is in the mingling of contraries, the extremity of sorrow, the extremity of joy, perfection of personality, the perfection of its surrender, overflowing turbulent energy, and marmorean stillness; and its red rose opens at the meeting of the two beams of the cross, and at the trysting-place of mortal and immortal, time and eternity. No new man has ever plucked that rose, or found that trysting-place, for he could but come to the understanding of himself, to the mastery of unlocking words, after long frequenting of the great Masters, hardly without ancestral memory of the like. Even knowledge is not enough, for the 'recklessness' Castiglione thought necessary in good manners is necessary in this likewise, and if a man has it not he will be gloomy, and had better to his marketing again.

* * *

August 1907

ANIMA HOMINIS

I

When I come home after meeting men who are strange to me, and sometimes even after talking to women, I go over all I have said in gloom and disappointment. Perhaps I have overstated everything from a desire to vex or startle, from hostility that is but fear; or all my natural thoughts have been drowned by an undisciplined sympathy. My fellow-diners have hardly seemed of mixed humanity, and how should I keep my head among images of good and evil, crude allegories?

But when I shut my door and light the candle, I invite a marmorean Muse, an art where no thought or emotion has come to mind because another man has thought or felt something different, for now there must be no reaction, action only, and the world must move my heart but to the heart's discovery of itself, and I begin to dream of eyelids that do not quiver before the bayonet: all my thoughts have ease and joy, I am all virtue and confidence. When I come to put in rhyme what I have found, it will be a hard toil, but for a moment I believe I have found myself and not my anti-self. It is only the shrinking from toil, perhaps, that convinces me that I have been no more myself than is the cat the medicinal grass it is eating in the garden.

How could I have mistaken for myself an heroic condition that from early boyhood has made me superstitious? That which comes as complete, as minutely organised, as are those elaborate, brightly lighted buildings and sceneries appearing in a moment, as I lie between sleeping and waking, must come from above me and beyond me. At times I remember that place in Dante where he sees in his chamber the 'Lord of Terrible Aspect', and how, seeming 'to rejoice inwardly that it was a marvel to see, speaking, he said many things among the which I could understand but few, and of these this: ego dominus tuus'; or should the conditions come, not, as it were, in a gesture — as the image of a man — but in some fine landscape, it is of Boehme, maybe, that I think, and of that country where we 'eternally solace ourselves in the excellent beautiful flourishing of all manner of flowers and forms, both trees and plants, and all kinds of fruit'.

II

When I consider the minds of my friends, among artists and emotional writers, I discover a like contrast. I have sometimes told one close friend that her only fault is a habit of harsh judgment with those who have not her sympathy, and she has written comedies where the wickedest people seem but bold children. She does not know why she has created that world where no one is ever judged, a high celebration of indulgence, but to me it seems that her ideal of beauty is the compensating dream of nature wearied out by over-much judgment. I know a famous actress who, in private life, is like the captain of some buccaneer ship holding his crew to good behaviour at the mouth of a blunderbuss, and upon the stage she excels in the representation of women who stir to pity and to desire because they need our protection, and is most adorable as one of those young queens imagined by Maeterlinck who have so little will, so little self, that they are like shadows sighing at the edge of the world. When I last saw her in her own house she lived in a torrent of words and movements, she could not listen, and all about her upon the walls were women drawn by Burne-Jones in his latest period. She had invited me in the

hope that I would defend those women, who were always listening, and are as necessary to her as a contemplative Buddha
to a Japanese Samurai, against a French critic who would persuade her to take into her heart in their stead a Post-Impres-
sionist picture of a fat, flushed woman lying naked upon a
Turkey carpet.

There are indeed certain men whose art is less an opposing
virtue than a compensation for some accident of health or circumstance. During the riots over the first production of *The
Playboy of the Western World*, Synge was confused, without
clear thought, and was soon ill — indeed the strain of that
week may perhaps have hastened his death — and he was, as
is usual with gentle and silent men, scrupulously accurate in
all his statements. In his art he made, to delight his ear and his
mind's eye, voluble daredevils who 'go romancing through a
romping lifetime...to the dawning of the Judgment Day'. At
other moments this man, condemned to the life of a monk by
bad health, takes an amused pleasure in 'great queens...
making themselves matches from the start to the end'. Indeed, in all his imagination he delights in fine physical life, in
life when the moon pulls up the tide. The last act of *Deirdre
of the Sorrows*, where his art is at its noblest, was written upon
his death-bed. He was not sure of any world to come, he was
leaving his betrothed and his unwritten play — 'O, what a
waste of time,' he said to me; he hated to die, and in the last
speeches of Deirdre and in the middle act he accepted death
and dismissed life with a gracious gesture. He gave to Deirdre
the emotion that seemed to him most desirable, most difficult,
most fitting, and maybe saw in those delighted seven years,
now dwindling from her, the fulfilment of his own life.

III

When I think of any great poetical writer of the past (a realist is a historian and obscures the cleavage by the record of his eyes), I comprehend, if I know the lineaments of his life, that the work is the man's flight from his entire horoscope, his blind struggle in the network of the stars. William Morris, a happy, busy, most irascible man, described dim colour and pensive emotion, following, beyond any man of his time, an indolent Muse; while Savage Landor topped us all in calm nobility when the pen was in his hand, as in the daily violence of his passion when he had laid it down. He had in his *Imaginary Conversations* reminded us, as it were, that the Venus de Milo is a stone, and yet he wrote when the copies did not come from the printer as soon as he expected: 'I have . . . had the resolution to tear in pieces all my sketches and projects and to forswear all future undertakings. I have tried to sleep away my time and pass two-thirds of the twenty-four hours in bed. I may speak of myself as a dead man.' I imagine Keats to have been born with that thirst for luxury common to many at the outsetting of the Romantic Movement, and not able, like wealthy Beckford, to slake it with beautiful and strange objects. It drove him to imaginary delights; ignorant, poor, and in poor health, and not perfectly well-bred, he knew himself driven from tangible luxury; meeting Shelley, he was resentful and suspicious because he, as Leigh Hunt recalls, 'being a little too sensitive on the score of his origin, felt inclined to see in every man of birth his natural enemy'.

IV

Some thirty years ago I read a prose allegory by Simeon Solomon, long out of print and unprocurable, and remember or seem to remember a sentence, 'a hollow image of fulfilled desire'. All happy art seems to me that hollow image, but when its lineaments express also the poverty or the exasperation that set its maker to the work, we call it tragic art. Keats but gave us his dream of luxury; but while reading Dante we never long escape the conflict, partly because the verses are at moments a mirror of his history, and yet more because that history is so clear and simple that it has the quality of art. I am no Dante scholar, and I but read him in Shadwell or in Dante Rossetti, but I am always persuaded that he celebrated the most pure lady poet ever sung and the Divine Justice, not merely because death took that lady and Florence banished her singer, but because he had to struggle in his own heart with his unjust anger and his lust; while, unlike those of the great poets who are at peace with the world and at war with themselves, he fought a double war. 'Always,' says Boccaccio, 'both in youth and maturity he found room among his virtues for lechery'; or as Matthew Arnold preferred to change the phrase, 'his conduct was exceeding irregular'. Guido Cavalcanti, as Rossetti translates him, finds 'too much baseness' in his friend:

> And still thy speech of me, heartfelt and kind,
> Hath made me treasure up thy poetry;
> But now I dare not, for thy abject life,
> Make manifest that I approve thy rhymes.

And when Dante meets Beatrice in Eden, does she not reproach him because, when she had taken her presence away, he followed, in spite of warning dreams, false images, and now, to save him in his own despite, she has 'visited . . . the Portals of the Dead', and chosen Virgil for his courier? While Gino da Pistoia complains that in his *Commedia* his 'lovely heresies . . . beat the right down and let the wrong go free':

Therefore his vain decrees, wherein he lied,
Must be like empty nutshells flung aside;
Yet through the rash false witness set to grow,
French and Italian vengeance on such pride
May fall like Antony on Cicero.

Dante himself sings to Giovanni Guirino 'at the approach of death':

The King, by whose rich grave his servants be
With plenty beyond measure set to dwell,
Ordains that I my bitter wrath dispel,
And lift mine eyes to the great Consistory.

V

We make out of the quarrel with others, rhetoric, but of the quarrel with ourselves, poetry. Unlike the rhetoricians, who get a confident voice from remembering the crowd they have won or may win, we sing amid our uncertainty; and, smitten even in the presence of the most high beauty by the knowledge of our solitude, our rhythm shudders. I think, too, that no fine poet, no matter how disordered his life, has ever, even in his mere life, had pleasure for his end. Johnson and Dowson, friends of my youth, were dissipated men, the one a drunkard, the other a drunkard and mad about women, and yet they had the gravity of men who had found life out and were awakening from the dream; and both, one in life and art and one in art and less in life, had a continual preoccupation with religion. Nor has any poet I have read of or heard of or met with been a sentimentalist. The other self, the anti-self or the antithetical self, as one may choose to name it, comes but to those who are no longer deceived, whose passion is reality. The sentimentalists are practical men who believe in money, in position, in a marriage bell, and whose understanding of happiness is to be so busy whether at work or at play that all is forgotten but the momentary aim. They find their pleasure in a cup that is filled from Lethe's wharf, and for the awakening, for the vision, for the revelation of reality, tradition offers us a different word — ecstasy. An old artist wrote to me of his wanderings by the quays of New York, and how he found there a woman nursing a sick child, and drew her story from her. She spoke, too, of other children who had died: a long tragic story. 'I wanted to paint her,' he wrote; 'if I denied myself any of the pain I could not believe in my own ecstasy.' We must not make a false faith by hiding from our thoughts the causes of doubt, for faith is the highest achievement of the human intellect, the only gift man can make to God, and therefore it must be offered in sincerity. Neither must we create, by hiding ugliness, a false beauty as our offering to the world. He only can create the greatest imaginable beauty who has endured all imaginable pangs, for only when we have seen and foreseen what we dread shall we be rewarded by that dazzling, unforeseen, wing-footed wanderer. We could not find him if he were not in some sense of our being, and yet of our being but as water with fire, a noise with silence. He is of all things not impossible the most difficult, for that only which comes easily can never be a portion of our being; 'soon got, soon gone', as the proverb says. I shall find the dark grow luminous, the void fruitful when I understand I have nothing, that the ringers in the tower have appointed for the hymen of the soul a passing bell.

The last knowledge has often come most quickly to turbulent men, and for a season brought new turbulence. When life puts away her conjuring tricks one by one, those that deceive us longest may well be the wine-cup and the sensual kiss, for our Chambers of Commerce and of Commons have not the divine architecture of the body, nor has their frenzy been ripened by the sun. The poet, because he may not stand within the sacred house but lives amid the whirlwinds that beset its threshold, may find his pardon.

VI

I think the Christian saint and hero, instead of being merely dissatisfied, make deliberate sacrifice. I remember reading once an autobiography of a man who had made a daring journey in disguise to Russian exiles in Siberia, and his telling how, very timid as a child, he schooled himself by wandering at night through dangerous streets. Saint and hero cannot be content to pass at moments to that hollow image and after become their heterogeneous selves, but would always, if they could, resemble the antithetical self. There is a shadow of type on type, for in all great poetical styles there is saint or hero, but when it is all over Dante can return to his chambering and Shakespeare to his 'pottle-pot'. They sought no impossible perfection but when they handled paper or parchment. So too will saint or hero, because he works in his own flesh and blood and not in paper or parchment, have more deliberate understanding of that other flesh and blood.

Some years ago I began to believe that our culture, with its doctrine of sincerity and self-realisation, made us gentle and passive, and that the Middle Ages and the Renaissance were right to found theirs upon the imitation of Christ or of some classic hero. Saint Francis and Caesar Borgia made themselves overmastering, creative persons by turning from the mirror to meditation upon a mask. When I had this thought I could see nothing else in life. I could not write the play I had planned, for all became allegorical, and though I tore up hundreds of pages in my endeavour to escape from allegory, my imagination became sterile for nearly five years and I only escaped at last when I had mocked in a comedy my own thought. I was always thinking of the element of imitation in style and in life, and of the life beyond heroic imitation. I find in an old diary: 'I think all happiness depends on the energy to assume the mask of some other life, on a re-birth as something not one's self, something created in a moment and perpetually renewed; in playing a game like that of a child where one loses the infinite pain of self-realisation, in a grotesque or solemn painted face put on that one may hide from the terror of judgment. . . . Perhaps all the sins and energies of the world are but the world's flight from an infinite blinding beam'; and again at an earlier date: 'If we cannot imagine ourselves as different from what we are, and try to assume that second self, we cannot impose a discipline upon ourselves though we may accept one from others. Active virtue, as distinguished from the passive acceptance of a code, is therefore theatrical, consciously dramatic, the wearing of a mask. . . . Wordsworth, great poet though he be, is so often flat and heavy partly because his moral sense, being a discipline he had not created, a mere obedience, has no theatrical element. This increases his popularity with the better kind of journalists and politicians who have written books.'

VII

I thought the hero found hanging upon some oak of Dodona an ancient mask, where perhaps there lingered something of Egypt, and that he changed it to his fancy, touching it a little here and there, gilding the eyebrows or putting a gilt line where the cheek-bone comes; that when at last he looked out of its eyes he knew another's breath came and went within his breath upon the carven lips, and that his eyes were upon the instant fixed upon a visionary world: how else could the god have come to us in the forest? The good, unlearned books say that He who keeps the distant stars within His fold comes without intermediary, but Plutarch's precepts and the experience of old women in Soho, ministering their witchcraft to servant-girls at a shilling apiece, will have it that a strange living man may win for Daimon[1] an illustrious dead man; but now I add another thought: the Daimon comes not as like to like but seeking its own opposite, for man and Daimon feed the hunger in one another's hearts. Because the ghost is simple, the man heterogeneous and confused, they are but knit together when the man has found a mask whose lineaments permit the expression of all the man most lacks, and it may be dreads, and of that only.

The more insatiable in all desire, the more resolute to refuse deception or an easy victory, the more close will be the bond, the more violent and definite the antipathy.

VIII

I think that all religious men have believed that there is a hand not ours in the events of life, and that, as somebody says in *Wilhelm Meister*, accident is destiny; and I think it was Heraclitus who said: the Daimon is our destiny. When I think of life as a struggle with the Daimon who would ever set us to the hardest work among those not impossible, I understand why there is a deep enmity between a man and his destiny, and why a man loves nothing but his destiny. In an Anglo-Saxon poem a certain man is called, as though to call him something that summed up all heroism, 'Doom eager'. I am persuaded that the Daimon delivers and deceives us, and that he wove that netting from the stars and threw the net from his

[1] I could not distinguish at the time between the permanent Daimon and the impermanent, who may be 'an illustrious dead man', though I knew the distinction was there. I shall deal with the matter in *A Vision*.
                                                             February 1924.

shoulder. Then my imagination runs from Daimon to sweetheart, and I divine an analogy that evades the intellect. I remember that Greek antiquity has bid us look for the principal stars, that govern enemy and sweetheart alike, among those that are about to set, in the Seventh House as the astrologers say; and that it may be 'sexual love', which is 'founded upon spiritual hate', is an image of the warfare of man and Daimon; and I even wonder if there may not be some secret communion, some whispering in the dark between Daimon and sweetheart. I remember how often women when in love grow superstitious, and believe that they can bring their lovers good luck; and I remember an old Irish story of three young men who went seeking for help in battle into the house of the gods at Slieve-na-mon. 'You must first be married,' some god told them, 'because a man's good or evil luck comes to him through a woman.'

I sometimes fence for half an hour at the day's end, and when I close my eyes upon the pillow I see a foil playing before me, the button to my face. We meet always in the deep of the mind, whatever our work, wherever our reverie carries us, that other Will.

IX

The poets finds and makes his mask in disappointment, the hero in defeat. The desire that is satisfied is not a great desire, nor has the shoulder used all its might that an unbreakable gate has never strained. The saint alone is not deceived, neither thrusting with his shoulder nor holding out unsatisfied hands. He would climb without wandering to the antithetical self of the world, the Indian narrowing his thought in meditation or driving it away in contemplation, the Christian copying Christ, the antithetical self of the classic world. For a hero loves the world till it breaks him, and the poet till it has broken faith; but while the world was yet debonair, the saint has turned away, and because he renounced experience itself, he will wear his mask as he finds it. The poet or the hero, no matter upon what bark they found their mask, so teeming their fancy, somewhat change its lineaments, but the saint, whose life is but a round of customary duty, needs nothing the whole world does not need, and day by day he scourges in his body the Roman and Christian conquerors: Alexander and Caesar are famished in his cell. His nativity is neither in disappointment nor in defeat, but in a temptation like that of Christ in the Wilderness, a contemplation in a single instant perpetually renewed of the Kingdoms of the World; all — because all renounced — continually present showing their empty thrones. Edwin Ellis, remembering that Christ also measured the sacrifice, imagined himself in a fine poem as meeting at Golgotha the phantom of 'Christ the Less', the Christ who might have lived a prosperous life without the knowledge of sin, and who now wanders 'companionless, a weary spectre day and night'.

> I saw him go and cried to him,
> 'Eli, thou hast forsaken me.'
> The nails were burning through each limb,
> He fled to find felicity.

And yet is the saint spared — despite his martyr's crown and his vigil of desire — defeat, disappointed love, and the sorrow of parting.

> O Night, that didst lead thus,
> O Night, more lovely than the dawn of light,
> O Night, that broughtest us
> Lover to lover's sight,
> Lover with loved in marriage of delight!

Upon my flowery breast,
Wholly for him, and save himself for none,
There did I give sweet rest
To my beloved one;
The fanning of the cedars breathed thereon.

When the first morning air
Blew from the tower, and waved his locks aside,
His hand, with gentle care,
Did wound me in the side,
And in my body all my senses died.

All things I then forgot,
My cheek on him who for my coming came;
All ceased and I was not,
Leaving my cares and shame
Among the lilies, and forgetting them.[1]

X

It is not permitted to a man who takes up pen or chisel, to seek originality, for passion is his only business, and he cannot but mould or sing after a new fashion because no disaster is like another. He is like those phantom lovers in the Japanese play who, compelled to wander side by side and never mingle, cry: 'We neither wake nor sleep and, passing our nights in a sorrow which is in the end a vision, what are these scenes of spring to us?' If when we have found a mask we fancy that it will not match our mood till we have touched with gold the cheek, we do it furtively, and only where the oaks of Dodona cast their deepest shadow, for could he see our handiwork the Daimon would fling himself out, being our enemy.

[1] Translated by Arthur Symons from 'San Juan de la Cruz'.

XI

Many years ago I saw, between sleeping and waking, a woman of incredible beauty shooting an arrow into the sky, and from the moment when I made my first guess at her meaning I have thought much of the difference between the winding movement of Nature and the straight line, which is called in Balzac's *Séraphita* the 'Mark of Man', but is better described as the mark of saint or sage. I think that we who are poets and artists, not being permitted to shoot beyond the tangible, must go from desire to weariness and so to desire again, and live but for the moment when vision comes to our weariness like terrible lightning, in the humility of the brutes. I do not doubt those heaving circles, those winding arcs, whether in one man's life or in that of an age, are mathematical, and that some in the world, or beyond the world, have foreknown the event and pricked upon the calendar the life-span of a Christ, a Buddha, a Napoleon: that every movement, in feeling or in thought, prepares in the dark by its own increasing clarity and confidence its own executioner. We seek reality with the slow toil of our weakness and are smitten from the boundless and the unforeseen. Only when we are saint or sage, and renounce experience itself, can we, in imagery of the Christian Cabbala, leave the sudden lightning and the path of the serpent and become the bowman who aims his arrow at the centre of the sun.

XII

The doctors of medicine have discovered that certain dreams of the night, for I do not grant them all, are the day's unfulfilled desire, and that our terror of desires condemned by the conscience has distorted and disturbed our dreams. They have only studied the breaking into dream of elements that have remained unsatisfied without purifying discouragement. We can satisfy in life a few of our passions and each passion but a little, and our characters indeed but differ because no two men bargain alike. The bargain, the compromise, is always threatened, and when it is broken we become mad or hysterical or are in some way deluded; and so when a starved or banished passion shows in a dream we, before awaking, break the logic that had given it the capacity of action and throw it into chaos again. But the passions, when we know that they cannot find fulfilment, become vision; and a vision, whether we wake or sleep, prolongs its power by rhythm and pattern, the wheel where the world is butterfly. We need no protection, but it does, for if we become interested in ourselves, in our own lives, we pass out of the vision. Whether it is we or the vision that create the pattern, who set the wheel turning, it is hard to say, but certainly we have a hundred ways of keeping it near us: we select our images from past times, we turn from our own age and try to feel Chaucer nearer than the daily paper. It compels us to cover all it cannot incorporate, and would carry us when it comes in sleep to that moment when even sleep closes her eyes and dreams begin to dream; and we are taken up into a clear light and are forgetful even of our own names and actions and yet in perfect possession of ourselves murmur like Faust, 'Stay, moment', and murmur in vain.

XIII

A poet, when he is growing old, will ask himself if he cannot keep his mask and his vision without new bitterness, new disappointment. Could he if he would, knowing how frail his vigour from youth up, copy Landor who lived loving and hating, ridiculous and unconquered, into extreme old age, all lost but the favour of his Muses?

The Mother of the Muses, we are taught,
Is Memory; she has left me; they remain,
And shake my shoulder, urging me to sing.

Surely, he may think, now that I have found vision and
mask I need not suffer any longer. He will buy perhaps some
small old house, where, like Ariosto, he can dig his garden,
and think that in the return of birds and leaves, or moon and
sun, and in the evening flight of the rooks he may discover
rhythm and pattern like those in sleep and so never awake out
of vision. Then he will remember Wordsworth withering into
eighty years, honoured and empty-witted, and climb to some
waste room and find, forgotten there by youth, some bitter
crust.

February 25, 1917

A PEOPLE'S THEATRE[1]

A LETTER TO LADY GREGORY

I

My dear Lady Gregory — Of recent years you have done all that is anxious and laborious in the supervision of the Abbey Theatre and left me free to follow my own thoughts. It is therefore right that I address to you this letter, wherein I shall explain, half for your ears, half for other ears, certain thoughts that have made me believe that the Abbey Theatre can never do all we had hoped. We set out to make a 'People's Theatre', and in that we have succeeded. But I did not know until very lately that there are certain things, dear to both our hearts, which no 'People's Theatre' can accomplish.

II

All exploitation of the life of the wealthy, for the eye and the ear of the poor and half-poor, in plays, in popular novels, in musical comedy, in fashion papers, at the cinema, in *Daily Mirror* photographs, is a travesty of the life of the rich; and if it were not would all but justify some Red Terror; and it impoverishes and vulgarises the imagination, seeming to hold up for envy and to commend a life where all is display and hurry, passion without emotion, emotion without intellect,

[1] I took the title from a book by Romain Rolland on some French theatrical experiments. 'A People's Theatre' is not quite the same thing as 'A Popular Theatre'. The essay was published in the *Irish Statesman* in the autumn of 1919.—1923.

and where there is nothing stern and solitary. The plays and
novels are the least mischievous, for they still have the old-
fashioned romanticism — their threepenny bit, if worn, is
silver yet — but they are without intensity and intellect and
cannot convey the charm of either as it may exist in those
they would represent. All this exploitation is a rankness that
has grown up recently among us and has come out of an historical necessity that has made the furniture and the clothes
and the brains, of all but the leisured and the lettered, copies
and travesties.

Shakespeare set upon the stage kings and queens, great historical or legendary persons about whom there is nothing
unreal except the circumstance of their lives which remain
vague and summary, because he could only write his best —
his mind and the mind of his audience being interested in emotion and intellect at their moment of union and at their
greatest intensity — when he wrote of those who controlled
the mechanism of life. Had they been controlled by it, intellect and emotion entangled by intricacy and detail could never
have mounted to that union which, as Swedenborg said of the
marriage of the angels, is a conflagration of the whole being.
But since great crowds, changed by popular education with its
eye always on some objective task, have begun to find reality
in mechanism alone,[1] our popular commercial art has substituted for Lear and Cordelia the real millionaire and the real
peeress, and seeks to make them charming by insisting perpetually that they have all that wealth can buy, or rather all
that average men and women would buy if they had wealth.
Shakespeare's groundlings watched the stage in terrified sympathy, while the British working-man looks perhaps at the

[1] I have read somewhere statistics that showed how popular education
has coincided with the lessening of Shakespeare's audience. In every
chief town before it began Shakespeare was constantly played.

photographs of these lords and ladies, whom he admires beyond measure, with the pleasant feeling that they will all be
robbed and murdered before he dies.

III

Then, too, that turning into ridicule of peasant and citizen
and all lesser men could but increase our delight when the
great personified spiritual power, but seems unnatural when
the great are but the rich. During an illness lately I read two
popular novels which I had borrowed from the servants. They
were good stories and half consoled me for the sleep I could
not get, but I was a long time before I saw clearly why everybody with less than a thousand a year was a theme of comedy
and everybody with less than five hundred a theme of farce.
Even Rosencrantz and Guildenstern, courtiers and doubtless
great men in their world, could be but foils for Hamlet because Shakespeare had nothing to do with objective truth, but
we who have nothing to do with anything else, in so far as we
are of our epoch, must not allow a greater style to corrupt us.

An artisan or a small shopkeeper feels, I think, when he sees
upon our Abbey stage men of his own trade, that they are
represented as he himself would represent them if he had the
gift of expression. I do not mean that he sees his own life expounded there without exaggeration, for exaggeration is selection and the more passionate the art the more marked is the
selection, but he does not feel that he has strayed into some
other man's seat. If it is comedy he will laugh at ridiculous
people, people in whose character there is some contortion,
but their station of life will not seem ridiculous. The best
stories I have listened to outside the theatre have been told me
by farmers or sailors when I was a boy, one or two by fellow-
travellers in railway carriages, and most had some quality of
romance, romance of a class and its particular capacity for

adventure; and our theatre is a people's theatre in a sense which no mere educational theatre can be, because its plays are to some extent a part of that popular imagination. It is very seldom that a man or woman bred up among the propertied or professional classes knows any class but his own, and that a class which is much the same all over the world, and already written of by so many dramatists that it is nearly impossible to see its dramatic situations with our own eyes, and those dramatic situations are perhaps exhausted — as Nietzsche thought the whole universe would be some day — and nothing left but to repeat the same combinations over again.

When the Abbey Manager sends us a play for our opinion and it is my turn to read it, if the handwriting of the MS. or of the author's accompanying letter suggests a leisured life I start prejudiced. There will be no fresh observation of character, I think, no sense of dialogue, all will be literary second-hand, at best what Rossetti called the 'soulless self-reflections of man's skill'. On the other hand, until the Abbey plays began themselves to be copied, a handwriting learned in a National School always made me expect dialogue written out by some man who had admired good dialogue before he had seen it upon paper. The construction would probably be bad, for there the student of plays has the better luck, but plays made impossible by rambling and redundance have often contained some character or some dialogue that has stayed in my memory for years. At first there was often vulgarity, and there still is in those comic love scenes which we invariably reject, and there is often propaganda with all its distortion, but these weigh light when set against life seen as if newly created. At first, in face of your mockery, I used to recommend some reading of Ibsen or Galsworthy, but no one has benefited by that reading or by anything but the Abbey audience and our own rejection of all gross propaganda and gross imitation of

the comic column in the newspapers. Our dramatists, and I
am not speaking of your work or Synge's but of those to
whom you and Synge and I gave an opportunity, have been
excellent just in so far as they have become all eye and ear,
their minds not smoking lamps, as at times they would have
wished, but clear mirrors.

Our players, too, have been vivid and exciting because they
have copied a life personally known to them, and of recent
years, since our Manager has had to select from the ordinary
stage-struck young men and women who have seen many
players and perhaps no life but that of the professional class, it
has been much harder, though players have matured more
rapidly, to get the old, exciting, vivid playing. I have never
recovered the good opinion of one recent Manager because I
urged him to choose instead some young man or woman from
some little shop who had never given his or her thoughts to
the theatre. 'Put all the names into a hat,' I think I said, 'and
pick the first that comes.' One of our early players was exceedingly fine in the old woman in *Riders to the Sea*. 'She has
never been to Aran, she knows nothing but Dublin, surely in
that part she is not objective, surely she creates from imagination,' I thought; but when I asked her she said, 'I copied from
my old grandmother.' Certainly it is this objectivity, this
making of all from sympathy, from observation, never from
passion, from lonely dreaming, that has made our players, at
their best, great comedians, for comedy is passionless.

We have been the first to create a true 'People's Theatre',
and we have succeeded because it is not an exploitation of
local colour, or of a limited form of drama possessing a temporary novelty, but the first doing of something for which the
world is ripe, something that will be done all over the world
and done more and more perfectly: the making articulate of
all the dumb classes each with its own knowledge of the

world, its own dignity, but all objective with the objectivity of the office and the workshop, of the newspaper and the street, of mechanism and of politics.

IV

Yet we did not set out to create this sort of theatre, and its success has been to me a discouragement and a defeat. Dante in that passage in the *Convito* which is, I think, the first passage of poignant autobiography in literary history, for there is nothing in Saint Augustine not formal and abstract beside it, in describing his poverty and his exile counts as his chief misfortune that he has had to show himself to all Italy and so publish his human frailties that men who honoured him unknown honour him no more. Lacking means, he had lacked seclusion, and he explains that men such as he should have but few and intimate friends. His study was unity of being, the subordination of all parts to the whole as in a perfectly proportioned human body — his own definition of beauty — and not, as with those I have described, the unity of things in the world; and like all subjectives he shrank, because of what he was, because of what others were, from contact with many men. Had he written plays he would have written from his own thought and passion, observing little and using little, if at all, the conversation of his time — and whether he wrote in verse or in prose his style would have been distant, musical, metaphorical, moulded by antiquity. We stand on the margin between wilderness and wilderness, that which we observe through our senses and that which we can experience only, and our art is always the description of one or the other. If our art is mainly from experience we have need of learned speech, of agreed symbols, because all those things whose names renew experience have accompanied that experience already

many times. A personage in one of Turgenev's novels is reminded by the odour of, I think, heliotrope, of some sweetheart that had worn it, and poetry is any flower that brings a
memory of emotion, while an unmemoried flower is prose,
and a flower pressed and named and numbered science; but
our poetical heliotrope need bring to mind no sweetheart of
ours, for it suffices that it crowned the bride of Paris, or
Peleus' bride. Neither poetry nor any subjective art can exist
but for those who do in some measure share its traditional
knowledge, a knowledge learned in leisure and contemplation.
Even Burns, except in those popular verses which are as lacking in tradition, as modern, as topical, as Longfellow, was, as
Henley said, not the founder but the last of a dynasty.

Once such men could draw the crowd because the circumstance of life changed slowly and there was little to disturb
contemplation, and so men repeated old verses and old stories,
and learned and simple had come to share in common much
allusion and symbol. Where the simple were ignorant they
were ready to learn and so became receptive, or perhaps even
to pretend knowledge like the clowns in the mediaeval poem
that describes the arrival of Chaucer's Pilgrims at Canterbury,
who that they may seem gentlemen pretend to know the
legends in the stained-glass windows. Shakespeare, more objective than Dante — for, alas, the world must move —, was
still predominantly subjective, and he wrote during the latest
crisis of history that made possible a theatre of his kind. There
were still among the common people many traditional songs
and stories, while Court and University, which were much
more important to him, had an interest Chaucer never shared
in great dramatic persons, in those men and women of
Plutarch, who made their death a ritual of passion; for what is
passion but the straining of man's being against some ob-
stacle that obstructs its unity?

You and I and Synge, not understanding the clock, set out to bring again the theatre of Shakespeare or rather perhaps of Sophocles. I had told you how at Young Ireland Societies and the like, young men when I was twenty had read papers to one another about Irish legend and history, and you yourself soon discovered the Gaelic League, then but a new weak thing, and taught yourself Irish. At Spiddal or near it an inn-keeper had sung us Gaelic songs, all new village work that though not literature had *naïveté* and sincerity. The writers, caring nothing for cleverness, had tried to express emotion, tragic or humorous, and great masterpieces, *The Grief of a Girl's Heart*, for instance, had been written in the same speech and manner and were still sung. We know that the songs of the Thames boatmen, to name but these, in the age of Queen Elizabeth had the same relation to great masterpieces. These Gaelic songs were as unlike as those to the songs of the music-hall with their clever ear-catching rhythm, the work of some mind as objective as that of an inventor or of a newspaper reporter. We thought we could bring the old folk-life to Dublin, patriotic feeling to aid us, and with the folk-life all the life of the heart, understanding heart, according to Dante's definition, as the most interior being; but the modern world is more powerful than any propaganda or even than any special circumstance, and our success has been that we have made a Theatre of the head, and persuaded Dublin playgoers to think about their own trade or profession or class and their life within it, so long as the stage curtain is up, in relation to Ireland as a whole. For certain hours of an evening they have objective modern eyes.

v

The objective nature and the subjective are mixed in different proportion as are the shadowed and the bright parts in the lunar phases. In Dante there was little shadow, in Shakespeare a larger portion, while you and Synge, it may be, resemble the moon when it has just passed its third quarter, for you have constant humour — and humour is of the shadowed part — much observation and a speech founded upon that of real life. You and he will always hold our audience, but both have used so constantly a measure of lunar light, have so elaborated style and emotion, an individual way of seeing, that neither will ever, till a classic and taught in school, find a perfect welcome.

The outcry against *The Playboy* was an outcry against its style, against its way of seeing; and when the audience called Synge 'decadent' — a favourite reproach from the objective everywhere — it was but troubled by the stench of its own burnt cakes. How could they that dreaded solitude love that which solitude had made? And never have I heard any that laugh the loudest at your comedies praise that musical and delicate style that makes them always a fit accompaniment for verse and sets them at times among the world's great comedies. Indeed, the louder they laugh the readier are they to rate them with the hundred ephemeral farces they have laughed at and forgotten. Synge they have at least hated. When you and Synge find such an uneasy footing, what shall I do there who have never observed anything, or listened with an attentive ear, but value all I have seen or heard because of the emotions they call up or because of something they remind me of that exists, as I believe, beyond the world? O yes, I am listened to — am I not a founder of the Theatre? — and here and there scattered solitaries delight in what I have made and return to hear it again; but some young Corkman, all eyes and ears, whose first rambling play we have just pulled together or half together, can do more than that. He will be played by players who have spoken dialogue like his every night for years, and sentences that it had been a bore to read will so delight the whole house that to keep my hands from clapping I shall have to remind myself that I gave my voice for the play's production and must not applaud my own judgment.

VI

I want to create for myself an unpopular theatre and an audience like a secret society where admission is by favour and never to many. Perhaps I shall never create it, for you and I and Synge have had to dig the stone for our statue and I am aghast at the sight of a new quarry, and besides I want so much — an audience of fifty, a room worthy of it (some great dining-room or drawing-room), half a dozen young men and women who can dance and speak verse or play drum and flute and zither, and all the while, instead of a profession, I but offer them 'an accomplishment'. However, there are my *Four Plays for Dancers* as a beginning, some masks by Mr. Dulac, music by Mr. Dulac and by Mr. Rummell. In most towns one can find fifty people for whom one need not build all on observation and sympathy, because they read poetry for their pleasure and understand the traditional language of passion. I desire a mysterious art, always reminding and half-reminding those who understand it of dearly loved things, doing its work by suggestion, not by direct statement, a complexity of rhythm, colour, gesture, not space-pervading like the intellect, but a memory and a prophecy: a mode of drama Shelley and Keats could have used without ceasing to be themselves, and for which even Blake in the mood of *The Book of Thel* might not have been too obscure. Instead of advertisements in the Press I need a hostess, and even the most accomplished hostess must choose with more than usual care, for I have noticed that city-living cultivated people, those whose names would first occur to her, set great value on painting, which is a form of property, and on music, which is a part of the organisation of life, while the lovers of literature, those who read a book many times, are either young men with little means or live far away from big towns.

What alarms me most is how a new art needing so elaborate a technique can make its first experiments before those who, as Molière said of the courtiers of his day, have seen so much. How shall our singers and dancers be welcomed by those who have heard Chaliapin in all his parts and who know all the dances of the Russians? Yet where can I find Mr. Dulac and Mr. Rummel or any to match them, but in London[1] or in Paris, and who but the leisured will welcome an elaborate art or pay for its first experiments? In one thing the luck might be upon our side. A man who loves verse and the visible arts has, in a work such as I imagined, the advantage of the professional player. The professional player becomes the amateur, the other has been preparing all his life, and certainly I shall not soon forget the rehearsal of *At the Hawk's Well*, when Mr. Ezra Pound, who had never acted on any stage, in the absence of our chief player rehearsed for half an hour. Even the forms of subjective acting that were natural to the professional stage have ceased. Where all now is sympathy and observation no Irving can carry himself with intellectual pride, nor any Salvini in half-animal nobility, both wrapped in solitude.

I know that you consider Ireland alone our business, and in that we do not differ, except that I care very little where a play of mine is first played so that it find some natural audience and good players. My rooks may sleep abroad in the fields for a while, but when the winter comes they will remember the

---

[1] I live in Dublin now, and indolence and hatred of travel will probably compel me to make my experiment there after all.—1923.

way home to the rookery trees. Indeed, I have Ireland especially in mind, for I want to make, or to help some man some day to make, a feeling of exclusiveness, a bond among chosen spirits, a mystery almost for leisured and lettered people. Ireland has suffered more than England from democracy, for since the Wild Geese fled, who might have grown to be leaders in manners and in taste, she has had but political leaders. As a drawing is defined by its outline and taste by its rejections, I too must reject and draw an outline about the thing I seek; and say that I seek, not a theatre but the theatre's anti-self, an art that can appease all within us that becomes uneasy as the curtain falls and the house breaks into applause.

VII

Meanwhile the Popular Theatre should grow always more objective; more and more a reflection of the general mind; more and more a discovery of the simple emotions that make all men kin, clearing itself the while of sentimentality, the wreckage of an obsolete popular culture, seeking always not to feel and to imagine but to understand and to see. Let those who are all personality, who can only feel and imagine, leave it, before their presence become a corruption and turn it from its honesty. The rhetoric of D'Annunzio, the melodrama and spectacle of the later Maeterlinck, are the insincerities of subjectives, who being very able men have learned to hold an audience that is not their natural audience. To be intelligible they are compelled to harden, to externalise and deform. The popular play left to itself may not lack vicissitude and development, for it may pass, though more slowly than the novel which need not carry with it so great a crowd, from the physical objectivity of Fielding and Defoe to the spiritual objectivity of Tolstoi and Dostoievsky, for beyond the whole we reach by unbiassed intellect there is another whole reached by resignation and the denial of self.

VIII

The two great energies of the world that in Shakespeare's day penetrated each other have fallen apart as speech and music fell apart at the Renaissance, and that has brought each to greater freedom, and we have to prepare a stage for the whole wealth of modern lyricism, for an art that is close to pure music, for those energies that would free the arts from imitation, that would ally acting to decoration and to the dance. We are not yet conscious, for as yet we have no philosophy, while the opposite energy is conscious. All visible history, the discoveries of science, the discussions of politics, are with it; but as I read the world, the sudden changes, or rather the sudden revelations of future changes, are not from visible history but from its anti-self. Blake says somewhere in a 'Prophetic Book' that things must complete themselves before they pass away, and every new logical development of the objective energy intensifies in an exact correspondence a counter-energy, or rather adds to an always deepening unanalysable longing. That counter-longing, having no visible past, can only become a conscious energy suddenly, in those moments of revelation which are as a flash of lightning. Are we approaching a supreme moment of self-consciousness, the two halves of the soul separate and face to face? A certain friend of mine has written upon this subject a couple of intricate poems called *The Phases of the Moon* and *The Double Vision* respectively, which are my continual study, and I must refer the reader to these poems for the necessary mathematical calculations. Were it not for that other gyre turning inward in exact measure with the outward whirl of its fellow, we would

fall in a generation or so under some tyranny that would cease
at last to be a tyranny, so perfect our acquiescence.

> Constrained, arraigned, baffled, bent and unbent
> By these wire-jointed jaws and limbs of wood,
> Themselves obedient,
> Knowing not evil and good;
>
> Obedient to some hidden magical breath.
> They do not even feel, so abstract are they,
> So dead beyond our death,
> Triumph that we obey.

[1919]

THE IRISH DRAMATIC MOVEMENT

YOUR ROYAL HIGHNESS, ladies and gentlemen, I have chosen as my theme the Irish Dramatic Movement, because when I remember the great honour that you have conferred upon me, I cannot forget many known and unknown persons. Perhaps the English committees would never have sent you my name if I had written no plays, no dramatic criticism, if my lyric poetry had not a quality of speech practised upon the stage, perhaps even — though this could be no portion of their deliberate thought — if it were not in some degree the symbol of a movement. I wish to tell the Royal Academy of Sweden of the labours, triumphs and troubles of my fellow-workers.

The modern literature of Ireland, and indeed all that stir of thought which prepared for the Anglo-Irish war, began when Parnell fell from power in 1891. A disillusioned and embittered Ireland turned from parliamentary politics; an event was conceived; and the race began, as I think, to be troubled by that event's long gestation. Dr. Hyde founded the Gaelic League, which was for many years to substitute for political argument a Gaelic grammar, and for political meetings village gatherings, where songs were sung and stories told in the Gaelic language. Meanwhile I had begun a movement in English, in the language in which modern Ireland thinks and does its business; founded certain societies where clerks, working men, men of all classes, could study the Irish poets, novelists and historians who had written in English, and as much of Gaelic literature as had been translated into English. But the great mass of our people, accustomed to interminable political speeches, read little, and so from the very start we felt that we must have a theatre of our own. The theatres of Dublin had nothing about them that we could call our own. They were empty buildings hired by the English travelling companies, and we wanted Irish plays and Irish players. When we thought of these plays we thought of everything that was romantic and poetical, because the nationalism we had called up — the nationalism every generation had called up in moments of discouragement — was romantic and poetical. It was not, however, until I met in 1896 Lady Gregory, a member of an old Galway family, who had spent her life between two Galway houses, the house where she was born, the house into which she married, that such a theatre became possible. All about her lived a peasantry who told stories in a form of English which has much of its syntax from Gaelic, much of its vocabulary from Tudor English, but it was very slowly that we discovered in that speech of theirs our most powerful dramatic instrument, not indeed until she herself began to write. Though my plays were written without dialect and in English blank verse, I think she was attracted to our movement because their subject-matter differed but little from the subject-matter of the country stories. Her own house has been protected by her presence, but the house where she was born was burned down by incendiaries some few months ago, and there has been like disorder over the greater part of Ireland. A trumpery dispute about an acre of land can rouse our people to monstrous savagery, and if in their war with the English auxiliary police they were shown no mercy, they showed none: murder answered murder. Yet their ignorance and violence can remember the noblest beauty. I have in Galway a little old tower, and when I climb to the top of it I can see at no great distance a green field where stood once the thatched cottage of a famous country beauty, the mistress of a small local landed proprietor. I have spoken to old men and women who remembered her, though all are dead now, and they spoke of her as the old men upon the wall of Troy spoke of Helen, nor did man and woman differ in their praise. One old woman of whose youth the neighbours cherished a scandalous tale said of her, 'I tremble all over when I think of her'; and there was another on the neighbouring mountain who said, 'The sun and the moon never shone on anybody so handsome, and her skin was so white that it looked blue, and she had two little blushes on her cheeks'. And there were men that told of the crowds that gathered to look at her upon a fair day, and of a man 'who got his death swimming a river', that he might look at her. It was a song written by the Gaelic poet Raftery that brought her such great fame, and the cottages still sing it, though there are not so many to sing it as when I was young:

> O star of light and O sun in harvest,
> O amber hair, O my share of the world,
> It is Mary Hynes, the calm and easy woman,
> Has beauty in her body and in her mind.

It seemed as if the ancient world lay all about us with its freedom of imagination, its delight in good stories, in man's force and woman's beauty, and that all we had to do was to make the town think as the country felt; yet we soon discovered that the town would only think town thoughts.

In the country you are alone with your own violence, your own ignorance and heaviness, and with the common tragedy of life, and if you have any artistic capacity you desire beautiful emotion; and, certain that the seasons will be the same always, care not how fantastic its expression. In the town, where everybody crowds upon you, it is your neighbour not yourself that you hate, and if you are not to embitter his life and your own life, perhaps even if you are not to murder him in some kind of revolutionary frenzy, somebody must teach reality and justice. You will hate that teacher for a while, calling his books and plays ugly, misdirected, morbid, or something of that kind, but you must agree with him in the end. We were to find ourselves in a quarrel with public opinion that compelled us against our own will and the will of our players to become always more realistic, substituting dialect for verse, common speech for dialect.

I had told Lady Gregory that I saw no likelihood of getting money for a theatre and so must put away that hope, and she promised to find the money among her friends. Her neighbour, Mr. Edward Martyn, paid for our first performances; and our first players came from England; but presently we began our real work with a company of Irish amateurs. Somebody had asked me at a lecture, 'Where will you get your actors?' and I had said, 'I will go into some crowded room, put the name of everybody in it on a different piece of paper, put all those pieces of paper into a hat and draw the first twelve'. I have often wondered at that prophecy, for though it was spoken probably to confound and confuse a questioner it was very nearly fulfilled. Our two best men actors were not indeed chosen by chance, for one was a stage-struck solicitors' clerk and the other a working man who had toured Ireland in a theatrical company managed by a Negro. I doubt if he had learned much in it, for its methods were rough and noisy, the Negro whitening his face when he played a white man, but, so strong is stage convention, blackening it when he played a black man. If a player had to open a letter on the stage I have no doubt that he struck it with the flat of his hand, as I have seen players do in my youth, a gesture that lost its meaning generations ago when blotting-paper was substituted for sand.

We got our women, however, from a little political society which described its object as educating the children of the poor, or, according to its enemies, teaching them a catechism that began with this question, 'What is the origin of evil?' and the answer, 'England'.

And they came to us for patriotic reasons and acted from precisely the same impulse that had made them teach, and yet two of them proved players of genius, Miss Allgood and Miss Maire O'Neill. They were sisters, one all simplicity, her mind shaped by folk-song and folk-story; the other sophisticated, lyrical and subtle. I do not know what their thoughts were as that strange new power awoke within them, but I think they must have suffered from a bad conscience, a feeling that the patriotic impulse had gone, that they had given themselves up to vanity or ambition. Yet I think it was that first misunderstanding of themselves made their peculiar genius possible, for had they come to us with theatrical ambitions they would have imitated some well-known English player and sighed for well-known English plays. Nor would they have found their genius if we had not remained for a long time obscure like the bird within its shell, playing in little halls, generally in some shabby out-of-the-way street. We could experiment and wait, with nothing to fear but political misunderstanding. We had little money and at first needed little, twenty-five pounds given by Lady Gregory and twenty pounds by myself and a few pounds picked up here and there. And our theatrical organisation was preposterous, players and authors all sitting together and settling by vote what play should be performed and who should play it. It took a series of disturbances, weeks of argument during which no performance could be given, before Lady Gregory and John Synge and I were put in control. And our relations with the public were even more disturbed. One play was violently attacked by the patriotic

Press because it described a married peasant woman who had a lover, and when we published the old Aran folk-tale upon which it was founded the Press said the tale had reached Aran from some decadent author of pagan Rome. Presently Lady Gregory wrote her first comedy. My verse plays were not long enough to fill an evening and so she wrote a little play on a country love story in the dialect of her neighbourhood. A countryman returns from America with a hundred pounds and discovers his old sweetheart married to a bankrupt farmer. He plays cards with the farmer, and by cheating against himself gives him the hundred pounds. The company refused to perform it because they said to admit an emigrant's return with a hundred pounds would encourage emigration. We produced evidence of returned emigrants with much larger sums, but were told that only made the matter worse. Then after interminable argument had worn us all out Lady Gregory agreed to reduce the sum to twenty, and the actors gave way. That little play was sentimental and conventional, but her next discovered her genius. She too had desired to serve, and that genius must have seemed miraculous to herself. She was in middle life, and had written nothing but a volume of political memoirs and had no interest in the theatre.

Nobody reading today her *Seven Short Plays* can understand why one of them, now an Irish classic, *The Rising of the Moon*, could not be performed for two years because of political hostility. A policeman discovers an escaped Fenian prisoner and lets him free, because the prisoner has aroused with some old songs the half-forgotten patriotism of his youth. The players would not perform it because they said it was an unpatriotic act to admit that a policeman was capable of patriotism. One well-known leader of the mob wrote to me, 'How can the Dublin mob be expected to fight the police if it looks upon them as capable of patriotism?' When performed at last the play was received with enthusiasm, but only to get us into new trouble. The chief Unionist Dublin newspaper denounced us for slandering His Majesty's forces, and Dublin Castle denied to us a privilege which we had shared with the other Dublin theatres of buying, for stage purposes, the cast-off clothes of the police. Castle and Press alike knew that the police had frequently let off political prisoners, but 'that only made the matter worse'. Every political party had the same desire to substitute for life, which never does the same thing twice, a bundle of reliable principles and assertions. Nor did religious orthodoxy like us any better than political; my *Countess Cathleen* was denounced by Cardinal Logue as an heretical play, and when I wrote that we would like to perform 'foreign masterpieces' a Nationalist newspaper declared that 'a foreign masterpiece is a very dangerous thing'. The little halls where we performed could hold a couple of hundred people at the utmost and our audience was often not more than twenty or thirty, and we performed but two or three times a month, and during our periods of quarrelling not even that. But there was no lack of leading articles, we were from the first a recognized public danger. Two events brought us victory: a friend gave us a theatre, and we found a strange man of genius, John Synge. After a particularly angry leading article I had come in front of the curtain and appealed to the hundred people of the audience for their support. When I came down from the stage an old friend, Miss Horniman, from whom I had been expecting a contribution of twenty pounds, said, 'I will find you a theatre'. She found and altered for our purpose what is now the Abbey Theatre, Dublin, and gave us a small subsidy for a few years.

I had met John Synge in Paris in 1896. Somebody had said, 'There is an Irishman living on the top floor of your hotel; I will introduce you'. I was very poor, but he was much poorer. He belonged to a very old Irish family and, though a simple courteous man, remembered it and was haughty and lonely. With just enough to keep him from starvation and not always from half-starvation, he had wandered about Europe, travelling third-class or upon foot, playing his fiddle to poor men on the road or in their cottages. He was the man that we needed, because he was the only man I have ever known incapable of a political thought or of a humanitarian purpose. He could walk the roadside all day with some poor man without any desire to do him good or for any reason except that he liked him. He was to do for Ireland, though more by his influence on other dramatists than by his direct influence, what Robert Burns did for Scotland. When Scotland thought herself gloomy and religious, Providence restored her imaginative spontaneity by raising up Robert Burns to commend drink and the Devil. I did not, however, see what was to come when I advised John Synge to go to a wild island off the Galway coast and study its life because that life 'had never been expressed in literature'. He had learned Gaelic at College and I told him that, as I would have told it to any young man who had learned Gaelic and wanted to write. When he found that wild island he became happy for the first time, escaping, as he said, 'from the nullity of the rich and the squalor of the poor'. He had bad health, he could not stand the island hardship long, but he would go to and fro between there and Dublin.

Burns himself could not have more shocked a gathering of Scots clergy than did he our players. Some of the women got about him and begged him to write a play about the rebellion of '98, and pointed out very truthfully that a play on such a patriotic theme would be a great success. He returned at the end of a fortnight with a scenario upon which he had toiled in his laborious way. Two women take refuge in a cave, a Protestant woman and a Catholic, and carry on an interminable argument about the merits of their respective religions. The Catholic woman denounces Henry VIII and Queen Elizabeth, and the Protestant woman the Inquisition and the Pope. They argue in low voices, because one is afraid of being ravished by the rebels and the other by the loyal soldiers. But at last either the Protestant or the Catholic says that she prefers any fate to remaining any longer in such wicked company and climbs out. The play was neither written nor performed, and neither then nor at any later time could I discover whether Synge understood the shock that he was giving. He certainly did not foresee in any way the trouble that his greatest play brought on us all.

When I had landed from a fishing yawl on the middle of the island of Aran, a few months before my first meeting with Synge, a little group of islanders, who had gathered to watch a stranger's arrival, brought me to 'the oldest man upon the island'. He spoke but two sentences, speaking them very slowly: 'If any gentleman has done a crime we'll hide him. There was a gentleman that killed his father, and I had him in my house six months till he got away to America.' It was a play founded on that old man's story Synge brought back with him. A young man arrives at a little public-house and tells the publican's daughter that he has murdered his father. He so tells it that he has all her sympathy, and every time he retells it, with new exaggerations and additions, he wins the sympathy of somebody or other, for it is the countryman's habit to be against the law. The countryman thinks the more terrible the crime, the greater must the provocation have been. The young man himself, under the excitement of his own story, becomes gay, energetic and lucky. He prospers in love, comes in first at the local races, and bankrupts the roulette tables afterwards. Then the father arrives with his head bandaged but very lively, and the people turn upon the impostor. To win back their esteem he takes up a spade to kill his father in earnest, but, horrified at the threat of what had sounded so well in the story, they bind him to hand over to the police. The father releases him and father and son walk off together, the son, still buoyed up by his imagination, announcing that he will be master henceforth. Picturesque, poetical, fantastical, a masterpiece of style and of music, the supreme work of our dialect theatre, his *Playboy* roused the populace to fury. We played it under police protection, seventy police in the theatre the last night, and five hundred, some newspaper said, keeping order in the streets outside. It is never played before any Irish audience for the first time without something or other being flung at the players. In New York a currant cake and a watch were flung, the owner of the watch claiming it at the stage door afterwards. The Dublin audience has, however, long since accepted the play. It has noticed, I think, that everyone upon the stage is somehow lovable and companionable, and that Synge has described, through an exaggerated symbolism, a reality which he loved precisely because he loved all reality. So far from being, as they had thought, a politician working in the interests of England, he was so little a politician that the world merely amused him and touched his pity. Yet when Synge died in 1909 opinion had hardly changed, we were playing to an almost empty theatre and were continually denounced. Our victory was won by those who had learned from him courage and sincerity but belonged to a different school. Synge's work, the work of Lady Gregory, my own *Cathleen ni Houlihan* and my *Hour-Glass* in its prose form, are characteristic of our first ambition. They bring the imagination and speech of the country, all that poetical tradition descended from the Middle Ages, to the people of the town.

Those who learned from Synge had often little knowledge of the country and always little interest in its dialect. Their plays are frequently attacks upon obvious abuses, the bribery at the appointment of a dispensary Doctor, the attempts of some local politician to remain friends with all parties. Indeed the young Ministers and party politicians of the Free State have had, I think, some of their education from our plays. Then, too, there are many comedies which are not political satires though they are concerned with the life of the politics-ridden people of the town. Of these Mr. Lennox Robinson's are the best known; his *Whiteheaded Boy* has been played in England and America. Of late it has seemed as if this school were coming to an end, for the old plots are repeated with slight variations and the characterisation grows mechanical. It is too soon yet to say what will come to us from the melodrama and tragedy of the last four years, but if we can pay our players and keep our theatre open something will come. We are burdened with debt, for we have come through war and civil war and audiences grow thin when there is firing in the streets. We have, however, survived so much that I believe in our luck, and think that I have a right to say my lecture ends in the middle or even, perhaps, at the beginning of the story. But certainly I have said enough to make you understand why, when I received from the hands of your King the great honour your Academy has conferred upon me, I felt that a young man's ghost should have stood upon one side of me and at the other a living woman sinking into the infirmity of age. Indeed I have seen little in this last week that would not have been memorable and exciting to Synge and to Lady Gregory, for Sweden has achieved more than we have hoped for our own country. I think most of all, perhaps, of that splendid spectacle of your Court, a family beloved and able that has gathered about it not the rank only but the intellect of its country. No like spectacle will in Ireland show its work of discipline and of taste, though it might satisfy a need of the race no institution created under the influence of English or American democracy can satisfy.

1924

INTRODUCTION TO FIGHTING THE WAVES

I

I WROTE *The Only Jealousy of Emer* for performance in a private house or studio, considering it, for reasons which I have explained, unsuited to a public stage. Then somebody put it on a public stage in Holland and Hildo van Krop made his powerful masks. Because the dramatist who can collaborate with a great sculptor is lucky, I rewrote the play not only to fit it for such a stage but to free it from abstraction and confusion. I have retold the story in prose which I have tried to make very simple, and left imaginative suggestion to dancers, singers, musicians. I have left the words of the opening and closing lyrics unchanged, for sung to modern music in the modern way they suggest strange patterns to the ear without obtruding upon it their difficult, irrelevant words. The masks get much of their power from enclosing the whole head; this makes the head out of proportion to the body, and I found some difference of opinion as to whether this was a disadvantage or not in an art so distant from reality; that it was not a disadvantage in the case of the Woman of the Sidhe all were agreed. She was a strange, noble, unforgettable figure.

I do not say that it is always necessary when one writes for a general audience to make the words of the dialogue so simple and so matter-of-fact; but it is necessary where the appeal is mainly to the eye and to the ear through songs and music. *Fighting the Waves* is in itself nothing, a mere occasion for sculptor and dancer, for the exciting dramatic music of George Antheil.

II

'It is that famous man Cuchulain. . . .' In the eighties of the
last century Standish O'Grady, his mind full of Homer, retold the story of Cuchulain that he might bring back an heroic
ideal. His work, which founded modern Irish literature, was
hasty and ill-constructed, his style marred by imitation of
Carlyle; twenty years later Lady Gregory translated the whole
body of Irish heroic legend into the dialect of the cottages in
those great books *Cuchulain of Muirthemne* and *Gods and Fighting Men*, her eye too upon life. In later years she often quoted
the saying of Aristotle: 'To think like a wise man, but express
oneself like the common people,' and always her wise man
was heroic man. Synge wrote his *Deirdre of the Sorrows* in
peasant dialect, but died before he had put the final touches to
anything but the last act, the most poignant and noble in Irish
drama. I wrote in blank verse, which I tried to bring as close
to common speech as the subject permitted, a number of connected plays — *Deirdre, At the Hawk's Well, The Green Helmet, On Baile's Strand, The Only Jealousy of Emer*. I would have
attempted the Battle of the Ford and the Death of Cuchulain,
had not the mood of Ireland changed.

III

When Parnell was dragged down, his shattered party gave
itself up to nine years' vituperation, and Irish imagination fled
the sordid scene. A. E.'s *Homeward Songs by the Way*; Padraic
Colum's little songs of peasant life; my own early poems;
Lady Gregory's comedies, where, though the dramatic tension
is always sufficient, the worst people are no wickeder than
children; Synge's *Well of the Saints* and *Playboy of the Western
World*, where the worst people are the best company, were as
typical of that time as Lady Gregory's translations. Repelled

by what had seemed the sole reality, we had turned to romantic dreaming, to the nobility of tradition.

About 1909 the first of the satirists appeared, 'The Cork Realists', we called them, men that had come to maturity amidst spite and bitterness. Instead of turning their backs upon the actual Ireland of their day, they attacked everything that had made it possible, and in Ireland and among the Irish in England made more friends than enemies by their attacks. James Joyce, the son of a small Parnellite organiser, had begun to write, but remained unpublished.

> An age is the reversal of an age;
> When strangers murdered Emmet, Fitzgerald, Tone,
> We lived like men that watch a painted stage.
> What matter for the scene, the scene once gone!
> It had not touched our lives; but popular rage,
> *Hysterica passio*, dragged this quarry down.
> None shared our guilt; nor did we play a part
> Upon a painted stage when we devoured his heart.

But even if there had been no such cause of bitterness, of self-contempt, we could not, considering that every man everywhere is more of his time than of his nation, have long kept the attention of our small public, no, not with the whole support, and that we never had, of the Garrets and Cellars. Only a change in European thought could have made that possible. When Stendhal described a masterpiece as a 'mirror dawdling down a lane', he expressed the mechanical philosophy of the French eighteenth century. Gradually literature conformed to his ideal; Balzac became old-fashioned; romanticism grew theatrical in its strain to hold the public; till, by the end of the nineteenth century, the principal characters in the most famous books were the passive analysts of events, or had been brutalised into the likeness of mechanical objects. But Europe is

changing its philosophy. Some four years ago the Russian
Government silenced the mechanists because social dialectic is
impossible if matter is trundled about by some limited force.
Certain typical books — *Ulysses*, Virginia Woolf's *The
Waves*, Mr. Ezra Pound's *Draft of XXX Cantos* — suggest a
philosophy like that of the *Samkara* school of ancient India,
mental and physical objects alike material, a deluge of experience breaking over us and within us, melting limits whether
of line or tint; man no hard bright mirror dawdling by the dry
sticks of a hedge, but a swimmer, or rather the waves themselves. In this new literature announced with much else by
Balzac in *Le Chef-d'œuvre inconnu*, as in that which it super-
seded, man in himself is nothing.

IV

I once heard Sir William Crookes tell half a dozen people
that he had seen a flower carried in broad daylight slowly
across the room by what seemed an invisible hand. His chemical research led to the discovery of radiant matter, but the
science that shapes opinion has ignored his other research that
seems to those who study it the slow preparation for the
greatest, perhaps the most dangerous, revolution in thought
Europe has seen since the Renaissance, a revolution that may,
perhaps, establish the scientific complement of certain philosophies that in all ancient countries sustained heroic art. We
may meet again, not the old simple celebration of life tuned
to the highest pitch, neither Homer nor the Greek dramatists,
something more deliberate than that, more systematised, more
external, more self-conscious, as must be at a second coming,
Plato's Republic, not the Siege of Troy.

I shall remind the Garrets and Cellars of certain signs, that
they may, as a Chinese philosopher has advised, shape things

at their beginning, when it is easy, not at the end, when it is difficult. I first name Mr. Sacheverell Sitwell's lovely 'Pastoral'; point out that he has celebrated those Minoan shepherds, those tamers of the wild bulls, their waists enclosed from childhood in wide belts of bronze, that they might attain wasp-like elegance; that he prefers them to the natural easy Sicilian shepherds, preferring as it were cowboys to those that 'watched their flocks by night'; then Dr. Gogarty's praise of 'the Submarine Men trained through a lifetime'; and remind them of their own satisfaction in that praise. Then they might, after considering the demand of the black, brown, green, and blue shirts, 'Power to the most disciplined', ask themselves whether D'Annunzio and his terrible drill at Fiume may not prove as symbolic as Shelley, whose art and life became so completely identified with romantic contemplation that young men in their late teens, when I was at that age, identified him with poetry itself.

Here in Ireland we have come to think of self-sacrifice, when worthy of public honour, as the act of some man at the moment when he is least himself, most completely the crowd. The heroic act, as it descends through tradition, is an act done because a man is himself, because, being himself, he can ask nothing of other men but room amid remembered tragedies; a sacrifice of himself to himself, almost, so little may he bargain, of the moment to the moment. I think of some Elizabethan play where, when mutineers threaten to hang the ship's captain, he replies: 'What has that to do with me?' So lonely is that ancient act, so great the pathos of its joy, that I have never been able to read without tears a passage in *Sigurd the Volsung* describing how the new-born child lay in the bed and looked 'straight on the sun'; how the serving-women washed him, bore him back to his mother, wife of the dead Sigmund; how 'they shrank in their rejoicing before the eyes of the child'; 'the best sprung from the best'; how though 'the spring morn smiled . . . the hour seemed awful to them'.

> But Hiordis looked on the Volsung,
>   on her grief and her fond desire.
> And the hope of her heart was quickened,
>   and her heart was a living fire;
> And she said: 'Now one of the earthly
>   on the eyes of my child hath gazed
> Nor shrunk before their glory,
>   nor stayed her love amazed:
> I behold thee as Sigmund beholdeth, —
>   and I was the home of thine heart —
> Woe's me for the day when thou wert not,
>   And the hour when we shall part!'

How could one fail to be moved in the presence of the central mystery of the faith of poets, painters, and athletes? I am carried forty years back and hear a famous old athlete wind up a speech to country lads — 'The holy people have above them the communion of saints; we the communion of the *Tuatha de Danaan* of Erin.'

Science has driven out the legends, stories, superstitions that protected the immature and the ignorant with symbol, and now that the flower has crossed our rooms, science must take their place and demonstrate as philosophy has in all ages, that States are justified, not by multiplying or, as it would seem, comforting those that are inherently miserable, but because sustained by those for whom the hour seems 'awful', and by those born out of themselves, the best born of the best.

Since my twentieth year, these thoughts have been in my mind, and now that I am old I sing them to the Garrets and the Cellars:

Move upon Newton's town,
The town of Hobbes and of Locke,
Pine, spruce, come down
Cliff, ravine, rock:
What can disturb the corn?
What makes its shudder and bend?
The rose brings her thorn,
The Absolute walks behind.

V

Yet it may be that our science, our modern philosophy, keep a subconscious knowledge that their raft, roped together at the end of the seventeenth century, must, if they so much as glance at that slow-moving flower, part and abandon us to the storm, or it may be, as Professor Richet suggests at the end of his long survey of psychical research from the first experiments of Sir William Crookes to the present moment, that all it can do is, after a steady scrutiny, to prove the poverty of the human intellect, that we are lost amid alien intellects, near but incomprehensible, more incomprehensible than the most distant stars. We may, whether it scrutinise or not, lacking its convenient happy explanations, plunge as Rome did in the fourth century according to some philosopher of that day into 'a fabulous, formless darkness'.

Should H. G. Wells afflict you,
Put whitewash in a pail;
Paint: 'Science — opium of the suburbs'
On some waste wall.

VI

'First I must cover up his face, I must hide him from the sea.' I am deeply grateful for a mask with the silver glitter of a fish, for a dance with an eddy like that of water, for music that suggested, not the vagueness, but the rhythm of the sea. A Dublin journalist showed his scorn for 'the new paganism' by writing: 'Mr. Yeats' play is not really original, for something of the kind doubtless existed in Ancient Babylon,' but a German psycho-analyst has traced the 'mother complex' back to our mother the sea — after all, Babylon was a modern inland city — to the loneliness of the first crab or crayfish that climbed ashore and turned lizard; while Gemistus Plethon not only substituted the sea for Adam and Eve, but, according to a friend learned in the Renaissance, made it symbolise the garden's ground or first original, 'that concrete universal which all philosophy is seeking'.

VII

'Everything he loves must fly,' everything he desires; Emer too must renounce desire, but there is another love, that which is like the man-at-arms in the Anglo-Saxon poem, 'doom eager'. Young, we discover an opposite through our love; old, we discover our love through some opposite neither hate nor despair can destroy, because it is another self, a self that we have fled in vain.

1932

ON D. H. LAWRENCE

[These two extracts are from letters to Olivia Shakespear, 22 and 25 May, 1933.]

. . . MY two sensations at the moment are Hulme's *Speculations* and *Lady Chatterley's Lover*. The first in an essay called *Modern Art* relates such opposites as *The Apes of God* and *Lady Chatterley*. Get somebody to lend you the last if you have not read it. Frank Harris's *Memoirs* are vulgar and immoral — the sexual passages were like holes burnt with a match in a piece of old newspaper; their appeal to physical sensation was hateful; but *Lady Chatterley* is noble. Its description of the sexual act is more detailed than in Harris, the language is sometimes that of cabmen and yet the book is all fire. Those two lovers, the gamekeeper and his employer's wife, each separated from their class by their love, and by fate, are poignant in their loneliness, and the coarse language of the one, accepted by both, becomes a forlorn poetry uniting their solitudes, something ancient, humble and terrible . . .

. . . Of course Lawrence is an emphasis directed against modern abstraction. I find the whole book interesting and not merely the sexual parts. They are something that he sets up as against the abstraction of an age that he thinks dead from the waist downward. Of course happiness is not where he seems to place it. We are happy when for everything inside us there is an equivalent something outside us. I think it was Goethe said this. One should add the converse. It is terrible to desire and not possess, and terrible to possess and not desire. Because of this we long for an age which has the unity which Plato somewhere defined as sorrowing and rejoicing over the same things. How else escape the Bank Holiday crowd?

I have bought a suit of rough blue serge.

Yours,
W. B. Yeats.

Read *Twenty Years a-Growing* or some of it. I once told you that you would be happy if you had twelve children and lived on limpets. There are limpets on the Great Blasket.

INTRODUCTION TO THE OXFORD
BOOK OF MODERN VERSE

*   *   *

III

Then in 1900 everybody got down off his stilts; henceforth nobody drank absinthe with his black coffee; nobody went mad; nobody committed suicide; nobody joined the Catholic church; or if they did I have forgotten.

Victorianism had been defeated, though two writers dominated the moment who had never heard of that defeat or did not believe in it; Rudyard Kipling and William Watson. Indian residence and associations had isolated the first, he was full of opinions, of politics, of impurities — to use our word — and the word must have been right, for he interests a critical audience to-day by the grotesque tragedy of 'Danny Deever', the matter but not the form of old street ballads, and by songs traditional in matter and form like the 'St. Helena Lullaby'. The second had reached maturity before the revolt began, his first book had been published in the early eighties. 'Wring the neck of rhetoric' Verlaine had said, and the public soon turned against William Watson, forgetting that at his best he had not rhetoric but noble eloquence. As I turn his pages I find verse after verse read long ago and still unforgettable, this to some journalist who, intoxicated perhaps by William Archer's translations from Ibsen, had described, it may be, some lyric elaborating or deepening its own tradition as of 'no importance to the age':

> Great Heaven! When these with clamour shrill
>   Drift out to Lethe's harbour bar
> A verse of Lovelace shall be still
>   As vivid as a pulsing star:

this, received from some Miltonic cliff that had it from a
Roman voice:

> The august, inhospitable, inhuman night
> Glittering magnificently unperturbed.

IV

Conflict bequeathed its bias. Folk-song, unknown to the
Victorians as their attempts to imitate it show, must, because
never declamatory or eloquent, fill the scene. If anybody will
turn these pages attending to poets born in the 'fifties, 'sixties,
and 'seventies, he will find how successful are their folk-
songs and their imitations. In Ireland, where still lives almost
undisturbed the last folk tradition of western Europe, the
songs of Campbell and Colum draw from that tradition their
themes, return to it, and are sung to Irish airs by boys and
girls who have never heard the names of the authors; but the
reaction from rhetoric, from all that was prepense and
artificial, has forced upon these writers now and again, as
upon my own early work, a facile charm, a too soft simplicity. In England came like temptations. *The Shropshire Lad*
is worthy of its fame, but a mile further and all had been
marsh. Thomas Hardy, though his work lacked technical
accomplishment, made the necessary correction through his
mastery of the impersonal objective scene. John Synge
brought back masculinity to Irish verse with his harsh disillusionment, and later, when the folk movement seemed to

support vague political mass excitement, certain poets began
to create passionate masterful personality.

V

We remembered the Gaelic poets of the seventeenth and
early eighteenth centuries wandering, after the flight of the
Catholic nobility, among the boorish and the ignorant,
singing their loneliness and their rage; James Stephens, Frank
O'Connor made them symbols of our pride: -

> The periwinkle, and the tough dog-fish
> At eventide have got into my dish!
> The great, where are they now! the great had said —
> This is not seemly, bring to him instead
> That which serves his and serves our dignity —
> And that was done.

> I am O'Rahilly:
> Here in a distant place I hold my tongue,
> Who once said all his say, when he was young!

I showed Lady Gregory a few weeks before her death a book
by Day Lewis. 'I prefer,' she said, 'those poems translated by
Frank O'Connor because they come out of original sin.' A
distinguished Irish poet said a month back — I had read him a
poem by Turner — 'We cannot become philosophic like the
English, our lives are too exciting.' He was not thinking of
such where public life is simple and exciting. We are not
many; Ireland has had few poets of any kind outside Gaelic.
I think England has had more good poets from 1900 to the
present day than during any period of the same length since
the early seventeenth century. There are no predominant
figures, no Browning, no Tennyson, no Swinburne, but more

than I have found room for have written two, three, or half a dozen lyrics that may be permanent.

During the first years of the century the best known were celebrators of the country-side or of the life of ships; I think of Davies and of Masefield; some few wrote in the manner of the traditional country ballad. Others, descended not from Homer but from Virgil, wrote what the young communist scornfully calls 'Belles-lettres': Binyon when at his best, as I think, of Tristram and Isoult: Sturge Moore of centaurs, amazons, gazelles copied from a Persian picture: De la Mare short lyrics that carry us back through *Christabel* or *Kubla Khan*.

> Through what wild centuries
> Roves back the rose?

The younger of the two ladies who wrote under the name of 'Michael Field' made personal lyrics in the manner of Walter Savage Landor and the Greek anthology.

None of these were innovators; they preferred to keep all the past their rival; their fame will increase with time. They have been joined of late years by Sacheverell Sitwell with his *Canons of Giant Art*, written in the recently rediscovered 'sprung verse', his main theme changes of colour, or historical phase, in Greece, Crete, India. *Agamemnon's Tomb*, however, describes our horror at the presence and circumstance of death and rises to great intensity.

VII

Robert Bridges seemed for a time, through his influence on Laurence Binyon and others less known, the patron saint of the movement. His influence — practice, not theory — was never deadening; he gave to lyric poetry a new cadence, a distinction as deliberate as that of Whistler's painting, an impulse moulded and checked like that in certain poems of Landor, but different, more in the nerves, less in the blood, more birdlike, less human; words often commonplace made unforgettable by some trick of speeding and slowing,

> A glitter of pleasure
> And a dark tomb,

or by some trick of simplicity, not the impulsive simplicity of youth but that of age, much impulse examined and rejected:

> I heard a linnet courting
>   His lady in the spring!
> His mates were idly sporting,
>   Nor stayed to hear him sing
>   His song of love. —
> I fear my speech distorting
>   His tender love.

Every metaphor, every thought a commonplace, emptiness everywhere, the whole magnificent.

VIII

A modern writer is beset by what Rossetti called 'the soulless self-reflections of man's skill'; the more vivid his nature, the greater his boredom, a boredom no Greek, no Elizabethan, knew in like degree, if at all. He may escape to the classics with the writers I have just described, or with much loss of self-control and coherence force language against its will into a powerful, artificial vividness. Edith Sitwell has a temperament of a strangeness so high-pitched that only through this artifice could it find expression. One cannot think of her in any other age or country. She has transformed

with her metrical virtuosity traditional metres reborn not to
be read but spoken, exaggerated metaphors into mythology,
carrying them from poem to poem, compelling us to go
backward to some first usage for the birth of the myth; if the
storm suggest the bellowing of elephants, some later poem
will display 'The elephant trunks of the sea'. Nature appears
before us in a hashish-eater's dream. This dream is double;
in its first half, through separated metaphor, through mythology, she creates, amid crowds and scenery that suggest the
Russian Ballet and Aubrey Beardsley's final phase, a perpetual
metamorphosis that seems an elegant, artificial childhood; in
the other half, driven by a necessity of contrast, a nightmare
vision like that of Webster, of the emblems of mortality. A
group of writers have often a persistent image. There are
'stars' in poem after poem of certain writers of the 'nineties
as though to symbolize an aspiration towards what is inviolate and fixed; and now in poem after poem by Edith
Sitwell or later writers are 'bones' — 'the anguish of the
skeleton', 'the terrible Gehenna of the bone'; Eliot has:

> No contact possible to flesh
> Allayed the fever of the bone.

and Elinor Wylie, an American whose exquisite work is
slighter than that of her English contemporaries because she
has not their full receptivity to the profound hereditary sadness
of English genius:

> Live like the velvet mole:
> Go burrow underground,
> And there hold intercourse
> With roots of trees and stones,
> With rivers at their source
> And disembodied bones.

Laurence Binyon, Sturge Moore, knew nothing of this image; it seems most persistent among those who, throwing aside tradition, seek something somebody has called 'essential form' in the theme itself. A fairly well-known woman painter in September drew my house, at that season almost hidden in foliage; she reduced the trees to skeletons as though it were mid-winter, in pursuit of 'essential form'. Does not intellectual analysis in one of its moods identify man with that which is most persistent in his body? The poets are haunted once again by the Elizabethan image, but there is a difference. Since Poincaré said 'space is the creation of our ancestors', we have found it more and more difficult to separate ourselves from the dead when we commit them to the grave; the bones are not dead but accursed, accursed because unchanging.

> The small bones built in the womb
> The womb that loathed the bones
> And cast out the soul.

Perhaps in this new, profound poetry, the symbol itself is contradictory, horror of life, horror of death.

IX

Eliot has produced his great effect upon his generation because he has described men and women that get out of bed or into it from mere habit; in describing this life that has lost heart his own art seems grey, cold, dry. He is an Alexander Pope, working without apparent imagination, producing his effects by a rejection of all rhythms and metaphors used by the more popular romantics rather than by the discovery of his own, this rejection giving his work an unexaggerated plainness that has the effect of novelty. He has the rhythmical flatness of *The Essay on Man* — despite Miss Sitwell's advocacy

I see Pope as Blake and Keats saw him — later, in *The Waste Land*, amid much that is moving in symbol and imagery there is much monotony of accent:

> When lovely woman stoops to folly and
> Paces about her room again, alone,
> She smooths her hair with automatic hand,
> And put a record on the gramophone.

I was affected, as I am by these lines, when I saw for the first time a painting by Manet. I longed for the vivid colour and light of Rousseau and Courbet, I could not endure the grey middle-tint — and even to-day Manet gives me an incomplete pleasure; he had left the procession. Nor can I put the Eliot of these poems among those that descend from Shakespeare and the translators of the Bible. I think of him as satirist rather than poet. Once only does that early work speak in the great manner:

> The host with someone indistinct
> Converses at the door apart,
> The nightingales are singing near
> The Convent of the Sacred Heart,
>
> And sang within the bloody wood
> When Agamemnon cried aloud,
> And let their liquid siftings fall
> To stain the stiff dishonoured shroud.

Not until *The Hollow Men* and *Ash-Wednesday*, where he is helped by the short lines, and in the dramatic poems where his remarkable sense of actor, chanter, scene, sweeps him away, is there rhythmical animation. Two or three of my friends attribute the change to an emotional enrichment from religion, but his religion compared to that of John Gray, Francis

Thompson, Lionel Johnson in *The Dark Angel*, lacks all strong emotion; a New England Protestant by descent, there is little self-surrender in his personal relation to God and the soul. *Murder in the Cathedral* is a powerful stage play because the actor, the monkish habit, certain repeated words, symbolise what we know, not what the author knows. Nowhere has the author explained how Becket and the King differ in aim; Becket's people have been robbed and persecuted in his absence; like the King he demands strong government. Speaking through Becket's mouth Eliot confronts a world growing always more terrible with a religion like that of some great statesman, a pity not less poignant because it tempers the prayer book with the results of mathematical philosophy.

> Peace. And let them be, in their exaltation.
> They speak better than they know, and beyond your
>   understanding,
> They know and do not know, that acting is suffering
> And suffering is action. Neither does the actor suffer
> Nor the patient act. But both are fixed
> In an eternal action, an eternal patience
> To which all must consent that it may be willed
> And which all must suffer that they may will it,
> That the pattern may subsist, for the pattern is the action
> And the suffering, that the wheel may turn and still
> Be forever still.

X

Ezra Pound has made flux his theme; plot, characterisation, logical discourse, seem to him abstractions unsuitable to a man of his generation. He is mid-way in an immense poem in *vers libre* called for the moment *The Cantos*, where the metamorphosis of Dionysus, the descent of Odysseus into Hades,

repeat themselves in various disguises, always in association
with some third that is not repeated. Hades may become the
hell where whatever modern men he most disapproves of
suffer damnation, the metamorphosis petty frauds practised by
Jews at Gibraltar. The relation of all the elements to one
another, repeated or unrepeated, is to become apparent when
the whole is finished. There is no transmission through time,
we pass without comment from ancient Greece to modern
England, from modern England to medieval China; the
symphony, the pattern, is timeless, flux eternal and therefore
without movement. Like other readers I discover at present
merely exquisite or grotesque fragments. He hopes to give the
impression that all is living, that there are no edges, no con-
vexities, nothing to check the flow; but can such a poem
have a mathematical structure? Can impressions that are in
part visual, in part metrical, be related like the notes of a
symphony; has the author been carried beyond reason by a
theoretical conception? His belief in his own conception is so
great that since the appearance of the first Canto I have tried
to suspend judgment.

When I consider his work as a whole I find more style than
form; at moments more style, more deliberate nobility and
the means to convey it than in any contemporary poet known
to me, but it is constantly interrupted, broken, twisted into
nothing by its direct opposite, nervous obsession, nightmare,
stammering confusion; he is an economist, poet, politician,
raging at malignants with inexplicable characters and motives,
grotesque figures out of a child's book of beasts. This loss of
self-control, common among uneducated revolutionists, is
rare — Shelley had it in some degree — among men of Ezra
Pound's culture and erudition. Style and its opposite can
alternate, but form must be full, sphere-like, single. Even
where there is no interruption he is often content, if certain

verses and lines have style, to leave unbridged transitions, unexplained ejaculations, that make his meaning unintelligible. He has great influence, more perhaps than any contemporary except Eliot, is probably the source of that lack of form and consequent obscurity which is the main defect of Auden, Day Lewis, and their school, a school which, as will presently be seen, I greatly admire. Even where the style is sustained throughout one gets an impression, especially when he is writing in *vers libre*, that he has not got all the wine into the bowl, that he is a brilliant improvisator translating at sight from an unknown Greek masterpiece:

> See, they return; ah, see the tentative
> Movements, and the slow feet,
> The trouble in the pace and the uncertain
> Wavering!
>
> See, they return, one, and by one,
> With fear, as half-awakened;
> As if the snow should hesitate
> And murmur in the wind,
>   and half turn back;
>
> These were the Wing'd-with-awe,
>   Inviolable.
> Gods of the winged shoe!
> With them the silver hounds,
>   sniffing the trace of air!

XI

When my generation denounced scientific humanitarian pre-occupation, psychological curiosity, rhetoric, we had not found what ailed Victorian literature. The Elizabethans had all these things, especially rhetoric. A friend writes 'all bravado went out of English literature when Falstaff turned into Oliver Cromwell, into England's bad conscience'; but he is wrong. Dryden's plays are full of it. The mischief began at the end of the seventeenth century when man became passive before a mechanised nature; that lasted to our own day with the exception of a brief period between Smart's *Song of David* and the death of Byron, wherein imprisoned man beat upon the door. Or I may dismiss all that ancient history and say it began when Stendhal described a masterpiece as a 'mirror dawdling down a lane'. There are only two long poems in Victorian literature that caught public attention; *The Ring and the Book* where great intellect analyses the suffering of one passive soul, weighs the persecutor's guilt, and *The Idylls of the King* where a poetry in itself an exquisite passivity is built about an allegory where a characterless king represents the soul. I read few modern novels, but I think I am right in saying that in every novel that has created an intellectual fashion from Huysmans's *La Cathédrale* to Ernest Hemingway's *Farewell to Arms*, the chief character is a mirror. It has sometimes seemed of late years, though not in the poems I have selected for this book, as if the poet could at any moment write a poem by recording the fortuitous scene or thought, perhaps it might be enough to put into some fashionable rhythm — 'I am sitting in a chair, there are three dead flies on a corner of the ceiling.'

Change has come suddenly, the despair of my friends in the 'nineties part of its preparation. Nature, steel-bound or stone-built in the nineteenth century, became a flux where man drowned or swam; the moment had come for some poet to cry 'the flux is in my own mind'.

XII

It was Turner who raised that cry, to gain upon the instant a control of plastic material, a power of emotional construction, Pound has always lacked. At his rare best he competes with Eliot in precision, but Eliot's genius is human, mundane, impeccable, it seems to say 'this man will never disappoint, never be out of character. He moves among objects for which he accepts no responsibility, among the mapped and measured.' Generations must pass before man recovers control of event and circumstance; mind has recognised its responsibility, that is all; Turner himself seems the symbol of an incomplete discovery. After clearing up some metaphysical obscurity he leaves obscure what a moment's thought would have cleared; author of a suave, sophisticated comedy he can talk about 'snivelling majorities'; a rich-natured friendly man he has in his satirical platonic dialogue *The Aesthetes* shot upon forbidden ground. The first romantic poets, Blake, Coleridge, Shelley, dazed by new suddenly opening vistas, had equal though different inconsistencies. I think of him as the first poet to read a mathematical equation, a musical score, a book of verse, with an equal understanding; he seems to ride in an observation balloon, blue heaven above, earth beneath an abstract pattern.

We know nothing but abstract patterns, generalisations, mathematical equations, though such the havoc wrought by newspaper articles and government statistics, two abstractions may sit down to lunch. But what about the imagery we call nature, the sensual scene? Perhaps we are always awake and asleep at the same time; after all going to bed is but a habit; is not sleep by the testimony of the poets our common mother? In *The Seven Days of the Sun*, where there is much exciting thought, I find:

But to me the landscape is like a sea
The waves of the hills
And the bubbles of bush and flower
And the springtide breaking into white foam!

It is a slow sea,
Mare tranquillum,
And a thousand years of wind
Cannot raise a dwarf billow to the moonlight.

But the bosom of the landscape lifts and falls
With its own leaden tide,
That tide whose sparkles are the lilliputian stars.

It is that slow sea
That sea of adamantine languor,
Sleep!

I recall Pater's description of the Mona Lisa; had the
individual soul of da Vinci's sitter gone down with the pearl
divers or trafficked for strange webs? or did Pater foreshadow
a poetry, a philosophy, where the individual is nothing, the
flux of *The Cantos* of Ezra Pound, objects without contour
as in *Le Chef-d'œuvre Inconnu*, human experience no longer
shut into brief lives, cut off into this place and that place, the
flux of Turner's poetry that within our minds enriches itself,
re-dreams itself, yet only in seeming — for time cannot be
divided? Yet one theme perplexes Turner, whether in
comedy, dialogue, poem. Somewhere in the middle of it all
da Vinci's sitter had private reality like that of the Dark Lady
among the women Shakespeare had imagined, but because
that private soul is always behind our knowledge, though
always hidden it must be the sole source of pain, stupefaction,
evil. A musician, he imagines Heaven as a musical com-

position, a mathematician, as a relation of curves, a poet, as a
dark, inhuman sea.

> The sea carves innumerable shells
> Rolling itself into crystalline curves
> The cressets of its faintest sighs
> Flickering into filigreed whorls,
> Its lustre into mother-of-pearl
> Its mystery into fishes' eyes
> Its billowing abundance into whales
> Around and under the Poles.

XIII

In *The Mutations of the Phoenix* Herbert Read discovers
that the flux is in the mind, not of it perhaps, but in it. The
Phoenix is finite mind rising in a nest of light from the sea or
infinite; the discovery of Berkeley in 'Siris' where light is
'perception', of Grosseteste, twelfth-century philosopher, who
defines it as 'corporeality, or that of which corporeality is
made'.

> All existence
>   past, present and to be
>   is in this sea fringe.
> There is no other temporal scene.

> The Phoenix burns spiritually
>   among the fierce stars
>   and in the docile brain's recesses.
> Its ultimate spark
> you cannot trace . . .

> Light burns the world in the focus of an eye.

XIV

To Dorothy Wellesley nature is a womb, a darkness; its surface is sleep, upon sleep we walk, into sleep drive the plough, and there lie the happy, the wise, the unconceived;

> They lie in the loam
> Laid backward by slice of the plough;
> They sit in the rock;
> In a matrix of amethyst crouches a man . . .

but unlike Turner or Read she need not prove or define, that was all done before she began to write and think. As though it were the tale of Mother Hubbard or the results of the last general election, she accepts what Turner and Read accept, sings her joy or sorrow in its presence, at times facile and clumsy, at times magnificent in her masculine rhythm, in the precision of her style. Eliot and Edith Sitwell have much of their intensity from a deliberate re-moulding or checking of past impulse, Turner much of his from a deliberate rejection of current belief, but here is no criticism at all. A new positive belief has given to her, as it gave to Shelley, an uncheckable impulse, and this belief is all the more positive because found, not sought; like certain characters in William Morris she has 'lucky eyes', her sail is full.

I knew nothing of her until a few months ago I read the opening passage in *Horses*, delighted by its changes in pace, abrupt assertion, then a long sweeping line, by its vocabulary modern and precise;

> Who, in the garden-pony carrying skeps
> Of grass or fallen leaves, his knees gone slack,
> Round belly, hollow back,
> Sees the Mongolian Tarpan of the Steppes?

Or, in the Shire with plaits and feathered feet,
The war-horse like the wind the Tartar knew?
Or, in the Suffolk Punch, spells out anew
The wild grey asses fleet
With stripe from head to tail, and moderate ears?

The swing from Stendhal has passed Turner; the individual soul, the betrayal of the unconceived at birth, are among her principal themes, it must go further still; that soul must become its own betrayer, its own deliverer, the one activity, the mirror turn lamp. Not that the old conception is untrue, new literature better than old. In the greater nations every phase has characteristic beauty — has not Nicholas of Cusa said reality is expressed through contradiction? Yet for me, a man of my time, through my poetical faculty living its history, after much meat fish seems the only possible diet. I have indeed read certain poems by Turner, by Dorothy Wellesley, with more than all the excitement that came upon me when, a very young man, I heard somebody read out in a London tavern the poems of Ernest Dowson's despair — that too living history.

XV

I have a distaste for certain poems written in the midst of the great war; they are in all anthologies, but I have substituted Herbert Read's *End of a War* written long after. The writers of these poems were invariably officers of exceptional courage and capacity, one a man constantly selected for dangerous work, all, I think, had the Military Cross; their letters are vivid and humorous, they were not without joy — for all skill is joyful — but felt bound, in the words of the best known, to plead the suffering of their men. In poems that had for a

time considerable fame, written in the first person, they made
that suffering their own. I have rejected these poems for the
same reason that made Arnold withdraw his *Empedocles on
Etna* from circulation; passive suffering is not a theme for
poetry. In all the great tragedies, tragedy is a joy to the man
who dies; in Greece the tragic chorus danced. When man has
withdrawn into the quicksilver at the back of the mirror no
great event becomes luminous in his mind; it is no longer
possible to write *The Persians*, *Agincourt*, *Chevy Chase*: some
blunderer has driven his car on to the wrong side of the road —
that is all.

If war is necessary, or necessary in our time and place, it is
best to forget its suffering as we do the discomfort of fever,
remembering our comfort at midnight when our temperature
fell, or as we forget the worse moments of more painful
disease. Florence Farr returning third class from Ireland found
herself among Connaught Rangers just returned from the
Boer War who described an incident over and over, and
always with loud laughter: an unpopular sergeant struck
by a shell turned round and round like a dancer wound in his
own entrails. That too may be a right way of seeing war, if
war is necessary; the way of the Cockney slums, of Patrick
Street, of the *Kilmainham Minut*, of *Johnny I hardly knew ye*,
of the medieval *Dance of Death*.

XVI

Ten years after the war certain poets combined the modern
vocabulary, the accurate record of the relevant facts learnt
from Eliot, with the sense of suffering of the war poets, that
sense of suffering no longer passive, no longer an obsession of
the nerves; philosophy had made it part of all the mind. Edith
Sitwell with her Russian Ballet, Turner with his *Mare Tran-*

quillum, Dorothy Wellesley, with her ancient names —
'Heraclitus added fire' — her moths, horses and serpents,
Pound with his descent into Hades, his Chinese classics, are
too romantic to seem modern. Browning, that he might seem
modern, created an ejaculating man-of-the-world good
humour; but Day Lewis, Madge, MacNeice, are modern
through the character of their intellectual passion. We have
been gradually approaching this art through that cult of
sincerity, that refusal to multiply personality which is characteristic of our time. They may seem obscure, confused,
because of their concentrated passion, their interest in associations hitherto untravelled; it is as though their words and
rhythms remained gummed to one another instead of separating and falling into order. I can seldom find more than half
a dozen lyrics that I like, yet in this moment of sympathy I
prefer them to Eliot, to myself — I too have tried to be
modern. They have pulled off the mask, the manner writers
hitherto assumed Shelley in relation to his dream, Byron,
Henley, to their adventure, their action. Here stands not this
or that man but man's naked mind.

Although I have preferred, and shall again, constrained
by a different nationality, a man so many years old, fixed
to some one place, known to friends and enemies, full
of mortal frailty, expressing all things not made mysterious
by nature with impatient clarity, I have read with some
excitement poets I had approached with distaste, delighted
in their pure spiritual objectivity as in something long
foretold.

Much of the war poetry was pacificist, revolutionary; it
was easier to look at suffering if you had somebody to blame
for it, or some remedy in mind. Many of these poets have
called themselves communists, though I find in their work
no trace of the recognized communist philosophy and the

practising communist rejects them. The Russian government in 1930 silenced its Mechanists, put Spinoza on his head and claimed him for grandfather; but the men who created the communism of the masses had Stendhal's mirror for a contemporary, believed that religion, art, philosophy, expressed economic change, that the shell secreted the fish. Perhaps all that the masses accept is obsolete — the Orangeman beats his drum every Twelfth of July — perhaps fringes, wigs, furbelows, hoops, patches, stocks, Wellington boots, start up as armed men; but were a poet sensitive to the best thought of his time to accept that belief, when time is restoring the soul's autonomy, it would be as though he had swallowed a stone and kept it in his bowels. None of these men have accepted it, communism is their *Deus ex Machina*, their Santa Claus, their happy ending, but speaking as a poet I prefer tragedy to tragi-comedy. No matter how great a reformer's energy a still greater is required to face, all activities expended in vain, the unreformed. 'God', said an old country-woman 'smiles alike when regarding the good and condemning the lost.' MacNeice, the anti-communist, expecting some descent of barbarism next turn of the wheel, contemplates the modern world with even greater horror than the communist Day Lewis, although with less lyrical beauty. More often I cannot tell whether the poet is communist or anti-communist. On what side is Madge? Indeed I know of no school where the poets so closely resemble each other. Spender has said that the poetry of belief must supersede that of personality, and it is perhaps a belief shared that has created their intensity, their resemblance; but this belief is not political. If I understand aright this difficult art the contemplation of suffering has compelled them to seek beyond the flux something unchanging, inviolate, that country where no ghost haunts, no beloved lures because it has neither past nor future.

This lunar beauty
Has no history
Is complete and early;
If beauty later
Bear any feature
It had a lover
And is another.

*   *   *

1936

MODERN POETRY: A BROADCAST

THE period from the death of Tennyson until the present moment has, it seems, more good lyric poets than any similar period since the seventeenth century — no great overpowering figures, but many poets who have written some three or four lyrics apiece which may be permanent in our literature. It did not always seem so; even two years ago I should have said the opposite; I should have named three or four poets and said there was nobody else who mattered. Then I gave all my time to the study of that poetry. There was a club of poets — you may know its name, 'The Rhymers' Club' — which first met, I think, a few months before the death of Tennyson and lasted seven or eight years. It met in a Fleet Street tavern called 'The Cheshire Cheese'. Two members of the Club are vivid in my memory: Ernest Dowson, timid, silent, a little melancholy, lax in body, vague in attitude; Lionel Johnson, determined, erect, his few words dogmatic, almost a dwarf but beautifully made, his features cut in ivory. His thought dominated the scene and gave the Club its character. Nothing of importance could be discovered, he would say, science must be confined to the kitchen or the workshop; only philosophy and religion could solve the great secret, and they said all their say years ago; a gentleman was a man who who understood Greek. I was full of crude speculation that made me ashamed. I remember praying that I might get my imagination fixed upon life itself, like the imagination of Chaucer. In those days I was a convinced ascetic, yet I envied Dowson his dissipated life. I thought it must be easy to think like Chaucer when you lived among those morbid, elegant,

tragic women suggested by Dowson's poetry, painted and
drawn by his friends Conder and Beardsley. You must all
know those famous lines that are in so many anthologies:

> Unto us they belong,
>   Us the bitter and gay,
> Wine and woman and song.

When I repeated those beautiful lines it never occurred to
me to wonder why the Dowson I knew seemed neither gay
nor bitter. A provincial, conscious of clumsiness and lack of
self-possession, I still more envied Lionel Johnson, who had
met, as I believed, everybody of importance. If one spoke of
some famous ecclesiastic or statesman he would say: 'I know
him intimately,' and quote some conversation that laid bare
that man's soul. He was never a satirist, being too courteous,
too just, for that distortion. One felt that these conversations
had happened exactly as he said. Years were to pass before I
discovered that Dowson's life, except when he came to the
Rhymers' or called upon some friend selected for an extreme
respectability, was a sordid round of drink and cheap harlots;
that Lionel Johnson had never met those famous men, that
he never met anybody, because he got up at nightfall, got
drunk at a public-house or worked half the night, sat the other
half, a glass of whisky at his elbow, staring at the brown
corduroy curtains that protected from dust the books that
lined his walls, imagining the puppets that were the true
companions of his mind. He met Dowson, but then Dowson
was nobody and he was convinced that he did Dowson good.
He had no interest in women, and on that subject was perhaps
eloquent. Some friends of mine saw them one moonlight
night returning from the 'Crown' public-house which had
just closed, their zig-zagging feet requiring the whole width

of Oxford Street, Lionel Johnson talking. My friend stood
still eavesdropping; Lionel Johnson was expounding a Father
of the Church. Their piety, in Dowson a penitential sadness, in
Lionel Johnson more often a noble ecstasy, was, as I think,
illuminated and intensified by their contrasting puppet-shows,
those elegant, tragic penitents, those great men in their
triumph. You may know Lionel Johnson's poem on the statue
of King Charles, or that characteristic poem that begins: 'Ah,
see the fair chivalry come, the Companions of Christ.' In my
present mood, remembering his scholarship, remembering
that his religious sense was never divided from his sense of the
past, I recall most vividly his 'Church of a Dream':

Sadly the dead leaves rustle in the whistling wind,
Around the weather-worn, grey church, low down the vale:
The Saints in golden vesture shake before the gale;
The glorious windows shake, where still they dwell en-
    shrined;
Old Saints by long-dead, shrivelled hands, long since de-
    signed:
There still, although the world autumnal be, and pale,
Still in their golden vesture the old Saints prevail;
Alone with Christ, desolate else, left by mankind.

Only one ancient priest offers the Sacrifice,
Murmuring holy Latin immemorial:
Swaying with tremulous hands the old censer full of spice,
In grey, sweet incense clouds; blue, sweet clouds mystical:
To him, in place of men, for he is old, suffice
Melancholy remembrances and vesperal.

There were other poets, generally a few years younger,
who having escaped that first wave of excitement lived tame

and orderly lives. But they, too, were in reaction against everything Victorian.

A church in the style of Inigo Jones opens on to a grass lawn a few hundred yards from the Marble Arch. It was designed by a member of the Rhymers' Club, whose architecture, like his poetry, seemed to exist less for his own sake than to illustrate his genius as a connoisseur. I have sometimes thought that masterpiece, perhaps the smallest church in London, the most appropriate symbol of all that was most characteristic in the art of my friends. Their poems seemed to say: 'You will remember us the longer because we are very small, very unambitious.' Yet my friends were most ambitious men; they wished to express life at its intense moments, those moments that are brief because of their intensity, and at those moments alone. In the Victorian era the most famous poetry was often a passage in a poem of some length, perhaps of great length, a poem full of thoughts that might have been expressed in prose. A short lyric seemed an accident, an interruption amid more serious work. Somebody has quoted Browning as saying that he could have written many lyrics had he thought them worth the trouble. The aim of my friends, my own aim, if it sometimes made us prefer the acorn to the oak, the small to the great, freed us from many things that we thought an impurity. Swinburne, Tennyson, Arnold, Browning, had admitted so much psychology, science, moral fervour. Had not Verlaine said of *In Memoriam*, 'When he should have been broken-hearted he had many reminiscences'? We tried to write like the poets of the Greek Anthology, or like Catullus, or like the Jacobean lyrists, men who wrote while poetry was still pure. We did not look forward or look outward, we left that to the prose writers; we looked back. We thought it was in the very nature of poetry to look back, to resemble those Swedenborgian angels who are described as moving for ever towards the dayspring of their youth. In this we were all, orderly and disorderly alike, in full agreement.

When I think of the Rhymers' Club and grow weary of those luckless men, I think of another circle that was in full agreement. It gathered round Charles Ricketts, one of the greatest connoisseurs of any age, an artist whose woodcuts prolonged the inspiration of Rossetti, whose paintings mirrored the rich colouring of Delacroix. When we studied his art we studied our double. We, too, thought always that style should be proud of its ancestry, of its traditional high breeding, that an ostentatious originality was out of place whether in the arts or in good manners. When the Rhymers' Club was breaking up I read enthusiastic reviews of the first book of Sturge Moore and grew jealous. He did not belong to the Rhymers' Club and I wanted to believe that we had all the good poets; but one evening Charles Ricketts brought me to a riverside house at Richmond and introduced me to Edith Cooper. She put into my unwilling hands Sturge Moore's book and made me read out and discuss certain poems. I surrendered. I took back all I had said against him. I was most moved by his poem called *The Dying Swan*:

> O silver-throated Swan
> Struck, struck! a golden dart
> Clean through thy breast has gone
> Home to thy heart.
> Thrill, thrill, O silver throat!
> O silver trumpet, pour
> Love for defiance back
> On him who smote!
> And brim, brim o'er
> With love; and ruby-dye thy track

> Down thy last living reach
> Of river, sail the golden light . . .
> Enter the sun's heart . . . even teach,
> O wondrous-gifted Pain, teach thou
> The god to love, let him learn how.

Edith Cooper herself seemed a dry, precise, precious, pious, finicking old maid; with an aunt, a Miss Bradley, she had written under the name of 'Michael Field' tragedies in the Elizabethan manner, which I seem to remember after forty or fifty years as occasionally powerful but spoilt by strained emotion and laboured metaphor; they had already fallen into oblivion, but under the influence of Charles Ricketts she had studied Greek and found a new character, a second youth. She had begun, though I did not know it for many years, a series of little poems, masterpieces of simplicity, which resemble certain of Landor's lyrics, though her voice is not so deep, but high, thin, and sweet.

> Thine elder that I am, thou must not cling
> To me, nor mournful for my love entreat:
> And yet, Alcaeus, as the sudden spring
> Is love, yea, and to veiled Demeter sweet.
> Sweeter than tone of harp, more gold than gold
> Is thy young voice to me; yet, ah, the pain
> To learn I am beloved now I am old,
> Who, in my youth, loved, as thou must, in vain.

And here is another, which because it hints at so much more than it says, is very moving.

> They bring me gifts, they honour me,
> Now I am growing old;
> And wondering youth crowds round my knee,
> As if I had a mystery
> And worship to unfold.

To me the tender, blushing bride
Doth come with lips that fail;
I feel her heart beat at my side
And cry: 'Like Ares in his pride,
Hail, noble bridegroom, hail!'

My generation, because it disliked Victorian rhetorical moral fervour, came to dislike all rhetoric. In France, where there was a similar movement, a poet had written, 'Take rhetoric and wring its neck'. People began to imitate old ballads because an old ballad is never rhetorical. I think of *A Shropshire Lad*, of certain poems by Hardy, of Kipling's *Saint Helena Lullaby*, and his *The Looking-Glass*. I will not read any of that famous poetry but a poem nobody ever heard of. When I was a young man, York Powell, an Oxford Don, was renowned for his miraculous learning, but only his few intimates, perhaps only those much younger than himself, knew that he was not the dry man he seemed. From the top of a bus, somewhere between Victoria and Walham Green, he pointed out to me a pawnshop he had once found very useful; I was in his rooms at Oxford when he replied to somebody who had asked him to become Proctor that the older he grew the less and less difference could he see between right and wrong. He used to frequent prizefights with my brother, a lad in his twenties, and it was in a Broadside, a mixture of hand-coloured prints and poetry published by my brother, and now long out of print, that I discovered the poem I am now about to read. It is a translation from the French of Paul Fort.

The pretty maid she died, she died, in love-bed as she lay;
They took her to the church-yard; all at the break of day;
They laid her all alone there: all in her white array;
They laid her all alone there: a-coffin'd in the clay:

And they came back so merrily: all at the dawn of day;
A-singing all so merrily: ' *The dog must have his day!* '
The pretty maid is dead, is dead; in love-bed as she lay;
And they are off afield to work: as they do every day.

The poems I have read resemble in certain characteristics all
modern poetry up to the Great War. The centaurs and
amazons of Sturge Moore, the Tristram and Isoult of Binyon's noble poem — there were always some long poems; my
Deirdre, my Cuchulain had been written about for centuries
and our public wished for nothing else. Here and there some
young revolutionist would boast that his eyes were on the
present or the future, or even denounce all poetry back to
Dante, but we were content; we wrote as men had always
written. Then established things were shaken by the Great
War. All civilised men had believed in progress, in a warless
future, in always-increasing wealth, but now influential young
men began to wonder if anything could last or if anything
were worth fighting for. In the third year of the War came
the most revolutionary man in poetry during my lifetime,
though his revolution was stylistic alone — T. S. Eliot published his first book. No romantic word or sound, nothing
reminiscent, nothing in the least like the painting of Ricketts
could be permitted henceforth. Poetry must resemble prose,
and both must accept the vocabulary of their time; nor must
there be any special subject-matter. Tristram and Isoult were
not a more suitable theme than Paddington Railway Station.
The past had deceived us: let us accept the worthless present.

> The morning comes to consciousness
> Of faint stale smells of beer
> From the sawdust-trampled street
> With all its muddy feet that press
> To early coffee-stands. . . .

> One thinks of all the hands
> That are raising dingy shades
> In a thousand furnished rooms.

We older writers disliked this new poetry, but were forced
to admit its satiric intensity. It was in Eliot that certain
revolutionary War poets, young men who felt they had been
dragged away from their studies, from their pleasant life, by
the blundering frenzy of old men, found the greater part of
their style. They were too near their subject-matter to do, as I
think, work of permanent importance, but their social passion,
their sense of tragedy, their modernity, have passed into
young influential poets of to-day: Auden, Spender, MacNeice,
Day Lewis, and others. Some of these poets are Communists,
but even in those who are not, there is an overwhelming social
bitterness. Some speak of the War in which none were old
enough to have served:

> I've heard them lilting at loom and belting,
> Lasses lilting before dawn of day;
> But now they are silent, not gamesome and gallant —
> The flowers of the town are rotting away.

> There was laughing and loving in the lanes at evening;
> Handsome were the boys then, and girls were gay.
> But lost in Flanders by medalled commanders
> The lads of the village are melted away.

This poetry is supported by critics who think it the poetry
of the future — in my youth I heard much of the music of the
future — and attack all not of their school. A poet of an older
school has named them 'the racketeers'. Sometimes they
attack Miss Edith Sitwell, who seems to me an important
poet, shaped as they are by the disillusionment that followed

the Great War. Among her fauns, cats, columbines, clowns, wicked fairies, into that phantasmagoria which reminds me of a ballet called *The Sleeping Beauty*, loved by the last of the Tsars, she interjects a nightmare horror of death and decay. I commend to you *The Hambone and the Heart*, and *The Lament of Edward Blastock*, as among the most tragic poems of our time. Her language is the traditional language of literature, but twisted, torn, complicated, jerked here and there by strained resemblances, unnatural contacts, forced upon it by terror or by some violence beating in her blood, some primitive obsession that civilisation can no longer exorcise. I find her obscure, exasperating, delightful. I think I like her best when she seems a child, terrified and delighted by the story it is inventing. I will read you a little poem she has called *Ass-Face*, but first I must explain its imagery which has taken me a couple of minutes to puzzle out, not because it is obscure, but because image follows image too quickly to be understood at a first hearing. I prefer to think of Ass-Face as a personality invented by some child at a nursery window after dark. The starry heavens are the lighted bars and saloons of public-houses, and the descending light is asses' milk which makes Ass-Face drunk. But this light is thought of the next moment as bright threads floating down in spirals to make a dress for Columbine, and the next moment after that as milk spirting on the sands of the sea — one thinks of the glittering foam — a sea which brays like an ass, and is covered because it is a rough sea by an ass's hide. Along the shore there are trees, and under these trees beavers are building Babel, and these beavers think that the noise Ass-Face makes in his drunkenness is Cain and Abel fighting. Then somehow as the vision ends the starlight has turned into the houses that the beavers are building. But their Babel and their houses are like white lace, and we are told that Ass-Face will spoil them all.

When you listen to this poem, you should become two people, one a sage who thinks perhaps that Ass-Face is the stupefying frenzy of nature, one a child listening to a poem as irrational as a 'Sing a Song of Sixpence':

> Ass-Face drank
> The asses' milk of the stars . . .
> The milky spirals as they sank
> From heaven's saloons and golden bars,
> Made a gown
> For Columbine,
> Spirting down
> On sands divine
> By the asses' hide of the sea
> (With each tide braying free).
> And the beavers building Babel
> Beneath each tree's thin beard,
> Said, 'Is it Cain and Abel
> Fighting again we heard?'
> It is Ass-Face, Ass-Face,
> Drunk on the milk of the stars,
> Who will spoil their houses of white lace —
> Expelled from the golden bars!

I think profound philosophy must come from terror. An abyss opens under our feet; inherited convictions, the presuppositions of our thoughts, those Fathers of the Church Lionel Johnson expounded, drop into the abyss. Whether we will or no we must ask the ancient questions: Is there reality anywhere? Is there a God? Is there a Soul? We cry with the Indian Sacred Book: 'They have put a golden stopper into the neck of the bottle; pull it! Let out reality!'

Some seven years after the close of the War, seven years

of meditation, came Turner's *Seven Days of the Sun*, Dorothy Wellesley's *Matrix*, Herbert Read's *Mutations of the Phoenix*, T. S. Eliot's *Waste Land*; long philosophical poems; and even now the young Communist poets complicate their short lyrics with difficult metaphysics.

If you are lovers of poetry, and it is for such that I speak, you know *The Waste Land*, but perhaps not the other poems that I have named, though you will certainly know Dorothy Wellesley's poem in praise of horses, and probably Turner's praise of a mountain in Mexico with a romantic name. To three, perhaps to all four of these writers, what we call the solid earth was manufactured by the human mind from unknown raw material. They do not think this because of Kant and Berkeley, who are an old story, but because of something that has got into the air since a famous French mathematician wrote 'Space is a creation of our ancestors'. Eliot's historical and scholarly mind seems to have added this further thought, probably from Nicholas of Cusa: reality is expressed in a series of contradictions, or is that unknowable something that supports the centre of the see-saw.

At the still point of the turning world. Neither flesh nor
    fleshless;
Neither from nor towards; at the still point, there the dance is,
But neither arrest nor movement. And do not call it fixity.
Where past and future are gathered. Neither movement from
    nor towards,
Neither ascent nor decline. Except for the point, the still
    point,
There would be no dance, and there is only the dance.

All are pessimists; Dorothy Wellesley thinks that the 'unconceived', as she calls those that have not yet been melted into that subjective creation we call the world, are alone happy. They are a part of the unknown raw material which the manufacturer has neglected. They have escaped the torture of the senses, the boredom of that automatic return of the same sensation Eliot has described. I will read you a passage from her poem *Matrix*:

> Where, then, are the unborn ones?
> Do they eternally go,
> Cloud-wracks of souls tormented,
> Through ether for ever?
>
> No such ventures theirs, no.
> They crowd in the core of the earth;
> They lie in the loam,
> Laid backward by slice of the plough;
> They sit in the rock:
> In a matrix of amethyst crouches a man,
> Pigmy, a part of the womb,
> Of the stone,
> For ever, for all time, now.
>
> All things there are his own:
> The light on water, the leaves,
> The spray of the wild yellow rose;
> Beautiful as to the born
> Are the stars to the unconceived;
> The twilight, the morn, of their sight,
> Are lovelier than to the born.

Turner, the poet, mathematician, musician, thinks that the horror of the world is in its beauty. Beautiful forms deceive us, because if we grasp them, they dissolve into what he calls

'confused sensation'; and destroy us because they drag us
under the machinery of nature; if it were possible he would,
like a Buddhist, or a connoisseur, kill or suspend desire. He
does not see men and women as the puppets of Eliot's poetry,
repeating over and over the same trivial movements, but as
the reflections of a terrible Olympus. I will read you his poem
upon the procession of the mannequins.

> I have seen mannequins,
> As white and gold as lilies,
> Swaying their tall bodies across the burnished floor
> Of *Reville* or *Paquin*;
> Writhing in colour and line,
> Curved tropical flowers
> As bright as thunderbolts,
> Or hooded in dark furs
> The sun's pale splash
> In English autumn woods.
>
> And I have watched these soft explosions of life
> As astronomers watch the combustion of stars.
> The violence of supernatural power
> Upon their faces,
> White orbits
> Of incalculable forces.
>
> And I have had no desire for their bodies
> But have felt the whiteness of a lily
> Upon my palate;
> And the solidity of their slender curves
> Like a beautiful mathematical proposition
> In my brain.

But in the expression of their faces
Terror.

Cruelty in the eyes, nostrils, and lips —
Pain
thou passion-flower, thou wreath, thou orbit,
thou spiritual rotation,
thou smile upon a pedestal,
Peony of the garden of Paradise!

Many Irish men and women must be listening, and they may wonder why I have said nothing of modern Irish poetry. I have not done so because it moves in a different direction and belongs to a different story. Modern Irish poetry began in the midst of that rediscovery of folk thought I described when quoting York Powell's translation from Paul Fort. The English movement, checked by the realism of Eliot, the social passion of the War poets, gave way to an impersonal philosophical poetry. Because Ireland has a still living folk tradition, her poets cannot get it out of their heads that they themselves, good-tempered or bad-tempered, tall or short, will be remembered by the common people. Instead of turning to impersonal philosophy, they have hardened and deepened their personalities. I could have taken as examples Synge or James Stephens, men I have never ceased to delight in. But I prefer to quote poetry of which you have probably never heard, though it is among the greatest lyric poetry of our time.

Some twelve years ago political enemies came to Senator Gogarty's house while they knew he would be in his bath and so unable to reach his revolver, made him dress, brought him to an empty house on the edge of the Liffey. They told him nothing, but he felt certain he was to be kept as hostage and shot after the inevitable execution of a certain man then in prison. Self-possessed and daring, he escaped, and while swimming the cold December river, vowed two swans to it if it would land him safely. I was present some weeks later when, in the presence of the Head of the State and other notables, the two swans were launched. That story shows the man — scholar, wit, poet, gay adventurer. In one poem, written years afterwards, the man who dedicated the swans dedicates the poems, and the mood has not changed:

> Tall unpopular men,
> Slim proud women who move
> As women walked in the islands when
> Temples were built to Love,
> I sing to you. With you
> Beauty at best can live,
> Beauty that dwells with the rare and few,
> Cold and imperative.
> He who had Caesar's ear
> Sang to the lonely and strong.
> Virgil made an austere
> Venus Muse of his song.

Here is another poem characteristic of those poems which have restored the emotion of heroism to lyric poetry:

> Our friends go with us as we go
>   Down the long path where Beauty wends,
> Where all we love forgathers, so
>   Why should we fear to join our friends?
>
> Who would survive them to outlast
>   His children; to outwear his fame —
> Left when the Triumph has gone past —
>   To win from Age, not Time, a name?

Then do not shudder at the knife
    That Death's indifferent hand drives home,
But with the Strivers leave the Strife,
    Nor, after Caesar, skulk in Rome.

When I have read you a poem I have tried to read it rhythmically; I may be a bad reader; or read badly because I am out of sorts, or self-conscious; but there is no other method. A poem is an elaboration of the rhythms of common speech and their association with profound feeling. To read a poem like prose, that hearers unaccustomed to poetry may find it easy to understand, is to turn it into bad, florid prose. If anybody reads or recites poetry as if it were prose from some public platform, I ask you, speaking for poets, living, dead, or unborn, to protest in whatever way occurs to your perhaps youthful minds; if they recite or read by wireless, I ask you to express your indignation by letter. William Morris, coming out of a hall where somebody had read or recited his *Sigurd the Volsung*, said: 'It cost me a lot of damned hard work to get that thing into verse.'

1936

A GENERAL INTRODUCTION FOR MY WORK[1]

I. THE FIRST PRINCIPLE

A POET writes always of his personal life, in his finest work out of its tragedy, whatever it be, remorse, lost love, or mere loneliness; he never speaks directly as to someone at the breakfast table, there is always a phantasmagoria. Dante and Milton had mythologies, Shakespeare the characters of English history or of traditional romance; even when the poet seems most himself, when he is Raleigh and gives potentates the lie, or Shelley 'a nerve o'er which do creep the else unfelt oppressions of this earth', or Byron when 'the soul wears out the breast' as 'the sword outwears its sheath', he is never the bundle of accident and incoherence that sits down to breakfast; he has been reborn as an idea, something intended, complete. A novelist might describe his accidence, his incoherence, he must not; he is more type than man, more passion than type. He is Lear, Romeo, Oedipus, Tiresias; he has stepped out of a play, and even the woman he loves is Rosalind, Cleopatra, never The Dark Lady. He is part of his own phantasmagoria and we adore him because nature has grown intelligible, and by so doing a part of our creative power. 'When mind is lost in the light of the Self', says the Prashna Upanishad, 'it dreams no more; still in the body it is lost in happiness.' 'A wise man seeks in Self', says the Chandogya Upanishad, 'those that are alive and those that are dead

[1] Written for a complete edition of Yeats's works which was never produced

and gets what the world cannot give.' The world knows nothing because it has made nothing, we know everything because we have made everything.

II. SUBJECT-MATTER

It was through the old Fenian leader John O'Leary I found my theme. His long imprisonment, his longer banishment, his magnificent head, his scholarship, his pride, his integrity, all that aristocratic dream nourished amid little shops and little farms, had drawn around him a group of young men; I was but eighteen or nineteen and had already, under the influence of *The Faerie Queene* and *The Sad Shepherd*, written a pastoral play, and under that of Shelley's *Prometheus Unbound* two plays, one staged somewhere in the Caucasus, the other in a crater of the moon; and I knew myself to be vague and incoherent. He gave me the poems of Thomas Davis, said they were not good poetry but had changed his life when a young man, spoke of other poets associated with Davis and *The Nation* newspaper, probably lent me their books. I saw even more clearly than O'Leary that they were not good poetry. I read nothing but romantic literature; hated that dry eighteenth-century rhetoric; but they had one quality I admired and admire: they were not separated individual men; they spoke or tried to speak out of a people to a people; behind them stretched the generations. I knew, though but now and then as young men know things, that I must turn from that modern literature Jonathan Swift compared to the web a spider draws out of its bowels; I hated and still hate with an ever growing hatred the literature of the point of view. I wanted, if my ignorance permitted, to get back to Homer, to those that fed at his table. I wanted to cry as all men cried, to laugh as all men laughed, and the Young Ireland poets when not writing mere politics had the same want, but they did not know that the common and its befitting language is the research of a lifetime and when found may lack popular recognition. Then somebody, not O'Leary, told me of Standish O'Grady and his interpretation of Irish legends. O'Leary had sent me to O'Curry, but his unarranged and uninterpreted history defeated my boyish indolence.

A generation before *The Nation* newspaper was founded the Royal Irish Academy had begun the study of ancient Irish literature. That study was as much a gift from the Protestant aristocracy which had created the Parliament as *The Nation* and its school, though Davis and Mitchel were Protestants; was a gift from the Catholic middle classes who were to create the Irish Free State. The Academy persuaded the English Government to finance an ordnance survey on a large scale; scholars, including that great scholar O'Donovan, were sent from village to village recording names and their legends. Perhaps it was the last moment when such work could be well done, the memory of the people was still intact, the collectors themselves had perhaps heard or seen the banshee; the Royal Irish Academy and its public with equal enthusiasm welcomed Pagan and Christian; thought the Round Towers a commemoration of Persian fire-worship. There was little orthodoxy to take alarm; the Catholics were crushed and cowed; an honoured great-uncle of mine — his portrait by some forgotten master hangs upon my bedroom wall — a Church of Ireland rector, would upon occasion boast that you could not ask a question he could not answer with a perfectly appropriate blasphemy or indecency. When several counties had been surveyed but nothing published, the Government, afraid of rousing dangerous patriotic emotion, withdrew support; large manuscript volumes remain containing much picturesque correspondence between scholars.

When modern Irish literature began, O'Grady's influence

predominated. He could delight us with an extravagance we were too critical to share; a day will come, he said, when Slieve-na-mon will be more famous than Olympus; yet he was no Nationalist as we understood the word, but in rebellion, as he was fond of explaining, against the House of Commons, not against the King. His cousin, that great scholar Hayes O'Grady, would not join our non-political Irish Literary Society because he considered it a Fenian body, but boasted that although he had lived in England for forty years he had never made an English friend. He worked at the British Museum compiling their Gaelic catalogue and translating our heroic tales in an eighteenth-century frenzy; his heroine 'fractured her heart', his hero 'ascended to the apex of the eminence' and there 'vibrated his javelin', and afterwards took ship upon 'colossal ocean's superficies'. Both O'Gradys considered themselves as representing the old Irish land-owning aristocracy; both probably, Standish O'Grady certainly, thought that England, because decadent and democratic, had betrayed their order. It was another member of that order, Lady Gregory, who was to do for the heroic legends in *Gods and Fighting Men* and in *Cuchulain of Muirthemne* what Lady Charlotte Guest's *Mabinogion* had done with less beauty and style for those of Wales. Standish O'Grady had much modern sentiment, his style, like that of John Mitchel forty years before, shaped by Carlyle; she formed her style upon the Anglo-Irish dialect of her neighbourhood, an old vivid speech with a partly Tudor vocabulary, a syntax partly moulded by men who still thought in Gaelic.

I had heard in Sligo cottages or from pilots at Rosses Point endless stories of apparitions, whether of the recent dead or of the people of history and legend, of that Queen Maeve whose reputed cairn stands on the mountain over the bay.

Then at the British Museum I read stories Irish writers of the 'forties and 'fifties had written of such apparitions, but they enraged me more than pleased because they turned the country visions into a joke. But when I went from cottage to cottage with Lady Gregory and watched her hand recording that great collection she has called *Visions and Beliefs* I escaped disfiguring humour.

Behind all Irish history hangs a great tapestry, even Christianity had to accept it and be itself pictured there. Nobody looking at its dim folds can say where Christianity begins and Druidism ends; 'There is one perfect among the birds, one perfect among the fish, and one among men that is perfect.' I can only explain by that suggestion of recent scholars — Professor Burkitt of Cambridge commended it to my attention — that St. Patrick came to Ireland not in the fifth century but towards the end of the second. The great controversies had not begun; Easter was still the first full moon after the Equinox. Upon that day the world had been created, the Ark rested upon Ararat, Moses led the Israelites out of Egypt; the umbilical cord which united Christianity to the ancient world had not yet been cut, Christ was still the half-brother of Dionysus. A man just tonsured by the Druids could learn from the nearest Christian neighbour to sign himself with the Cross without sense of incongruity, nor would his children acquire that sense. The organised clans weakened Church organisation, they could accept the monk but not the bishop.

A modern man, *The Golden Bough* and *Human Personality* in his head, finds much that is congenial in St. Patrick's Creed as recorded in his Confessions, and nothing to reject except the word 'soon' in the statement that Christ will soon judge the quick and the dead. He can repeat it, believe it even, without a thought of the historic Christ, or ancient Judea, or of anything subject to historical conjecture and shifting evidence;

I repeat it and think of 'the Self' in the Upanishads. Into this tradition, oral and written, went in later years fragments of Neo-Platonism, cabbalistic words — I have heard the words 'tetragrammaton agla' in Doneraile — the floating debris of mediaeval thought, but nothing that did not please the solitary mind. Even the religious equivalent for Baroque and Rococo could not come to us as thought, perhaps because Gaelic is incapable of abstraction. It came as cruelty. That tapestry filled the scene at the birth of modern Irish literature, it is there in the Synge of *The Well of the Saints*, in James Stephens, and in Lady Gregory throughout, in all of George Russell that did not come from the Upanishads, and in all but my later poetry.

Sometimes I am told in commendation, if the newspaper is Irish, in condemnation if English, that my movement perished under the firing squads of 1916; sometimes that those firing squads made our realistic movement possible. If that statement is true, and it is only so in part, for romance was everywhere receding, it is because in the imagination of Pearse and his fellow soldiers the Sacrifice of the Mass had found the Red Branch in the tapestry; they went out to die calling upon Cuchulain:

> Fall, Hercules, from Heaven in tempests hurled
> To cleanse the beastly stable of this world.

In one sense the poets of 1916 were not of what the newspapers call my school. The Gaelic League, made timid by a modern popularisation of Catholicism sprung from the aspidistra and not from the root of Jesse, dreaded intellectual daring and stuck to dictionary and grammar. Pearse and MacDonagh and others among the executed men would have done, or attempted, in Gaelic what we did or attempted in English.

Our mythology, our legends, differ from those of other European countries because down to the end of the seventeenth century they had the attention, perhaps the unquestioned belief, of peasant and noble alike; Homer belongs to sedentary men, even to-day our ancient queens, our mediaeval soldiers and lovers, can make a pedlar shudder. I can put my own thought, despair perhaps from the study of present circumstance in the light of ancient philosophy, into the mouth of rambling poets of the seventeenth century, or even of some imagined ballad singer of to-day, and the deeper my thought the more credible, the more peasant-like, are ballad singer and rambling poet. Some modern poets contend that jazz and music-hall songs are the folk art of our time, that we should mould our art upon them; we Irish poets, modern men also, reject every folk art that does not go back to Olympus. Give me time and a little youth and I will prove that even 'Johnny, I hardly knew ye' goes back.

Mr. Arnold Toynbee in an annex to the second volume of *The Study of History* describes the birth and decay of what he calls the Far Western Christian culture; it lost at the Synod of Whitby its chance of mastering Europe, suffered final ecclesiastical defeat in the twelfth century with 'the thoroughgoing incorporation of the Irish Christendom into the Roman Church. In the political and literary spheres' it lasted unbroken till the seventeenth century. He then insists that if 'Jewish Zionism and Irish Nationalism succeed in achieving their aims, then Jewry and Irishry will each fit into its own tiny niche . . . among sixty or seventy national communities', find life somewhat easier, but cease to be 'the relic of an independent society . . . the romance of Ancient Ireland has at last come to an end . . . Modern Ireland has made up her mind, in our generation, to find her level as a willing inmate in our workaday Western world.'

If Irish literature goes on as my generation planned it, it may do something to keep the 'Irishry' living, nor will the work of the realists hinder, nor the figures they imagine, nor those described in memoirs of the revolution. These last especially, like certain great political predecessors, Parnell, Swift, Lord Edward, have stepped back into the tapestry. It may be indeed that certain characteristics of the 'Irishry' must grow in importance. When Lady Gregory asked me to annotate her *Visions and Beliefs* I began, that I might understand what she had taken down in Galway, an investigation of contemporary spiritualism. For several years I frequented those mediums who in various poor parts of London instruct artisans or their wives for a few pence upon their relations to their dead, to their employers, and to their children; then I compared what she had heard in Galway, or I in London, with the visions of Swedenborg, and, after my inadequate notes had been published, with Indian belief. If Lady Gregory had not said when we passed an old man in the woods, 'That man may know the secret of the ages', I might never have talked with Shri Purohit Swāmi nor made him translate his Master's travels in Tibet, not helped him translate the Upanishads. I think I now know why the gamekeeper at Coole heard the footsteps of a deer on the edge of the lake where no deer had passed for a hundred years, and why a certain cracked old priest said that nobody had been to hell or heaven in his time, meaning thereby that the Rath had got them all; that the dead stayed where they had lived, or near it, sought no abstract region of blessing or punishment but retreated, as it were, into the hidden character of their neighbourhood. I am convinced that in two or three generations it will become generally known that the mechanical theory has no reality, that the natural and supernatural are knit together, that to escape a dangerous fanaticism we must study a new science; at that moment Europeans may find something attractive in a Christ posed against a background not of Judaism but of Druidism, not shut off in dead history, but flowing, concrete, phenomenal.

I was born into this faith, have lived in it, and shall die in it; my Christ, a legitimate deduction from the Creed of St. Patrick as I think, is that Unity of Being Dante compared to a perfectly proportioned human body, Blake's 'Imagination', what the Upanishads have named 'Self': nor is this unity distant and therefore intellectually understandable, but imminent, differing from man to man and age to age, taking upon itself pain and ugliness, 'eye of newt, and toe of frog'.

Subconscious preoccupation with this theme brought me *A Vision*, its harsh geometry an incomplete interpretation. The 'Irishry' have preserved their ancient 'deposit' through wars which, during the sixteenth and seventeenth centuries, became wars of extermination; no people, Lecky said at the opening of his *Ireland in the Eighteenth Century*, have undergone greater persecution, nor did that persecution altogether cease up to our own day. No people hate as we do in whom that past is always alive, there are moments when hatred poisons my life and I accuse myself of effeminacy because I have not given it adequate expression. It is not enough to have put it into the mouth of a rambling peasant poet. Then I remind myself that though mine is the first English marriage I know of in the direct line, all my family names are English, and that I owe my soul to Shakespeare, to Spenser and to Blake, perhaps to William Morris, and to the English language in which I think, speak, and write, that everything I love has come to me through English; my hatred tortures me with love, my love with hate. I am like the Tibetan monk who dreams at his initiation that he is eaten by a wild beast and learns on waking that he himself is eater and eaten. This is Irish hatred and solitude, the hatred of human life that made

Swift write *Gulliver* and the epitaph upon his tomb, that can still make us wag between extremes and doubt our sanity.

Again and again I am asked why I do not write in Gaelic. Some four or five years ago I was invited to dinner by a London society and found myself among London journalists, Indian students, and foreign political refugees. An Indian paper says it was a dinner in my honour; I hope not; I have forgotten, though I have a clear memory of my own angry mind. I should have spoken as men are expected to speak at public dinners; I should have paid and been paid conventional compliments; then they would speak of the refugees; from that on all would be lively and topical, foreign tyranny would be arraigned, England seem even to those confused Indians the protector of liberty; I grew angrier and angrier; Wordsworth, that typical Englishman, had published his famous sonnet to François Dominique Toussaint, a Santo Domingo Negro:

> There's not a breathing of the common wind
> That will forget thee

in the year when Emmet conspired and died, and he remembered that rebellion as little as the half hanging and the pitch cap that preceded it by half a dozen years. That there might be no topical speeches I denounced the oppression of the people of India; being a man of letters, not a politician, I told how they had been forced to learn everything, even their own Sanskrit, through the vehicle of English till the first discoverer of wisdom had become bywords for vague abstract facility. I begged the Indian writers present to remember that no man can think or write with music and vigour except in his mother tongue. I turned a friendly audience hostile, yet when I think of that scene I am unrepentant and angry.

I could no more have written in Gaelic than can those

Indians write in English; Gaelic is my national language, but it is not my mother tongue.

III. STYLE AND ATTITUDE

Style is almost unconscious. I know what I have tried to do, little what I have done. Contemporary lyric poems, even those that moved me — *The Stream's Secret, Dolores* — seemed too long, but an Irish preference for a swift current might be mere indolence, yet Burns may have felt the same when he read Thomson and Cowper. The English mind is meditative, rich, deliberate; it may remember the Thames valley. I planned to write short lyrics or poetic drama where every speech would be short and concentrated, knit by dramatic tension, and I did so with more confidence because young English poets were at that time writing out of emotion at the moment of crisis, though their old slow-moving meditation returned almost at once. Then, and in this English poetry has followed my lead, I tried to make the language of poetry coincide with that of passionate, normal speech. I wanted to write in whatever language comes most naturally when we soliloquise, as I do all day long, upon the events of our own lives or of any life where we can see ourselves for the moment. I sometimes compare myself with the mad old slum women I hear denouncing and remembering; 'How dare you', I heard one say of some imaginary suitor, 'and you without health or a home!' If I spoke my thoughts aloud they might be as angry and as wild. It was a long time before I had made a language to my liking; I began to make it when I discovered some twenty years ago that I must seek, not as Wordsworth thought, words in common use, but a powerful and passionate syntax, and a complete coincidence between period and stanza. Because I need a passionate syntax for passionate subject-matter I compel myself to accept those traditional metres that have developed with the language. Ezra Pound, Turner, Lawrence wrote admirable free verse, I could not. I would lose myself, become joyless like those mad old women. The translators of the Bible, Sir Thomas Browne, certain translators from the Greek when translators still bothered about rhythm, created a form midway between prose and verse that seems natural to impersonal meditation; but all that is personal soon rots; it must be packed in ice or salt. Once when I was in delirium from pneumonia I dictated a letter to George Moore telling him to eat salt because it was a symbol of eternity; the delirium passed, I had no memory of that letter, but I must have meant what I now mean. If I wrote of personal love or sorrow in free verse, or in any rhythm that left it unchanged, amid all its accidence, I would be full of self-contempt because of my egotism and indiscretion, and foresee the boredom of my reader. I must choose a traditional stanza, even what I alter must seem traditional. I commit my emotion to shepherds, herdsmen, camel-drivers, learned men, Milton's or Shelley's Platonist, that tower Palmer drew. Talk to me of originality and I will turn on you with rage. I am a crowd, I am a lonely man, I am nothing. Ancient salt is best packing. The heroes of Shakespeare convey to us through their looks, or through the metaphorical patterns of their speech, the sudden enlargement of their vision, their ecstasy at the approach of death: 'She should have died hereafter', 'Of many thousand kisses, the poor last', 'Absent thee from felicity awhile'. They have become God or Mother Goddess, the pelican, 'My baby at my breast', but all must be cold; no actress has ever sobbed when she played Cleopatra, even the shallow brain of a producer has never thought of such a thing. The supernatural is present, cold winds blow across our hands, upon our faces, the thermometer falls, and because of that cold we are hated by journalists and groundlings. There may be in this or that detail painful tragedy, but in the whole work none. I have heard Lady Gregory say, rejecting some play in the modern manner sent to the Abbey Theatre, 'Tragedy must be a joy to the man who dies'. Nor is it any different with lyrics, songs, narrative poems; neither scholars nor the populace have sung or read anything generation after generation because of its pain. The maid of honour whose tragedy they sing must be lifted out of history with timeless pattern, she is one of the four Maries, the rhythm is old and familiar, imagination must dance, must be carried beyond feeling into the aboriginal ice. Is ice the correct word? I once boasted, copying the phrase from a letter of my father's, that I would write a poem 'cold and passionate as the dawn'.

When I wrote in blank verse I was dissatisfied; my vaguely mediaeval *Countess Cathleen* fitted the measure, but our Heroic Age went better, or so I fancied, in the ballad metre of *The Green Helmet*. There was something in what I felt about Deirdre, about Cuchulain, that rejected the Renaissance and its characteristic metres, and this was a principal reason why I created in dance plays the form that varies blank verse with lyric metres. When I speak blank verse and analyse my feelings, I stand at a moment of history when instinct, its traditional songs and dances, its general agreement, is of the past. I have been cast up out of the whale's belly though I still remember the sound and sway that came from beyond its ribs, and, like the Queen in Paul Fort's ballad, I smell of the fish of the sea. The contrapuntal structure of the verse, to employ a term adopted by Robert Bridges, combines the past and present. If I repeat the first line of *Paradise Lost* so as to emphasise its five feet I am among the folk singers — 'Of mán's first dísobédience ánd the frúit', but speak it as I should I cross it with another emphasis, that of passionate prose — 'Of mán's

fírst disobédience and the frúit', or 'Of mán's fírst dís-
obedience and the frúit'; the folk song is still there, but a
ghostly voice, an unvariable possibility, an unconscious norm.
What moves me and my hearer is a vivid speech that has no
laws except that it must not exorcise the ghostly voice. I am
awake and asleep, at my moment of revelation, self-possessed
in self-surrender; there is no rhyme, no echo of the beaten
drum, the dancing foot, that would overset my balance.
When I was a boy I wrote a poem upon dancing that had one
good line: 'They snatch with their hands at the sleep of the
skies.' If I sat down and thought for a year I would discover
that but for certain syllabic limitations, a rejection or acceptance of certain elisions, I must wake or sleep.

The Countess Cathleen could speak a blank verse which I
had loosened, almost put out of joint, for her need, because
I thought of her as mediaeval and thereby connected her with
the general European movement. For Deirdre and Cuchulain
and all the other figures of Irish legend are still in the whale's
belly.

IV. WHITHER?

The young English poets reject dream and personal emotion; they have thought out opinions that join them to this or
that political party; they employ an intricate psychology,
action in character, not as in the ballads character in action,
and all consider that they have a right to the same close
attention that men pay to the mathematician and the metaphysician. One of the more distinguished has just explained
that man has hitherto slept but must now awake. They are
determined to express the factory, the metropolis, that they
may be modern. Young men teaching school in some picturesque cathedral town, or settled for life in Capri or in
Sicily, defend their type of metaphor by saying that it comes

naturally to a man who travels to his work by Tube. I am indebted to a man of this school who went through my work at my request, crossing out all conventional metaphors, but they seem to me to have rejected also those dream associations which were the whole art of Mallarmé. He had topped a previous wave. As they express not what the Upanishads call 'that ancient Self' but individual intellect, they have the right to choose the man in the Tube because of his objective importance. They attempt to kill the whale, push the Renaissance higher yet, out-think Leonardo; their verse kills the folk ghost and yet would remain verse. I am joined to the 'Irishry' and I expect a counter-Renaissance. No doubt it is part of the game to push that Renaissance; I make no complaint; I am accustomed to the geometrical arrangement of history in *A Vision*, but I go deeper than 'custom' for my convictions. When I stand upon O'Connell Bridge in the half-light and notice that discordant architecture, all those electric signs, where modern heterogeneity has taken physical form, a vague hatred comes up out of my own dark and I am certain that wherever in Europe there are minds strong enough to lead others the same vague hatred rises; in four or five or in less generations this hatred will have issued in violence and imposed some kind of rule of kindred. I cannot know the nature of that rule, for its opposite fills the light; all I can do to bring it nearer is to intensify my hatred. I am no Nationalist, except in Ireland for passing reasons; State and Nation are the work of intellect, and when you consider what comes before and after them they are, as Victor Hugo said of something or other, not worth the blade of grass God gives for the nest of the linnet.

1937

IRELAND AFTER THE REVOLUTION

I ASSUME that some tragic crisis shall so alter Europe and all opinion that the Irish Government will teach the great majority of its school-children nothing but ploughing, harrowing, sowing, curry-combing, bicycle-cleaning, drill-driving, parcel-making, bale-pushing, tin-can-soldering, door-knob-polishing, threshold-whitening, coat-cleaning, trouser-patching, and playing upon the squiffer, all things that serve human dignity, unless indeed it decide that these things are better taught at home, in which case it can leave the poor children at peace.

Having settled that matter I return to more important things. Teach nothing but Greek, Gaelic, mathematics, and perhaps one modern language. I reject Latin because it was a language of the Graeco-Roman decadence, all imitation and manner and other feminine tricks; the much or little Latin necessary for a priest, doctor or lawyer should be part of professional training and come later. D'Arbois de Jubainville worked on old Irish for thirty years because it brought him back to the civilisation immediately behind that of Homer, and when I prepared *Oedipus at Colonus* for the Abbey stage I saw that the wood of the Furies in the opening scene was any Irish haunted wood. No passing beggar or fiddler or benighted countryman has ever trembled or been awe-struck by nymph-haunted or Fury-haunted wood described in Roman poetry. Roman poetry is founded upon documents, not upon belief.

Translate into modern Irish all that is most beautiful in old and middle Irish, what Frank O'Connor and Augusta

Gregory, let us say, have translated into English; let every schoolmaster point out where in his neighbourhood this or that thing happened, or is said to have happened, but teach Irish and Greek together, make the pupil translate Greek into Irish, Irish into Greek. The old Irish poets lay in a formless matrix; the Greek poets kept the richness of those dreams and yet were completely awake. Sleep has no bottom, waking no top. Irish can give our children love of the soil underfoot; but only Greek, co-ordination or intensity.

When I was a very young man, fresh from my first study of Elizabethan drama, I began to puzzle my elders with the question: 'Why has the audience deteriorated?' I would go on to explain that the modern theatre audience was as inferior to the Elizabethan as that was to the Greek; I spoke of the difficult transition from topic to topic in Shakespearean dialogue, of the still more difficult in those long speeches of Chapman; we could not give that close attention to-day. And then I would compare the Elizabethan plot broken up into farce and spectacle with the elaborate unity of Greek drama; no Elizabethan had the Greek intensity. No one could answer my question, nor could I myself, for I still half-believed in progress. But I can answer it now: civilisation rose to its high-tide mark in Greece, fell, rose again in the Renaissance but not to the same level. But we may, if we choose, not now or soon but at the next turn of the wheel, push ourselves up, being ourselves the tide, beyond that first mark. But no, these things are fated: we may be pushed up.

Mathematics should be taught because being certainty with-out reality it is the modern key to power, but not till the child is thirteen or fourteen years old and has begun to reason. Children before that age are the only born mimics, and they learn all through mimicry and should be taught languages and nothing else, though not so many that they will lose intensity of expression in their own, and these languages should be taught by word of mouth. Greek and Irish they should speak as fluently as they now speak English. If Irish is to become the national tongue the change must come slowly, almost imperceptibly; a sudden or forced change of language may be the ruin of the soul. England has forced English upon the schools and colleges of India, and now after generations of teaching no Indian can write or speak animated English and his mother tongue is despised and corrupted. Catholic Ireland is but slowly recovering from its change of language in the eighteenth century. Irishmen learn English at their mother's knee, English is now their mother-tongue, and a sudden change would bring a long barren epoch.

Let schools teach what is too difficult for grown men but is easy to the imitation or docility of childhood; English, history, and geography and those pleasant easy things which are the most important of all should be taught by father and mother, ancestral tradition, and the child's own reading, and if the child lack this teaching let father, mother, and child be ashamed, as they are if it lack breeding and manners. I would restore the responsibilities of the family.

[1938]

W. B. YEATS
SELECTED PROSE

AUTOBIOGRAPHICAL WRITINGS

REVERIES OVER CHILDHOOD AND YOUTH

*　　*　　*

IV

BECAUSE I had found it hard to attend to anything less interesting than my thoughts, I was difficult to teach. Several of my uncles and aunts had tried to teach me to read, and because they could not, and because I was much older than children who read easily, had come to think, as I have learnt since, that I had not all my faculties. But for an accident they might have thought it for a long time. My father was staying in the house and never went to church, and that gave me the courage to refuse to set out one Sunday morning. I was often devout, my eyes filling with tears at the thought of God and of my own sins, but I hated church. My grandmother tried to teach me to put my toes first to the ground because I suppose I stumped on my heels, and that took my pleasure out of the way there. Later on when I had learnt to read I took pleasure in the words of the hymn, but never understood why the choir took three times as long as I did in getting to the end; and the part of the service I liked, the sermon and passages of the Apocalypse and Ecclesiastes, were no compensation for all the repetitions and for the fatigue of so much standing. My father said if I would not go to church he would teach me to read. I think now that he wanted to make me go for my grandmother's sake and could think of no other way. He was an angry and impatient teacher and flung the reading-book at my head, and next Sunday I decided to go to church.

My father had, however, got interested in teaching me, and only shifted the lesson to a week-day till he had conquered my wandering mind. My first clear image of him was fixed on my imagination, I believe, but a few days before the first lesson. He had just arrived from London and was walking up and down the nursery floor. He had a very black beard and hair, and one cheek bulged out with a fig that was there to draw the pain out of a bad tooth. One of the nurses (a nurse had come from London with my brothers and sisters) said to the other that a live frog, she had heard, was best of all. Then I was sent to a dame-school kept by an old woman who stood us in rows and had a long stick like a billiard cue to get at the back rows. My father was still at Sligo when I came back from my first lesson and asked me what I had been taught. I said I had been taught to sing, and he said, 'Sing then', and I sang —

> Little drops of water,
> Little grains of sand,
> Make the mighty ocean
> And the pleasant land

high up in my head. So my father wrote to the old woman that I was never to be taught to sing again, and afterwards other teachers were told the same thing. Presently my elder sister came on a long visit and she and I went to a little two-storeyed house in a poor street where an old gentlewoman taught us spelling and grammar. When we had learned our lesson well, we were allowed to look at a sword presented to her father who had led troops in India or China and to spell out a long complimentary inscription on the silver scabbard. As we walked to her house or home again we held a large umbrella before us, both gripping the handle and guiding ourselves by looking out of a round hole gnawed in the cover by a mouse. When I had got beyond books of one syllable, I began to spend my time in a room called the library, though there were no books in it that I can remember except some old novels I never opened and a many-volumed encyclopaedia published towards the end of the eighteenth century. I read this encyclopaedia a great deal and can remember a long passage considering whether fossil wood despite its appearance might not be only a curiously shaped stone.

My father's unbelief had set me thinking about the evidences of religion and I weighed the matter perpetually with great anxiety, for I did not think I could live without religion. All my religious emotions were, I think, connected with clouds and cloudy glimpses of luminous sky, perhaps because of some Bible picture of God's speaking to Abraham or the like. At least I can remember the sight moving me to tears. One day I got a decisive argument for belief. A cow was about to calve, and I went to the field where the cow was with some farm-hands who carried a lantern, and next day I heard that the cow had calved in the early morning. I asked everybody how calves were born, and because nobody would tell me, made up my mind that nobody knew. They were the gift of God, that much was certain, but it was plain that nobody had ever dared to see them come, and children must come in the same way. I made up my mind that when I was a man I would wait up till calf or child had come. I was certain there would be a cloud and a burst of light and God would bring the calf in the cloud out of the light. That thought made me content until a boy of twelve or thirteen, who had come on a visit for the day, sat beside me in a hay-loft and explained all the mechanism of sex. He had learnt all about it from an elder boy whose pathic he was (to use a term he would not have understood) and his description, given, as I can see now, as if he were telling of any other fact of physical life, made me miserable for weeks. After the first impression wore off, I began to doubt if he had spoken truth, but one day I discovered a passage in the encyclopaedia that, though I only partly understood its long words, confirmed what he had said. I did not know enough to be shocked at his relation to the elder boy, but it was the first breaking of the dream of childhood.

My realization of death came when my father and mother and my two brothers and my two sisters were on a visit. I was in the library when I heard feet running past and heard somebody say in the passage that my younger brother, Robert, had died. He had been ill for some days. A little later my sister and I sat at the table, very happy, drawing ships with their flags half-mast high. We must have heard or seen that the ships in the harbour had their flags at half-mast. Next day at breakfast I heard people telling how my mother and the servant had heard the banshee crying the night before he died. It must have been after this that I told my grand-mother I did not want to go with her when she went to see old bed-ridden people because they would soon die.

     ★   ★   ★

XIII

Our house for the first year or so was on the top of a cliff, so that in stormy weather the spray would soak my bed at night, for I had taken the glass out of the window, sash and all. A literary passion for the open air was to last me for a few years. Then for another year or two we had a house over-looking the harbour where the one great sight was the going and coming of the fishing fleet. We had one regular servant, a fisherman's wife, and the occasional help of a big, red-faced girl who ate a whole pot of jam while my mother was at church and accused me of it. Some such arrangement lasted until long after the time I write of, and until my father going into the kitchen by chance found a girl, engaged during a passing need, in tears at the thought of leaving our other servant, and promised that they should never be parted. I have no doubt that we lived at the harbour for my mother's sake. She had, when we were children, refused to take us to a seaside place because she heard it possessed a bathing-box, but she loved the activities of a fishing village. When I think of her, I almost always see her talking over a cup of tea in the kitchen with our servant, the fisherman's wife, on the only themes outside our house that seemed of interest — the fishing-people of Howth, or the pilots and fishing-people of Rosses Point. She read no books, but she and the fisherman's wife would tell each other stories that Homer might have told, pleased with any moment of sudden intensity and laughing together over any point of satire. There is an essay called *Village Ghosts* in my *Celtic Twilight* which is but a record of one such afternoon, and many a fine tale has been lost because it had not occurred to me soon enough to keep notes. My father was always praising her to my sisters and to me, because she pretended to nothing she did not feel. She would write him letters telling of her delight in the tumbling clouds, but she did not care for pictures, and never went to an exhibition even to see a picture of his, nor to his studio to see the day's work, neither now nor when they were first married. I remember all this very clearly and little after it until her mind had gone in a stroke of paralysis and she had found, liberated at last from financial worry, perfect happiness feeding the birds at a London window. She had always, my father would say, intensity, and that was his chief word of praise; and once he added to the praise, 'No spendthrift ever had a poet for a son, though a miser might.'

XIV

The great event of a boy's life is the awakening of sex. He will bathe many times a day, or get up at dawn and having stripped leap to and fro over a stick laid upon two chairs, and hardly know, and never admit, that he had begun to take pleasure in his own nakedness, nor will he understand the change until some dream discovers it. He may never understand at all the greater change in his mind.

It all came upon me when I was close upon seventeen like the bursting of a shell. Somnambulistic country girls, when it is upon them, throw plates about or pull them with long hairs in simulation of the poltergeist, or become mediums for some genuine spirit-mischief, surrendering to their desire of the marvellous. As I look backward, I seem to discover that my passions, my loves and my despairs, instead of being my enemies, a disturbance and an attack, became so beautiful that I had to be constantly alone to give them my whole attention. I notice that now, for the first time, what I saw when alone is more vivid in my memory than what I did or saw in company.

A herd had shown me a cave some hundred and fifty feet below the cliff path and a couple of hundred above the sea, and told me that an evicted tenant called Macrom, dead some fifteen years, had lived there many years, and shown me a rusty nail in the rock which had served perhaps to hold up some wooden protection from wind and weather. Here I stored a tin of cocoa and some biscuits, and instead of going to my bed, would slip out on warm nights and sleep in the cave on the excuse of catching moths. One had to pass over a rocky ledge, safe enough for any one with a fair head, yet seeming, if looked at from above, narrow and sloping; and a remonstrance from a stranger who had seen me climbing along it doubled my delight in the adventure. When, however, upon a bank holiday, I found lovers in my cave, I was not content with it again till I heard that the ghost of Macrom had been seen a little before the dawn, stooping over his fire in the cave-mouth. I had been trying to cook eggs, as I had read in some book, by burying them in the earth under a fire of sticks.

At other times, I would sleep among the rhododendrons and rocks in the wilder part of the grounds of Howth Castle. After a while my father said I must stay indoors half the night, meaning that I should get some sleep in my bed; but I, knowing that I would be too sleepy and comfortable to get up again, used to sit over the kitchen fire till half the night was gone. Exaggerated accounts spread through the school, and sometimes when I did not know a lesson some master would banter me about the way my nights were spent. My interest in science began to fade, and presently I said to myself, 'It has all been a misunderstanding.' I remembered how soon I tired of my specimens, and how little I knew after all my years of collecting, and I came to believe that I had gone through so much labour because of a text, heard for the first time in Saint John's Church in Sligo, and copied Solomon, who had knowledge of hyssop and of tree, that I might be certain of my own wisdom. I still carried my green net, but I began to play at being a sage, a magician or a poet. I had many idols, and as I climbed along the narrow ledge I was now Manfred on his glacier, and now Prince Athanase with his solitary lamp, but I soon chose Alastor for my chief of men and longed to share his melancholy, and maybe at last to disappear from everybody's sight as he disappeared drifting in a boat along some slow-moving river between great trees. When I thought of women they were modelled on those in my favourite poets and loved in brief tragedy, or like the girl in *The Revolt of Islam*, accompanied their lovers through all manner of wild places, lawless women without homes and without children.

XV

My father's influence upon my thoughts was at its height. We went to Dublin by train every morning, breakfasting in his studio. He had taken a large room with a beautiful eighteenth-century mantelpiece in a York Street tenement-house, and at breakfast he read passages from the poets, and always from the play or poem at its most passionate moment. He never read me a passage because of its speculative interest, and indeed did not care at all for poetry where there was generalization or abstraction however impassioned. He would read out the first speeches of the *Prometheus Unbound*, but never the ecstatic lyricism of that famous fourth act; and another day the scene where Coriolanus comes to the house of Aufidius and tells the impudent servants that his home is under the canopy. I have seen *Coriolanus* played a number of times since then, and read it more than once, but that scene is more vivid than the rest, and it is my father's voice that I hear and not Irving's or Benson's. He did not care even for a fine lyric passage unless he felt some actual man behind its elaboration of beauty, and he was always looking for the lineaments of some desirable, familiar life. When the spirits sang their scorn of Manfred, and Manfred answered, 'O sweet and melancholy voices',[1] I was told that they could not, even in anger, put off their spiritual sweetness. He thought Keats a greater poet than Shelley, because less abstract, but did not read him, caring little, I think, for any of that most

[1]　　　'I hear
Your voices, sweet and melancholy sounds' . . .
　　　　　　　Manfred, Act I, Scene I.

beautiful poetry which has come in modern times from the influence of painting. All must be an idealization of speech, and at some moment of passionate action or somnambulistic reverie. I remember his saying that all contemplative men were in a conspiracy to overrate their state of life, and that all writers were of them, excepting the great poets. Looking backwards, it seems to me that I saw his mind in fragments, which had always hidden connections I only now begin to discover. He disliked the Victorian poetry of ideas, and Wordsworth but for certain passages or whole poems. He said one morning over his breakfast that he had discovered in the shape of the head of a Wordsworthian scholar, an old and greatly respected clergyman whose portrait he was painting, all the animal instincts of a prize-fighter. He despised the formal beauty of Raphael, that calm which is not an ordered passion but an hypocrisy, and attacked Raphael's life for its love of pleasure and its self-indulgence. In literature he was always Pre-Raphaelite, and carried into literature principles that, while the Academy was still unbroken, had made the first attack upon academic form.

He no longer read me anything for its story, and all our discussion was of style.

XVI

I began to make blunders when I paid calls or visits, and a woman I had known and liked as a child told me I had changed for the worse. I wanted to be wise and eloquent, an essay on the younger Ampère had helped me to this ambition, and when I was alone I exaggerated my blunders and was miserable. I had begun to write poetry in imitation of Shelley and of Edmund Spenser, play after play — for my father exalted dramatic poetry above all other kinds — and I

invented fantastic and incoherent plots. My lines but seldom
scanned, for I could not understand the prosody in the books,
although there were many lines that taken by themselves had
music. I spoke them slowly as I wrote and only discovered
when I read them to somebody else that there was no common
music, no prosody. There were, however, moments of
observation; for, even when I caught moths no longer, I still
noticed all that passed; how the little moths came out at sunset, and how after that there were only a few big moths till
dawn brought little moths again; and what birds cried out at
night as if in their sleep.

XVII

At Sligo, where I still went for my holidays, I stayed with
my uncle, George Pollexfen, who had come from Ballina to
fill the place of my grandfather, who had retired. My grandfather had no longer his big house, his partner William
Middleton was dead, and there had been legal trouble. He
was no longer the rich man he had been, and his sons and
daughters were married and scattered. He had a tall, bare
house overlooking the harbour, and had nothing to do but
work himself into a rage if he saw a mud-lighter mismanaged
or judged from the smoke of a steamer that she was burning
cheap coal, and to superintend the making of his tomb.
There was a Middleton tomb and a long list of Middletons on
the wall, and an almost empty space for Pollexfen names, but
he had said, because there was a Middleton there he did not
like, 'I am not going to lie with those old bones'; and already
one saw his name in large gilt letters on the stone fence of the
new tomb. He ended his walk at Saint John's churchyard
almost daily, for he liked everything neat and compendious as
upon shipboard, and if he had not looked after the tomb

himself the builder might have added some useless ornament. He had, however, all his old skill and nerve. I was going to Rosses Point on the little trading steamer and saw him take the wheel from the helmsman and steer her through a gap in the Channel wall, and across the sand, an unheard-of course, and at the journey's end bring her alongside her wharf at Rosses without the accustomed zigzagging or pulling on a rope but in a single movement. He took snuff when he had a cold, but had never smoked nor taken alcohol; and when in his eightieth year his doctor advised a stimulant, he replied, 'No, no, I am not going to form a bad habit.'

My brother had partly taken my place in my grandmother's affections. He had lived permanently in her house for some years now, and went to a Sligo school where he was always bottom of his class. My grandmother did not mind that, for she said, 'He is too kindhearted to pass the other boys.' He spent his free hours going here and there with crowds of little boys, sons of pilots and sailors, as their well-liked leader, arranging donkey races or driving donkeys tandem, an occupation which requires all one's intellect because of their obstinacy. Besides he had begun to amuse everybody with his drawings; and in half the pictures he paints to-day I recognize faces that I have met at Rosses or the Sligo quays. It is long since he has lived there, but his memory seems as accurate as the sight of the eye.

*   *   *

XXI

At Ballisodare an event happened that brought me back to the superstitions of my childhood. I do not know when it was, for the events of this period have as little sequence as those of childhood. I was staying with cousins at Avena House, a young man a few years older, and a girl of my own age and perhaps her sister who was a good deal older. My girl cousin had often told me of strange sights she had seen at Ballisodare or Rosses. An old woman three or four feet in height and leaning on a stick had once come to the window and looked in at her, and sometimes she would meet people on the road who would say, 'How is So-and-so?', naming some member of her family, and she would know, though she could not explain how, that they were not people of this world. Once she had lost her way in a familiar field, and when she found it again the silver mounting on a walking-stick belonging to her brother which she carried had vanished. An old woman in the village said afterwards, 'You have good friends amongst them, and the silver was taken instead of you.'

Though it was all years ago, what I am going to tell now must be accurate, for no great while ago she wrote out her unprompted memory of it all and it was the same as mine. She was sitting under an old-fashioned mirror reading and I was reading in another part of the room. Suddenly I heard a sound as if somebody was throwing a shower of peas at the mirror. I got her to go into the next room and rap with her knuckles on the other side of the wall to see if the sound could come from there, and while I was alone a great thump came close to my head upon the winscot and on a different wall of the room. Later in the day a servant heard a heavy footstep going through the empty house, and that night, when I and my two cousins went for a walk, she saw the ground under some trees all in a blaze of light. I saw nothing, but presently we crossed the river and went along its edge where, they say, there was a village destroyed, I think in the wars of the seventeenth century, and near an old graveyard. Suddenly we all saw a light moving over the river where there is a great rush of waters. It was like a very brilliant torch. A moment later the girl saw a man coming towards us who disappeared in the water. I kept asking myself if I could be deceived. Perhaps after all, though it seemed impossible, somebody was walking in the water with a torch. But we could see a small light low down on Knocknarea seven miles off, and it began to move upward over the mountain slope. I timed it on my watch and in five minutes it reached the summit, and I, who had often climbed the mountain, knew that no human footstep was so speedy.

From that on I wandered about raths and faery hills and questioned old women and old men and, when I was tired out or unhappy, began to long for some such end as True Thomas found. I did not believe with my intellect that you could be carried away body and soul, but I believed with my emotions and the belief of the countrypeople made that easy. Once when I had crawled into the stone passage in some rath of the third Rosses, the pilot who had come with me called down the passage: 'Are you all right, sir?'

And one night as I came near the village of Rosses on the road from Sligo, a fire blazed up on a green bank at my right side seven or eight feet above me, and another fire suddenly answered from Knocknarea. I hurried on doubting, and yet hardly doubting in my heart that I saw again the fires that I had seen by the river at Ballisodare. I began occasionally telling people that one should believe whatever had been believed in all countries and periods, and only reject any part of it after much evidence, instead of starting all over afresh and only believing what one could prove. But I was always ready to deny or turn into a joke what was for all that my secret fanaticism. When I had read Darwin and Huxley and believed as they did, I had wanted, because an established authority was upon my side, to argue with everybody.

*   *   *

XXIV

From our first arrival in Dublin, my father had brought
me from time to time to see Edward Dowden. He and my
father had been college friends and were trying, perhaps, to
take up again their old friendship. Sometimes we were asked
to breakfast, and afterwards my father would tell me to read
out one of my poems. Dowden was wise in his encourage-
ment, never overpraising and never unsympathetic, and he
would sometimes lend me books. The orderly, prosperous
house where all was in good taste, where poetry was rightly
valued, made Dublin tolerable for a while, and for perhaps a
couple of years he was an image of romance. My father
would not share my enthusiasm and soon, I noticed, grew
impatient at these meetings. He would sometimes say that he
had wanted Dowden when they were young to give himself
to creative art, and would talk of what he considered Dowden's failure in life. I know now that he was finding in his
friend what he himself had been saved from by the conversation of the Pre-Raphaelites. 'He will not trust his nature,' he
would say, or 'He is too much influenced by his inferiors,' or
he would praise *Renunciants*, one of Dowden's poems, to
prove what Dowden might have written. I was not influenced, for I had imagined a past worthy of that dark,
romantic face. I took literally his verses, touched here and
there with Swinburnian rhetoric, and believed that he had
loved, unhappily and illicitly; and when through the practice
of my art I discovered that certain images about the love of
woman were the properties of a school, I but changed my
fancy and thought of him as very wise.

I was constantly troubled about philosophic questions. I
would say to my fellow-students at the art schools, 'Poetry
and sculpture exist to keep our passions alive'; and somebody

would say, 'We would be much better without our passions.' Or I would have a week's anxiety over the problem: do the arts make us happier, or more sensitive and therefore more unhappy? And I would say to Hughes or Sheppard, 'If I cannot be certain they make us happier I will never write again.' If I spoke of these things to Dowden he would put the question away with good-humoured irony: he seemed to condescend to everybody and everything and was now my sage. I was about to learn that if a man is to write lyric poetry he must be shaped by nature and art to some one out of half a dozen traditional poses, and be lover or saint, sage or sensualist, or mere mocker of all life; and that none but that stroke of luckless luck can open before him the accumulated expression of the world. And this thought before it could be knowledge was an instinct.

I was vexed when my father called Dowden's irony timidity, but after many years his impression has not changed, for he wrote to me but a few months ago, 'It was like talking to a priest. One had to be careful not to remind him of his sacrifice.' Once after breakfast Dowden read us some chapters of the unpublished *Life of Shelley*, and I who had made the *Prometheus Unbound* my sacred book was delighted with all he read. I was chilled, however, when he explained that he had lost his liking for Shelley and would not have written it but for an old promise to the Shelley family. When it was published, Matthew Arnold made sport of certain conventionalities and extravagances that were, my father and I had come to see, the violence or clumsiness of a conscientious man hiding from himself a lack of sympathy.

Though my faith was shaken, it was only when he urged me to read George Eliot that I became angry and disillusioned and worked myself into a quarrel or half-quarrel. I had read all Victor Hugo's romances and a couple of Balzac's and was

in no mind to like her. She seemed to have a distrust or a distaste for all in life that gives one a springing foot. Then, too,
she knew so well how to enforce her distaste by the authority
of her mid-Victorian science or by some habit of mind of its
breeding, that I, who had not escaped the fascination of what
I loathed, doubted while the book lay open whatsoever my
instinct knew of splendour. She disturbed me and alarmed
me, but when I spoke of her to my father, he threw her aside
with a phrase, 'O, she was an ugly woman who hated handsome men and handsome women'; and he began to praise
Wuthering Heights.

Only the other day, when I got a volume of Dowden's
letters, did I discover that the friendship between Dowden
and my father had long been an antagonism. My father had
written from Fitzroy Road in the 'sixties that the brotherhood,
by which he meant the poet Edwin Ellis, Nettleship and himself, 'abhorred Wordsworth'; and Dowden, not remembering that another week would bring a different mood and
abhorrence, had written a pained and solemn letter. My
father had answered that Dowden believed too much in the
intellect, that all valuable education was but a stirring up of
the emotions and that this did not mean excitability. 'In the
completely emotional man,' he wrote, 'the least awakening
of feeling is a harmony in which every chord of every feeling
vibrates. Excitement is the feature of an insufficiently emotional nature, the harsh vibrating discourse of but one or two
chords.' Living in a free world accustomed to the gay exaggeration of the talk of equals, of men who talk and write to
discover truth and not for popular instruction, he had already,
when both men were in their twenties, decided, it is plain, that
Dowden was a provincial.

XXV

It was only when I began to study psychical research and mystical philosophy that I broke away from my father's influence. He had been a follower of John Stuart Mill and so had never shared Rossetti's conviction that it mattered to nobody whether the sun went round the earth or the earth round the sun. But through this new research, this reaction from popular science, I had begun to feel that I had allies for my secret thought.

Once when I was in Dowden's drawing-room a servant announced my late headmaster. I must have got pale or red, for Dowden with some ironical, friendly remark brought me into another room and there I stayed until the visitor was gone. A few months later, when I met the headmaster again, I had more courage. We chanced upon one another in the street and he said, 'I want you to use your influence with So-and-so, for he is giving all his time to some sort of mysticism and he will fail in his examination.' I was in great alarm, but I managed to say something about the children of this world being wiser than the children of light. He went off with a brusque 'Good morning.' I do not think that even at that age I would have been so grandiloquent but for my alarm. He had, however, aroused all my indignation. My new allies and my old had alike sustained me. 'Intermediate examinations', which I had always refused, meant money for pupil and for teacher, and that alone. My father had brought me up never when at school to think of the future or of any practical result. I have even known him to say, 'When I was young, the definition of a gentleman was a man not wholly occupied in getting on.' And yet this master wanted to withdraw my friend from the pursuit of the most important of all the truths. My friend, now in his last year at school, was a 'show boy', and had beaten all Ireland again and again, but now he and I were reading Baron Reichenbach on Odic Force and manuals published by the Theosophical Society. We spent a good deal of time in the Kildare Street Museum passing our hands over the glass cases, feeling or believing we felt the Odic Force flowing from the big crystals. We also found pins blindfolded and read papers on our discoveries to the Hermetic Society that met near the roof in York Street. I had, when we first made our Society, proposed for our consideration that whatever the great poets had affirmed in their finest moments was the nearest we could come to an authoritative religion, and that their mythology, their spirits of water and wind, were but literal truth. I had read *Prometheus Unbound* with this thought in mind and wanted help to carry my study through all literature. I was soon to vex my father by defining truth as 'the dramatically appropriate utterance of the highest man'. And if I had been asked to define the 'highest man', I would have said perhaps, 'We can but find him as Homer found Odysseus when he was looking for a theme.'

My friend had written to some missionary society to send him to the South Seas, when I offered him Renan's *Life of Christ* and a copy of *Esoteric Buddhism*. He refused both, but a few days later while reading for an examination in Kildare Street Library, he asked in an idle moment for *Esoteric Buddhism* and came out an esoteric Buddhist. He wrote to the missionaries withdrawing his letter and offered himself to the Theosophical Society as a *chela*. He was vexed now at my lack of zeal, for I had stayed somewhere between the books, held there perhaps by my father's scepticism. I said, and he thought it was a great joke though I was serious, that even if I were certain in my own mind, I did not know 'a single person with a talent for conviction'. For a time he made me ashamed of my world and its lack of zeal, and I wondered if his world

(his father was a notorious Orange leader) where everything
was a matter of belief was not better than mine. He himself
proposed the immediate conversion of the other 'show boy',
a clever little fellow, now a Dublin mathematician and still
under five feet. I found him a day later in much depression.
I said, 'Did he refuse to listen to you?' 'Not at all,' was the
answer, 'for I had only been talking for a quarter of an hour
when he said he believed.' Certainly those minds, parched by
many examinations, were thirsty.

Sometimes a Professor of Oriental Languages at Trinity
College, a Persian, came to our Society and talked of the
magicians of the East. When he was a little boy, he had seen
a vision in a pool of ink, a multitude of spirits singing in
Arabic, 'Woe unto those that do not believe in us.' And we
persuaded a Brahmin philosopher to come from London and
stay for a few days with the only one among us who had
rooms of his own. It was my first meeting with a philosophy
that confirmed my vague speculations and seemed at once
logical and boundless. Consciousness, he taught, does not
merely spread out its surface but has, in vision and in contemplation, another motion and can change in height and in
depth. A handsome young man with the typical face of
Christ, he chaffed me good-humouredly because he said I
came at breakfast and began some question that was interrupted by the first caller, waited in silence till ten or eleven
at night when the last caller had gone, and finished my
question.

*   *   *

XXVII

I had begun to frequent a club founded by Mr. Oldham,
and not from natural liking, but from a secret ambition. I

wished to become self-possessed, to be able to play with hostile minds as Hamlet played, to look in the lion's face, as it were, with unquivering eyelash. In Ireland harsh argument which had gone out of fashion in England was still the manner of our conversation, and at this club Unionist and Nationalist could interrupt one another and insult one another without the formal and traditional restraint of public speech. Sometimes they would change the subject and discuss Socialism, or a philosophical question, merely to discover their old passions under a new shape. I spoke easily and, I thought, well till someone was rude and then I would become silent or exaggerate my opinion to absurdity, or hesitate and grow confused, or be carried away myself by some party passion. I would spend hours afterwards going over my words and putting the wrong ones right. Discovering that I was only self-possessed with people I knew intimately, I would often go to a strange house where I knew I would spend a wretched hour for schooling's sake. I did not discover that Hamlet had his self-possession from no schooling but from indifference and passion-conquering sweetness, and that less heroic minds can but hope it from old age.

*   *   *

XXIX

From these debates, from O'Leary's conversation, and from the Irish books he lent or gave me has come all I have set my hand to since. I had begun to know a great deal about the Irish poets who had written in English. I read with excitement books I should find unreadable to-day, and found romance in lives that had neither wit nor adventure. I did not deceive myself; I knew how often they wrote a cold and abstract language, and yet I who had never wanted to see the

houses where Keats and Shelley lived would ask everybody
what sort of place Inchedony was, because Callanan had
named after it a bad poem in the manner of *Childe Harold*.
Walking home from a debate, I remember saying to some
college student, 'Ireland cannot put from her the habits
learned from her old military civilization and from a Church
that prays in Latin. Those popular poets have not touched her
heart, her poetry when it comes will be distinguished and
lonely.' O'Leary had once said to me, 'Neither Ireland nor
England knows the good from the bad in any art, but Ireland
unlike England does not hate the good when it is pointed out
to her.' I began to plot and scheme how one might seal with
the right image the soft wax before it began to harden. I had
noticed that Irish Catholics among whom had been born so
many political martyrs had not the good taste, the household
courtesy and decency of the Protestant Ireland I had known,
yet Protestant Ireland seemed to think of nothing but getting
on in the world. I thought we might bring the halves together if we had a national literature that made Ireland
beautiful in the memory, and yet had been freed from provincialism by an exacting criticism, a European pose.

XXX

Someone at the Young Ireland Society gave me a newspaper that I might read some article or letter. I began idly
reading verses describing the shore of Ireland as seen by a
returning, dying emigrant. My eyes filled with tears and yet
I knew the verses were badly written — vague, abstract
words such as one finds in a newspaper. I looked at the end
and saw the name of some political exile who had died but a
few days after his return to Ireland. They had moved me
because they contained the actual thoughts of a man at a

passionate moment of life, and when I met my father I was full of the discovery. We should write out our own thoughts in as nearly as possible the language we thought them in, as though in a letter to an intimate friend. We should not disguise them in any way; for our lives give them force as the lives of people in plays give force to their words. Personal utterance, which had almost ceased in English literature, could be as fine an escape from rhetoric and abstraction as drama itself. But my father would hear of nothing but drama; personal utterance was only egotism. I knew it was not, but as yet did not know how to explain the difference. I tried from that on to write out of my emotions exactly as they came to me in life, not changing them to make them more beautiful. 'If I can be sincere and make my language natural, and without becoming discursive, like a novelist, and so indiscreet and prosaic,' I said to myself, 'I shall, if good luck or bad luck make my life interesting, be a great poet; for it will be no longer a matter of literature at all.' Yet when I reread those early poems which gave me so much trouble, I find little but romantic convention, unconscious drama. It is so many years before one can believe enough in what one feels even to know what the feeling is.

XXXI

Perhaps a year before we returned to London, a Catholic friend brought me to a spiritualistic séance at the house of a young man lately arrested under a suspicion of Fenianism, but released for lack of evidence. He and his friends had been sitting weekly about a table in the hope of spiritual manifestation and one had developed mediumship. A drawer full of books had leaped out of the table when no one was touching it, a picture had moved upon the wall. There were some half-dozen of us, and our host began by making passes until the medium fell asleep sitting upright in his chair. Then the lights were turned out, and we sat waiting in the dim light of a fire. Presently my shoulders began to twitch and my hands. I could easily have stopped them, but I had never heard of such a thing and I was curious. After a few minutes the movement became violent and I stopped it. I sat motionless for a while and then my whole body moved like a suddenly unrolled watch-spring, and I was thrown backward on the wall. I again stilled the movement and sat at the table. Everybody began to say I was a medium, and that if I would not resist some wonderful thing would happen. I remembered that Balzac had once desired to take opium for the experience' sake, but would not because he dreaded the surrender of his will. We were now holding each other's hands and presently my right hand banged the knuckles of the woman next to me upon the table. She laughed, and the medium, speaking for the first time, and with difficulty, out of his mesmeric sleep, said, 'Tell her there is great danger.' He stood up and began walking round me making movements with his hands as though he were pushing something away. I was now struggling vainly with this force which compelled me to movements I had not willed, and my movements became so violent that the table was broken. I tried to pray, and because I could not remember a prayer, repeated in a loud voice —

> 'Of Man's first disobedience and the fruit
> Of that forbidden tree whose mortal taste
> Brought death into the world, and all our woe . . .
> Sing, Heavenly Muse.'

My Catholic friend had left the table and was saying a Paternoster and Ave Maria in the corner. Presently all became still and so dark that I could not see anybody. I described it to somebody next day as like going out of a noisy political meeting on to a quiet country road. I said to myself, 'I am now in a trance but I no longer have any desire to resist.' But when I turned my eyes to the fireplace I could see a faint gleam of light, so I thought, 'No, I am not in a trance.' Then I saw shapes faintly appearing in the darkness, and thought, 'They are spirits'; but they were only the spiritualists and my friend at her prayers. The medium said in a faint voice, 'We are through the bad spirits.' I said, 'Will they ever come again, do you think?' and he said, 'No, never again, I think,' and in my boyish vanity I thought it was I who had banished them.

For years afterwards I would not go to a séance or turn a table and would often ask myself what was that violent impulse that had run through my nerves. Was it a part of myself — something always to be a danger perhaps; or had it come from without, as it seemed?

XXXII

I had published my first book of poems by subscription, O'Leary finding many subscribers, and a book of stories, when I heard that my grandmother was dead and went to Sligo for the funeral. She had asked to see me, but by some mistake I was not sent for. She had heard that I was much about with a beautiful, admired woman and feared that I did not speak of marriage because I was poor, and wanted to say to me, 'Women care nothing about money.' My grandfather was dying also and only survived her a few weeks. I went to see him and wondered at his handsome face now sickness had refined it, and noticed that he foretold the changes in the weather by indications of the light and of the temperature that would have meant nothing to another. As

I sat there my old childish fear returned and I was glad to get away. I stayed with my uncle whose house was opposite where my grandfather lived, and walking home one day we met the doctor. The doctor said there was no hope and that my grandfather should be told, but my uncle would not allow it. He said, 'It would make a man mad to know he was dying.' In vain the doctor pleaded that he had never known a man not made calmer by the knowledge. I listened sad and angry, but my uncle always took a low view of human nature, his very tolerance which was exceedingly great came from his hoping nothing of anybody. Before he had given way my grandfather lifted up his arms and cried out, 'There she is,' and fell backward dead. Before he was dead, old servants of that house where there had never been noise or disorder began their small pilferings, and after his death there was a quarrel over the disposition of certain mantelpiece ornaments of no value.

XXXIII

For some months now I have lived with my own youth and childhood, not always writing indeed but thinking of it almost every day, and I am sorrowful and disturbed. It is not that I have accomplished too few of my plans, for I am not ambitious; but when I think of all the books I have read, and of the wise words I have heard spoken, and of the anxiety I have given to parents and grandparents, and of the hopes that I have had, all life weighed in the scales of my own life seems to me a preparation for something that never happens.

[1915]

I BECAME AN AUTHOR

How did I begin to write? I have nothing to say that may help young writers, except that I hope they will not begin as I did. I spent longer than most schoolboys preparing the next day's work, and yet learnt nothing, and would always have been at the bottom of my class but for one or two subjects that I hardly had to learn at all. My father would say: 'You cannot fix your mind on anything that does not interest you, and it is to study what does not that you are sent to school.' I did not suffer from the 'poetic temperament', but from some psychological weakness. Greater poets than I have been great scholars. Even to-day I struggle against a lack of confidence, when among average men, come from that daily humiliation, and because I do not know what they know. I can toil through a little French poetry, but nothing remains of the Greek, Latin and German I tried to learn. I have only one memory of my schooldays that gives me pleasure; though in both my English and Irish schools I was near the bottom of the class, my friends were at the top, for then, as now, I hated fools. When I would find out if some man can be trusted, I asked if he associates with his betters. In the Irish school my chief friend was Charles Johnson, son of the Orange leader. He beat all Ireland in the Intermediate examinations, and when I met him in America years afterwards he said: 'There is nothing I cannot learn and nothing I want to learn.' Some instinct drew us together, it was to him I used to read my poems. They were all plays — except one long poem in Spenserian stanzas, which some woman of whom I remember nothing, not even if she was pretty, borrowed and lost out of her carriage when shopping. I recall three plays, not of any merit, one vaguely Elizabethan, its scene a German forest, one an imitation of Shelley, its scene a crater in the moon, one of somebody's translations from the Sanscrit, its scene an Indian temple. Charles Johnson admired parts of these poems so much that I doubt if he ever thought I had fulfilled their promise. A fragment, or perhaps all that was written, of the Indian play, I put near the opening of my *Collected Poems* because when I put it there he was still living, and it is still there because I have forgotten to take it out. I have sometimes wondered if I did not write poetry to find a cure for my own ailment, as constipated cats do when they eat valerian. But that will not do, because my interest in proud, confident people began before I had been much humiliated. Some people say I have an affected manner, and if that is true, as it may well be, it is because my father took me when I was ten or eleven to Irving's famous 'Hamlet'. Years afterwards I walked the Dublin streets when nobody was looking, or nobody that I knew, with that strut Gordon Craig has compared to a movement in a dance, and made the characters I created speak with his brooding broken wildness. Two months ago, describing the Second Coming, I wrote this couplet:

> What brushes fly and gnat aside?
> Irving and his plume of pride.

Nobody should think a young poet pathetic and weak, or that he has a lonely struggle. I think some old and famous men may think that they had in their schooldays their most satisfying fame; certainly I had about me a little group whose admiration for work that had no merit justified my immense self-confidence.

When eighteen or nineteen I wrote a pastoral play under the influence of Keats and Shelley, modified by that of Jonson's 'Sad Shepherd', and one of my friends showed it to some Trinity undergraduates who were publishing the *Dublin University Review*, an ambitious political and literary periodical that lasted for a few months — I cannot remember who, except that it was not Charles Johnston, who had passed for the Indian Civil Service, gone to India, and would stay there till he tired of it. I was at the Art Schools because painting was the family trade, and because I did not think I could pass the matriculation examination for Trinity. The undergraduates liked the poem and invited me to read it to a man four or five years older than the rest of us, Bury, in later years a classical historian and editor of Gibbon. I was excited, not merely because he would decide the acceptance or rejection of my play, but because he was a schoolmaster and I had never met a schoolmaster in private life. Once when I was at Edward Dowden's the head of my old school was announced, but I turned so pale or so red that Dowden brought me into another room. Perhaps I could get Bury to explain why I had been told to learn so many things that I had not been able to fix my attention upon anything.

I thought a man brought his convictions into everything he did; I had said to the photographer when he was arranging his piece of iron shaped like a horse-shoe to keep my head in position: 'Because you have only white and black paper instead of light and shadow you cannot represent Nature. An artist can, because he employs a kind of symbolism.' To my surprise, instead of showing indignation at my attack upon his trade, he replied: 'A photograph is mechanical.' Even to-day I have the same habit of thought, but only when thinking of pre-eminent men. A few days ago I read of some University meeting where, when somebody said: 'Nobody to-day believes in a personal devil,' Lord Acton said: 'I do'; and I knew that because the Cambridge Universal History, which he had planned, contains nothing about a personal devil's influence upon events, Lord Acton was a picturesque liar. For some reason which I cannot recollect I was left alone with Bury and said, after a great effort to overcome my shyness: 'I know you will defend the ordinary system of education by saying that it strengthens the will, but I am convinced that it only seems to do so because it weakens the impulses.' He smiled and looked embarrassed, but said nothing.

My pastoral play *The Island of Statues* appeared in the review. I have not looked at it for many years, but nothing I did at that time had merit. Two lyrics from it are at the beginning of my *Collected Poems*, not because I liked them but because when I put them there friends that had were still living. Immediately after its publication, or just before, I fell under the influence of two men who were to influence deeply the Irish intellectual movement — old John O'Leary the Fenian leader, in whose library I found the poets of Young Ireland; and Standish O'Grady, who had rewritten in vigorous romantic English certain ancient Irish heroic legends. Because of the talk of these men, and the books the one lent and the other wrote, I turned my back on foreign themes, decided that the race was more important than the individual, and began my 'Wanderings of Oisin'; it was published with many shorter poems by subscription, John O'Leary finding almost all the subscribers. Henceforth I was one of the rising poets. I lived in London and had many friends, and when I could not earn the twenty shillings a week which in those days bought bed and board for man or boy, I could stay with my family or a Sligo relative. In this I was more fortunate than Isadora Duncan who was to write of her first London years: 'I had renown and the favour of princes and not enough to eat.' As a professional writer I was clumsy, stiff and sluggish; when I reviewed a book I had to write my own heated thoughts because I did not know how to get thoughts out of my subject; when I wrote a poem half a dozen lines sometimes took as many days because I was determined to put the natural words in the natural order, my imagination still full of poetic diction. It was that old difficulty of my school work over again, except that I had now plenty of time.

[1938]

FOUR YEARS: 1887-1891

*   *   *

II

I COULD not understand where the charm had gone that I had felt, when as a schoolboy of twelve or thirteen I had played among the unfinished houses [at Bedford Park], once leaving the marks of my two hands, blacked by a fall among some paint, upon a white balustrade.

Yet I was in all things Pre-Raphaelite. When I was fifteen or sixteen my father had told me about Rossetti and Blake and given me their poetry to read; and once at Liverpool on my way to Sligo I had seen *Dante's Dream* in the gallery there, a picture painted when Rossetti had lost his dramatic power and to-day not very pleasing to me, and its colour, its people, its romantic architecture had blotted all other pictures away. It was a perpetual bewilderment that when my father, moved perhaps by some memory of his youth, chose some theme from poetic tradition, he would soon weary and leave it unfinished. I had seen the change coming bit by bit and its defence elaborated by young men fresh from the Paris art schools. 'We must paint what is in front of us,' or 'A man must be of his own time,' they would say, and if I spoke of Blake or Rossetti they would point out his bad drawing and tell me to admire Carolus Duran and Bastien-Lepage. Then, too, they were very ignorant men; they read nothing, for nothing mattered but 'knowing how to paint', being in reaction against a generation that seemed to have wasted its time upon so many things. I thought myself alone in hating these young men, their contempt for the past, their monopoly of the future, but in a few months I was to discover others of my own age who thought as I did, for it is not true that youth looks before it with the mechanical gaze of a well-drilled soldier. Its quarrel is not with the past, but with the present, where its elders are so obviously powerful and no cause seems lost if it seem to threaten that power. Does cultivated youth ever really love the future, where the eye can discover no persecuted Royalty hidden among oak leaves, though from it certainly does come so much proletarian rhetoric?

I was unlike others of my generation in one thing only. I am very religious, and deprived by Huxley and Tyndall, whom I detested, of the simple-minded religion of my childhood, I had made a new religion, almost an infallible Church of poetic tradition, of a fardel of stories, and of personages, and of emotions, inseparable from their first expression, passed on from generation to generation by poets and painters with some help from philosophers and theologians. I wished for a world where I could discover this tradition perpetually, and not in pictures and in poems only, but in tiles round the chimney-piece and in the hangings that kept out the draught. I had even created a dogma: 'Because those imaginary people are created out of the deepest instinct of man, to be his measure and his norm, whatever I can imagine those mouths speaking may be the nearest I can go to truth.' When I listened they seemed always to speak of one thing only: they, their loves, every incident of their lives, were steeped in the supernatural. Could even Titian's *Ariosto* that I loved beyond other portraits have its grave look, as if waiting for some perfect final event, if the painters before Titian had not learned portraiture while painting into the corner of compositions full of saints and Madonnas their kneeling patrons?

At seventeen years old I was already an old-fashioned brass cannon full of shot, and nothing had kept me from going off but a doubt as to my capacity to shoot straight.

*   *   *

V

Presently a hansom drove up to our door at Bedford Park with Miss Maud Gonne, who brought an introduction to my father from old John O'Leary, the Fenian leader. She vexed my father by praise of war, war for its own sake, not as the creator of certain virtues but as if there were some virtue in excitement itself. I supported her against my father, which vexed him the more, though he might have understood that, apart from the fact that Carolus Duran and Bastien-Lepage were somehow involved, a man young as I could not have differed from a woman so beautiful and so young. To-day, with her great height and the unchangeable lineaments of her form, she looks the Sibyl I would have had played by Florence Farr, but in that day she seemed a classical impersonation of the Spring, the Virgilian commendation 'She walks like a goddess' made for her alone. Her complexion was luminous, like that of apple-blossom through which the light falls, and I remember her standing that first day by a great heap of such blossoms in the window. In the next few years I saw her always when she passed to and fro between Dublin and Paris, surrounded, no matter how rapid her journey and how brief her stay at either end of it, by cages full of birds, canaries, finches of all kinds, dogs, a parrot, and once a full-grown hawk from Donegal.

*   *   *

VI

Some quarter of an hour's walk from Bedford Park, out on
the high road to Richmond, lived W. E. Henley, and I, like
many others, began under him my education. His portrait, a
lithograph by Rothenstein, hangs over my mantelpiece among
portraits of other friends. He is drawn standing, but because
doubtless of his crippled legs he leans forward, resting his el-
bows upon some slightly suggested object — a table or a win-
dow-sill. His heavy figure and powerful head, the disordered
hair standing upright, his short irregular beard and moustache,
his lined and wrinkled face, his eyes steadily fixed upon some
object in complete confidence and self-possession, and yet as in
half-broken reverie, all are there exactly as I remember him. I
have seen other portraits and they too show him exactly as I
remember him, as though he had but one appearance and that
seen fully at the first glance and by all alike. He was most
human — human, I used to say, like one of Shakespeare's
characters — and yet pressed and pummelled, as it were, into
a single attitude, almost into a gesture and a speech as by some
overwhelming situation. I disagreed with him about everything, but I admired him beyond words. With the exception
of some early poems founded upon old French models I disliked his poetry, mainly because he wrote in *vers libre*, which
I associated with Tyndall and Huxley, and Bastien-Lepage's
clownish peasant staring with vacant eyes at her great boots;
and filled it with unimpassioned description of a hospital ward
where his leg had been amputated. I wanted the strongest passions, passions that had nothing to do with observation, and
metrical forms that seemed old enough to have been sung by
men half asleep or riding upon a journey. Furthermore, Pre-
Raphaelitism affected him as some people are affected by a cat
in the room, and though he professed himself at our first meet-

ing without political interests or convictions, he soon grew
into a violent Unionist and Imperialist. I used to say when I
spoke of his poems, 'He is like a great actor with a bad part;
yet who would look at Hamlet in the grave scene if Salvini
played the grave-digger?' and I might so have explained much
that he said and did. I meant that he was like a great actor of
passion — character-acting meant nothing to me for many
years — and an actor of passion will display some one quality
of soul, personified again and again, just as a great poetical
painter, Titian, Botticelli, Rossetti, may depend for his greatness upon a type of beauty which presently we call by his
name. Irving, the last of the sort on the English stage, and in
modern England and France it is the rarest sort, never moved
me but in the expression of intellectual pride, and though I
saw Salvini but once I am convinced that his genius was a kind
of animal nobility. Henley, half inarticulate — 'I am very
costive,' he would say — beset with personal quarrels, built up
an image of power and magnanimity till it became, at moments, when seen as it were by lightning, his true self. Half his
opinions were the contrivance of a subconsciousness that
sought always to bring life to the dramatic crisis and expression to that point of artifice where the true self could find its
tongue. Without opponents there had been no drama, and in
his youth Ruskinism and Pre-Raphaelitism, for he was of my
father's generation, were the only possible opponents. How
could one resent his prejudice when, that he himself might
play a worthy part, he must find beyond the common rout,
whom he derided and flouted daily, opponents he could
imagine moulded like himself? Once he said to me in the
height of his Imperial propaganda, 'Tell those young men in
Ireland that this great thing must go on. They say Ireland is
not fit for self-government, but that is nonsense. It is as fit as
any other European country, but we cannot grant it.' And

then he spoke of his desire to found and edit a Dublin newspaper. It would have expounded the Gaelic propaganda then
beginning, though Dr. Hyde had, as yet, no League, our old
stories, our modern literature — everything that did not demand any shred or patch of government. He dreamed of a
tyranny, but it was that of Cosimo de' Medici.

VII

We gathered on Sunday evenings in two rooms, with fold-
ing doors between, and hung, I think, with photographs from
Dutch masters, and in one room there was always, I think, a
table with cold meat. I can recall but one elderly man — Dunn
his name was — rather silent and full of good sense, an old
friend of Henley's. We were young men, none as yet established in his own or in the world's opinion, and Henley was
our leader and our confidant. One evening, I found him alone
amused and exasperated. 'Young A——,' he cried, 'has just
been round to ask my advice. Would I think it a wise thing if
he bolted with Mrs. B——? "Have you quite determined to
do it?" I asked him. "Quite." "Well," I said, "in that case I
refuse to give you any advice."' Mrs. B—— was a beautiful
talented woman, who, as the Welsh Triad said of Guinevere,
'was much given to being carried off'. I think we listened to
him, and often obeyed him, partly because he was quite plainly
not upon the side of our parents. We might have a different
ground of quarrel, but the result seemed more important than
the ground, and his confident manner and speech made us believe, perhaps for the first time, in victory. And besides, if he
did denounce, and in my case he certainly did, what we held
in secret reverence, he never failed to associate it with things or
persons that did not move us to reverence. Once I found him
just returned from some art congress in Liverpool or in Man-

chester. 'The Salvation Armyism of art', he called it, and gave a grotesque description of some city councillor he had found admiring Turner. He, who hated all that Ruskin praised, thereupon had derided Turner, and finding the city councillor the next day on the other side of the gallery, admiring some Pre-Raphaelite there, derided that Pre-Raphaelite. The third day Henley discovered the poor man on a chair in the middle of the room staring disconsolately upon the floor. He terrified us also and certainly I did not dare, and I think none of us dared, to speak our admiration for book or picture he condemned, but he made us feel always our importance, and no man among us could do good work, or show the promise of it, and lack his praise. I can remember meeting of a Sunday night Charles Whibley, Kenneth Grahame, author of *The Golden Age*, Barry Pain, now a well-known novelist, R. A. M. Stevenson, art critic and a famous talker, George Wyndham, later on a Cabinet Minister and Irish Chief Secretary, and now or later Oscar Wilde, who was some ten years older than the rest of us. But faces and names are vague to me, and while faces that I met but once may rise clearly before me, a face met on many a Sunday has perhaps vanished. Kipling came sometimes, I think, but I never met him; and Stepniak, the Nihilist, whom I knew well elsewhere but not there, said, 'I cannot go more than once a year, it is too exhausting.' Henley got the best out of us all, because he had made us accept him as our judge and we knew that his judgment could neither sleep, nor be softened, nor changed, nor turned aside. When I think of him, the antithesis that is the foundation of human nature being ever in my sight, I see his crippled legs as though he were some Vulcan perpetually forging swords for other men to use; and certainly I always thought of C——, a fine classical scholar, a pale and seemingly gentle man, as our chief swordsman and bravo. When Henley founded his weekly newspaper, first the *Scots*, afterwards the *National Observer*, this young man wrote articles and reviews notorious for savage wit; and years afterwards when the *National Observer* was dead, Henley dying, and our cavern of outlaws empty, I met him in Paris very sad and, I think, very poor. 'Nobody will employ me now,' he said. 'Your master is gone,' I answered, 'and you are like the spear in an old Irish story that had to be kept dipped in poppy-juice that it might not go about killing people on its own account.' I wrote my first good lyrics and tolerable essays for the *National Observer*, and as I always signed my work could go my own road in some measure. Henley often revised my lyrics, crossing out a line or a stanza and writing in one of his own, and I was comforted by my belief that he also rewrote Kipling, then in the first flood of popularity. At first, indeed, I was ashamed of being rewritten and thought that others were not, and only began investigation when the editorial characteristics — epigrams, archaisms, and all — appeared in the article upon Parish fashions and in that upon opium by an Egyptian Pasha. I was not compelled to full conformity, for verse is plainly stubborn; and in prose, that I might avoid unacceptable opinions, I wrote nothing but ghost or faery stories, picked up from my mother or some pilot at Rosses Point, and Henley saw that I must needs mix a palette fitted to my subject-matter. But if he had changed every 'has' into 'hath' I would have let him, for had not we sunned ourselves in his generosity? 'My young men outdo me and they write better than I,' he wrote in some letter praising Charles Whibley's work, and to another friend with a copy of my *Man Who Dreamed of Faeryland*: 'See what a fine thing has been written by one of my lads.'

*　　　*　　　*

X

I saw a good deal of Wilde at that time — was it 1887 or 1888? — I have no way of fixing the date except that I had published my first book, *The Wanderings of Oisin*, and that Wilde had not yet published his *Decay of Lying*. He had, before our first meeting, reviewed my book and despite its vagueness of intention, and the inexactness of its speech, praised without qualification; and what was worth more than any review, he had talked about it; and now he asked me to eat my Christmas dinner with him, believing, I imagine, that I was alone in London. He had just renounced his velveteen, and even those cuffs turned backward over the sleeves, and had begun to dress very carefully in the fashion of the moment. He lived in a little house at Chelsea that the architect Godwin had decorated with an elegance that owed something to Whistler. There was nothing mediaeval nor Pre-Raphaelite, no cupboard door with figures upon flat gold, no peacock-blue, no dark background. I remember vaguely a white drawing-room with Whistler etchings, 'let into' white panels, and a dining-room all white, chairs, walls, mantelpiece, carpet, except for a diamond-shaped piece of red cloth in the middle of the table under a terra-cotta statuette, and, I think, a red-shaded lamp hanging from the ceiling to a little above the statuette. It was perhaps too perfect in its unity, his past of a few years before had gone too completely, and I remember thinking that the perfect harmony of his life there, with his beautiful wife and his two young children, suggested some deliberate artistic composition.

He commended and dispraised himself during dinner by attributing characteristics like his own to his country: 'We Irish are too poetical to be poets; we are a nation of brilliant failures, but we are the greatest talkers since the Greeks.' When dinner was over he read to me from the proofs of *The Decay of Lying* and when he came to the sentence, 'Schopenhauer has analysed the pessimism that characterises modern thought, but Hamlet invented it. The world has become sad because a puppet was once melancholy,' I said, 'Why do you change "sad" to "melancholy"?' He replied that he wanted a full sound at the close of his sentence, and I thought it no excuse and an example of the vague impressiveness that spoilt his writing for me. Only when he spoke, or when his writing was the mirror of his speech, or in some simple faery-tale, had he words exact enough to hold a subtle ear. He alarmed me, though not as Henley did, for I never left his house thinking myself fool or dunce. He flattered the intellect of every man he liked; he made me tell him long Irish stories and compared my art of story-telling to Homer's; and once when he had described himself as writing in the census paper 'age 19, profession genius, infirmity talent' the other guest, a young journalist fresh from Oxford or Cambridge, said, 'What should I have written?' and was told that it should have been 'profession talent, infirmity genius'. When, however, I called, wearing shoes a little too yellow — unblackened leather had just become fashionable — I realized their extravagance when I saw his eyes fixed upon them; and another day Wilde asked me to tell his little boy a faery-story, and I had but got as far as 'Once upon a time there was a giant' when the little boy screamed and ran out of the room. Wilde looked grave and I was plunged into the shame of clumsiness that afflicts the young. And when I asked for some literary gossip for some provincial newspaper, that paid me a few shillings a month, I was told that writing literary gossip was no job for a gentleman.

Though to be compared to Homer passed the time pleasantly, I had not been greatly perturbed had he stopped me with 'Is it a long story?' as Henley would certainly have done. I was abashed before him as wit and man of the world alone. I remember that he deprecated the very general belief in his success or his efficiency, and, I think, with sincerity. One form of success had gone: he was no more the lion of the season and he had not discovered his gift for writing comedy, yet I think I knew him at the happiest moment of his life. No scandal had touched his name, his fame as a talker was growing among his equals, and he seemed to live in the enjoyment of his own spontaneity. One day he began, 'I have been inventing a Christian heresy', and he told a detailed story, in the style of some early Father, of how Christ recovered after the Cruci- fixion, and escaping from the tomb, lived on for many years, the one man upon earth who knew the falsehood of Christian- ity. Once Saint Paul visited his town and he alone in the car- penters' quarter did not go to hear him preach. Henceforth the other carpenters noticed that, for some unknown reason, he kept his hands covered. A few days afterwards I found Wilde with smock frocks in various colours spread out upon the floor in front of him, while a missionary explained that he did not object to the heathen going naked upon week-days, but insisted upon clothes in church. He had brought the smock frocks in a cab that the only art-critic whose fame had reached Central Africa might select a colour; so Wilde sat there weigh- ing all with a conscious ecclesiastic solemnity.

*   *   *

XII

I cannot remember who first brought me to the old stable beside Kelmscott House, William Morris's house at Hammer- smith, and to the debates held there upon Sunday evenings by the Socialist League. I was soon of the little group who had

supper with Morris afterwards. I met at these suppers very
constantly Walter Crane, Emery Walker, in association with
Cobden-Sanderson, the printer of many fine books, and less
constantly Bernard Shaw and Cockerell, now of the Fitzwilliam Museum, Cambridge, and perhaps but once or twice
Hyndman the Socialist and the Anarchist Prince Kropotkin.
There, too, one always met certain more or less educated
workmen, rough of speech and manner, with a conviction to
meet every turn. I was told by one of them, on a night when
I had done perhaps more than my share of the talking, that I
had talked more nonsense in one evening than he had heard in
the whole course of his past life. I had merely preferred Parnell, then at the height of his career, to Michael Davitt, who
had wrecked his Irish influence by international politics. We
sat round a long unpolished and unpainted trestle table of new
wood in a room where hung Rossetti's *Pomegranate*, a portrait
of Mrs. Morris, and where one wall and part of the ceiling
were covered by a great Persian carpet. Morris had said somewhere or other that carpets were meant for people who took
their shoes off when they entered a house and were most in
place upon a tent floor. I was a little disappointed in the house,
for Morris was an ageing man content at last to gather beautiful things rather than to arrange a beautiful house. I saw the
drawing-room once or twice, and there alone all my sense of
decoration, founded upon the background of Rossetti's pictures, was satisfied by a big cupboard painted with a scene
from Chaucer by Burne-Jones; but even there were objects,
perhaps a chair or a little table, that seemed accidental, bought
hurriedly perhaps and with little thought, to make wife or
daughter comfortable. I had read as a boy, in books belonging
to my father, the third volume of *The Earthly Paradise*, and
The Defence of Guenevere, which pleased me less, but had not
opened either for a long time. *The Man Who Never Laughed*

Again had seemed the most wonderful of tales till my father had accused me of preferring Morris to Keats, got angry about it, and put me altogether out of countenance. He had spoiled my pleasure, for now I questioned while I read and at last ceased to read; nor had Morris written as yet those prose romances that became after his death so great a joy that they were the only books I was ever to read slowly that I might not come too quickly to the end. It was now Morris himself that stirred my interest, and I took to him first because of some little tricks of speech and body that reminded me of my old grandfather in Sligo, but soon discovered his spontaneity and joy and made him my chief of men. To-day I do not set his poetry very high, but for an odd altogether wonderful line, or thought; and yet, if some angel offered me the choice, I would choose to live his life, poetry and all, rather than my own or any other man's. A reproduction of his portrait by Watts hangs over my mantelpiece with Henley's, and those of other friends. Its grave wide-open eyes, like the eyes of some dreaming beast, remind me of the open eyes of Titian's *Ariosto*, while the broad vigorous body suggests a mind that has no need of the intellect to remain sane, though it give itself to every fantasy: the dreamer of the Middle Ages. It is 'the fool of Faery . . . wide and wild as a hill', the resolute European image that yet half remembers Buddha's motionless meditation, and has no trait in common with the wavering, lean image of hungry speculation, that cannot but because of certain famous Hamlets of our stage fill the mind's eye. Shakespeare himself foreshadowed a symbolic change, that is, a change in the whole temperament of the world, for though he called his Hamlet 'fat' and even 'scant of breath', he thrust between his fingers agile rapier and dagger.

The dream world of Morris was as much the antithesis of daily life as with other men of genius, but he was never conscious of the antithesis and so knew nothing of intellectual suffering. His intellect, unexhausted by speculation or casuistry, was wholly at the service of hand and eye, and whatever he pleased he did with an unheard-of ease and simplicity, and if style and vocabulary were at times monotonous, he could not have made them otherwise without ceasing to be himself. Instead of the language of Chaucer and Shakespeare, its warp fresh from field and market — if the woof were learned — his age offered him a speech, exhausted from abstraction, that only returned to its full vitality when written learnedly and slowly.

The roots of his antithetical dream were visible enough: a never idle man of great physical strength and extremely irascible — did he not fling a badly baked plum-pudding through the window upon Christmas Day? — a man more joyous than any intellectual man of our world, he called himself 'the idle singer of an empty day', created new forms of melancholy, and faint persons, like the knights and ladies of Burne-Jones, who are never, no, not once in forty volumes, put out of temper. A blunderer who had said to the only unconverted man at a Socialist picnic in Dublin, to prove that equality came easy, 'I was brought up a gentleman and now as you can see associate with all sorts,' and left wounds thereby that rankled after twenty years, a man of whom I have heard it said, 'He is always afraid that he is doing something wrong and generally is,' he wrote long stories with apparently no other object than that his persons might show to one another, through situations of poignant difficulty, the most exquisite tact.

He did not project, like Henley or like Wilde, an image of himself, because having all his imagination set upon making and doing he had little self-knowledge. He imagined instead new conditions of making and doing; and in the teeth of those scientific generalizations that cowed my boyhood, I can see some like imagining in every great change, and believe that the first flying-fish first leaped, not because it sought 'adaptation' to the air, but out of horror of the sea.

*   *   *

XV

I had various women friends on whom I would call towards five o'clock mainly to discuss my thoughts that I could not bring to a man without meeting some competing thought, but partly because their tea and toast saved my pennies for the 'bus-ride home; but with women, apart from their intimate exchanges of thought, I was timid and abashed. I was sitting on a seat in front of the British Museum feeding pigeons when a couple of girls sat near and began enticing my pigeons away, laughing and whispering to one another, and I looked straight in front of me, very indignant, and presently went into the Museum without turning my head towards them. Since then I have often wondered if they were pretty or merely very young. Sometimes I told myself very adventurous love-stories with myself for hero, and at other times I planned out a life of lonely austerity, and at other times mixed the ideals and planned a life of lonely austerity mitigated by periodical lapses. I had still the ambition, formed in Sligo in my teens, of living in imitation of Thoreau on Innisfree, a little island in Lough Gill, and when walking through Fleet Street very homesick I heard a little tinkle of water and saw a fountain in a shop-window which balanced a little ball upon its jet, and began to remember lake water. From the sudden remembrance came my poem *Innisfree*, my first lyric with anything in its rhythm of my own music. I had begun to loosen rhythm as an escape from rhetoric and from that emotion of the crowd that rhetoric brings, but I only understood vaguely and occasionally that I must for my special purpose use nothing but the common syntax. A couple of years later I would not have written that first line with its conventional archaism — 'Arise and go' — nor the inversion in the last stanza. Passing another day by the new Law Courts, a building that I admired because it was Gothic — 'It is not very good,' Morris had said, 'but it is better than anything else they have got and so they hate it' — I grew suddenly oppressed by the great weight of stone, and thought, 'There are miles and miles of stone and brick all round me,' and presently added, 'If John the Baptist or his like were to come again and had his mind set upon it, he could make all these people go out into some wilderness leaving their buildings empty,' and that thought, which does not seem very valuable now, so enlightened the day that it is still vivid in the memory. I spent a few days at Oxford copying out a seventeenth-century translation of Poggio's *Liber Facetiarum* or the *Hypnerotomachia* of Poliphili for a publisher — I forget which, for I copied both — and returned very pale to my troubled family. I had lived upon bread and tea because I thought that if antiquity found locust and wild honey nutritive, my soul was strong enough to need no better. I was always planning some great gesture, putting the whole world into one scale of the balance and my soul into the other and imagining that the whole world somehow kicked the beam. More than thirty years have passed and I have seen no forcible young man of letters brave the metropolis without some like stimulant; and all after two or three, or twelve or fifteen years, according to obstinacy, have understood that we achieve, if we do achieve, in little sedentary stitches as though we were making lace. I had one unmeasured advantage from my stimulant: I could ink my socks, that they might not show through my shoes, with a most haughty mind, imagining myself, and my torn

tackle, somewhere else, in some far place 'under the canopy
... i' the city of kites and crows'.

In London I saw nothing good and constantly remembered
that Ruskin had said to some friend of my father's, 'As I go to
work at the British Museum I see the faces of the people become daily more corrupt.' I convinced myself for a time that
on the same journey I saw but what he saw. Certain old
women's faces filled me with horror, faces that are no longer
there, or if they are pass before me unnoticed: the fat
blotched faces, rising above double chins, of women who
have drunk too much beer and eaten much meat. In Dublin I
had often seen old women walking with erect heads and
gaunt bodies, talking to themselves with loud voices, mad
with drink and poverty, but they were different, they belonged to romance. Da Vinci had drawn women who looked
so, and so carried their bodies.

*   *   *

XVII

I had already met most of the poets of my generation. I had
said, soon after the publication of *The Wanderings of Oisin*, to
the editor of a series of shilling reprints, who had set me to
compile tales of the Irish faeries, 'I am growing jealous of
other poets and we will all grow jealous of each other unless
we know each other and so feel a share in each other's
triumph.' He was a Welshman, lately a mining engineer,
Ernest Rhys, a writer of Welsh translations and original poems,
that have often moved me greatly though I can think of no
one else who has read them. He was perhaps a dozen years
older than myself and through his work as editor knew everybody who would compile a book for seven or eight pounds.
Between us we founded The Rhymers' Club, which for some

years was to meet every night in an upper room with a sanded
floor in an ancient eating-house in Fleet Street called the
Cheshire Cheese. Lionel Johnson, Ernest Dowson, Victor
Plarr, Ernest Radford, John Davidson, Richard Le Gallienne,
T. W. Rolleston, Selwyn Image, Edwin Ellis, and John Todhunter came constantly for a time, Arthur Symons and Herbert Horne, less constantly, while William Watson joined but
never came and Francis Thompson came once but never
joined; and sometimes if we met in a private house, which we
did occasionally, Oscar Wilde came. It had been useless to
invite him to the Cheshire Cheese, for he hated Bohemia.
'Olive Schreiner,' he said once to me, 'is staying in the East
End because that is the only place where people do not wear
masks upon their faces, but I have told her that I live in the
West End because nothing in life interests me but the mask.'

We read our poems to one another and talked criticism and
drank a little wine. I sometimes say when I speak of the club,
'We had such-and-such ideas, such-and-such a quarrel with
the great Victorians, we set before us such-and-such aims,' as
though we had many philosophical ideas. I say this because I
am ashamed to admit that I had these ideas and that whenever
I began to talk of them a gloomy silence fell upon the room.
A young Irish poet, who wrote excellently but had the worst
manners, was to say a few years later, 'You do not talk like a
poet, you talk like a man of letters,' and if all the Rhymers had
not been polite, if most of them had not been to Oxford or
Cambridge, the greater number would have said the same
thing. I was full of thought, often very abstract thought, longing all the while to be full of images, because I had gone to the
art schools instead of a university. Yet even if I had gone to a
university, and learned all the classical foundations of English
literature and English culture, all that great erudition which
once accepted frees the mind from restlessness, I should have

had to give up my Irish subject-matter, or attempt to found a new tradition. Lacking sufficient recognized precedent, I must needs find out some reason for all I did. I knew almost from the start that to overflow with reasons was to be not quite well-born; and when I could I hid them, as men hide a disagreeable ancestry; and that there was no help for it seeing that my country was not born at all. I was of those doomed to imperfect achievement, and under a curse, as it were, like some race of birds compelled to spend the time needed for the making of the nest in argument as to the convenience of moss and twig and lichen. Le Gallienne and Davidson, and even Symons, were provincial at their setting out, but their provincialism was curable, mine incurable; while the one conviction shared by all the younger men, but principally by Johnson and Horne, who imposed their personalities upon us, was an opposition to all ideas, all generalizations that can be explained and debated. Symons fresh from Paris would sometimes say, 'We are concerned with nothing but impressions,' but that itself was a generalization and met but stony silence. Conversation constantly dwindled into 'Do you like So-and-so's last book?' 'No, I prefer the book before it,' and I think that but for its Irish members, who said whatever came into their heads, the club would not have survived its first difficult months. I saw — now ashamed that I saw 'like a man of letters', now exasperated at the indifference of these poets to the fashion of their own river-bed — that Swinburne in one way, Browning in another, and Tennyson in a third, had filled their work with what I called 'impurities', curiosities about politics, about science, about history, about religion; and that we must create once more the pure work.

Our clothes were for the most part unadventurous like our conversation, though I indeed wore a brown velveteen coat, a loose tie, and a very old Inverness cape, discarded by my father twenty years before and preserved by my Sligo-born mother whose actions were unreasoning and habitual like the seasons. But no other member of the club, except Le Gallienne, who wore a loose tie, and Symons, who had an Inverness cape that was quite new and almost fashionable, would have shown himself for the world in any costume but 'that of an English gentleman'. 'One should be quite unnoticeable,' Johnson explained to me. Those who conformed most carefully to the fashion in their clothes generally departed farthest from it in their handwriting, which was small, neat, and studied, one poet — which, I forget — having founded his upon the handwriting of George Herbert. Dowson and Symons I was to know better in later years when Symons became a very dear friend, and I never got behind John Davidson's Scottish roughness and exasperation, though I saw much of him, but from the first I devoted myself to Lionel Johnson. He and Horne and Image and one or two others shared a man-servant and an old house in Charlotte Street, Fitzroy Square, typical figures of transition, doing as an achievement of learning and of exquisite taste what their predecessors did in careless abundance. All were Pre-Raphaelite, and sometimes one might meet in the rooms of one or other a ragged figure, as of some fallen dynasty, Simeon Solomon, the Pre-Raphaelite painter, once the friend of Rossetti and of Swinburne, but fresh now from some low public-house. Condemned to a long term of imprisonment for a criminal offence, he had sunk into drunkenness and misery. Introduced one night, however, to some man who mistook him, in the dim candlelight, for another Solomon, a successful academic painter and R.A., he started to his feet in a rage with, 'Sir, do you dare to mistake me for that mountebank?' Though not one had hearkened to the feeblest caw, or been spattered by the smallest dropping from any Huxley, Tyndall, Carolus Duran, Bastien-Lepage bundle of old twigs I began by suspecting them of lukewarmness, and even backsliding, and I owe it to that suspicion that I never became intimate with Horne, who lived to become the greatest English authority upon Italian life in the fifteenth century and to write the one standard work on Botticelli. Connoisseur in several arts, he had designed a little church in the manner of Inigo Jones for a burial-ground near the Marble Arch. Though I now think his little church a masterpiece, its style was more than a century too late to hit my fancy, at two- or three-and-twenty; and I accused him of leaning towards that eighteenth century —

> That taught a school
> Of dolts to smooth, inlay, and clip, and fit
> Till, like the certain wands of Jacob's wit,
> Their verses tallied.

Another fanaticism delayed my friendship with two men, who are now my friends and in certain matters my chief instructors. Somebody, probably Lionel Johnson, brought me to the studio of Charles Ricketts and Charles Shannon, certainly heirs of the great generation, and the first thing I saw was a Shannon picture of a lady and child, arrayed in lace, silk and satin, suggesting that hated century. My eyes were full of some more mythological mother and child and I would have none of it and I told Shannon that he had not painted a mother and child, but elegant people expecting visitors, and I thought that a great reproach. Somebody writing in the *Germ* had said that a picture of a pheasant and an apple was merely a picture of something to eat, and I was so angry with the indifference to subject, which was the commonplace of all art criticism since Bastien-Lepage, that I could at times see nothing else but subject. I thought that, though it might not matter to the man himself whether he loved a white woman or a black, a female pickpocket or a regular communicant of the Church of England, if only he loved strongly, it certainly did matter to his relations and even under some circumstances to his whole neighbourhood. Sometimes indeed, like some father in Molière, I ignored the lover's feelings altogether and even refused to admit that a trace of the devil, perhaps a trace of colour, may lend piquancy, especially if the connection be not permanent.

Among these men, of whom so many of the greatest talents were to live such passionate lives and die such tragic deaths, one serene man, T. W. Rolleston, seemed always out of place; it was I who brought him there, intending to set him to some work in Ireland later on. I have known young Dublin working-men slip out of their workshop to see the second Thomas Davis passing by, and can even remember a conspiracy, by some three or four, to make him 'the leader of the Irish race at home and abroad,' and all because he had regular features; and when all is said Alexander the Great and Alcibiades were personable men, and the Founder of the Christian religion was the only man who was neither a little too tall nor a little too short, but exactly six feet high. We in Ireland thought as do the plays and ballads, not understanding that, from the first moment wherein Nature foresaw the birth of Bastien-Lepage, she has only granted great creative power to men whose faces are contorted with extravagance or curiosity, or dulled with some protecting stupidity.

I had now met all those who were to make the nineties of the last century tragic in the history of literature, but as yet we were all seemingly equal, whether in talent or in luck, and scarce even personalities to one another. I remember saying one night at the Cheshire Cheese, when more poets than usual had come, 'None of us can say who will succeed, or even who

has or has not talent. The only thing certain about us is that we
are too many.'

XVIII

I have described what image — always opposite to the
natural self or the natural world — Wilde, Henley, Morris
copied or tried to copy, but I have not said if I found an image
for myself. I know very little about myself and much less of
that anti-self: probably the woman who cooks my dinner or
the woman who sweeps out my study knows more than I. It
is perhaps because Nature made me a gregarious man, going
hither and thither looking for conversation, and ready to deny
from fear or favour his dearest conviction, that I love proud
and lonely things. When I was a child and went daily to the
sexton's daughter for writing lessons, I found one poem in her
School Reader that delighted me beyond all others: a fragment of some metrical translation from Aristophanes wherein
the birds sing scorn upon mankind. In later years my mind
gave itself to gregarious Shelley's dream of a young man, his
hair blanched with sorrow, studying philosophy in some
lonely tower, or of his old man, master of all human knowledge, hidden from human sight in some shell-strewn cavern
on the Mediterranean shore. One passage above all ran perpetually in my ears: —

> Some feign that he is Enoch: others dream
> He was pre-Adamite, and has survived
> Cycles of generation and of ruin.
> The sage, in truth, by dreadful abstinence,
> And conquering penance of the mutinous flesh,
> Deep contemplation and unwearied study,
> In years outstretched beyond the date of man,

May have attained to sovereignty and science
Over those strong and secret things and thoughts
Which others fear and know not.

MAHMUD

                              I would talk
With this old Jew.

HASSAN

                    Thy will is even now
Made known to him where he dwells in a sea-cavern
'Mid the Demonesi, less accessible
Than thou or God! He who would question him
Must sail alone at sunset, where the stream
Of Ocean sleeps around those foamless isles,
When the young moon is westering as now,
And evening airs wander upon the wave;
And, when the pines of that bee-pasturing isle,
Green Erebinthus, quench the fiery shadow
Of his gilt prow within the sapphire water,
Then must the lonely helmsman cry aloud
'Ahasuerus!' and the caverns round
Will answer 'Ahasuerus!' If his prayer
Be granted, a faint meteor will arise,
Lighting him over Marmora; and a wind
Will rush out of the sighing pine-forest,
And with the wind a storm of harmony
Unutterably sweet, and pilot him
Through the soft twilight to the Bosphorus:
Thence, at the hour and place and circumstance
Fit for the matter of their conference,
The Jew appears. Few dare, and few who dare
Win the desired communion.

Already in Dublin, I had been attracted to the Theosophists because they had affirmed the real existence of the Jew, or of his like, and, apart from whatever might have been imagined by Huxley, Tyndall, Carolus Duran and Bastien-Lepage, I saw nothing against his reality. Presently having heard that Madame Blavatsky had arrived from France, or from India, I thought it time to look the matter up. Certainly if wisdom existed anywhere in the world it must be in some lonely mind admitting no duty to us, communing with God only, conceding nothing from fear or favour. Have not all peoples, while bound together in a single mind and taste, believed that such men existed and paid them that honour, or paid it to their mere shadow, which they have refused to philanthropists and to men of learning?

*   *   *

XX

At the British Museum Reading-Room I often saw a man of thirty-six, or thirty-seven, in a brown velveteen coat, with a gaunt resolute face, and an athletic body, who seemed, before I heard his name, or knew the nature of his studies, a figure of romance. Presently I was introduced, where or by what man or woman I do not remember. He was called Liddell Mathers, but would soon, under the touch of 'The Celtic Movement', become MacGregor Mathers, and then plain MacGregor. He was the author of *The Kabbala Unveiled*, and his studies were two only — magic and the theory of war, for he believed himself a born commander and all but equal in wisdom and in power to that old Jew. He had copied many manuscripts on magic ceremonial and doctrine in the British Museum, and was to copy many more in Continental libraries, and it was through him mainly that I began certain studies and

experiences, that were to convince me that images well up before the mind's eye from a deeper source than conscious or
subconscious memory. I believe that his mind in those early
days did not belie his face and body — though in later years it
became unhinged, as Don Quixote's was unhinged — for he
kept a proud head amid great poverty. One that boxed with
him nightly has told me that for many weeks he could knock
him down, though Mathers was the stronger man, and only
knew long after that during those weeks Mathers starved. He
had spoken to me, I think at our first introduction, of a society
which sometimes called itself — it had a different name among
its members — 'The Hermetic Students', and in May or June
1887 I was initiated into that society in a Charlotte Street
studio, and being at a most receptive age, shaped and isolated.
Mathers was its governing mind, a born teacher and organizer.
One of those who incite — less by spoken word than by what
they are — imaginative action. We paid some small annual
subscription, a few shillings for rent and stationery, but no
poor man paid even that and all found him generous of time
and thought. With Mathers I met an old white-haired Oxford-
shire clergyman, the most panic-stricken person I have ever
known, though Mathers' introduction had been, 'He unites us
to the great adepts of antiquity.' This old man took me aside
that he might say, 'I hope you never invoke spirits — that is a
very dangerous thing to do. I am told that even the planetary
spirits turn upon us in the end.' I said, 'Have you ever seen an
apparition?' 'O yes, once,' he said. 'I have my alchemical
laboratory in a cellar under my house where the Bishop cannot
see it. One day I was walking up and down there when I heard
another footstep walking up and down beside me. I turned
and saw a girl I had been in love with when I was a young
man, but she died long ago. She wanted me to kiss her. O no,
I would not do that.' 'Why not?' I said. 'O, she might have

got power over me.' 'Has your alchemical research had any success?' I said. 'Yes, I once made the elixir of life. A French alchemist said it had the right smell and the right colour' (the alchemist may have been Eliphas Lévi, who visited England in the 'sixties, and would have said anything), 'but the first effect of the elixir is that your nails fall out and your hair falls off. I was afraid that I might have made a mistake and that nothing else might happen, so I put it away on a shelf. I meant to drink it when I was an old man, but when I got it down the other day it had all dried up.'

Soon after my first meeting with Mathers he emerged into brief prosperity, becoming for two or three years Curator of a private museum at Forest Hill, and marrying a young and beautiful wife, the sister of the philosopher, Henri Bergson. His house at Forest Hill was soon a romantic place to a little group, Florence Farr — she too had been initiated — myself, and some dozen fellow-students. I think that it was she, her curiosity being insatiable, who first brought a tale of marvel and that she brought it in mockery and in wonder. Mathers had taken her for a walk through a field of sheep and had said, 'Look at the sheep. I am going to imagine myself a ram,' and at once all the sheep ran after him; another day he had tried to quell a thunderstorm by making symbols in the air with a Masonic sword, but the storm had not been quelled; and then came the crowning wonder. He had given her a piece of cardboard on which was a coloured geometrical symbol and had told her to hold it to her forehead and she had found herself walking upon a cliff above the sea, seagulls shrieking overhead. I did not think the ram story impossible, and even tried half a dozen times to excite a cat by imagining a mouse in front of its nose, but still some chance movement of the flock might have deceived her. But what could have deceived her in that final marvel? Then another brought a like report, and presently my own turn came. He gave me a cardboard symbol and I closed my eyes. Sight came slowly, there was not that sudden miracle as if the darkness had been cut with a knife, for that miracle is mostly a woman's privilege, but there rose before me mental images that I could not control: a desert and a black Titan raising himself up by his two hands from the middle of a heap of ancient ruins. Mathers explained that I had seen a being of the order of Salamanders because he had shown me their symbol, but it was not necessary even to show the symbol, it would have been sufficient that he imagined it. I had already written in my diary, under some date in 1887, that Madame Blavatsky's 'Masters' were 'trance personalities', and I must have meant such beings as my black Titan, only more lasting and more powerful. I had found when a boy in Dublin on a table in the Royal Irish Academy a pamphlet on Japanese art and read there of an animal painter so remarkable that horses he had painted upon a temple wall had slipped down after dark and trampled the neighbours' fields of rice. Somebody had come into the temple in the early morning, had been startled by a shower of water-drops, had looked up and seen painted horses still wet from the dew-covered fields, but now 'trembling into stillness'.

I had soon mastered Mathers' symbolic system, and discovered that for a considerable minority — whom I could select by certain unanalysable characteristics — the visible world would completely vanish, and that world summoned by the symbol take its place. One day when alone in a third-class carriage, in the very middle of the railway bridge that crosses the Thames near Victoria, I smelt incense. I was on my way to Forest Hill; might it not come from some spirit Mathers had called up? I had wondered when I smelt it at Madame Blavatsky's if there might be some contrivance, some secret censer, but that explanation was no longer possible. I believed that Salamander of his but an image, and presently I found analogies between smell and image. That smell must be thought-created, but what certainty had I that what had taken me by surprise could be from my own thought, and if a thought could affect the sense of smell, why not the sense of touch? Then I discovered among that group of students that surrounded Mathers a man who had fought a cat in his dreams and awaked to find his breast covered with scratches. Was there an impassable barrier between those scratches and the trampled fields of rice? It would seem so, and yet all was uncertainty. What fixed law would our experiments leave to our imagination?

*　　*　　*

XXI

I generalized a great deal and was ashamed of it. I thought it was my business in life to be an artist and a poet, and that there could be no business comparable to that. I refused to read books and even to meet people who excited me to generalization, all to no purpose. I said my prayers much as in childhood, though without the old regularity of hour and place, and I began to pray that my imagination might somehow be rescued from abstraction and become as preoccupied with life as had been the imagination of Chaucer. For ten or twelve years more I suffered continual remorse, and only became content when my abstractions had composed themselves into picture and dramatization. My very remorse helped to spoil my early poetry, giving it an element of sentimentality through my refusal to permit it any share of an intellect which I considered impure. Even in practical life I only very gradually began to use generalizations, that have since become the foundation of all I have done, or shall do, in Ireland. For all I know all men may have been so timid, for I am persuaded that our intellects at twenty contain all the truths we shall ever find, but as yet we do not know truths that belong to us from opinions caught up in casual irritation or momentary fantasy. As life goes on we discover that certain thoughts sustain us in defeat, or give us victory, whether over ourselves or others, and it is these thoughts, tested by passion, that we call convictions. Among subjective men (in all those, that is, who must spin a web out of their own bowels) the victory is an intellectual daily re-creation of all that exterior fate snatches away, and so that fate's antithesis; while what I have called 'the Mask' is an emotional antithesis to all that comes out of their internal nature. We begin to live when we have conceived life as tragedy.

[1921]

*   *   *

IRELAND AFTER PARNELL

*　　*　　*

At the top of the house, and at the time I remember best in the same room with the young Scotsman, lived Mr. George Russell (A.E.), and the house and the society were divided into his adherents and those of the engineer; and I heard of some quarrelling between the factions. The rivalry was subconscious. Neither had willingly opposed the other in any matter of importance. The engineer had all the financial responsibility, and George Russell was, in the eyes of the community, saint and genius. Had either seen that the question at issue was the leadership of mystical thought in Dublin, he would, I think, have given way, but the dispute seemed trivial. At the weekly meetings, anything might be discussed; no chairman called a speaker to order; an atheistic workman could denounce religion, or a pious Catholic confound theosophy with atheism; and the engineer, precise and practical, disapproved. He had an object. He wished to make converts for a definite form of belief, and here an enemy, if a better speaker, might make all the converts. He wished to confine discussion to members of the society, and had proposed in committee, I was told, a resolution on the subject; while Russell, who had refused to join my National Literary Society, because the party of Harp and Pepperpot had set limits to discussion, resisted, and at last defeated him. In a couple of years some new dispute arose; he resigned, and founded a society which drew doctrine and method from America or London; and Russell became, as he is to-day, the one masterful influence among young Dublin

men and women who love religious speculation, but have no
historical faith.

When Russell and I had been at the art schools six or seven
years before, he had been almost unintelligible. He had seemed
incapable of coherent thought, and perhaps was so at certain
moments. The idea came upon him, he has told me, that if he
spoke he would reveal that he had lost coherence; and for the
three days that the idea lasted he spent the hours of daylight
wandering upon the Dublin mountains, that he might escape
the necessity for speech. I used to listen to him at that time,
mostly walking through the streets at night, for the sake of
some stray sentence, beautiful and profound, amid many
words that seemed without meaning; and there were others,
too, who walked and listened, for he had become, I think, to
all his fellow-students, sacred, as the fool is sacred in the East.
We copied the model laboriously, he would draw without
research into the natural form, and call his study *Saint John in
the Wilderness*; but I can remember the almost scared look and
the half-whisper of a student, now a successful sculptor, who
said, pointing to the modelling of a shoulder, 'That is too
easy, a great deal too easy!' For with brush and pencil he was
too coherent.

We derided each other, told absurd tales to one another's
discredit, but we never derided him, or told tales to his discredit. He stood outside the sense of comedy his friend John
Eglinton has called 'the social cement' of our civilization; and
we would 'gush' when we spoke of him, as men do when
they praise something incomprehensible. But when he painted
there was no difficulty in comprehending. How could that
ease and rapidity of composition, so far beyond anything that
we could attain to, belong to a man whose words seemed
often without meaning?

A few months before I had come to Ireland he had sent me

some verses, which I had liked till Edwin Ellis had laughed me from my liking by proving that no line had a rhythm that agreed with any other, and that, the moment one thought he had settled upon some scheme of rhyme, he would break from it without reason. But now his verse was clear in thought and delicate in form. He wrote without premeditation or labour. It had, as it were, organized itself, and grown as nervous and living as if it had, as Dante said of his own work, paled his cheek. The Society he belonged to published a little magazine, and he had asked the readers to decide whether they preferred his prose or his verse, and it was because they so willed it that he wrote the little transcendental verses afterwards published in *Homeward; Songs by the Way.*

Life was not expensive in that house, where, I think, no meat was eaten; I know that out of the sixty or seventy pounds a year which he earned as accountant in a Dublin shop, he saved a considerable portion for his private charity; and it was, I think, his benevolence that gave him his lucidity of speech, and, perhaps, of writing. If he convinced himself that any particular activity was desirable in the public interest or in that of his friends, he had at once the ardour that came to another from personal ambition. He was always surrounded with a little group of infirm or unlucky persons, whom he explained to themselves and to others, turning cat to griffin, goose to swan. In later years he was to accept the position of organizer of a co-operative banking system, before he had even read a book upon economics or finance, and within a few months to give evidence before a Royal Commission upon the system, as an acknowledged expert, though he had brought to it nothing but his impassioned versatility.

At the time I write of him, he was the religious teacher, and that alone — his painting, his poetry, and his conversation all subservient to that one end. Men watched him with awe or with bewilderment; it was known that he saw visions continually, perhaps more continually than any modern man since Swedenborg; and when he painted and drew in pastel what he had seen, some accepted the record without hesitation, others, like myself, noticing the academic Graeco-Roman forms, and remembering his early admiration for the works of Gustave Moreau, divined a subjective element, but no one doubted his word. One might not think him a good observer, but no one could doubt that he reported with the most scrupulous care what he believed himself to have seen; nor did he lack occasional objective corroboration. Walking with some man in his park — his demesne, as we say in Ireland — he had seen a visionary church at a particular spot, and the man had dug and uncovered its foundations; then some woman had met him with, 'O, Mr. Russell, I am so unhappy,' and he had replied, 'You will be perfectly happy this evening at seven o'clock,' and left her to her blushes. She had an appointment with a young man for seven o'clock. I had heard of this a day or so after the event, and I asked him about it, and was told it had suddenly come into his head to use those words; but why he did not know. He and I often quarrelled, because I wanted him to examine and question his visions, and write them out as they occurred; and still more because I thought symbolic what he thought real like the men and women that had passed him on the road. Were they so much a part of his subconscious life that they would have vanished had he submitted them to question; were they like those voices that only speak, those strange sights that only show themselves for an instant, when the attention has been withdrawn; that phantasmagoria of which I had learnt something in London: and had his verse and his painting a like origin? And was that why the same hand that painted a certain dreamy, lovely sandy shore, now in the Dublin Municipal Gallery, could with great rapidity fill many canvases with poetical commonplace; and why, after writing *Homeward; Songs by the Way*, where all is skilful and much exquisite, he would never again write a perfect book? Was it precisely because in Swedenborg alone the conscious and the subconscious became one — as in that marriage of the angels, which he has described as a contact of the whole being — so completely one indeed that Coleridge thought Swedenborg both man and woman?

Russell's influence, which was already great, had more to support it than his versatility, or the mystery that surrounded him, for his sense of justice, and the daring that came from his own confidence in it, had made him the general counsellor. He would give endless time to a case of conscience, and no situation was too difficult for his clarity; and certainly some of the situations were difficult. I remember his being summoned to decide between two ladies who had quarrelled about a vacillating admirer, and called each other, to each other's faces, the worst names in our somewhat anaemic modern vocabulary; and I have heard of his success on an occasion when I think no other but Dostoievsky's idiot could have avoided offence. The Society was very young, and, as its members faced the world's moral complexities as though they were the first that ever faced them, they drew up very vigorous rules. One rule was that if any member saw a fault growing upon any other member, it was his duty to point it out to that member. A certain young man became convinced that a certain young woman had fallen in love with him; and, as an unwritten rule pronounced love and the spiritual life incompatible, that was a heavy fault. As the young man felt the delicacy of the situation, he asked for Russell's help, and side by side they braved the offender, who, I was told, received their admonishment with surprised humility, and promised amendment. His voice would often become high, and lose its self-possession during intimate conversation, and I especially could put him in a rage; but the moment the audience became too large for intimacy, or some exciting event had given formality to speech, he would be at the same moment impassioned and impersonal. He had, and has, the capacity, beyond that of any man I have known, to put with entire justice not only the thoughts, but the emotions of the most opposite parties and personalities, as it were dissolving some public or private uproar into drama by Corneille or by Racine; and men who have hated each other must sometimes have been reconciled, because each heard his enemy's argument put into better words than he himself had found for his own; and this gift was in later years to give him political influence, and win him respect from Irish Nationalist and Unionist alike. It is, perhaps, because of it — joined to a too literal acceptance of those noble images of moral tradition which are so like late Graeco-Roman statues — that he has come to see all human life as a mythological system, where, though all cats are griffins, the more dangerous griffins are only found among politicians he has not spoken to, or among authors he has but glanced at; while those men and women who bring him their confessions and listen to his advice carry but the snowiest of swan's plumage. Nor has it failed to make him, as I think, a bad literary critic; demanding plays and poems where the characters must attain a stature of seven feet, and resenting as something perverse and morbid all abatement from that measure. I sometimes wonder what he would have been had he not met in early life the poetry of Emerson and Walt Whitman, writers who have begun to seem superficial precisely because they lack the Vision of Evil; and those translations of the Upanishads, which it is so much harder to study by the sinking flame of Indian tradition than by the serviceable lamp of Emerson and Walt Whitman.

We are never satisfied with the maturity of those whom we have admired in boyhood; and because we have seen their whole circle — even the most successful life is but a segment— we remain to the end their harshest critics. One old school-fellow of mine will never believe that I have fulfilled the promise of some rough unscannable verses that I wrote before I was eighteen. Does any imaginative man find in maturity the admiration that his first half-articulate years aroused in some little circle; and is not the first success the greatest? Certainly, I demanded of Russell some impossible things, and if I had any influence upon him — and I have little doubt that I had, for we were very intimate — it may not have been a good influence, for I thought there could be no aim for poet or artist except expression of a 'Unity of Being' like that of a 'perfectly proportioned human body' — though I would not at the time have used that phrase. I remember that I was ironic and indignant when he left the art schools because his 'will was weak, and must grow weaker if he followed any emotional pursuit'; as, later, when he let the readers of a magazine decide between his prose and his verse. I now know that there are men who cannot possess 'Unity of Being', who must not seek it or express it — and who, so far from seeking an anti-self, a Mask that delineates a being in all things the opposite to their natural state, can but seek the suppression of the anti-self, till the natural state alone remains. These are those who must seek no image of desire, but await that which lies beyond their mind — unities not of the mind, but unities of Nature, unities of God — the man of science, the moralist, the humanitarian, the politician, Saint Simeon Stylites upon his pillar, Saint Anthony in his cavern, all whose preoccupation is to seem nothing; to hollow their hearts till they are void and without form, to summon a creator by revealing chaos, to become the lamp for another's wick and oil; and indeed it may be that it

has been for their guidance in a very special sense that the
'perfectly proportioned human body' suffered crucifixion.
For them Mask and Image are of necessity morbid, turning
their eyes upon themselves, as though they were of those who
can be law unto themselves, of whom Chapman has written,
'Neither is it lawful that they should stoop to any other law,'
whereas they are indeed of those who can but ask, 'Have I
behaved as well as So-and-so?' 'Am I a good man according
to the commandments?' or, 'Do I realize my own nothing-
ness before God?' 'Have my experiments and observations
excluded the personal factor with sufficient rigour?' Such men
do not assume wisdom or beauty as Shelley did, when he
masked himself as Ahasuerus, or as Prince Athanase, nor do
they pursue an Image through a world that had else seemed an
uninhabitable wilderness till, amid the privations of that pursuit, the Image is no more named Pandemos, but Urania; for
such men must cast all Masks away and fly the Image, till that
Image, transfigured because of their cruelties of self-abase-
ment, becomes itself some Image or epitome of the whole
natural or supernatural world, and itself pursues. The whole-
ness of the supernatural world can only express itself in personal form, because it has no epitome but man, nor can the
Hound of Heaven fling itself into any but an empty heart. We
may know the fugitives from other poets because, like George
Herbert, like Francis Thompson, like George Russell, their
imaginations grow more vivid in the expression of something
which they have not themselves created, some historical religion or cause. But if the fugitive should live, as I think Russell
does at times, as it is natural for a Morris or a Henley or a
Shelley to live, hunters and pursuers all, his art surrenders itself
to moral or poetical commonplace, to a repetition of thoughts
and images that have no relation to experience.

I think that Russell would not have disappointed even my

hopes had he, instead of meeting as an impressionable youth with our modern subjective romanticism, met with some form of traditional belief, which condemned all that romanticism admires and praises, indeed, all images of desire; for such condemnation would have turned his intellect towards the images of his vision. It might, doubtless, have embittered his life, for his strong intellect would have been driven out into the impersonal deeps where the man shudders; but it would have kept him a religious teacher, and set him, it may be, among the greatest of that species; politics, for a vision-seeking man, can be but half achievement, a choice of an almost easy kind of skill instead of that kind which is, of all those not impossible, the most difficult. Is it not certain that the Creator yawns in earthquake and thunder and other popular displays, but toils in rounding the delicate spiral of a shell?

XV

I heard the other day of a Dublin man recognizing in London an elderly man who had lived in that house in Ely Place in his youth, and of that elderly man, at the sudden memory, bursting into tears. Though I have no such poignant memories, for I was never of it, never anything but a dissatisfied critic, yet certain vivid moments come back to me as I write. . . . Russell has just come in from a long walk on the Two Rock mountain, very full of his conversation with an old religious beggar, who kept repeating, 'God possesses the heavens, but He covets the earth — He covets the earth.'

.   .   .   .   .

I get in talk with a young man who has taken the orthodox side in some debate. He is a stranger, but explains that he has inherited magical art from his father, and asks me to his rooms to see it in operation. He and a friend of his kill a black cock, and burn herbs in a big bowl, but nothing happens except that the friend repeats again and again, 'O, my God,' and when I ask him why he has said that, does not know that he has spoken; and I feel that there is something very evil in the room.

    .   .   .   .   .

We are sitting round the fire one night, and a member, a woman, tells a dream that she has just had. She dreamed that she saw monks digging in a garden. They dug down till they found a coffin, and when they took off the lid she saw that in the coffin lay a beautiful young man in a dress of gold brocade. The young man railed against the glory of the world, and when he had finished, the monks closed the coffin reverently, and buried it once more. They smoothed the ground, and then went on with their gardening.

    .   .   .   .   .

I have a young man with me, an official of the National Literary Society, and I leave him in the reading-room with Russell, while I go upstairs to see the young Scotsman. I return after some minutes to find that the young man has become a Theosophist, but a month later, after an interview with a friar, to whom he gives an incredible account of his new beliefs, he goes to Mass again.

[1922]

HODOS CHAMELIONTOS

I

WHEN staying with Hyde in Roscommon, I had driven over to Lough Kay, hoping to find some local memory of the old story of Tumaus Costello, which I was turning into a story now called *Proud Costello, Macdermot's Daughter, and the Bitter Tongue*. I was rowed up the lake that I might find the island where he died; I had to find it from Hyde's account in the *Love-Songs of Connacht*, for when I asked the boatman, he told the story of Hero and Leander, putting Hero's house on one island, and Leander's on another. Presently we stopped to eat our sandwiches at the 'Castle Rock', an island all castle. It was not an old castle, being but the invention of some romantic man, seventy or eighty years ago. The last man who had lived there had been Dr. Hyde's father, and he had but stayed a fortnight. The Gaelic-speaking men in the district were accustomed, instead of calling some specially useless thing a 'white elephant', to call it 'The Castle on the Rock'. The roof was, however, still sound, and the windows unbroken. The situation in the centre of the lake, that has little wood-grown islands, and is surrounded by wood-grown hills, is romantic, and at one end, and perhaps at the other too, there is a stone platform where meditative persons might pace to and fro. I planned a mystical Order which should buy or hire the castle, and keep it as a place where its members could retire for a while for contemplation, and where we might establish mysteries like those of Eleusis and Samothrace; and for ten years to come my most impassioned thought was a vain attempt to

345

find philosophy and to create ritual for that Order. I had an unshakable conviction, arising how or whence I cannot tell, that invisible gates would open as they opened for Blake, as they opened for Swedenborg, as they opened for Boehme, and that this philosophy would find its manuals of devotion in all imaginative literature, and set before Irishmen for special manual an Irish literature which, though made by many minds, would seem the work of a single mind, and turn our places of beauty or legendary association into holy symbols. I did not think this philosophy would be altogether pagan, for it was plain that its symbols must be selected from all those things that had moved men most during many, mainly Christian, centuries.

I thought that for a time I could rhyme of love, calling it *The Rose*, because of the Rose's double meaning; of a fisherman who had 'never a crack' in his heart; of an old woman complaining of the idleness of the young, or of some cheerful fiddler, all those things that 'popular poets' write of, but that I must some day — on that day when the gates began to open — become difficult or obscure. With a rhythm that still echoed Morris I prayed to the Red Rose, to Intellectual Beauty:—

> Come near, come near, come near — Ah, leave me still
> A little space for the rose-breath to fill!
> Lest I no more hear common things . . .
> But seek alone to hear the strange things said
> By God to the bright hearts of those long dead,
> And learn to chaunt a tongue men do not know.

I do not remember what I meant by 'the bright hearts', but a little later I wrote of spirits 'with mirrors in their hearts'.

My rituals were not to be made deliberately, like a poem, but all got by that method Mathers had explained to me, and with this hope I plunged without a clue into a labyrinth of images, into that labyrinth that we are warned against in those *Oracles* which antiquity has attributed to Zoroaster, but modern scholarship to some Alexandrian poet: 'Stoop not down to the darkly splendid world wherein lieth continually a faithless depth and Hades wrapped in cloud, delighting in unintelligible images.'

[1922]

*　　*　　*

THE STIRRING OF THE BONES

*   *   *

IV

*   *   *

I had in my head a project to reconcile old and new that gave Maud Gonne and myself many stirring conversations upon journeys by rail to meetings in Scotland, in Dublin, or in the Midlands. Should we not persuade the organizations in Dublin and in London, when the time drew near for the unveiling of our statue, or even perhaps for the laying of its foundation-stone, to invite the leaders of Parnellite or Anti-Parnellite, of the new group of Unionists who had almost changed sides in their indignation at the over-taxation of Ireland, to lay their policy before our Convention — could we not then propose and carry that the Convention sit permanently, or appoint some Executive Committee to direct Irish policy and report from time to time? The total withdrawal from Westminster had been proposed in the 'seventies, before the two devouring heads were of equal strength — for our Cerberus had but two — and now that the abstract head seemed the stronger, would be proposed again, but the Convention could send them thither, not as an independent power, but as its delegation, and only when and for what purpose the Convention might decide. I dreaded some wild Fenian movement, and with literature perhaps more in my mind than politics, dreamed of that Unity of Culture which might begin with some few men controlling some form of administration.

I began to talk my project over with various organizers, who often interrupted their attention, which was perhaps only politeness, with some new jibe at Mr. Dillon or Mr. Redmond. I thought I had Maud Gonne's support, but when I overheard her conversation, she commonly urged the entire withdrawal of the Irish Members, or if she did refer to my scheme, it was to suggest the sending to England of eighty ragged and drunken Dublin beggars or eighty pugilists 'to be paid by results'.

She was the first who spoke publicly or semi-publicly of the withdrawal of the Irish Members as a practical policy for our time, so far as I know, but others may have been considering it. A nation in crisis becomes almost like a single mind, or rather like those minds I have described that become channels for parallel streams of thought, each stream taking the colour of the mind it flows through. These streams are not set moving, as I think, through conversation or publication, but through 'telepathic contact' at some depth below that of normal consciousness; and it is only years afterwards, when future events have shown the theme's importance, that we discover that they are different expressions of a common theme. That self-moving, self-creating nation necessitated an Irish centre of policy, and I planned a premature impossible peace between those two devouring heads because I was sedentary and thoughtful; but Maud Gonne was not sedentary, and I noticed that before some great event she did not think but became exceedingly superstitious. Are not such as she aware, at moments of great crisis, of some power beyond their own minds; or are they like some good portrait-painter of my father's generation and only think when the model is under their eye? Once upon the eve of some demonstration, I found her with many caged larks and finches which she was about to set free for the luck's sake.

I abandoned my plans on discovering that our young men, not yet educated by Mr. Birrell's University, would certainly shout down every one they disagreed with, and that their finance was so extravagant that we must content ourselves with a foundation-stone and an iron rail to protect it, for there could never be a statue; while she carried out every plan she made.

Her power over crowds was at its height, and some portion of the power came because she could still, even when pushing an abstract principle to what seemed to me an absurdity, keep her own mind free, and so when men and women did her bidding they did it not only because she was beautiful, but because that beauty suggested joy and freedom. Besides, there was an element in her beauty that moved minds full of old Gaelic stories and poems, for she looked as though she lived in an ancient civilization where all superiorities whether of the mind or the body were a part of public ceremonial, were in some way the crowd's creation, as the entrance of the Pope into Saint Peter's is the crowd's creation. Her beauty, backed by her great stature, could instantly affect an assembly, and not, as often with our stage beauties, because obvious and florid, for it was incredibly distinguished, and if — as must be that it might seem that assembly's very self, fused, unified, and solitary — her face, like the face of some Greek statue, showed little thought, her whole body seemed a master-work of long labouring thought, as though a Scopas had measured and calculated, consorted with Egyptian sages, and mathematicians out of Babylon, that he might out-face even Artemisia's sepulchral image with a living norm.

But in that ancient civilization abstract thoughts scarce existed, while she but rose partially and for a moment out of raging abstraction; and for that reason, as I have known another woman do, she hated her own beauty, not its effect upon others, but its image in the mirror. Beauty is from the anti-thetical self, and a woman can scarce but hate it, for not only does it demand a painful daily service, but it calls for the denial or the dissolution of the self.

> How many centuries spent
> The sedentary soul
> In toils of measurement
> Beyond eagle or mole,
> Beyond hearing or seeing
> Or Archimedes' guess,
> To raise into being
> That loveliness?

V

On the morning of the great procession, the greatest in living memory, the Parnellite and Anti-Parnellite members of Parliament, huddled together like cows in a storm, gather behind our carriage, and I hear John Redmond say to certain of his late enemies, 'I went up nearer the head of the procession, but one of the marshals said, "This is not your place, Mr. Redmond; your place is further back." "No," I said, "I will stay here." "In that case," he said, "I will lead you back." ' Later on I can see by the pushing and shouldering of a delegate from South Africa how important place and precedence is; and noticing that Maud Gonne is cheered everywhere, and that the Irish Members march through street after street without welcome, I wonder if their enemies have not intended their humiliation.

    •   •   •   •   •   •

We are at the Mansion House Banquet, and John Dillon is making the first speech he has made before a popular Dublin

audience since the death of Parnell; and I have several times to
keep my London delegates from interrupting. Dillon is very
nervous, and as I watch him the abstract passion begins to rise
within me, and I am almost overpowered by an instinct of
cruelty; I long to cry out, 'Had Zimri peace who slew his
master?'

    •   •   •   •   •

Is our Foundation Stone still unlaid when the more important streets are decorated for Queen Victoria's Jubilee?

I find Maud Gonne at her hotel talking to a young working-
man who looks very melancholy. She had offered to speak at
one of the regular meetings of his Socialist society about Queen
Victoria, and he has summoned what will be a great meeting
in the open air. She has refused to speak, and he says that her
refusal means his ruin, as nobody will ever believe that he had
any promise at all. When he has left without complaint or
anger, she gives me very cogent reasons against the open-air
meeting, but I can think of nothing but the young man and
his look of melancholy. He has left his address, and presently,
at my persuasion, she drives to his tenement, where she finds
him and his wife and children crowded into a very small space
— perhaps there was only one room — and, moved by the
sight, promises to speak. The young man is James Connolly
who, with Padraic Pearse, is to make the Insurrection of 1916
and to be executed.

    •   •   •   •   •

The meeting is held in College Green and is very crowded,
and Maud Gonne speaks, I think, standing upon a chair. In
front of her is an old woman with a miniature of Lord Edward Fitzgerald, which she waves in her excitement, crying
out, 'I was in it before she was born.' Maud Gonne tells how
that morning she had gone to lay a wreath upon a martyr's

tomb at Saint Michael's Church, for it is the one day in the year when such wreaths are laid, but had been refused admission because it is the Jubilee. Then she pauses, and after that her voice rises to a cry, 'Must the graves of our dead go undecorated because Victoria has her Jubilee?'

.   .   .   .   .

It is eight or nine at night, and she and I have come from the City Hall, where the Convention has been sitting, that we may walk to the National Club in Rutland Square, and we find a great crowd in the street, who surround us and accompany us. Presently I hear a sound of breaking glass, the crowd has begun to stone the windows of decorated houses, and when I try to speak that I may restore order, I discovered that I have lost my voice through much speaking at the Convention. I can only whisper and gesticulate, and as I am thus freed from responsibility, I share the emotion of the crowd, and perhaps even feel as they feel when the glass crashes. Maud Gonne has a look of exultation as she walks with her laughing head thrown back.

Later that night Connolly carries in procession a coffin with the words 'British Empire' upon it, and police and mob fight for its ownership, and at last, that the police may not capture it, it is thrown into the Liffey. And there are fights between police and window-breakers, and I read in the morning papers that many have been wounded; some two hundred heads have been dressed at the hospitals; an old woman killed by baton blows, or perhaps trampled under the feet of the crowd; and that two thousand pounds' worth of decorated plate-glass windows have been broken. I count the links in the chain of responsibility, run them across my fingers, and wonder if any link there is from my workshop.

.   .   .   .   .

Queen Victoria visits the city, and Dublin Unionists have gathered together from all Ireland some twelve thousand children and built for them a grandstand, and bought them sweets and buns that they may cheer. A week later Maud Gonne marches forty thousand children through the streets of Dublin, and in a field beyond Drumcondra, and in the presence of a priest of their Church, they swear to cherish towards England, until the freedom of Ireland has been won, an undying enmity.

How many of these children will carry bomb or rifle when a little under or a little over thirty?

[1922]

*   *   *

DRAMATIS PERSONAE

*   *   *

III

PRESENTLY, perhaps after Arthur Symons had gone, Lady Gregory called, reminded me that we had met in London though but for a few minutes at some fashionable house. A glimpse of a long vista of trees, over an undergrowth of clipped laurels, seen for a moment as the outside car approached her house on my first visit, is a vivid memory. Coole House, though it has lost the great park full of ancient trees, is still set in the midst of a thick wood, which spreads out behind the house in two directions, in one along the edges of a lake which, as there is no escape for its water except a narrow subterranean passage, doubles or trebles its size in winter. In later years I was to know the edges of that lake better than any spot on earth, to know it in all the changes of the seasons, to find there always some new beauty. Wondering at myself, I remember that when I first saw that house I was so full of the mediaevalism of William Morris that I did not like the gold frames, some deep and full of ornament, round the pictures in the drawing-room; years were to pass before I came to understand the earlier nineteenth and later eighteenth century, and to love that house more than all other houses. Every generation had left its memorial; every generation had been highly educated; eldest sons had gone the grand tour, returning with statues or pictures; Mogul or Persian paintings had been brought from the Far East by a Gregory chairman of the East

India Company, great earthenware ewers and basins, great silver bowls, by Lady Gregory's husband, a famous Governor of Ceylon, who had married in old age, and was now some seven years dead; but of all those Gregorys, the least distinguished, judged by accepted standards, most roused my interest — a Richard who at the close of the eighteenth century was a popular brilliant officer in the Guards. He was accused of pleading ill-health to escape active service, and though exonerated by some official inquiry, resigned his commission, gave up London and his friends. He made the acquaintance of a schoolgirl, carried her off, put her into a little house in Coole demesne, afterwards the steward's house, where she lived disguised as a boy until his father died. They married, and at the end of last century the people still kept the memory of her kindness and her charity. One of the latest planted of the woods bore her name, and is, I hope, still called, now that the Government Foresters are in possession, 'The Isabella Wood'. While compelled to live in boy's clothes she had called herself 'Jack the Sailor' from a song of Dibdin's. Richard had brought in bullock-carts through Italy the marble copy of the Venus de' Medici in the drawing-room, added to the library the Greek and Roman Classics bound by famous French and English binders, substituted for the old straight avenue two great sweeping avenues each a mile or a little more in length. Was it he or his father who had possessed the Arab horses, painted by Stubbs? It was perhaps Lady Gregory's husband, a Trustee of of the English National Gallery, who had bought the greater number of the pictures. Those that I keep most in memory are a Canaletto, a Guardi, a Zurbarán. Two or three that once hung there had, before I saw those great rooms, gone to the National Gallery, and the fine portraits by Augustus John and Charles Shannon were still to come. The mezzotints and engravings of the masters and friends of the old Gregorys that

hung round the small downstairs breakfast-room, Pitt, Fox,
Lord Wellesley, Palmerston, Gladstone, many that I have forgotten, had increased generation by generation, and among
them Lady Gregory had hung a letter from Burke to the
Gregory that was chairman of the East India Company saying
that he committed to his care, now that he himself had grown
old, the people of India. In the hall, or at one's right hand as
one ascended the stairs, hung Persian helmets, Indian shields,
Indian swords in elaborate sheaths, stuffed birds from various
parts of the world, shot by whom nobody could remember,
portraits of the members of Grillion's Club, illuminated ad-
dresses presented in Ceylon or Galway, signed photographs or
engravings of Tennyson, Mark Twain, Browning, Thackeray,
at a later date paintings of Galway scenery by Sir Richard Burton, bequeathed at his death, and etchings by Augustus John.
I can remember somebody saying: 'Balzac would have given
twenty pages to the stairs.' The house itself was plain and box-
like, except on the side towards the lake, where somebody,
probably Richard Gregory, had enlarged the drawing-room
and dining-room with great bow windows. Edward Martyn's
burnt house had been like it doubtless, for it was into such
houses men moved, when it was safe to leave their castles, or
the thatched cottages under castle walls; architecture did not
return until the cut stone Georgian houses of a later date.

IV

Lady Gregory, as I first knew her, was a plainly dressed
woman of forty-five, without obvious good looks, except the
charm that comes from strength, intelligence and kindness.
One who knew her at an earlier date speaks of dark skin, of an
extreme vitality, and a portrait by Mrs. Jopling that may have
flattered shows considerable beauty. When her husband died,

she had given up her London house, had devoted herself to the estate and to her son, spending little that mortgages might be paid off. The house had become her passion. That passion grew greater still when the house took its place in the public life of Ireland. She was a type that only the superficial observer could identify with Victorian earnestness, for her point of view was founded, not on any narrow modern habit, but upon her sense of great literature, upon her own strange feudal, almost mediaeval youth. She was a Persse — a form of the name Shakespeare calls Percy — descended from some Duke of Northumberland; her family had settled in the seventeenth century somewhere in the midlands, but finding, the legend declares, the visits of Lord Clanricarde, going and returning between his estate and Dublin, expensive, they had moved that they might be no longer near the high road and bought vast tracts of Galway land. Roxborough House, small and plain, but interesting for its high-pitched roof — the first slate roof built in Galway — was beside the road from Gort to Loughrea, a few yards from the bounding wall of a demesne that was nine miles round. Three or four masons were, during Lady Gregory's girlhood, continually busy upon the wall. On the other side of the road rose the Slievoughter range, feeding grouse and wild deer. The house contained neither pictures nor furniture of historic interest. The Persses had been soldiers, farmers, riders to hounds and, in the time of the Irish Parliament, politicians; a bridge within the wall commemorated the victory of the Irish Volunteers in 1782, but all had lacked intellectual curiosity until the downfall of their class had all but come. In the latter half of the nineteenth century Lady Gregory was born, an older and a younger sister gave birth to Sir Hugh Lane and to that John Shawe-Taylor who, by an act of daring I must presently describe, made the settlement of the Land Question possible.

Popular legend attributes to all the sons of the house daring and physical strength; some years ago, Free State Ministers were fond of recounting the adventures of Lady Gregory's 'Seven Brothers', who, no matter who objected to their rents, or coveted their possessions, were safe 'because had one been killed, the others would have run down and shot the assassin'; how the wildest of the brothers, excluded by some misdemeanour from a Hunt Ball, had turned a hose on the guests; how, a famous shot, he had walked into a public-house in a time of disturbance and put a bullet through every number on the clock. They had all the necessities of life on the mountain, or within the walls of their demesne, exporting great quantities of game, ruling their tenants, as had their fathers before, with a despotic benevolence, were admired, and perhaps loved, for the Irish people, however lawless, respect a rule founded upon some visible supremacy. I heard an old man say once to Lady Gregory: 'There was never a man that could hold a bow with your brothers.' Those brothers were figures from the eighteenth century. Sir Jonah Barrington might have celebrated their lives, but their mother and the mother of John Shawe-Taylor were of the nineteenth in one of their characteristics. Like so many Irish women of the upper classes, who reacted against the licence, the religious lassitude of the immediate past, they were evangelical Protestants, and set out to convert their neighbourhood. Few remember how much of this movement was a genuine enthusiasm; that one of its missionaries who travelled Ireland has written her life, has described meetings in peasant cottages where everybody engaged in religious discussion, has said that she was everywhere opposed and slandered by the powerful and the wealthy because upon the side of the poor. I can turn from the pages of her book with sympathy. Were I a better man and a more ignorant I had liked just such a life. But that missionary would have met with no sympathy at Roxborough, except, it may be, among those boisterous brothers or from one studious girl, for Roxborough Protestantism was on the side of wealth and power. All there had an instinctive love for their country or their neighbourhood, the mail-boat had not yet drawn the thoughts of the wealthy classes elsewhere. My great-grand-mother Corbet, the mistress of Sandymount Castle, had been out of Ireland but once. She had visited her son, afterwards Governor of Penang, at his English school, carrying a fort-night's provisions, so great were the hazards of the crossing; but that was some two generations earlier. Their proselytism expressed their love, they gave what they thought best. But the born student of the great literature of the world cannot proselytize, and Augusta Persse, as Lady Gregory was then named, walked and discussed Shakespeare with a man but little steadier than her brothers, a scholar of Trinity, in later years a famous botanist, a friendship ended by her alarmed mother. Was it earlier or later that she established a little shop upon the estate and herself sold there that she might compel the shopkeepers to bring down their exorbitant prices? Other well-born women of that time, Ruskin's Rose among them, did the same. Born in 1852, she had passed her formative years in comparative peace, Fenianism a far-off threat; and her mar-riage with Sir William Gregory in her twenty-ninth year, visits to Ceylon, India, London, Rome, set her beyond the reach of the bitter struggle between landlord and tenant of the late 'seventies and early 'eighties. She knew Ireland always in its permanent relationships, associations — violence but a brief interruption —, never lost her sense of feudal responsibility, not of duty as the word is generally understood, but of bur-dens laid upon her by her station and her character, a choice constantly renewed in solitude. 'She has been,' said an old man to me, 'like a serving-maid among us. She is plain and simple, like the Mother of God, and that was the greatest lady that ever lived.' When in later years her literary style became in my ears the best written by woman, she had made the people a part of her soul; a phrase of Aristotle's had become her motto: 'To think like a wise man, but to express oneself like the common people.'

*   *   *

VII

It was now that George Moore came into our affairs, brought by Edward Martyn, who invited him to find a cast for *The Heather Field*. They were cousins and inseparable friends, bound one to the other by mutual contempt. When I told Martyn that Moore had good points, he replied: 'I know Moore a great deal longer than you do. He has no good points.' And a week or two later Moore said: 'That man Martyn is the most selfish man alive. He thinks that I am damned and he doesn't care.' I have described their friendship in a little play called *The Cat and the Moon*; the speaker is a blind beggar-man, and Laban is a townland where Edward Martyn went to chapel: . . . 'Did you ever know a holy man but had a wicked man for his comrade and his heart's darling? There is not a more holy man in the barony than the man who has the big house at Laban, and he goes knocking about the roads day and night with that old lecher from the county of Mayo, and he a woman-hater from the day of his birth. And well you know and all the neighbours know what they talk of by daylight and candlelight. The old lecher does be telling over all the sins he committed, or maybe never committed at all, and the man of Laban does be trying to head him off and quiet him down that he may quit telling them.' Moore and Martyn were indeed in certain characteristics typical peasants, the peasant sinner, the peasant saint. Moore's grandfather or great-grandfather had been a convert, but there were Catholic marriages. Catholic families, beaten down by the Penal Laws, despised by Irish Protestants, by the few English Catholics they met, had but little choice as to where they picked their brides; boys, on one side of old family, grew up squireens, half-sirs, peasants who had lost their tradition, gentlemen who had lost theirs. Lady Gregory once told me what marriage coarsened the Moore blood, but I have forgotten.

George Moore had a ceaseless preoccupation with painting and the theatre, within certain limits a technical understanding of both; whatever idea possessed him, courage and explosive power; but sacrificed all that seemed to other men good breeding, honour, friendship, in pursuit of what he considered the root facts of life. I had seen him once in the Cheshire Cheese. I had with me some proof-sheets of the Ellis and Yeats study of Blake's philosophy, and the drooping tree on the second page of *The Book of Thel* stirred him to eloquence. His 'How beautiful, how beautiful!' is all I can remember. Then one evening, in a narrow empty street between Fleet Street and the river, I heard a voice resounding as if in a funnel, someone in a hansom cab was denouncing its driver, and Moore drove by. Then I met him in Arthur Symons' flat in the Temple. He threw himself into a chair with the remark: 'I wish that woman would wash.' He had just returned from an assignation with his mistress, a woman known to Symons personally, to me by repute, an accomplished, witty, somewhat fashionable woman. All his friends suffered in some way; good behaviour was no protection, for it was all chance whether the facts he pursued were in actual life or in some story that amused him. Had 'that woman' prided herself upon her cleanliness, he would, had he decided upon a quarrel, have said with greater publicity: 'I wish that woman would wash.' His pursuit had now and then unfortunate results. 'What has depressed you, Moore?' said an acquaintance. 'I have been paying attention to a certain woman. I had every reason to think she liked me. I came to the point to-day and was turned down completely.' 'You must have said something wrong.' 'No, what I said was all right.' 'What was it?' 'I said I was clean and healthy and she could not do better.' Upon occasion it made him brutal and witty. He and I went to the town of Galway for a Gaelic festival that coincided with some assembly of priests. When we lunched at the Railway Hotel the room was full of priests. A Father Moloney, supposed to know all about Greek Art, caught sight of Moore and introduced himself. He probably knew nothing about Moore, except that he was some kind of critic, for he set out upon his favourite topic with: 'I have always considered it a proof of Greek purity that though they left the male form uncovered, they invariably draped the female.' 'Do you consider, Father Moloney,' said Moore in a voice that rang through the whole room, 'that the female form is inherently more indecent than the male?' Every priest turned a stern and horrified eye upon Father Moloney, who sat hunched up and quivering.

I have twice known Moore alarmed and conscience-struck, when told that he had injured somebody's financial prospects — a financial prospect is a root fact — but he attacked with indifference so long as nothing suffered but his victim's dignity or feelings. To injure a famous scholar in a quarrel not his he had printed all the scandalous stories he could rake together, or invent, in a frenzy of political hatred. I had remonstrated in vain, except that he cut out a passage describing his victim as 'a long pink pig', yet when he thought he might have deprived that scholar of a post he was miserable.

He had gone to Paris straight from his father's racing stables, from a house where there was no culture, as Symons and I understood that word, acquired copious inaccurate French, sat among art students, young writers about to become famous, in some café; a man carved out of a turnip, looking out of astonished eyes. I see him as that circle saw him, for I have in memory Manet's caricature. He spoke badly and much in a foreign tongue, read nothing, and was never to attain the discipline of style. 'I wrote a play in French,' he said, 'before I had seen dialogue on paper.' I doubt if he had read a play of Shakespeare's even at the end of his life. He did not know that style existed until he returned to Ireland in middle life; what he learned, he learned from conversation, from acted plays, from pictures. A revolutionary in revolt against the ignorant Catholicism of Mayo, he chose for master Zola as another might have chosen Karl Marx. Even to conversation and acted plays, he gave an inattentive ear, instincts incapable of clear expression deafened him and blinded him; he was Milton's lion rising up, pawing out of the earth, but, unlike that lion, stuck half-way. He reached to middle life ignorant even of small practical details. He said to a friend: 'How do you keep your pants from falling about your knees?' 'O,' said the friend, 'I put my braces through the little tapes that are sewn there for the purpose.' A few days later, he thanked the friend with emotion. Upon a long country bicycle ride with another friend, he had stopped because his pants were about his knees, had gone behind a hedge, had taken them off, and exchanged them at a cottage for a tumbler of milk. Only at pictures did he look undeafened and unblinded, for they impose their silence upon us. His *Modern Painting* has colloquial animation and surprise that might have grown into a roundness and ripeness of speech that is a part of style had not ambition made him in later life prefer sentences a Dublin critic has compared to ribbons of tooth-paste squeezed out of a tube. When the Irish Theatre was founded, he had published *A*

Mummer's Wife, which had made a considerable sensation, for it was the first realistic novel in the language, the first novel where every incident was there not because the author thought it beautiful, exciting or amusing, but because certain people who were neither beautiful, exciting, nor amusing must have acted in that way: the root facts of life, as they are known to the greatest number of people, that and nothing else. Balzac would have added his wisdom. Moore had but his blind ambition. *Esther Waters* should have been a greater novel, for the scene is more varied. Esther is tempted to steal a half-crown; Balzac might have made her steal it and keep our sympathy, but Moore must create a personification of motherly goodness, almost an abstraction. Five years later he begged a number of his friends to read it. 'I have just read it,' he said. 'It has done me good, it radiates goodness.' He had wanted to be good as the mass of men understand goodness. In later life he wrote a long preface to prove that he had a mistress in Mayfair.

*   *   *

XIX

Moore had inherited a large Mayo estate, and no Mayo country gentleman had ever dressed the part so well. He lacked manners, but had manner; he could enter a room so as to draw your attention without seeming to, his French, his knowledge of painting, suggested travel and leisure. Yet nature had denied to him the final touch: he had a coarse palate. Edward Martyn alone suspected it. When Moore abused the waiter or the cook, he had thought, 'I know what he is hiding.' In a London restaurant on a night when the soup was particularly good, just when Moore had the spoon at his lip, he said: 'Do you mean to say you are going to drink that?'

Moore tasted the soup, then called the waiter, and ran through the usual performance. Martyn did not undeceive him, content to chuckle in solitude. Moore had taken a house in Upper Ely Place; he spent a week at our principal hotel while his furniture was moving in: he denounced the food to the waiter, to the manager, went down to the kitchen and denounced it to the cook. 'He has written to the proprietress,' said the manager, 'that the steak is like brown paper. How can you believe a word such a man would say, a steak cannot be like brown paper.' He had his own bread sent in from the baker and said on the day he left: 'How can these people endure it?' 'Because,' said the admiring head-waiter, 'they are not *comme il faut*.' A little later I stayed with him and wrote to Lady Gregory: 'He is boisterously enduring the sixth cook.' Then from Sligo a few days later: 'Moore dismissed the sixth cook the day I left — six in three weeks. One brought in a policeman, Moore had made so much noise. He dragged the policeman into the dining-room and said: "Is there a law in this country to compel me to eat this abominable omelette?" '

Sometimes Moore, instead of asking us to accept for true some monstrous invention, would press a spontaneous action into deliberate comedy; starting in bad blood or blind passion, he would all in a moment see himself as others saw him. When he arrived in Dublin, all the doors in Upper Ely Place had been painted white by an agreement between the landlord and the tenants. Moore had his door painted green, and three Miss Beams — no, I have not got the name quite right — who lived next door protested to the landlord. Then began a correspondence between Moore and the landlord wherein Moore insisted on his position as an art critic, that the whole decoration of his house required a green door — I imagine that he had but wrapped the green flag around him — then the indignant young women bought a copy of *Esther Waters*, tore it up, put the fragments into a large envelope, wrote thereon: 'Too filthy to keep in the house,' dropped it into his letter-box. I was staying with Moore, I let myself in with a latch-key some night after twelve, and found a note on the hall table asking me to put the door on the chain. As I was undressing, I heard Moore trying to get in; when I had opened the door and pointed to the note he said: 'Oh, I forgot. Every night I go out at eleven, at twelve, at one, and rattle my stick on the railing to make the Miss Beams' dogs bark.' Then I saw in the newspapers that the Miss Beams had hired organ-grinders to play under Moore's window when he was writing, that he had prosecuted the organ-grinders. Moore had a large garden on the other side of the street, a blackbird sang there; he received his friends upon Saturday evening and made a moving speech upon the bird. 'I enjoy its song. If I were the bad man people say I am, could I enjoy its song?' He wrote every morning at an open window on the ground floor, and one morning saw the Miss Beams' cat cross the street, and thought, 'That cat will get my bird.' He went out and filled his pocket with stones, and whenever he saw the cat, threw a stone. Somebody, perhaps the typist, must have laughed, for the rest of the tale fills me with doubt. I was passing through Dublin just on my way to Coole; he came to my hotel. 'I remembered how early that cat got up. I thought it might get the blackbird if I was not there to protect it, so I set a trap. The Miss Beams wrote to the Society for the Prevention of Cruelty to Animals, and I am carrying on a correspondence with its secretary, cat versus bird.' (Perhaps after all, the archives of the Society do contain that correspondence. The tale is not yet incredible.) I passed through Dublin again, perhaps on my way back. Moore came to see me in seeming great depression. 'Remember that trap?' 'Yes.' 'Remember that bird?' 'Yes.' 'I have caught the bird.'

Moore gave a garden party during the annual festival of the
Gaelic League; there was a Gaelic play by Douglas Hyde
based upon a scenario of Moore's, and to this garden party he
invited the Catholic Archbishop, beginning the letter with:
'Cher confrère.' The Archbishop did not answer. He had already in a letter to the Press invited the Archbishop to institute
a stage censorship. 'But, my dear Yeats, Archbishops are educated men. If there is some difficulty about a play, I will call
upon him. I will explain. He will approve the play. No more
mob rule. No more such trouble as we had about *The Countess
Cathleen*. No more letters to the Press signed "Father of a
Family".'

[1935]

*   *   *

ESTRANGEMENT

*   *   *

II

LAST night there was a debate in the Arts Club on a political question. I was for a moment tempted to use arguments merely to answer something said, but did not do so, and noticed that every argument I had been tempted to use was used by somebody or other. Logic is a machine, one can leave it to itself; unhelped it will force those present to exhaust the subject, the fool is as likely as the sage to speak the appropriate answer to any statement, and if an answer is forgotten somebody will go home miserable. You throw your money on the table and you receive so much change.

Style, personality — deliberately adopted and therefore a mask — is the only escape from the hot-faced bargainers and the money-changers.

*   *   *

VII

It seems to me that true love is a discipline, and it needs so much wisdom that the love of Solomon and Sheba must have lasted, for all the silence of the Scriptures. Each divines the secret self of the other, and refusing to believe in the mere daily self, creates a mirror where the lover or the beloved sees an image to copy in daily life; for love also creates the Mask.

*   *   *

XXIII

All my life I have been haunted with the idea that the poet should know all classes of men as one of themselves, that he should combine the greatest possible personal realization with the greatest possible knowledge of the speech and circumstances of the world. Fifteen or twenty years ago I remember longing, with this purpose, to disguise myself as a peasant and wander through the West, and then to ship as sailor. But when one shrinks from all business with a stranger, and is unnatural with all who are not intimate friends, because one underrates or overrates unknown people, one cannot adventure forth. The artist grows more and more distinct, more and more a being in his own right as it were, but more and more loses grasp of the always more complex world. Some day setting out to find knowledge, like some pilgrim to the Holy Land, he will become the most romantic of characters. He will play with all masks.

XXIV

Tragedy is passion alone, and rejecting character, it gets form from motives, from the wandering of passion; while comedy is the clash of character. Eliminate character from comedy and you get farce. Farce is bound together by incident alone. In practice most works are mixed: Shakespeare being tragi-comedy. Comedy is joyous because all assumption of a part, of a personal mask, whether of the individualized face of comedy or of the grotesque face of farce, is a display of energy, and all energy is joyous. A poet creates tragedy from his own soul, that soul which is alike in all men. It has not joy, as we understand that word, but ecstasy, which is from the contemplation of things vaster than the individual and imperfectly seen, perhaps, by all those that still live. The masks of tragedy contain neither character nor personal energy. They are allied to decoration and to the abstract figures of Egyptian temples. Before the mind can look out of their eyes the active will perishes, hence their sorrowful calm. Joy is of the will which labours, which overcomes obstacles, which knows triumph. The soul knows its changes of state alone, and I think the motives of tragedy are not related to action but to changes of state. I feel this but do not see clearly, for I am hunting truth into its thicket and it is my business to keep close to the impressions of sense, to common daily life. Yet is not ecstasy some fulfilment of the soul in itself, some slow or sudden expansion of it like an overflowing well? Is not this what is meant by beauty?

*   *   *

XXVIII

This morning I got a letter telling me of A—— C——'s illness. I did not recognize her son's writing at first, and my mind wandered, I suppose because I was not well. I thought my mother was ill and that my sister was asking me to come at once: then I remembered that my mother died years ago and that more than kin was at stake. She has been to me mother, friend, sister and brother. I cannot realize the world without her — she brought to my wavering thoughts steadfast nobility. All the day the thought of losing her is like a conflagration in the rafters. Friendship is all the house I have.

*   *   *

XLVI

Ireland has grown sterile, because power has passed to men who lack the training which requires a certain amount of wealth to ensure continuity from generation to generation, and to free the mind in part from other tasks. A gentleman is a man whose principal ideas are not connected with his personal needs and his personal success. In old days he was a clerk or a noble, that is to say, he had freedom because of inherited wealth and position, or because of a personal renunciation. The names are different to-day, and I would put the artist and the scholar in the category of the clerk, yet personal renunciation is not now sufficient or the *hysterica passio* of Ireland would be inspiration, or perhaps it is sufficient but is impossible without inherited culture. For without culture or holiness, which are always the gift of a very few, a man may renounce wealth or any other external thing, but he cannot renounce hatred, envy, jealousy, revenge. Culture is the sanctity of the intellect.

[1926]

*   *   *

THE DEATH OF SYNGE

*　　*　　*

VI

I THINK that all happiness depends on the energy to assume the mask of some other self; that all joyous or creative life is a rebirth as something not oneself, something which has no memory and is created in a moment and perpetually renewed. We put on a grotesque or solemn painted face to hide us from the terrors of judgment, invent an imaginative saturnalia where one forgets reality, a game like that of a child, where one loses the infinite pain of self-realization. Perhaps all the sins and energies of the world are but its flight from an infinite blinding beam.

*　　*　　*

XXX

Went to S——'s the other night — everybody either too tall or too short, crooked or lop-sided. One woman had an excited voice, an intellect without self-possession, and there was a man with a look of a wood-kern, who kept bringing the conversation back and back to Synge's wrongdoing in having made a girl in the *Playboy* admire a man who had hamstrung 'mountain ewes'. He saw nothing else to object to but that one thing. He declared that the English would not give Home Rule because they thought Ireland cruel, and no Irishman should write a sentence to make them go on thinking that. There arose before my mind an image of this man arguing about Ireland with an endless procession of second-rate men. At last I said, 'When a country produces a man of genius he never is what it wants or believes it wants; he is always unlike its idea of itself. In the eighteenth century Scotland believed itself religious, moral and gloomy, and its national poet Burns came not to speak of these things but to speak of lust and drink and drunken gaiety. Ireland, since the Young Irelanders, has given itself up to apologetics. Every impression of life or impulse of imagination has been examined to see if it helped or hurt the glory of Ireland or the political claim of Ireland. A sincere impression of life became at last impossible, all was apologetics. There was no longer an impartial imagination, delighting in whatever is naturally exciting. Synge was the rushing up of the buried fire, an explosion of all that had been denied or refused, a furious impartiality, an indifferent turbulent sorrow. His work, like that of Burns, was to say all the people did not want to have said. He was able to do this because Nature had made him incapable of a political idea.' The wood-kern made no answer, did not understand a word I said, perhaps; but for the rest of the evening he kept saying to this person or to that person that he objected to nothing but the passage about the 'mountain ewes'.

[1928]

*　　　*　　　*

THE BOUNTY OF SWEDEN

EVERY now and then, when something has stirred my imagination, I begin talking to myself. I speak in my own person and dramatize myself, very much as I have seen a mad old woman do upon the Dublin quays, and sometimes detect myself speaking and moving as if I were still young, or walking perhaps like an old man with fumbling steps. Occasionally, I write out what I have said in verse, and generally for no better reason than because I remember that I have written no verse for a long time. I do not think of my soliloquies as having different literary qualities. They stir my interest, by their appropriateness to the men I imagine myself to be, or by their accurate description of some emotional circumstance, more than by any aesthetic value. When I begin to write I have no object but to find for them some natural speech, rhythm and syntax, and to set it out in some pattern, so seeming old that it may seem all men's speech, and though the labour is very great, I seem to have used no faculty peculiar to myself, certainly no special gift. I print the poem and never hear about it again, until I find the book years after with a page dog-eared by some young man, or marked by some young girl with a violet, and when I have seen that, I am a little ashamed, as though somebody were to attribute to me a delicacy of feeling I should but do not possess. What came so easily at first, and amidst so much drama, and was written so laboriously at the last, cannot be counted among my possessions.

On the other hand, if I give a successful lecture, or write a vigorous, critical essay, there is immediate effect; I am confident that on some one point, which seems to me of great importance, I know more than other men, and I covet honour.

*   *   *

IX

The next night there is a reception at the Palace, and the Nobel Prize winners are among the guests. We wait in a long gallery for our turn to enter the throne-room, and upon the black coats of the civilians, as upon the grey and silver of the Guards, lie the chains of the three Swedish Orders. Among the black-coated men are men of learning, men of letters, men of science, much of the intellect of Sweden. What model has made all this, one wonders: Goethe's Weimar, or Sweden's own eighteenth-century Courts? There may be, must be, faults of commission or omission, but where else could a like assembly be gathered? I who have never seen a Court, find myself before the evening is ended moved as if by some religious ceremony, though to a different end, for here it is Life herself that is praised. Presently we walk through lines of sentries, in the costume of Charles XII, the last of Sweden's great military Kings, and then bow as we pass rapidly before the tall seated figures of the Royal Family. They seem to be like stage royalties. Just such handsome men and women would have been chosen by a London manager staging, let us say, some dramatized version of *The Prisoner of Zenda.* One has a general impression of youthful distinction, even the tall, slight figure of the old King seems young. Then we pass from the throne-room into a vast hall hung with Gobelins tapestries, which seem in the distance to represent scenes like those in a Watteau or in a Fragonard. Their green colour by contrast turns the marble pillars above into a dusky silver. At the end of the hall musicians are sitting in a high marble gallery, and in the side galleries are women in white dresses, many very young and handsome. Others upon the level of the floor sit grouped together, making patches of white among the brilliant uniforms and the black coats. We are shepherded to our places, and the musicians play much Swedish music, which I cannot describe, for I know nothing of music. During our first long wait all kinds of pictures had passed before me in reverie and now my imagination renews its excitement. I had thought how we Irish had served famous men and famous families, and had been, so long as our nation had intellect enough to shape anything of itself, good lovers of women, but had never served any abstract cause, except the one, and that we personified by a woman, and I wondered if the service of woman could be so different from that of a Court. I had thought how, before the emigration of our poor began, our gentlemen had gone all over Europe, offering their swords at every Court, and that many had stood, just as I, but with an anxiety I could but imagine, for their future hung upon a frown or a smile. I had run through old family fables and histories, to find if any man of my blood has so stood, and had thought that there were men living, meant by nature for that vicissitude, who had served a woman through all folly, because they had found no Court to serve. Then my memory had gone back twenty years to that summer when a friend read out to me at the end of each day's work Castiglione's commendations and descriptions of that

Court of Urbino where youth for certain brief years imposed upon drowsy learning the discipline of its joy, and I remembered a cry of Bembo's made years after, 'Would that I were a shepherd that I might look down daily upon Urbino.' I had repeated to myself what I could remember of Ben Jonson's address to the Court of his time, 'Thou art a beautiful and brave spring and waterest all the noble plants of this Island. In thee the whole Kingdom dresseth itself and is ambitious to use thee as her glass. Beware then thou render men's figures truly and teach them no less to hate their deformities, than to love their forms. . . . Thy servant but not slave, Ben Jonson.'

And now I begin to imagine some equivalent gathering to that about me, called together by the heads of some State where every democratic dream had been fulfilled, and where all men had started level and only merit, acknowledged by all the people, ruled. The majority so gathered, certainly all who had supreme authority, would have reached that age when an English novelist becomes eligible for the Order of Merit. Times of disturbance might indeed carry into power some man of comparative youth, of fifty or sixty years perhaps, but I think of normal times. Here and there one would notice sons and daughters, perhaps even the more dutiful grandsons and granddaughters, but in the eyes of those, though not in their conversation, an acute observer might discover disquiet and a restless longing for the moment when they could slip away to some night-club's compensating anarchy. In the conversation of old and young there would be much sarcasm, great numbers of those tales which we all tell to one another's disadvantage. For all men would display to others' envy the trophies won in their life of struggle.

* * *

XIII

On Friday we visit the great Town Hall, which is the greatest work of Swedish art, a master-work of the Romantic movement. The Royal Palace had taken ninety years to build, and been the organizing centre of the art of its time, and this new magnificence, its narrow windows opening out upon a formal garden, its tall tower rising from the quayside, has taken ten years. It, too, has been an organizing centre, but for an art more imaginative and amazing. Here there is no important French influence, for all that has not come out of the necessities of site and material, no matter in what school the artist studied, carries the mind backward to Byzantium. I think of but two comparable buildings, the Pennsylvania terminus in New York, and the Catholic Cathedral at Westminster, but the Pennsylvania terminus, noble in austerity, is the work of a single mind, elaborating a suggestion from a Roman Bath, a mind that — supported by the American deference to authority — has been permitted to refuse everything not relevant to a single dominating idea. The starting-hours of the trains are upon specially designed boards, of a colour that makes them harmonize with the general design, and all other advertisements are forbidden, even in the stations that the trains pass immediately after leaving or before entering the terminus. The mood of severity must be prolonged or prepared for. The Catholic Cathedral is of a greater magnificence in general design, but being planted in a country where public opinion rules and the subscribers to every fund expect to have their way, is half ruined by ignoble decoration, the most ignoble of all planned and paid for by my countrymen. The Town Hall of Stockholm, upon the other hand, is decorated by many artists, working in harmony with one another and with the design of the building

as a whole, and yet all in seeming perfect freedom. In England
and Ireland public opinion compels the employment of the
worst artists, while here the authority of a Prince and the
wisdom of a Socialist Minister of culture, and the approval of
the most educated of all nations, have made possible the employment of the best. These myth-makers and mask-makers
worked as if they belonged to one family, and the great walls
where the roughened surface of the bricks, their carefully
varied size and tint, takes away all sense of mechanical finish;
the mosaic-covered walls of the 'Golden Room'; the paintings hung upon the walls of the committee-rooms; the
fresco paintings upon the greater surfaces with their subjects
from Swedish mythology; the wrought iron and the furniture, where all suggests history, and yet is full of invention;
the statuary in marble and in bronze, now mythological in
subject, now representations of great Swedes, modelled
naked as if they had come down from some Roman heaven;
all that suggestion of novelty and of an immeasurable past;
all that multitude and unity, could hardly have been possible,
had not love of Stockholm and belief in its future so filled
men of different minds, classes, and occupations that they
almost attained the supreme miracle, the dream that has
haunted all religions, and loved one another. No work comparable in method or achievement has been accomplished
since the Italian cities felt the excitement of the Renaissance,
for in the midst of our individualistic anarchy, growing
always, as it seemed, more violent, have arisen once more subordination, design, a sense of human need.
[1924]

*   *   *

*　　*　　*

III
SUBJECT FOR A POEM. APRIL 30TH

DEATH of a friend. To describe how mixed with one's grief comes the thought that the witness of some foolish word or act of one's own is gone.

Describe Byzantium as it is in the system towards the end of the first Christian millennium. A walking mummy. Flames at the street corners where the soul is purified, birds of hammered gold singing in the golden trees, in the harbour, offering their backs to the wailing dead that they may carry them to Paradise.

These subjects have been in my head for some time, especially the last.

*　　*　　*

VIII

Burke is only tolerable in his impassioned moments, but no matter what Swift talks of, one delights in his animation and clarity. I think the reason is that Swift always thought in English and is learned in that tongue. The writers who seem most characteristic of his time, Pope in his verse for instance, and the great orators, think in French or in Latin. How much of my reading is to discover the English and Irish originals of my thought, its first language, and, where no such originals exist, its relation to what original did. I seek more than idioms, for thoughts become more vivid when I find they were thought out in historical circumstances which affect those in which I live, or, which is perhaps the same thing, were thought first by men my ancestors may have known. Some of my ancestors may have seen Swift, and probably my Huguenot grandmother who asked burial near Bishop King spoke both to Swift and Berkeley. I have before me an ideal expression in which all that I have, clay and spirit alike, assists; it is as though I most approximate towards that expression when I carry with me the greatest possible amount of hereditary thought and feeling, even national and family hatred and pride.

Our poetry and prose are often abstract and foreign. I am a poor French scholar, yet in old days I felt my sentences take a French form. Yet we must not put an artificial emphasis on what is English or Irish, for if we do we no longer find new richness. I think of that supreme ceremony wherein the Mormon offers his wisdom to his ancestors. But our language and thought are broken from the past by hurry, even when we do not think in any foreign tongue. I can hear Swift's voice in his letters speaking the sentences at whatever pace makes their sound and idiom expressive. He speaks and we listen at leisure.

Burke, whether he wrote a pamphlet or prepared a speech, wrote for men in an assembly, whereas Swift wrote for men sitting at table or fireside — from that come his animation and his naturalness. Upon the other hand the sense of an assembly, of an exceptional occasion, rouses Burke to his great moments of passion.

*　　　*　　　*

XXX
RENVYLE. JULY 23RD

I have talked most of a long motor journey, talked even when I was hoarse. Why? Surely because I was timid, because I felt the other man was judging me, because I endowed his silence with all kinds of formidable qualities. Being on trial I must cajole my judge.

*   *   *

XXXIII
A LETTER TO MICHAEL'S SCHOOLMASTER

Dear Sir,

My son is now between nine and ten and should begin Greek at once and be taught by the Berlitz method that he may read as soon as possible that most exciting of all stories, the *Odyssey*, from that landing in Ithaca to the end. Grammar should come when the need comes. As he grows older he will read to me the great lyric poets and I will talk to him about Plato. Do not teach him one word of Latin. The Roman people were the classic decadence, their literature form without matter. They destroyed Milton, the French seventeenth and our own eighteenth century, and our schoolmasters even to-day read Greek with Latin eyes. Greece, could we but approach it with eyes as young as its own, might renew our youth. Teach him mathematics as thoroughly as his capacity permits. I know that Bertrand Russell must, seeing that he is such a featherhead, be wrong about everything, but as I have no mathematics I cannot prove it. I do not want my son to be as helpless. Do not teach him one word of geography. He has lived on the Alps, crossed a number of rivers and when he is fifteen I shall urge him to climb the Sugar Loaf. Do not teach him a word of history. I shall take him to Shakespeare's history plays, if a commercialised theatre permit, and give him all the historical novels of Dumas, and if he cannot pick up the rest he is a fool. Don't teach him one word of science, he can get all he wants in the newspapers and in any case it is no job for a gentleman. If you teach him Greek and mathematics and do not let him forget the French and German that he already knows you will do for him all that one man can do for another. If he wants to learn Irish after he is well founded in Greek, let him — it will clear his eyes of the Latin miasma. If you will not do what I say, whether the curriculum or your own will restrain, and my son comes from school a smatterer like his father, may your soul lie chained on the Red Sea bottom.

*　　*　　*

XXXV

SEPTEMBER 15TH

Reading Hone's unpublished life of Berkeley I get that sense of unreality before the historical figure that I had before the portrait in the Fellows' Room in Trinity College, Dublin. That philanthropic serene Bishop, that pasteboard man, never wrote the *Commonplace Book*. Attracted beyond expression by Berkeley's thought I have been repelled by the man as we have received him from tradition, a saint and sage who takes to tar water, who turns from the most overwhelming philosophic generalisations since Plato to convert negroes, and who in *Siris* writes as if he had forgotten it. But now that I reject the saint and sage I find Berkeley lovable. The Berkeley of the *Commonplace Book* wore an alien mask, the mask of preposterous benevolence that prevailed in sculpture and painting down to the middle of the nineteenth century — the monument to the Prince Consort on Leinster Lawn — to hide his clamorous, childlike, naïve, mischievous curiosity. The mischief of a man is malicious; when he pulls the skeleton out of the cupboard he calculates the whole effect, but Berkeley knew nothing of men and women. He loved discourse for its own sake as a child does, and said out of the contented solitude of a child the most embarrassing things. What did he really say in those three sermons to undergraduates that got him into such a political mess? — not quite, I think, what he says in that irrational essay on *Passive Obedience* written to save his face. Was the Bermuda project more than a justification for curiosity and discourse? Was not that curiosity already half satisfied when he drew the plans of his learned city — a steeple in the centre and markets in the corners?

He left behind those three earnest Fellows of College who might have liked converting negroes — even to-day there is a T.C.D. mission to savage parts — and took to America a portrait painter and a couple of pleasant young men of fortune, and when he got there associated with fox-hunters and American 'Immaterialist' disciples. When Walpole refused the money he came home without apparent regret — and, as I think, with relief. His curiosity was satisfied. Had an American disciple turned Boswell and had the genius for the task, we would have had another *Commonplace Book*, the old theme with vivid new illustrations drawn from the passing show. He returned to Ireland, the eighteenth-century mask — itself one of those abstractions he denounced — clapped firmly on his face. There is a famine in Ireland; a Bishop must be benevolent, beside a child has never thought of being anything else, but his curiosity is even more powerful. Had he not been told in America of Indians that cured all kinds of things with a concoction of tar? He had already put the mathematicians and philosophers by the ears, why not the doctors? And the tar water, and the cures it worked, what a subject for discourse! Could he not lead his reader — especially if that reader drank tar water every morning — from tar to light? Newton, made ignorant by his very knowledge, his contact with other men, his lack of childish solitude, had postulated an Ether, an abstraction, a something that did not exist because unperceived. If this is a foundation stuff it has visibility, light — mind and light the Siamese twins that constitute the whole of reality. But he is also the burned child so he writes as if he had never heard of Immaterialism, he becomes a materialist stoic philosopher, playing with some harmless symbol. The American Samuel Johnson and his Irish disciples will understand that this light, this intellectual Fire, is that continuity which holds together 'the perceptions', that it is a substitute for the old symbol God. Is it to adjust his mask more carefully, to pose himself as it were against remote antiquity, or a need for symbol that makes him talk of the Neo-platonic Trinity?

When I think of him, I think of my father, and of others born into the Anglo-Irish solitude, of their curiosity, their discourse, their spontaneity, their irresponsibility, their innocence, their sense of mystery as they grow old, their readiness to dress up at the suggestion of others though never quite certain what dress they wear.

Berkeley the Bishop was a humbug. His wife, that charming daughter who played the viol, Queen Caroline, Ministers of State, imposed it upon him; but he was meant for a Greek tub or an Indian palm tree. Only once in his life was he free, when, still an undergraduate, he filled the *Commonplace Book* with snorts of defiance.

Descartes, Locke, and Newton took away the world and gave us its excrement instead. Berkeley restored the world.

I think of the Nirvana Song of the Japanese monk: 'I sit on the mountain side and look up at the little farm — I say to the old farmer: "How many times have you mortgaged your land and paid off the mortgagee?" I take pleasure in the sound of the reeds.'

Berkeley has brought back to us the world that only exists because it shines and sounds. A child, smothering its laughter because the elders are standing round, has opened once more the great box of toys.

[Written April 7—November 18, 1936; published 1944]

*   *   *

LETTERS

To Katharine Tynan

[*After September 6, 1888*]   *3 Blenheim Road*

Dear Miss Tynan, Last time I wrote, if I remember correctly, I left many things unanswered. I wrote, I think, in much hurry about 'forms' for *Oisin*. (By the way I imagine Kegan Paul will charge full 5/-.)

I will go and see Ranking as soon as ever I have a day; at present the folklore still is not quite off my hands — the folklore and Aesop. Ranking lives now at the very other side of London.

You ask about Aesop. Nutt, the publisher, is bringing out a reprint of a very scarce copy of Aesop published by Caxton. And I am making a copy for the printers. York Powell, who got me the job, made a mistake and thought the only copy was at Oxford in the Bodleian. And so I had a very pleasant week in his rooms down there. I am now — when folklore gives me time — finishing it in the British Museum. Where, by the way, I saw Renan wandering about yesterday looking very like an old fat priest.

I have not done very badly these last few months. And it has been lucky, as my father's finishing the story in *Atalanta* has left him once more dependent on stray drawings. Not that I have done well exactly. However, I have had as much work as I could do — only badly paid. Did you read my article in *Providence Journal*? I got £5 for Aesop only but will get about another £1. I do not yet know what fairy book will bring. I have had £5 as an instalment. I forgot to ask you if you read the 'Phantom Ship' in *Providence Journal*. I mean to review

Todhunter there. The worst of me is that if my work is good it is done very very slowly — the notes to folklore book were done quickly and they are bad or at any rate not good. Introduction is better. Douglas Hyde gave me much help with footnotes, etc.

I had almost forgotten to say how gladly I will do some sort of a sketch for you and your doings for the American friend. But please tell me some more about it. Am I to describe your house and surroundings and yourself just, or do a general sketch of your literary life? Will you not tell me, in any case, some of the things you want said and should I do it at once? I shall have more time shortly. Could you tell me of any article of the kind you wish? Or shall I go my own road? I would sooner go yours. There must be several things you wish said. And have you any dates that are landmarks in your literary life and development? How long should it be?

The other day I met a most curious and interesting man — I do not wish to say yet whether he be of interest in himself, but his opinions are — at Madame Blavatsky's, where I go about once every six weeks. Do you remember an interview in the *Pall Mall* with a man called Russell, an American, who came over to England with his wife to teach gesture according to the system of some French philosopher? That was the man. We left Madame's at 11 and walked up and down Notting Hill till 1 o'c in the morning, talking philosophy. He was going to stop with the Shellys for a while; on his return I shall see more of him. The interesting thing about him is that he is a dandy as well as a philosopher. A perpetual paradox. He is naturally insignificant in looks, but by dint of elaborate training in gesture has turned himself into quite a striking looking person. There was a sketch of him in the *Pall Mall*. He is the most interesting person I have met at Madame's lately; as a rule one meets the penitent frivolous there. Still frivolous, only dull as well. She devours them, as she herself says, like the locust in the Apocalypse.

Lately I have read much of George Meredith's poems. They are certainly very beautiful, and have far more suavity and serenity than I had expected. Henley is very cobwebby after them and not very spontaneous. To me Henley's great fault is his form. It is never accidental but always preconceived. His poems are forced into a mould. I dislike the school to which he belongs. A poem should be a law to itself as plants and beasts are. It may be ever so much finished, but all finish should merely make plain that law. Read Meredith's *Love in the Valley*. It is full of a curious intricate richness.

I enclose a couple of lyrics of my own for your opinion. One is made out of three lines of verse I picked up in Sligo — Old Irish verse.

I have had a great deal of trouble over the folklore, the publishers first making me strike out 100 pages, on the ground that the book was too long and then, when two thirds was in print, add as many pages of fresh matter — because they had made a wrong calculation, and I had to set to work copying out and looking over material again, as the pages struck out had to do with the section already in type. It is, however, at last off my hands, almost.

Hear the ballad book has been reviewed in the *Saturday* but whether favourably or Saturdayishly I know not.

You would have been much amused to have seen my departure from Oxford. All the while I was there, one thing only troubled my peace of mind — the politeness of the man-servant. It was perpetually 'Wine, sir? Coffee, sir? Anything, sir?' At every 'sir', I said to myself, 'That means an extra shilling, in *his* mind, at least.' When I was going I did not know what to give him, but gave him five shillings. Then suddenly thought I had given him too little. I tried a joke.

My jokes had been all failures so far with him. It went explosively and I departed sadly knowing I had given too much.

I have corrected the two first parts of 'Oisin'. The second part is much more coherent than I had hoped. You did not hear the second part. It is the most inspired but the least artistic of the three. The last has most art. Because I was in complete solitude — no one near me but old and reticent people — when I wrote it. It was the greatest effort of all my things. When I had finished it I brought it round to read to my Uncle George Pollexfen and could hardly read, so collapsed I was. My voice quite broken. It really was a kind of vision. It beset me day and night. Not that I ever wrote more than a few lines in a day. But those few lines took me hours. All the rest of the time I walked about the roads thinking of it. I wait impatiently the proofs of it. With the other parts I am disappointed — they seem only shadows of what I saw. But the third must have got itself expressed — it kept me from my sleep too long. Yet the second part is more deep and poetic. It is not inspiration that exhausts one, but art. The first parts I felt. I saw the second. Yet there too, perhaps, only shadows have got themselves on to paper. And I am like the people who dream some wonderful thing and get up in the middle of the night and write it and find next day only scribbling on the paper.

I have added to the book the last scene of 'The Island of Statues' with a short argument to make all plain. I am sure the 'Island' is good of its kind.

I was then living a quite harmonious poetic life. Never thinking out of my depth. Always harmonious, narrow, calm. Taking small interest in people but most ardently moved by the more minute kinds of natural beauty. 'Mosada' was then written and a poem called 'Time and Vivien' which you have not seen. It is second in my book. Everything done then was quite passionless. The 'Island' was the last. Since I have left the 'Island', I have been going about on shoreless seas. Nothing anywhere has clear outline. Everything is cloud and foam. 'Oisin' and the 'Seeker' are the only readable result. In the second part of 'Oisin' under disguise of symbolism I have said several things to which I only have the key. The romance is for my readers. They must not even know there is a symbol anywhere. They will not find out. If they did, it would spoil the art. Yet the whole poem is full of symbols — if it be full of aught but clouds. The early poems I know to be quite coherent, and at no time are there clouds in my details, for I hate the soft modern manner. The clouds began about four years ago. I was finishing the 'Island'. They came and robbed Naschina of her shadow. As you will see, the rest is cloudless, narrow and calm.

I meant to wind up this so long letter before this, but in order to propitiate you for all this literariness must add a more human sheet or half-sheet.

Charley Johnston was at Madame Blavatsky's the other day with that air of clever insolence and elaborate efficiency he has ripened to such perfection. The before mentioned penitent frivolous delight in him.

If you only saw him talking French and smoking cigarettes with Madame's niece. He looked a veritable peacock. Such an air too of the world-worn man of society about him, as if he also were one of the penitent frivolous instead of a crusading undergraduate.

You will have to read straight through my book of folk-lore. It was meant for Irish poets. They should draw on it for plots and atmosphere. You will find plenty of workable subjects. I will expect to hear, as soon as you get the book, your opinion of my introduction — a very few pages it is, too.

Hyde is the best of all the Irish folklorists. His style is

perfect — so sincere and simple — so little literary.

I have been looking out in vain for the longer review of Todhunter in the *Irish Monthly*. Has the *Freeman* reviewed him yet, or the *Nation*? What of the Pan Celtic? They sent me a prospectus. Should I join? Would it help my book or could I be of any use as a member living over here?

When I see *Atalanta* with your poem, you will hear from me again. Your friend always,

W. B. YEATS

The *Saturday* has reviewed us Saturdayishly. Henley says he has nothing to do with it. Have not seen review yet. Went to Henley's (where Heaven knows there is little inducement to go) to find out for Miss O'Leary, and heard the interesting question of the thickness of steaks in different parts of the world discussed at great length.

Everyone is very kind there — but, the Lord deliver us from journalists! I met Sladen, the Australian poet, and liked him. He much admires your poems. Henley praises 'St. Francis', thinks it the best of yours he has seen. His book has been a great success. The expenses were very heavy, as a large number of copies were printed expensively on Japanese paper. At midsummer he had made twopence profit. There has been a good sale since.

This very long letter has grown bit by bit. Several times I thought it had come to an end, but there being no stamps in the near neighbourhood, each time adding a bit. When my story, which I am once more at work on, came to a check at any time, I took up this letter and added a bit.

Outside my window the balcony is covered with a whirl of fire-red leaves from the virginia creeper. To-day it is raining and blowing and they are flying hither and thither or gathered in corners, sodden with wet. How saddening is this old age of the year. All summer the wooden pilasters of the balcony have been covered with greenest leaves and pinkest sweet-pie flower. Now even the horse-chestnut has begun to wither. The chestnuts fall every now and then with quite a loud rustle and thud and the whole house at the garden side is covered with a crimson ruin of creeper and the sunflowers are all leaning down weighted by their heavy seeds.

Has Ashe King reviewed the ballad book? A review in *Truth* would help it. Has it sold at all well? I see it for sale at Irish Exhibition.

A copy should be sent to British Museum. Irish publishers are careless about this as I found in folklore hunts.

P.S. (2) Just got your letter. Could you send me the sketch of you in *Nation*? The description of your own which you refer to would much help.

Certainly I will try and get to see Mr. Rankin as soon as I can.

Proofs I will send one of these days with pleasure; just now I am going through them with Todhunter. Tomorrow or next day I will send them or the first batches, the rest after.

I have an amusing piece of news you may not have heard. Charles Johnston has followed Madame Blavatsky's niece to Moscow and will there be married to her. He will be back in London with his wife on October the 8th. They told nobody about it. The girl's mother — says Madame — cries unceasingly and Madame herself says they are 'Flap Doodles'. Johnston *was* in the running for Mahatmaship and now how are the mighty fallen! Theosophy despairs, only the young wife of the dandy philosopher of gesture throws up her eyes and says 'Oh, that beautiful young man and how wicked of Theosophy to try and prevent people from falling in love!' Madame covers them with her lambent raillery.

The future Mrs. Johnston is very nice, decidedly pretty,

with a laugh like bells of silver, and speaks several languages and is not older than Johnston. If you only heard Madame Blavatsky trying to pronounce Ballykilbeg!

Your poem on Fluffy is very good, full of unstrained naivety, but will write about it when I see the 'Children of Lir'. Want to catch post now and get some afternoon tea, which I hear clattering below.

This letter is none of your 'cock-boats' but a regular 'three-decker' of a letter.

To Lady Gregory

[*Postmark Oct 3, 1897*]   *Manchester*

My dear Lady Gregory: I find that Miss Gonne has to return to London for a few hours before going to Dublin. She goes first to a meeting at Hanley (wherever that is). I shall go with her. We had a long and exhausting political meeting this morning and will have another to-night. After the meeting this morning Miss Gonne and myself went to the picture gallery to see a Rossetti that is there. She is very kind and friendly, but whether more than that I cannot tell. I have been explaining the Celtic movement and she is enthusiastic over it in its more mystical development, and tells me that her cousin Miss May Gonne, who is clever I think, will be anxious to help to act or whatever we like. She will, Miss Gonne thinks, go to Dublin to work on committee etc if we like. She and Miss Gonne are going to some place in the West, if Miss Gonne can make time, to see visions. I told Miss Gonne what Lady Mayo said about her losing a lot of money at Aix les Bains (I spell that word obscurely to hide my ignorance) and she says it is quite accurate except that she won £100 instead of losing. This is a very feeble letter, the sort of thing one

writes when one is ten years old. 'It is a fine day. How are
you? A tree has fallen into the pond. I have a new canary' etc.
You know the style, but I have been chairman of a noisy
meeting for three hours and am very done up. I have a
speech to prepare for to-night. Everything went smoothly
this morning in spite of anonymous letters warning us to
keep a bodyguard at the door. Perhaps the disturbance waits
for to-night. I find the infinite triviality of politics more
trying than ever. We tear each other's character in pieces for
things that don't matter to anybody. Yours

W. B. YEATS

To John Quinn

4th October 1907   *Nassau Hotel*

My dear Quinn, Very many thanks for your long letter
which I was very glad indeed to get. I have just come up from
Coole for the production of a new play called *The Country
Dressmaker*. It is by a new writer called Fitzmaurice. A harsh,
strong, ugly comedy. It really gives a much worse view of the
people than *The Playboy*. Even I rather dislike it, though I
admire its sincerity, and yet it was received with enthusiasm.
The truth is that the objection to Synge is not mainly that he
makes the country people unpleasant or immoral, but that
he has got a standard of morals and intellect. They never
minded Boyle, whose people are a sordid lot, because they
knew what he was at. They understood his obvious moral,
and they don't mind Fitzmaurice because they don't think
he is at anything, but they shrink from Synge's harsh, independent, heroical, clean, wind-swept view of things. They
want their clerical conservatory where the air is warm and
damp. Of course, we may not get through to-morrow night,
but the row won't be very bad. Nothing is ever persecuted

but the intellect, though it is never persecuted under its own name. I don't think it would be wise for me to write a reply to that absurd article by McManus. As I never now write about politics people would think I was paying him off or his party off for *The Playboy*. I argued that question at the meeting not because I thought I would convince anybody but because the one thing that seemed possible was that all should show, players and playwrights, that we weren't afraid. The result has been that we have doubled the enthusiasm of our own following. The principal actors are now applauded at their entrances with a heartiness unknown before, and both Lady Gregory and myself received several times last spring what newspaper writers call 'an ovation'. We have lost a great many but the minority know that we are in earnest, and if only our finances hold out we will get the rest . . .

We have had another performance of *The Country Dressmaker* since I wrote, and the success was greater than before. The dear *Freeman*, or rather its evening issue which is called by another name, has congratulated us on having got a play at last 'to which nobody can take the slightest exception' or some such words, and yet Fitzmaurice, who wrote it, wrote it with the special object of showing up the sordid side of country life. He thinks himself a follower of Synge, which he is not. I have no doubt that there will be enthusiasm to-night, and that the author, who has been thirsting for the crown of martyrdom, will be called before the curtain for the third night running. We are putting the play on again next week owing to its success.

Synge has just had an operation on his throat and has come through it all right. I am to see him to-day for the first time. When he woke out of the ether sleep his first words, to the great delight of the doctor, who knows his plays, were: 'May God damn the English, they can't even swear without vulgarity.' This tale delights the Company, who shudder at the bad language they have to speak in his plays. I don't think he has done much this summer owing to bad health but he will probably set to work now . . .

Augustus John has been staying at Coole. He came there to do an etching of me for the collected edition. Shannon was busy when I was in London and the collected edition was being pushed on so quickly that I found I couldn't wait for him. I don't know what John will make of me. He made a lot of sketches with the brush and the pencil to work the etching from when he went home. I felt rather a martyr going to him. The students consider him the greatest living draughtsman, the only modern who can draw like an old master . . . He exaggerates every little hill and hollow of the face till one looks like a gypsy, grown old in wickedness and hardship. If one looked like any of his pictures the country women would take the clean clothes off the hedges when one passed, as they do at the sight of a tinker. He is himself a delight, the most innocent-wicked man I have ever met. He wears earrings, his hair down over his shoulders, a green velvet collar . . . He climbed to the top of the highest tree in Coole garden and carved a symbol there. Nobody else has been able to get up there to know what it is; even Robert stuck half way. He is a magnificent looking person, and looks the wild creature he is. His best work is etching. He is certainly a great etcher, with a savage imagination. Yours ever

                                                    W. B. YEATS

To John Quinn

7th January 1908   *18 Woburn Buildings*

Dear Quinn . . . I have arranged about the Shannon portrait and for the price you said. I am giving the first sitting to-morrow, and will ask you to let me have the right to publish a reproduction of the portrait in some book of mine. He has just done a drawing of me which is very charming, but by an unlucky accident most damnably like Keats. If I publish it by itself everybody will think it an affectation of mine. I have had adventures in trying to get a suitable portrait. My father always sees me through a mist of domestic emotion, or so I think; and Mancini, who filled me with joy, has turned me into a sort of Italian bandit, or half bandit half café king, certainly a joyous Latin, impudent, immoral, and reckless. Augustus John, who has made a very fine thing of me, has made me a sheer tinker, drunken, unpleasant and disreputable, but full of wisdom — a melancholy English Bohemian, capable of everything except living joyously on the surface.

I am going to put the lot one after the other: my father's emaciated portrait that was the frontispiece for *The Tables of the Law* beside Mancini's brazen image, and Augustus John's tinker to pluck the nose of Shannon's idealist. Nobody will believe they are the same man. And I shall write an essay upon them and describe them as all the different personages that I have dreamt of being but have never had the time for. I shall head it with what Wordsworth said about some marble bust of himself: 'No, that is not Mr. Wordsworth, the poet, that is Mr. Wordsworth, the Chancellor of the Exchequer.' . . . Yours ever

W. B. YEATS

To J. B. Yeats

November 29th 1909   *18 Woburn Buildings*

My dear Father: I'm here again in London, for the time. I came over to read my play to Mrs. Campbell. She wrote to me to come at 1.15, lunch and read it afterwards (this was yesterday week). I went and word was sent down with apologies she wasn't yet ready. On towards two she and lunch appeared. After lunch she listened, much interrupted by the parrot, to Act I with great enthusiasm. I was just starting Act II when a musician arrived, to play some incidental music she was to speak through in some forthcoming performance. She said: 'This won't delay me long, not more than ten minutes,' and then began an immense interminable quarrel with the musician about his music. After an hour and a half of this I said 'I think I had better go and put off an invitation to dinner I had for to-night.' She begged me to do so — full of apologies. I went away and returned at 6.30 just as the musician left. I then started Act II. A deaf man sat there whose mission was, it seemed, to say irrelevant enthusiastic things to Mrs. Campbell. I got through Act II well. Mrs. Campbell still enthusiastic. Then there came in telephone messages and I was asked to stay to dinner and read it afterwards. At dinner there was young Campbell and his wife and two other relations of hers, probably poor ones. After dinner arrived Mrs. Campbell's dressmaker, this would also take only a few minutes. Presently there was a mighty stir upstairs and somebody sent down in an excited way, like a messenger in a Greek Tragedy, to say that the dress was 6 inches too short in front. At half past ten there was a consultation in the drawing room as to whether somebody shouldn't go up and knock at Mrs. Campbell's door. It was decided that somebody should but everybody refused to be the one. I wanted to go home but I was told on no account must I do that. At half past 11 Mrs. Campbell came down, full of apologies, it would only be a few minutes longer. At twelve young Campbell's wife, who is an American heiress, and therefore independent, announced that she was going home and did, taking her husband. I sat on with the relations, whose business it seems was to entertain me. We sighed together at the amount it would cost us in taxi cabs to get home. At half past twelve Mrs. Campbell came in so tired that she had to lean on her daughter to get into the room. I said: 'This is absurd! You must go to your bed, and I must go home.' She said: 'No, I must hear the end of a play the same day as I hear the beginning.' I began to read. She did not know one word I was saying. She started to quarrel with me, because she supposed I had given a long speech which she wanted to a minor character and because of certain remarks which I applied to my heroine which she thought applied to her. She said at intervals, in an exasperated sleepy voice: 'No, I am not a slut and I do not like fools.' Finally I went home and I'm trying to find a halcyon day on which to read her the play again. I've even had to assure her by letter that it was not she but my heroine who liked fools.

I am dining out a great deal. I sat next the Prime Minister at a men's dinner party given by Edmund Gosse the other night. I started off rather badly, for Edmund Gosse whispered to me in the few minutes before dinner: 'Mind, no politics.' And then introduced me to Lord Cromer and Lord Cromer's first sentence was: 'We had a very interesting debate in the House of Lords this afternoon.' I being still wax under Gosse's finger replied: 'Oh I look on at English politics as a child does at a race course, taking sides by the colour of the jockeys' coats. And I often change sides in the middle of a race.' This rather chilled the conversation and somebody said to me presently: 'Lord Cromer is interested in nothing but politics.' I got on better with Asquith. I found him an exceedingly well read man, especially, curiously enough, in poetry. Not a man of really fine culture, I think, but exceedingly charming and well read. We talked a good deal about

Ireland and the new University and education. I told him how I had met a girl of 12 in a railway carriage who had never heard of Gladstone or Parnell, and he said that comes from bad education. Presently he said: 'I see you've had a lively time over Shaw's play and that the state of things is so perfect in Dublin that we need not bring it under the censorship.' He meant this as a compliment, for we had, of course, to fight the censorship, and the report of the Commission, so far as it touches on Ireland, supports us in having done so. Then he began asking about anti-clericalism in Dublin.

I've also been meeting lately General Ian Hamilton, a man of the really finest culture, as fine as that of anybody I've ever met. A very gentle person, and his friends say of him that he is the greatest soldier in the English army.

Next Sunday the Abbey Company does *Blanco* for the Stage Society. I think it will be a fine performance and it will help our reputation. Yours

W. B. YEATS

To J. B. Yeats

November 21st, 1912   *18 Woburn Buildings*

My dear Father, I have a great project, would you like to write your autobiography? My plan is to go to a publisher and arrange that you should be paid chapter by chapter on the receipt of the MS. at the rate of £1 per 1,000 words up to say £50. This £50 to be a first charge on the book. I shall try and arrange so that you will keep the serial rights. You will probably get very decent terms for some of the chapters in America. You could go on as you please, quick or slow, and say what you pleased. I suggest — but this is only to start your imagination working — that in your first chapter or chapters you describe old relations and your childhood. You have often told us most interesting things, pictures of old Ireland that should not be lost. Then, you could describe your school life and then weave a chapter round Sandymount. Isaac Butt would come into this. Later on, your memories of Potter and Nettleship and Wilson would have real historical importance. When you came to the later period, you could use once more what you have already written about York Powell, then, if you liked, you could talk about Synge and about America. I will get the publisher to illustrate the book. There are your own pictures to choose from, the portrait of Isaac Butt, of course, and pictures in the Tate Gallery by Potter and at Aberdeen by Wilson, and Mrs. Nettleship has still those early designs of Nettleship's and would probably be glad to have them published and him praised. You might do a wonderful book. You could say anything about anything, for after all, you yourself would be the theme, there would be no need to be afraid of egotism, for as Oscar Wilde said, that is charming in a book because we can close it whenever we like, and open it again when the mood comes. I think you might really do a wonderful book, and I think a profitable one. It would tell people about those things that are not old enough to be in the histories or new enough to be in the reader's mind, and these things are always the things that are least known. If you agree, the book can be done, for even if the publisher lacked faith, I know I could get the money. The point is, can you write it for £1 a thousand words in the first instance? You wouldn't have to hurry, and I think that in the long run it might produce a very considerable sum for you. I would do all the bargaining and make the publisher collect the pictures for illustrations. Probably, a good deal that you have written recently would fit in somewhere. The first chapter or two might be difficult, but after that, I know by experience of my own books that your thought would go on branching and blossoming in all directions; in the end, it might grow to longer than 50,000 words but I do not say it might not be shorter. The great thing is to do it in some form, long or short. An ordinary 6/- book is expected to be about 60,000 words, but if the pictures turn out well, though no longer, it might be a guinea book and very profitable indeed, for there would be nothing to pay for copyrights of pictures. If it were much less than 60,000 words, one could still — with the pictures to help — charge 6/-. Let me know as soon as you can and I will arrange the whole thing at once. Yours

W. B. YEATS

To J. B. Yeats

March 14 [?1916]   *18 Woburn Buildings*

My dear Father: The typist has just sent me a letter of yours dated Feb 12. I had not noticed when it came that you asked me a question. You ask for examples of 'imitation' in poetry. I suggest that the corresponding things are drama and the pictorial element and that in poetry those who lack these are rhetoricians. I feel in Wyndham Lewis's Cubist pictures an element corresponding to rhetoric arising from his confusion of the abstract with the rhythmical. Rhythm implies a living body, a breast to rise and fall, or limbs that dance, while the abstract is incompatible with life. The Cubist is abstract. At the same time you must not leave out rhythm and this rhythm is not imitation. Impressionism by leaving it out brought all this rhetoric of the abstract upon us. I have just been turning over a book of Japanese paintings. Everywhere there is delight in form, repeated yet varied, in curious patterns of lines, but these lines are all an ordering of natural objects though they are certainly not imitation. In every case the artist one feels has had to *consciously* and deliberately arrange his subject. It was the impressionists' belief that this arrangement should be only unconscious and instinctive that brought this violent reaction. They are right in believing that this should be conscious, but wrong in substituting abstract scientific thought for conscious feeling. If I delight in rhythm I love nature though she is not rhythmical. I express my love in rhythm. The more I express it the less can I forget her.

I think Keats perhaps greater than Shelley and beyond words greater than Swinburne because he makes pictures one cannot forget and sees them as full of rhythm as a Chinese painting. Swinburne's poetry, all but some early poems, is as abstract as a cubist picture. Carlyle is abstract — ideas, never things or only their common worn out images taken up from some preacher, and to-day he is as dead as Macpherson's *Ossian*. Insincere and theatrical, he saw nothing. His moral zeal cast before his mind perpetually 'God', 'Eternity', 'Work', and these ideas corresponding to no exact pictures have their analogy in all art which is without imitation. I doubt if I have made myself plain. I separate the rhythmical and the abstract. They are brothers but one is Abel and one is Cain. In poetry they are not confused for we know that poetry is rhythm, but in music-hall verses we find an abstract cadence, which is vulgar because it is apart from imitation. This cadence is a mechanism, it never suggests a voice shaken with joy or sorrow as poetical rhythm does. It is but the noise of a machine and not the coming and going of the breath.

It is midnight and I must stop. Yours

W. B. YEATS

I am back again in London.

To Olivia Shakespear

March 22 [Postmark 1923]   *82 Merrion Square*

My dear Olivia: I think things are mending here — my own
projects in that matter postponed but not abandoned — the
war seems fading out. In spite of all that has happened, I
find constant evidence of ability or intensity which makes one
hopeful. I was on a committee of the Senate the other day,
which is considering legislation based on a series of blue
books, with elaborate maps of coalfields etc, issued by the
revolutionary government at the start of its war with England.
It spent many thousands upon collecting evidence and over
publication. Then again when the news came in of Michael
Collins' death, one of the Ministers recited to the Cabinet —
or to seven Ministers — the entire *Adonais* of Shelley. One
strange thing is the absence of personal bitterness. Senators
whose houses have been burnt (one man has lost archives
going back to, I think, the 16th century) speak as if it were
some impersonal tragedy, some event caused by storm or
earthquake. Our debates are without emotion, dull, business-
like and well attended. We have just legalized, after detailed
discussion, and approved, changes in local government, and
in the poor laws, made in the very midst of the revolutionary
war, changes that have meant considerable economy and
better treatment of the poor.

My armed guard very much on the alert just now (many
republicans are I think in town for a conference) and I was
challenged last night on the stairs. I was in my stocking feet
so as not to wake the children. I give my guard detective
stories to train them in the highest tradition of their profession. Last week the theatres were ordered to close by the
republicans and all closed except the Abbey (which I thought

would go up in flames and so removed my father's portraits from the vestibule) but next day all theatres were open again at the command of the government.

George is almost well again — not quit of quarantine — but able to go out for short walks, and to be gay and cheerful. Pound sends me a postcard from S. Marino addressed to me at the Senate and heads it 'from the last republic'.

Yes I would greatly like Binyon's *Blake* which I saw at Ricketts' and admired. Yours affectionately

W. B. YEATS

My plans are still government policy but are postponed till peace has come by other means. They will be used not to bring peace but to lay War's ghost. At least so I am told officially. Unofficially I hear that the War party carried the day (this all very private). Certainly peace seems coming. Only isolated shots now at night; but one is sure of nothing.

To Olivia Shakespear

May 25 [Postmark 1926]   *Thoor Ballylee*

My dear Olivia: We are at our Tower and I am writing poetry as I always do here, and as always happens, no matter how I begin, it becomes love poetry before I am finished with it. I have lots of subjects in my head including a play about Christ meeting the worshippers of Dionysus on the mountain side — no doubt that will somehow become love poetry too. I have brought but two books, Baudelaire and Mac-Kenna's *Plotinus*. Plotinus is a most ardent and wonderful person. I am also writing answers to a long series of questions sent me by a reader of *A Vision*, and Plotinus helps me there. Do you remember the story of Buddha who gave a flower to some one, who in his turn gave another a silent gift and so from man to man for centuries passed on the doctrine of the Zen school? One feels at moments as if one could with a touch convey a vision — that the mystic way and sexual love use the same means — opposed yet parallel existences (I cannot spell and there is no dictionary in the house).

An old beggar has just called I knew here twenty years ago as wandering piper but now he is paralysed and cannot play. He was lamenting the great houses burned or empty — 'The gentry have kept the shoes on my feet, and the coat on my back and the shilling in my pocket — never once in all the forty and five years that I have been upon the road have I asked a penny of a farmer.' I gave him five shillings and he started off in the rain for the nearest town — five miles — I rather fancy to drink it.

The last I gave to was at Coole and he opened the conversation by saying to Lady Gregory — 'My lady you are in the winter of your age' — they are all full of contemplation and elaborate of speech and have their regular track.

My moods fill me with surprise and some alarm. The other day I found at Coole a reproduction of a drawing of two charming young persons in the full stream of their Saphoistic enthusiasm, and it got into my dreams at night and made a great racket there, and yet I feel spiritual things are very near me. I think I shall be able to feel [word indecipherable] for those more remote parts of the System that are hardly touched in *A Vision*. I suppose to grow old is to grow impersonal, to need nothing and to seek nothing for oneself — at least it may be thus.

As you see I have no news, for nothing happens in this blessed place, but a stray beggar or a heron. Yours affectionately

W. B. YEATS

To Olivia Shakespear

March 2 [1929]   *Via Americhe 12–8*
                                                 Rapallo

My dear Olivia, It is long since I have written — partly cold
which has made the corner of the room where my desk and
note-paper are look very unpleasant, and partly certain days
in bed with rheumatism. No matter how bad the weather I
can make myself write verse — if I have it in my head — but
little else. Now we are thawing. I am writing *Twelve poems for
music* — have done three of them (and two other poems) —
no[t] so much that they may be sung as that I may define
their kind of emotion to myself. I want them to be all emotion and all impersonal. One of the three I have written is
my best lyric for some years I think. They are the opposite of
my recent work and all praise of joyous life, though in the
best of them it is a dry bone on the shore that sings the praise.
Last night I saw in a dream strange ragged excited people
singing in a crowd. The most visible were a man and woman
who were I think dancing. The man was swinging round his
head a weight at the end of a rope or leather thong, and I
knew that he did not know whether he would strike her dead
or not, and both had their eyes fixed on each other, and both
sang their love for one another. I suppose it was Blake's old
thought 'sexual love is founded upon spiritual hate' — I will
probably find I have written it in a poem in a few days —
though my remembering my dream may prevent that — by
making my criticism work upon it. (At least there is evidence
to that effect.)

   To-night we dine with Ezra — the first dinner-coated meal
since I got here — to meet Hauptmann who does not know a
word of English but is fine to look at — after the fashion of

William Morris. Auntille — how do you spell him? — and his lady will be there and probably a certain Basil Bunting, one of Ezra's more savage disciples. He got into jail as a pacifist and then for assaulting the police and carrying concealed weapons and he is now writing up Antille's music. George and I keep him at a distance and yet I have no doubt that just such as he surrounded Shakespeare's theatre, when it was denounced by the first puritans.

I have turned from Browning — to me a dangerous influence — to Morris and read through his *Defence of Guenevere* and some unfinished prose fragments with great wonder. I have come to fear the world's last great poetic period is over

> Though the great song return no more
> There's keen delight in what we have —
> A rattle of pebbles on the shore
> Under the receding wave.

The young do not feel like that — George does not, nor Ezra — but men far off feel it — in Japan for instance. Yours affectionately

W. B. YEATS

I knew nothing of your illness until it was over. I hope all is very well now. I shall be in London on May 1 and stay perhaps a fortnight, so keep some hours for me.

To Olivia Shakespear

May 31 [*1932*]   *42 Fitzwilliam Square*

My dear Olivia: You will have known why I have not written, for you will have seen Lady Gregory['s] death in the papers. I had come to Dublin for a few days to see about

Abbey business. On Sunday night at 11.30 I had a telephone message from her solicitor who had been trying to find me all day. I took the first train in the morning but she had died in the night. She was her indomitable self to the last but of that I will not write, or not now.

We have taken a little house at Rathfarnham just outside Dublin. It has the most beautiful gardens I have seen round a small house, and all well stocked. I shall step out from my study into the front garden — but as I write the words I know that I am heartbroken for Coole and its great woods. A queer Dublin sculptor dressed like a workman and in filthy clothes, a man who lives in a kind of slum and has slum children, came the day after Lady Gregory's death 'to pay his respects'. He walked from room to room and then stood where hang the mezzotints and engravings of those under or with whom (I cannot spell to-night — that word looks wrong) the Gregorys have served, Fox, Burke and so on, and after standing silent said 'All the nobility of earth'. I felt he did not mean it for that room alone but for lost tradition. How much of my own verse has not been but the repetition of those words. Yours

W. B. YEATS

To Olivia Shakespear

Feb 27 [*Postmark Feb 28, 1934*]   *Riversdale*

My dear Olivia: I come out of my reveries to write to you. I do nothing all day long but think of the drama I am building up in my *Lady Gregory*. I have drawn Martyn and his house, Lady Gregory and hers, have brought George Moore upon the scene, finished a long analysis of him, which pictures for the first time this preposterous person. These first chapters are

sensations and exciting and will bring George much household money when she sends them out to English and American magazines. I am just beginning on Woburn Buildings,
building up the scene there — alas the most significant image
of those years must be left out. This first part will probably be
made up of extracts from letters to Lady Gregory and my
comments. My first fifty pages — probably to be published
before the rest — will bring me to about 1900. They begin
where my old autobiography ends. It is curious how one's
life falls into definite sections — in 1897 a new scene was set,
new actors appeared.

I do not find anything the matter [with] the Swami['s]
book, it is his master's book that is incredible. I have so many
wonders that I have gone completely to the miracle workers.
Did you see old Budge's interview in the *Daily Express* of,
I think, Jan 14? Egyptian magicians had, he said, 'materialized'
in his presence the souls of men who were excavating for him
twenty-four miles away. He had given orders to the 'materialized' forms that the men miles away had carried [out]. He
says he has now mastered from certain inscriptions the whole
method of Egyptian magic and is putting the knowledge into
the hands of men sworn never to publish it.

Here is our most recent event. Next door is a large farm-
house in considerable grounds. People called —— live there,
'blue shirts' of local importance, and until one day two weeks
ago they had many dogs. 'Blue shirts' are upholding law,
incarnations of public spirit, rioters in the cause of peace, and
George hates 'Blue shirts'. She was delighted when she
caught their collie-dog in our hen-house and missed a white
hen. I was going into town and she said as I started 'I will
write to complain. If they do nothing I will go to the police.'
When I returned in the evening she was plunged in gloom.
Her letter sent by our gardener had been replied to at once

in these words: 'Sorry, have done away with collie-dog' —
note the Hitler touch — a little later came the gardener. In
his presence, Mrs. —— had drowned four dogs. A fifth had
revived, when taken out of the water, and as it was not her
own dog but a stray she had hunted it down the road with a
can tied to its tail. There was a sixth dog, she said, but as it had
been with her for some time she would take time to think
whether to send it to the dogs' home or drown it. I tried to
console George — after all she was only responsible for the
the death of the collie and so on. But there was something
wrong. At last it came. The white hen had returned. Was she
to write and say so? I said 'No; you feel a multi-murderess and
if you write, Mrs. —— will feel she is.' 'But she will see the
hen.' 'Put it in the pot.' 'It is my best layer.' However I insisted and the white hen went into the pot. Yours
affectionately

W. B. YEATS

ESSAYS, STORIES, INTRODUCTIONS, SPEECHES AND OTHER PROSE

INTRODUCTION TO *FAIRY AND FOLK TALES OF THE IRISH PEASANTRY*

DR. CORBETT, Bishop of Oxford and Norwich, lamented long ago the departure of the English fairies. 'In Queen Mary's time' he wrote —

> 'When Tom came home from labour,
>   Or Cis to milking rose,
> Then merrily, merrily went their tabor,
>   And merrily went their toes.'

But now, in the times of James, they had all gone, for 'they were of the old profession', and 'their songs were Ave Maries'. In Ireland they are still extant, giving gifts to the kindly, and plaguing the surly. 'Have you ever seen a fairy or such like?' I asked an old man in County Sligo. 'Amn't I annoyed with them,' was the answer. 'Do the fishermen along here know anything of the mermaids?' I asked a woman of a village in County Dublin. 'Indeed, they don't like to see them at all,' she answered, 'for they always bring bad weather.' 'Here is a man who believes in ghosts,' said a foreign sea-captain, pointing to a pilot of my acquaintance. 'In every house over there,' said the pilot, pointing to his native village of Rosses, 'there are several.' Certainly that now old and much respected dogmatist, the Spirit of the Age, had in no manner made his voice heard down there. In a little while, for he has gotten a consumptive appearance of late, he will be covered over decently in his grave, and another will grow, old and much respected, in his place, and never be heard of down there, and after him another and another and another. Indeed, it is a question whether any of these personages will ever be heard of outside the newspaper offices and lecture-rooms and drawing-rooms and eel-pie houses of the cities, or if the Spirit of the Age is at any time more than a froth. At any rate, whole troops of their like will not change the Celt much. Giraldus Cambrensis found the people of the western islands a trifle paganish. 'How many gods are there?' asked a priest, a little while ago, of a man from the Island of Innistor. 'There is one on Innistor; but this seems a big place,' said the man, and the priest held up his hands in horror, as Giraldus had, just seven centuries before. Remember, I am not blaming the man; it is very much better to believe in a number of gods than in none at all, or to think there is only one, but that he is a little sentimental and impracticable, and not constructed for the nineteenth century. The Celt, and his cromlechs, and his pillar-stones, these will not change much — indeed, it is doubtful if anybody at all changes at any time. In spite of hosts of deniers, and asserters, and wise-men, and professors, the majority still are averse to sitting down to dine thirteen at table, or being helped to salt, or walking under a ladder, or seeing a single magpie flirting his chequered tail. There are, of course, children of light who have set their faces against all this, though even a newspaper man, if you entice him into a cemetery at midnight, will believe in phantoms, for every one is a visionary, if you scratch him deep enough. But the Celt is a visionary without scratching.

Yet, be it noticed, if you are a stranger, you will not readily get ghost and fairy legends, even in a western village. You must go adroitly to work, and make friends with the children, and the old men, with those who have not felt the pressure

of mere daylight existence, and those with whom it is growing less, and will have altogether taken itself off one of these
days. The old women are most learned, but will not so readily
be got to talk, for the fairies are very secretive, and much resent being talked of; and are there not many stories of old
women who were nearly pinched into their graves or
numbed with fairy blasts?

At sea, when the nets are out and the pipes are lit, then will
some ancient hoarder of tales become loquacious, telling his
histories to the tune of the creaking of the boats. Holy-eve
night, too, is a great time, and in old days many tales were to be
heard at wakes. But the priests have set faces against wakes.

In the Parochial Survey of Ireland it is recorded how the
story-tellers used to gather together of an evening, and if any
had a different version from the others, they would all recite
theirs and vote, and the man who had varied would have to
abide by their verdict. In this way stories have been handed
down with such accuracy, that the long tale of Deirdre was,
in the earlier decades of this century, told almost word for
word, as in the very ancient MSS. in the Royal Dublin
Society. In one case only it varied, and then the MS. was
obviously wrong — a passage had been forgotten by the
copyist. But this accuracy is rather in the folk and bardic
tales than in the fairy legends, for these vary widely, being
usually adapted to some neighbouring village or local fairy-
seeing celebrity. Each county has usually some family, or
personage, supposed to have been favoured or plagued,
especially by the phantoms, as the Hackets of Castle Hacket,
Galway, who had for their ancestor a fairy, or John-o'-Daly
of Lisadell, Sligo, who wrote 'Eileen Aroon', the song the
Scotch have stolen and called 'Robin Adair', and which
Handel would sooner have written than all his oratorios,[1] and

[1] He lived some time in Dublin and heard it then.

the 'O'Donahue of Kerry'. Round these men stories tended to group themselves, sometimes deserting more ancient heroes for the purpose. Round poets have they gathered especially, for poetry in Ireland has always been mysteriously connected with magic.

These folk-tales are full of simplicity and musical occurrences, for they are the literature of a class for whom every incident in the old rut of birth, love, pain, and death has cropped up unchanged for centuries: who have steeped everything in the heart: to whom everything is a symbol. They have the spade over which man has leant from the beginning. The people of the cities have the machine, which is prose and a *parvenu*. They have few events. They can turn over the incidents of a long life as they sit by the fire. With us nothing has time to gather meaning, and too many things are occurring for even a big heart to hold. It is said the most eloquent people in the world are the Arabs, who have only the bare earth of the desert and a sky swept bare by the sun. 'Wisdom has alighted upon three things,' goes their proverb; 'the hand of the Chinese, the brain of the Frank, and the tongue of the Arab.' This, I take it, is the meaning of that simplicity sought for so much in these days by all the poets, and not to be had at any price.

The most notable and typical story-teller of my acquaintance is one Paddy Flynn, a little, bright-eyed, old man, living in a leaky one-roomed cottage of the village of B——, 'The most gentle — *i.e.* fairy — place in the whole of the County Sligo,' he says, though others claim that honour for Drumahair or for Drumcliff. A very pious old man, too! You may have some time to inspect his strange figure and ragged hair, if he happen to be in a devout humour, before he comes to the doings of the gentry. A strange devotion! Old tales of Columkill, and what he said to his mother.

'How are you to-day, mother?' 'Worse!' 'May you be worse to-morrow'; and on the next day, 'How are you to-day, mother?' 'Worse!' 'May you be worse to-morrow'; and on the next, 'How are you to-day, mother?' 'Better, thank God.' 'May you be better to-morrow.' In which undutiful manner he will tell you Columkill inculcated cheerfulness. Then most likely he will wander off into his favourite theme — how the Judge smiles alike in rewarding the good and condemning the lost to unceasing flames. Very consoling does it appear to Paddy Flynn, this melancholy and apocalyptic cheerfulness of the Judge. Nor seems his own cheerfulness quite earthly — though a very palpable cheerfulness. The first time I saw him he was cooking mushrooms for himself; the next time he was asleep under a hedge, smiling in his sleep. Assuredly some joy not quite of this steadfast earth lightens in those eyes — swift as the eyes of a rabbit — among so many wrinkles, for Paddy Flynn is very old. A melancholy there is in the midst of their cheerfulness — a melancholy that is almost a portion of their joy, the visionary melancholy of purely instinctive natures and of all animals. In the triple solitude of age and eccentricity and partial deafness he goes about much pestered by children.

As to the reality of his fairy and spirit-seeing powers, not all are agreed. One day we were talking of the Banshee. 'I have seen it,' he said, 'down there by the water "batting" the river with its hands.' He it was who said the fairies annoyed him.

Not that the Sceptic is entirely afar even from these western villages. I found him one morning as he bound his corn in a merest pocket-handkerchief of a field. Very different from Paddy Flynn — Scepticism in every wrinkle of his face, and a travelled man, too! — a foot-long Mohawk Indian tattooed on one of his arms to evidence the matter. 'They who travel,' says a neighbouring priest, shaking his head over him, and quoting Thomas à Kempis, 'seldom come home holy.' I had mentioned ghosts to this Sceptic. 'Ghosts,' said he; 'there are no such things at all, at all, but the gentry, they stand to reason; for the devil, when he fell out of heaven, took the weak-minded ones with him, and they were put into the waste places. And that's what the gentry are. But they are getting scarce now, because their time's over, ye see, and they're going back. But ghosts, no! And I'll tell ye something more I don't believe in — the fire of hell'; then, in a low voice, 'that's only invented to give the priests and the parsons something to do.' Thereupon this man, so full of enlightenment, returned to his corn-binding.

The various collectors of Irish folk-lore have, from our point of view, one great merit, and from the point of view of others, one great fault. They have made their work literature rather than science, and told us of the Irish peasantry rather than of the primitive religion of mankind, or whatever else the folk-lorists are on the gad after. To be considered scientists they should have tabulated all their tales in forms like grocers' bills — item the fairy king, item the queen. Instead of this they have caught the very voice of the people, the very pulse of life, each giving what was most noticed in his day. Croker and Lover, full of the ideas of harum-scarum Irish gentility, saw everything humorised. The impulse of the Irish literature of their time came from a class that did not — mainly for political reasons — take the populace seriously, and imagined the country as a humorists's Arcadia; its passion, its gloom, its tragedy, they knew nothing of. What they did was not wholly false; they merely magnified an irresponsible type, found oftenest among boatmen, carmen, and gentlemen's servants, into the type of a whole nation, and created the stage Irishman. The writers of 'forty-eight, and the famine combined, burst their bubble. Their work had the dash as well as the shallowness of an ascendant and idle class, and in Croker is touched everywhere with beauty — a gentle Arcadian beauty. Carleton, a peasant born, has in many of his stories — I have been only able to give a few of the slightest — more especially in his ghost stories, a much more serious way with him, for all his humour. Kennedy, an old bookseller in Dublin, who seems to have had a something of genuine belief in the fairies, came next in time. He has far less literary faculty, but is wonderfully accurate, giving often the very words the stories were told in. But the best book since Croker is Lady Wilde's *Ancient Legends*. The humour has all given way to pathos and tenderness. We have here the innermost heart of the Celt in the moments he has grown to love through years of persecution, when, cushioning himself about with dreams, and hearing fairy-songs in the twilight, he ponders on the soul and on the dead. Here is the Celt, only it is the Celt dreaming.

Besides these are two writers of importance, who have published, so far, nothing in book shape — Miss Letitia Maclintock and Mr. Douglas Hyde. Miss Maclintock writes accurately and beautifully the half Scotch dialect of Ulster; and Mr. Douglas Hyde is now preparing a volume of folk tales in Gaelic, having taken them down, for the most part, word for word among the Gaelic speakers of Roscommon and Galway. He is, perhaps, most to be trusted of all. He knows the people thoroughly. Others see a phase of Irish life; he understands all its elements. His work is neither humorous nor mournful; it is simply life. I hope he may put some of his gatherings into ballads, for he is the last of our ballad-writers of the school of Walsh and Callanan — men whose work seems fragrant with turf smoke. And this brings to mind the chap-books. They are to be found brown with turf smoke on cottage shelves, and are, or were, sold on every hand by the pedlars, but cannot be found in any library of this city of the Sassanach. 'The Royal Fairy Tales', 'The Hibernian Tales', and 'The Legends of the Fairies' are the fairy literature of the people.

Several specimens of our fairy poetry are given. It is more like the fairy poetry of Scotland than of England. The personages of English fairy literature are merely, in most cases, mortals beautifully masquerading. Nobody ever believed in such fairies. They are romantic bubbles from Provence. Nobody ever laid new milk on their doorstep for them.

As to my own part in this book, I have tried to make it representative, as far as so few pages would allow, of every kind of Irish folk-faith. The reader will perhaps wonder that in all my notes I have not rationalised a single hobgoblin. I seek for shelter to the words of Socrates.

Phaedrus. I should like to know, Socrates, whether the place is not somewhere here at which Boreas is said to have carried off Orithyia from the banks of the Ilissus?

Socrates. That is the tradition.

Phaedrus. And is this the exact spot? The little stream is delightfully clear and bright; I can fancy that there might be maidens playing near.

Socrates. I believe the spot is not exactly here, but about a quarter-of-a-mile lower down, where you cross to the temple of Artemis, and I think that there is some sort of an altar of Boreas at the place.

Phaedrus. I do not recollect; but I beseech you to tell me, Socrates, do you believe this tale?

Socrates. The wise are doubtful, and I should not be singular, if, like them, I also doubted. I might have a rational explanation that Orithyia was playing with Pharmacia, when a northern gust carried her over the neighbouring rocks; and this being the manner of her death, she was said to have been carried away by Boreas. There is a discrepancy, however, about the locality. According to another version of the story, she was taken from the Areopagus, and not from this place. Now I quite acknowledge that these allegories are very nice, but he is not to be envied who has to invent them; much labour and ingenuity will be required of him; and when he has once begun, he must go on and rehabilitate centaurs and chimeras dire. Gorgons and winged steeds flow in apace, and numberless other inconceivable and portentous monsters. And if he is sceptical about them, and would fain reduce them one after another to the rules of probability, this sort of crude philosophy will take up all his time. Now, I have certainly not time for such inquiries. Shall I tell you why? I must first know myself, as the Delphian inscription says; to be curious about that which is not my business, while I am still in ignorance of my own self, would be ridiculous. And, therefore, I say farewell to all this; the common opinion is enough for me. For, as I was saying, I want to know not about this, but about myself. Am I, indeed, a wonder more complicated and swollen with passion than the serpent Typhoo, or a creature of gentler and simpler sort, to whom nature has given a diviner and lowlier destiny?

FROM *MYTHOLOGIES*

A VISIONARY

A YOUNG man came to see me at my lodgings the other night, and began to talk of the making of the earth and the heavens and much else. I questioned him about his life and his doings. He had written many poems and painted many mystical designs since we met last, but latterly had neither written nor painted, for his whole heart was set upon making his character vigorous and calm, and the emotional life of the artist was bad for him, he feared. He recited his poems readily, however. He had them all in his memory. Some indeed had never been written down. Suddenly it seemed to me that he was peering about him a little eagerly. 'Do you see anything, X——?' I said. 'A shining, winged woman, covered by her long hair, is standing near the doorway,' he answered, or some such words. 'Is it the influence of some living person who thinks of us, and whose thoughts appear to us in that symbolic form?' I said; for I am well instructed in the ways of the visionaries and in the fashion of their speech. 'No,' he replied; 'for if it were the thoughts of a person who is alive I should feel the living influence in my living body, and my heart would beat and my breath would fail. It is a spirit. It is some one who is dead or who has never lived.'

I asked what he was doing, and found he was clerk in a large shop. His pleasure, however, was to wander about upon the hills, talking to half-mad and visionary peasants, or to persuade queer and conscience-stricken persons to deliver up the keeping of their troubles into his care. Another night, when I was with him in his own lodging, more than one turned up to talk over their beliefs and disbeliefs, and sun them as it were in the subtle light of his mind. Sometimes visions come to him as he talks with them, and he is rumoured to have told divers people true matters of their past days and distant friends, and left them hushed with dread of their strange teacher, who seems scarce more than a boy, and is so much more subtle than the oldest among them.

The poetry he recited me was full of his nature and his visions. Sometimes it told of other lives he believes himself to have lived in other centuries, sometimes of people he had talked to, revealing them to their own minds. I told him I would write an article upon him and it, and was told in turn that I might do so if I did not mention his name, for he wished to be always 'unknown, obscure, impersonal'. Next day a bundle of his poems arrived, and with them a note in these words: 'Here are copies of verses you said you liked. I do not think I could ever write or paint any more. I prepare myself for a cycle of other activities in some other life. I will make rigid my roots and branches. It is not now my turn to burst into leaves and flowers.'

The poems were all endeavours to capture some high, impalpable mood in a net of obscure images. There were fine passages in all, but these were often embedded in thoughts which have evidently a special value to his mind, but are to other men the counters of an unknown coinage. At other times the beauty of the thought was obscured by careless writing as though he had suddenly doubted if writing was not a foolish labour. He had frequently illustrated his verses with drawings, in which an imperfect anatomy did not altogether smother a beauty of feeling. The faeries in whom he believes have given him many subjects, notably Thomas of Ercildoune sitting motionless in the twilight while a young and beautiful creature leans softly out of the shadow and whispers in his ear. He had delighted above all in strong effects of colour: spirits who have upon their heads instead of hair the feathers of peacocks; a phantom reaching from a swirl of flame towards a star; a spirit passing with a globe of iridescent crystal — symbol of the soul — half shut within his hand. But always under this largess of colour lay some appeal to human sympathy. This appeal draws to him all those who, like himself, seek for illumination or else mourn for a joy that has gone. One of these especially comes to mind. A winter or two ago he spent much of the night walking up and down upon the mountain talking to an old peasant who, dumb to most men, poured out his cares for him. Both were unhappy: X—— because he had then first decided that art and poetry were not for him, and the old peasant because his life was ebbing out with no achievement remaining and no hope left him. The peasant was wandering in his mind with prolonged sorrow. Once he burst out with, 'God possesses the heavens — God possesses the heavens — but He covets the world'; and once he lamented that his old neighbours were gone, and that all had forgotten him: they used to draw a chair to the fire for him in every cabin, and now they said, 'Who is that old fellow there?' 'The fret' (Irish for doom) 'is over me,' he repeated, and then went on to talk once more of God and Heaven. More than once also he said, waving his arm towards the mountain, 'Only myself knows what happened under the thorn-tree forty years ago'; and as he said it the tears upon his face glistened in the moonlight.

[1891]

RED HANRAHAN

HANRAHAN, the hedge schoolmaster, a tall, strong, red-haired young man, came into the barn where some of the men of the village were sitting on Samhain Eve. It had been a dwelling-house, and when the man that owned it had built a better one, he had put the two rooms together, and kept it for a place to store one thing or another. There was a fire on the old hearth, and there were dip candles stuck in bottles, and there was a black quart bottle upon some boards that had been put across two barrels to make a table. Most of the men were sitting beside the fire, and one of them was singing a long wandering song, about a Munster man and a Connacht man that were quarrelling about their two provinces.

Hanrahan went to the man of the house and said, 'I got your message'; but when he had said that, he stopped, for an old mountainy man that had a shirt and trousers of unbleached flannel, and that was sitting by himself near the door, was looking at him, and moving an old pack of cards about in his hands and muttering. 'Don't mind him,' said the man of the house; 'he is only some stranger came in a while ago, and we bade him welcome, it being Samhain night, but I think he is not in his right wits. Listen to him now and you will hear what he is saying.'

They listened then, and they could hear the old man muttering to himself as he turned the cards, 'Spades and Diamonds, Courage and Power; Clubs and Hearts, Knowledge and Pleasure.'

'That is the kind of talk he has been going on with for the last hour,' said the man of the house, and Hanrahan turned his eyes from the old man as if he did not like to be looking at him.

'I got your message,' Hanrahan said then. ' "He is in the barn with his three first cousins from Kilchriest," the messenger said, "and there are some of the neighbours with them." '

'It is my cousin over there is wanting to see you,' said the man of the house, and he called over a young frieze-coated man, who was listening to the song, and said, 'This is Red Hanrahan you have the message for.'

'It is a kind message, indeed,' said the young man, 'for it comes from your sweetheart, Mary Lavelle.'

'How would you get a message from her, and what do you know of her?'

'I don't know her, indeed, but I was in Loughrea yesterday, and a neighbour of hers that had some dealings with me was saying that she bade him send you word, if he met any one from this side in the market, that her mother has died from her, and if you have a mind yet to join with herself, she is willing to keep her word to you.'

'I will go to her indeed,' said Hanrahan.

'And she bade you make no delay, for if she has not a man in the house before the month is out, it is likely the little bit of land will be given to another.'

When Hanrahan heard that, he rose up from the bench he had sat down on. 'I will make no delay indeed,' he said; 'there is a full moon, and if I get as far as Kilchriest to-night, I will reach to her before the setting of the sun to-morrow.'

When the others heard that, they began to laugh at him for being in such haste to go to his sweetheart, and one asked him if he would leave his school in the old lime-kiln, where he was giving the children such good learning. But he said the children would be glad enough in the morning to find the place empty, and no one to keep them at their task; and as for his school he could set it up again in any place, having as he had his little inkpot hanging from his neck by a chain, and his big Virgil and his primer in the skirt of his coat.

Some of them asked him to drink a glass before he went, and a young man caught hold of his coat, and said he must not leave them without singing the song he had made in praise of Venus and of Mary Lavelle. He drank a glass of whiskey, but he said he would not stop but would set out on his journey.

'There's time enough, Red Hanrahan,' said the man of the house. 'It will be time enough for you to give up sport when you are after your marriage, and it might be a long time before we will see you again.'

'I will not stop,' said Hanrahan; 'my mind would be on the roads all the time, bringing me to the woman that sent for me, and she lonesome and watching till I come.'

Some of the others came about him, pressing him that had been such a pleasant comrade, so full of songs and every kind of trick and fun, not to leave them till the night would be over, but he refused them all, and shook them off, and went to the door. But as he put his foot over the threshold, the strange old man stood up and put his hand that was thin and withered like a bird's claw on Hanrahan's hand, and said: 'It is not Hanrahan, the learned man and the great songmaker, that should go out from a gathering like this, on a Samhain night. And stop here, now,' he said, 'and play a hand with me; and here is an old pack of cards has done its work many a night before this, and old as it is, there has been much of the riches of the world lost and won over it.'

One of the young men said, 'It isn't much of the riches of the world has stopped with yourself, old man,' and he looked at the old man's bare feet, and they all laughed. But Hanrahan did not laugh, but he sat down very quietly, without a word. Then one of them said, 'So you will stop with us after all,

Hanrahan'; and the old man said, 'He will stop indeed, did you not hear me asking him?'

They all looked at the old man then as if wondering where he came from. 'It is far I am come,' he said; 'through France I have come, and through Spain, and by Lough Greine of the hidden mouth, and none has refused me anything.' And then he was silent and nobody liked to question him, and they began to play. There were six men at the boards playing, and the others were looking on behind. They played two or three games for nothing, and then the old man took a fourpenny bit, worn very thin and smooth, out from his pocket, and he called to the rest to put something on the game. Then they all put down something on the boards, and little as it was it looked much, from the way it was shoved from one to another, first one man winning it and then his neighbour. And sometimes the luck would go against a man and he would have nothing left, and then one or another would lend him something, and he would pay it again out of his winnings, for neither good nor bad luck stopped long with any one.

And once Hanrahan said as a man would say in a dream, 'It is time for me to be going the road'; but just then a good card came to him, and he played it out, and all the money began to come to him. And once he thought of Mary Lavelle, and he sighed; and that time his luck went from him, and he forgot her again.

But at last the luck went to the old man and it stayed with him, and all they had flowed into him, and he began to laugh little laughs to himself, and to sing over and over to himself, 'Spades and Diamonds, Courage and Power,' and so on, as if if it were a verse of a song.

And after a while anyone looking at the men, and seeing the way their bodies were rocking to and fro, and the way they kept their eyes on the old man's hands, would think they had drink taken, or that the whole store they had in the world was put on the cards; but that was not so, for the quart bottle had not been disturbed since the game began, and was nearly full yet, and all that was on the game was a few sixpenny bits and shillings, and maybe a handful of coppers.

'You are good men to win and good men to lose,' said the old man; 'you have play in your hearts.' He began then to shuffle the cards and to mix them, very quick and fast, till at last they could not see them to be cards at all, but you would think him to be making rings of fire in the air, as little lads would make them with whirling a lighted stick; and after that it seemed to them that all the room was dark, and they could see nothing but his hands and the cards.

And all in a minute a hare made a leap out from between his hands, and whether it was one of the cards that took that shape, or whether it was made out of nothing in the palms of his hands, nobody knew, but there it was running on the floor of the barn, as quick as any hare that ever lived.

Some looked at the hare, but more kept their eyes on the old man, and while they were looking at him a hound made a leap out between his hands, the same way as the hare did, and after that another hound and another, till there was a whole pack of them following the hare round and round the barn.

The players were all standing up now, with their backs to the boards, shrinking from the hounds, and nearly deafened with the noise of their yelping, but as quick as the hounds were they could not overtake the hare, but it went round, till at the last it seemed as if a blast of wind burst open the barn door, and the hare doubled and made a leap over the boards where the men had been playing, and went out of the door and away through the night, and the hounds over the boards and through the door after it.

Then the old man called out, 'Follow the hounds, follow the hounds, and it is a great hunt you will see to-night,' and he went out after them. But used as the men were to go hunting after hares, and ready as they were for any sport, they were in dread to go out into the night, and it was only Hanrahan that rose up and that said, 'I will follow, I will follow on.'

'You had best stop here, Hanrahan,' the young man that was nearest him said, 'for you might be going into some great danger.' But Hanrahan said, 'I will see fair play, I will see fair play,' and he went stumbling out of the door like a man in a dream, and the door shut after him as he went.

He thought he saw the old man in front of him, but it was only his own shadow that the full moon cast on the road before him, but he could hear the hounds crying after the hare over the wide green fields of Granagh, and he followed them very fast, for there was nothing to stop him; and after a while he came to smaller fields that had little walls of loose stones around them, and he threw the stones down as he crossed them, and did not wait to put them up again; and he passed by the place where the river goes underground at Ballylee, and he could hear the hounds going before him up towards the head of the river. Soon he found it harder to run, for it was uphill he was going, and clouds came over the moon, and it was hard for him to see his way, and once he left the path to take a short-cut, but his foot slipped into a bog-hole and he had to come back to it. And how long he was going he did not know, or what way he went, but at last he was up on the bare mountain, with nothing but the rough heather about him, and he could neither hear the hounds nor any other thing. But their cry began to come to him again, at first far off and then very near, and when it came quite close to him, it went up all of a sudden into the air, and there was the sound of hunting over his head; then it went away northward till he could hear nothing at all. 'That's not fair,' he said, 'that's not fair.' And he could walk no longer, but sat down on the heather where he was, in the heart of Slieve Echtge, for all the strength had gone from him, with the dint of the long journey he had made.

And after a while he took notice that there was a door close to him, and a light coming from it, and he wondered that being so close to him he had not seen it before. And he rose up, and tired as he was he went in at the door, and although it was night-time outside, it was daylight he found within. And presently he met with an old man that had been gathering summer thyme and yellow flag-flowers, and it seemed as if all the sweet smells of the summer were with them. And the old man said, 'It is a long time you have been coming to us, Hanrahan the learned man and the great songmaker.'

And with that he brought him into a very big shining house, and every grand thing Hanrahan had ever heard of, and every colour he had ever seen, was in it. There was a high place at the end of the house, and on it there was sitting in a high chair a woman, the most beautiful the world ever saw, having a long pale face and flowers about it, but she had the tired look of one that had been long waiting. And there were sitting on the step below her chair four grey old women, and the one of them was holding a great cauldron in her lap; and another a great stone on her knees, and heavy as it was it seemed light to her; and another of them had a very long spear that was made of pointed wood; and the last of them had a sword that was without a scabbard.

Hanrahan stood looking at them for a long time, but none of them spoke any word to him or looked at him at all. And he had it in his mind to ask who that woman in the chair was, that was like a queen, and what she was waiting for; but ready as he was with his tongue and afraid of no person, he was in dread now to speak to so beautiful a woman, and in so grand a place. And then he thought to ask what were the four things the four grey old women were holding like great treasures, but he could not think of the right words to bring out.

Then the first of the old women rose up, holding the cauldron between her two hands, and she said, 'Pleasure,' and Hanrahan said no word. Then the second old woman rose up with the stone in her hands, and she said, 'Power'; and the third old woman rose up with a spear in her hand, and she said, 'Courage'; and the last of the old women rose up having the sword in her hands, and she said, 'Knowledge.' And everyone, after she had spoken, waited as if for Hanrahan to question her, but he said nothing at all. And then the four old women went out of the door, bringing their four treasures with them, and as they went out one of them said, 'He has no wish for us'; and another said, 'He is weak, he is weak'; and another said, 'He is afraid'; and the last said, 'His wits are gone from him.' And then they all said, 'Echtge, daughter of the Silver Hand, must stay in her sleep. It is a pity, it is a great pity.'

And then the woman that was like a queen gave a very sad sigh, and it seemed to Hanrahan as if the sigh had the sound in it of hidden streams; and if the place he was in had been ten times grander and more shining than it was, he could not have hindered sleep from coming on him; and he staggered like a drunken man and lay down there and then.

When Hanrahan awoke, the sun was shining on his face, but there was white frost on the grass around him, and there was ice on the edge of the stream he was lying by, and that goes running on through Doire-caol and Drim-na-rod. He knew by the shape of the hills and by the shining of Lough Greine in the distance that he was upon one of the hills of Slieve Echtge, but he was not sure how he came there; for all that had happened in the barn had gone from him, and all of his journey but the soreness of his feet and the stiffness in his bones.

It was a year after that, there were men of the village of Cappaghtagle sitting by the fire in a house on the roadside, and Red Hanrahan that was now very thin and worn, and his hair very long and wild, came to the half-door and asked leave to come in and rest himself; and they bid him welcome because it was Samhain night. He sat down with them, and they gave him a glass of whiskey out of a quart bottle; and they saw the little inkpot hanging about his neck, and knew he was a scholar, and asked for stories about the Greeks.

He took the Virgil out of the big pocket of his coat, but the cover was very black and swollen with the wet, and the page when he opened it was very yellow, but that was no great matter, for he looked at it like a man that had never learned to read. Some young man that was there began to laugh at him then, and to ask why did he carry so heavy a book with him when he was not able to read it.

It vexed Hanrahan to hear that, and he put the Virgil back in his pocket and asked if they had a pack of cards among them, for cards were better than books. When they brought out the cards he took them and began to shuffle them, and while he was shuffling them something seemed to come into his mind, and he put his hand to his face like one that is trying to remember, and he said, 'Was I ever here before, or where was I on a night like this?' and then of a sudden he stood up and let the cards fall to the floor, and he said, 'Who was it brought me a message from Mary Lavelle?'

'We never saw you before now, and we never heard of Mary Lavelle,' said the man of the house. 'And who is she,' he said, 'and what is it you are talking about?'

'It was this night a year ago, I was in a barn, and there were men playing cards, and there was money on the table, they were pushing it from one to another here and there — and I got a message, and I was going out of the door to look for my sweetheart that wanted me, Mary Lavelle.' And then Hanrahan called out very loud, 'Where have I been since then? Where was I for the whole year?'

'It is hard to say where you might have been in that time,' said the oldest of the men, 'or what part of the world you may have travelled; and it is like enough you have the dust of many roads on your feet; for there are many go wandering and forgetting like that,' he said, 'when once they have been given the touch.'

'That is true,' said another of the men. 'I knew a woman went wandering like that through the length of seven years; she came back after, and she told her friends she had often been glad enough to eat the food that was put in the pig's trough. And it is best for you to go to the priest now,' he said, 'and let him take off you whatever may have been put upon you.'

'It is to my sweetheart I will go, to Mary Lavelle,' said Hanrahan; 'it is too long I have delayed, how do I know what might have happened her in the length of a year?'

He was going out of the door then, but they all told him it was best for him to stop the night, and to get strength for the journey; and indeed he wanted that, for he was very weak, and when they gave him food he ate it like a man that had never seen food before, and one of them said, 'He is eating as if he had trodden on the hungry grass.' It was in the white light of the morning he set out, and the time seemed long to him till he could get to Mary Lavelle's house. But when he came to it, he found the door broken, and the thatch dropping from the roof, and no living person to be seen. And when he asked the neighbours what had happened her, all they could say was that she had been put out of the house, and had married some labouring man, and they had gone looking for work to London or Liverpool or some big place. And whether she found a worse place or a better he never knew, but anyway he never met with her or with news of her again.

[1903]

THE DEATH OF HANRAHAN THE RED

It came about gradually that Hanrahan ceased to stray from the neighbourhood of the Steep Place of the Strangers, making even his necessary journeys to the town for food seldomer and seldomer. The little leather bag in which there was still some silver and copper money, hung by the hearth-side undisturbed; nor did he seem to endure the pangs of half-starvation, although his hand had grown heavy on the staff and his cheeks hollow. His favourite business was to sit looking into the long narrow lake which cherishes the gaunt image of the Rock of the Bogs, and to wander in a little wood of larch and hazel and ash upon its border; and as the days passed it was as though he became incorporate with some more poignant and fragile world whose marchlands are the intense colours and silences of this world. Sometimes he would hear in the little wood a fitful music which was forgotten like a dream the moment it had ceased, and once in the deep silence of noon he heard there a sound like the continuous clashing of many swords; while at sundown and at moonrise the lake grew like a gateway of ivory and silver, and from its silence arose faint lamentations, a vague shivering laughter, and many pale and beckoning hands.

He was sitting looking into the water one autumn evening close to the place where the sacrilegious men-at-arms had fallen heaped together, while the piper of the Shee who had lured them over the edge of the Steep Place of the Strangers, rode through the upper air whirling his torch; when a cry began towards the east, at first distant and indistinct, but get-

ting nearer and louder as the shadows gathered. 'I am beautiful; I am beautiful,' were the words; 'the birds in the air, the
moths under the leaves, the flies over the water look at me;
for they never saw anyone as beautiful as I am. I am young;
I am young; look at me, mountains; look at me, perishing
woods; for my body will gleam like the white waters when
you have been hurried away. You and the races of men, and
the races of beasts, and the races of the fish and the winged
races are dropping like a guttering candle; but I laugh aloud
remembering my youth!' The cry would cease from time to
time as though in exhaustion and then begin once more, 'I am
beautiful, I am beautiful,' and repeat the same words and in
the same monotonous chant. Presently the hazel-branches at
the edge of the little wood trembled for a moment, and an old
woman forced her way from among them and passed Hanrahan with slow deliberate steps. Her face was the colour of
earth and incredibly wrinkled, and her white hair hung about
it in tangled and discoloured locks, and through her tattered
clothes showed here and there her dark, weather-roughened
skin. She passed with wide open eyes and lifted head and arms
hanging straight down; and was lost in the shadow of the
mountains towards the west. Hanrahan looked after her with
a shudder; for he recognized crazy Whinny Byrne, who went
from barony to barony begging her bread and crying always
the same cry; and remembered that she was once so wise that
the women of her village sought her counsel in all things; and
had so beautiful a voice that men and women came from a
distance of many miles to hear her sing at wake or wedding;
but the people of the Shee stole her wits a summer night fifty
years before, while she sat crooning to herself on the edge of
the sea, and dreaming of Cleena, who rushes with unwrinkled
feet among the foam.

The cry died away up the hillside, the last faint murmurs

coming, as it seemed, out of the purple deep where the first stars were glimmering like little fluttering white moths.

A cold wind was creeping among the reeds, and Hanrahan began to shiver and to sigh, and to think of the hearth where his fire of turf would be still making a little warm and kind, if dwindling, world under the broken thatch. He toiled slowly up the hill bowed as by an immense burden that grew the greater as he passed, where he had seen the unhappy lovers, that are in fairy-land, walking on the dark air with august feet, because the thought of them made his exile from beauty and from youth so bitterly poignant. The old yew above his cabin looked the more malignant from dwelling at so great a height an outcast from among its kind, and seemed to uplift its dark branches like withered hands threatening the stars, and the blue deep they swim in, with the coming of decay and shadowy old age.

He mounted upon the rock, whose partial shelter had doubtless enabled the yew to root itself firmly, before its branches received the burden of all the winds; and looked towards the south, for there he had been last loved and made his last verses. A little black spot was moving from the hills and woods, between the Hill of Awley and the lake of Castle Dargan, and, while he watched, it grew larger and larger, until he knew it for a wide-winged bird, and then for a spotted eagle with something glittering in its claws. It came swiftly towards him, flying straight onward as if upon a long journey or pondering some hidden purpose; and when it was nearly overhead he saw that the glittering thing was a large fish which still writhed from side to side. Suddenly the fish made a last struggle and leaped out of its claws, and fell with gasping mouth into the branches of the yew-tree. Hanrahan had not eaten since the previous morning, and then but little, and, though he had been scarcely aware of his hunger hitherto, his

hunger came upon him now, and so fiercely that he had gladly
buried his teeth into the living fish. He hurled a heavy stone at
the eagle, which had begun to circle with great clamour about
the tree, and having filled his cap with like stones, drove it
screaming over the mountain eastward. He began then to
climb the tree with a passionate haste, and had almost come to
where the fish hung in the fork between two branches, glittering like a star among the green smoke of some malevolent fire
lighted by the People from under the Sea, when a branch
broke under his hand and he fell heavily upon a rock, and
from this rebounded again, striking first his back and then his
head, and becoming unconscious at the last blow. The fire had
already consumed his goods, and now those creatures of earth
and air and water, that once endured his curse, had taken him
in a subtle ambuscade.

A face was bent over him when he awoke, and, despite his
weakness and bewilderment and suffering, he shuddered when
the turf fire, now red and leaping, gleamed on the broken and
blackened teeth and on the mud-stiffened tatters of Whinny
Byrne. She watched him intently a little, for her slow senses
appeared to need time to assure her that he was not dead; and
then laid down the wet cloth which had bathed the blood
from his face; and began stirring a pot, from which she drew
presently a couple of potatoes and held them towards him
with an inarticulate murmur. In so much of the night as was
not spent in short and feverish sleep, he saw her moving hither
and thither, or bending over the hearth with her wrinkled
hands spread out above its flame; and once or twice he caught
the words of her monotonous chant, subdued into a feeble
murmur. At the dawn he half raised himself with many pains
and pointed to the leather bag by the hearth-side. Whinny
opened the bag and took out a little copper and silver money,
but let it fall back again, not seeming to understand its pur-

pose; perhaps because she was accustomed to beg, not for money, but for potatoes and for fragments of bread and meat, and perhaps because the persuasion of her own beauty was coming upon her with a double passion in the exultation of the dawn. She went out and brought an armful of heather and heaped it over him, saying something about the morning being 'cold, cold, and cold', and brought a dozen more armfuls and heaped them by the first until he was well covered; and went away down the mountain-side; her cry of 'I am beautiful, I am beautiful,' dying slowly in the distance.

Hanrahan lay through the day, enduring much pain; and scarce able even to wonder if Whinny Byrne had left him for good, or but to come again and divide with him the gains of her begging. A little after sundown he heard her voice on the hillside, and that night she made up his fire and cooked her potatoes and divided them with him as before. Some days passed in this way, and the weight of his flesh was heavy about him, but gradually as he grew weaker it seemed to him that there were powers close at hand, and growing always more numerous, who might, in the wink o' an eye, break down the rampart the sensuality of pain had builded about him, and receive him into their world. Even as it was he had moments when he heard faint ecstatic reedy voices, crying from the roof-tree or from the flame of the earth; while at other moments the room was brimmed with a penetrating music. After a little, weakness brought a vanishing of pain and a slow blossoming of silence in which, like faint light through a mist, the ecstatic reedy voices came continually.

One morning he heard music, somewhere outside the door, and as the day passed it grew louder and louder until it drowned the ecstatic reedy voices and even Whinny's voice upon the hillside at sundown. About midnight, and in a moment, the walls seemed to melt away and to leave his bed

floating in a misty and pale light, which glimmered on each
side to an incalculable distance; and after the first blinding of
his eyes he saw that it was full of faint and great figures rushing
hither and thither. At the same moment the music became so
distinct, that he understood it was but the continuous clashing
of swords. 'I am dead,' he repeated, 'and in the midst of the
music of heaven. O Cherubim and Seraphim, receive my
soul!' At his cry the light where it was nearest filled with
sparks of more intense light; and he saw that these were the
points of swords turned towards his heart, and then a sudden
flame, dazzling, as it seemed, like a divine passion, swept over
all the light and went out, and he was in darkness. At first he
could see nothing, for it was as dark as though he were enclosed in black marble; but gradually the firelight began to
glimmer upon Whinny Byrne, who was bending over it, with
her eyes fixed upon the bed. She got up and came towards
him, and the ecstatic reedy voices began crying again, while a
faint dove-grey light crept over the room, coming from he
knew not what secret world. He saw the withered earthen
face and withered earthen arms, and for all his weakness
shrank farther towards the wall; and then faint white arms,
wrought as of glistening cloud, came out of the mud-stiffened
tatters and were clasped about his body; and a voice that
sounded faint and far, but was of a marvellous distinctness,
whispered in his ears: 'You will seek me no longer upon the
breasts of women.'

'Who are you?' he murmured.

'I am of those,' was the answer, 'who dwell in the minds of
the crazy and the diseased and the dying, and you are mine
until the world is melted like wax. Look, they have lighted our
wedding tapers!' And he saw that the air was crowded with
pale hands, and that each hand held a long taper like a rush-
light.

Whinny Byrne sat by the body until morning, and then began begging from barony to barony again, her monotonous chant keeping time to the beat of her wrinkled heels in the clinging dust: 'I am beautiful; I am beautiful; the birds in the air, the moths under the leaves, the flies over the waters look at me, for they never saw anyone beautiful as I am. I am young; I am young; look at me, mountains; look at me, perishing woods; for my body will gleam like the white waters when you have been hurried away. You and the races of men, and the races of beasts, and the races of the fish and the winged races are dropping like a guttering candle; but I laugh aloud remembering my youth!' She did not return at nightfall or ever again to the shepherd's cabin; and it was only after some days that turf-cutters found the body of Owen Hanrahan the Red, and gathering a concourse of mourners and of keening women gave him a burying worthy of so great a poet.

[1896]

'DUST HATH CLOSED HELEN'S EYE'

I

I HAVE been lately to a little group of houses, not many enough to be called a village, in the barony of Kiltartan in County Galway, whose name, Ballylee, is known through all the west of Ireland. There is the old square castle,[1] Ballylee, inhabited by a farmer and his wife, and a cottage where their daughter and their son-in-law live, and a little mill with an old miller, and old ash-trees throwing green shadows upon a little river and great stepping-stones. I went there two or three times last year to talk to the miller about Biddy Early, a wise woman that lived in Clare some years ago, and about her saying, 'There is a cure for all evil between the two mill-wheels of Ballylee,' and to find out from him or another whether she meant the moss between the running waters or some other herb. I have been there this summer, and I shall be there again before it is autumn, because Mary Hynes, a beautiful woman whose name is still a wonder by turf fires, died there sixty years ago; for our feet would linger where beauty has lived its life of sorrow to make us understand that it is not of the world. An old man brought me a little way from the mill and the castle, and down a long, narrow boreen that was nearly lost in brambles and sloe-bushes, and he said, 'That is the little old foundation of the house, but the most of it is taken for building walls, and the goats have ate those bushes

[1] Ballylee Castle, or Thoor Ballylee, as I have named it to escape from the too magnificent word 'castle,' is now my property, and I spend my summers or some part of them there. (1924.)

444

that are growing over it till they've got cranky, and they won't grow any more. They say she was the handsomest girl in Ireland, her skin was liked dribbled snow' — he meant driven snow, perhaps, — 'and she had blushes in her cheeks. She had five handsome brothers, but all are gone now!' I talked to him about a poem in Irish, Raftery, a famous poet, made about her, and how it said, 'There is a strong cellar in Ballylee.' He said the strong cellar was the great hole where the river sank underground, and he brought me to a deep pool, where an otter hurried away under a grey boulder, and told me that many fish came up out of the dark water at early morning 'to taste the fresh water coming down from the hills'.

I first heard of the poem from an old woman who lives about two miles farther up the river, and who remembers Raftery and Mary Hynes. She says, 'I never saw anybody so handsome as she was, and I never will till I die,' and that he was nearly blind, and had 'no way of living but to go round and to mark some house to go to, and then all the neighbours would gather to hear. If you treated him well he'd praise you, but if you did not, he'd fault you in Irish. He was the greatest poet in Ireland, and he'd make a song about that bush if he chanced to stand under it. There was a bush he stood under from the rain, and he made verses praising it, and then when the water came through he made verses dispraising it.' She sang the poem to a friend and to myself in Irish, and every word was audible and expressive, as the words in a song were always, as I think, before music grew too proud to be the garment of words, flowing and changing with the flowing and changing of their energies. The poem is not as natural as the best Irish poetry of the last century, for the thoughts are arranged in a too obviously traditional form, so the old poor half-blind man who made it has to speak as if he were a rich farmer offering the best of everything to the woman he loves, but it has naïve and tender phrases. The friend that was with me has made some of the translation, but some of it has been made by the countrypeople themselves. I think it has more of the simplicity of the Irish verses than one finds in most translations.

Going to Mass by the will of God,
The day came wet and the wind rose;
I met Mary Hynes at the cross of Kiltartan,
And I fell in love with her then and there.

I spoke to her kind and mannerly,
As by report was her own way;
And she said, 'Raftery, my mind is easy,
You may come to-day to Ballylee.'

When I heard her offer I did not linger,
When her talk went to my heart my heart rose.
We had only to go across the three fields,
We had daylight with us to Ballylee.

The table was laid with glasses and a quart measure,
She had fair hair, and she sitting beside me;
And she said, 'Drink, Raftery, and a hundred welcomes,
There is a strong cellar in Ballylee.'

O star of light and O sun in harvest,
O amber hair, O my share of the world,
Will you come with me upon Sunday
Till we agree together before all the people?

I would not grudge you a song every Sunday evening,
Punch on the table, or wine if you would drink it,
But, O King of Glory, dry the roads before me,
Till I find the way to Ballylee.

There is sweet air on the side of the hill
When you are looking down upon Ballylee;
When you are walking in the valley picking nuts and black-
  berries,
There is music of the birds in it and music of the Sidhe.

What is the worth of greatness till you have the light
Of the flower of the branch that is by your side?
There is no god to deny it or to try and hide it,
She is the sun in the heavens who wounded my heart.

There was no part of Ireland I did not travel,
From the rivers to the tops of the mountains,
To the edge of Lough Greine whose mouth is hidden,
And I saw no beauty but was behind hers.

Her hair was shining, and her brows were shining too;
Her face was like herself, her mouth pleasant and sweet.
She is the pride, and I give her the branch,
She is the shining flower of Ballylee.

It is Mary Hynes, the calm and easy woman,
Has beauty in her mind and in her face.
If a hundred clerks were gathered together,
They could not write down a half of her ways.

An old weaver, whose son is supposed to go away among
the Sidhe (the faeries) at night, says, 'Mary Hynes was the
most beautiful thing ever made. My mother used to tell me
about her, for she'd be at every hurling, and wherever she was
she was dressed in white. As many as eleven men asked her in
marriage in one day, but she wouldn't have any of them. There
was a lot of men up beyond Kilbecanty one night sitting together drinking, and talking of her, and one of them got up

and set out to go to Ballylee and see her; but Cloone Bog was open then, and when he came to it he fell into the water, and they found him dead there in the morning. She died of the fever that was before the famine.' Another old man says he was only a child when he saw her, but he remembered that 'the strongest man that was among us, one John Madden, got his death of the head of her, cold he got crossing rivers in the night-time to get to Ballylee.' This is perhaps the man the other remembered, for tradition gives the one thing many shapes. There is an old woman who remembers her, at Derry-brien among the Echtge hills, a vast desolate place, which has changed little since the old poem said, 'the stag upon the cold summit of Echtge hears the cry of the wolves', but still mindful of many poems and of the dignity of ancient speech. She says, 'The sun and the moon never shone on anybody so handsome, and her skin was so white that it looked blue, and she had two little blushes on her cheeks.' And an old wrinkled woman who lives close by Ballylee, and has told me many tales of the Sidhe, says, 'I often saw Mary Hynes, she was handsome indeed. She had two bunches of curls beside her cheeks, and they were the colour of silver. I saw Mary Molloy that was drowned in the river beyond, and Mary Guthrie that was in Ardrahan, but she took the sway of them both, a very comely creature. I was at her wake too — she had seen too much of the world. She was a kind creature. One day I was coming home through that field beyond, and I was tired, and who should come out but the Poison Glegeal (the shining flower), and she gave me a glass of new milk.' This old woman meant no more than some beautiful bright colour by the colour of silver, for though I knew an old man — he is dead now — who thought she might know 'the cure for all the evils in the world', that the Sidhe knew, she has seen too little gold to know its colour. But a man by the shore at Kinvara, who is too young to remember Mary Hynes, says, 'Everybody says there is no one at all to be seen now so handsome; it is said she had beautiful hair, the colour of gold. She was poor, but her clothes every day were the same as Sunday, she had such neatness. And if she went to any kind of a meeting, they would all be killing one another for a sight of her, and there was a great many in love with her, but she died young. It is said that no one that has a song made about them will ever live long.'

Those who are much admired are, it is held, taken by the Sidhe, who can use ungoverned feeling for their own ends, so that a father, as an old herb-doctor told me once, may give his child into their hands, or a husband his wife. The admired and desired are only safe if one says 'God bless them' when one's eyes are upon them. The old woman that sang the song thinks, too, that Mary Hynes was 'taken', as the phrase is, 'for they have taken many that are not handsome, and why would they not take her? And people came from all parts to look at her, and maybe there were some that did not say "God bless her."' An old man who lives by the sea at Duras has as little doubt that she was taken, 'for there are some living yet can remember her coming to the pattern[1] there beyond, and she was said to be the handsomest girl in Ireland.' She died young because the gods loved her, for the Sidhe are the gods, and it may be that the old saying, which we forget to understand literally, meant her manner of death in old times. These poor countrymen and countrywomen in their beliefs, and in their emotions, are many years nearer to that old Greek world, that set beauty beside the fountain of things, than are our men of learning. She 'had seen too much of the world'; but these old men and women, when they tell of her, blame another and not her, and though they can be hard, they grow gentle as the

[1] A 'pattern', or 'patron', is a festival in honour of a saint.

old men of Troy grew gentle when Helen passed by on the walls.

The poet who helped her to so much fame has himself a great fame throughout the west of Ireland. Some think that Raftery was half blind, and say, 'I saw Raftery, a dark man, but he had sight enough to see her,' or the like, but some think he was wholly blind, as he may have been at the end of his life. Fable makes all things perfect in their kind, and her blind people must never look on the world and the sun. I asked a man I met one day, when I was looking for a pool *na mna Sidhe* where women of Faery have been seen, how Raftery could have admired Mary Hynes so much if he had been altogether blind. He said, 'I think Raftery was altogether blind, but those that are blind have a way of seeing things, and have the power to know more, and to feel more, and to do more, and to guess more than those that have their sight, and a certain wit and a certain wisdom is given to them.' Everybody, indeed, will tell you that he was very wise, for was he not not only blind but a poet? The weaver, whose words about Mary Hynes I have already given, says, 'His poetry was the gift of the Almighty, for there are three things that are the gift of the Almighty — poetry and dancing and principles. That is why in the old times an ignorant man coming down from the hillside would be better behaved and have better learning than a man with education you'd meet now, for they got it from God'; and a man at Coole says, 'When he put his finger to one part of his head, everything would come to him as if it was written in a book'; and an old pensioner at Kiltartan says, 'He was standing under a bush one time, and he talked to it, and it answered him back in Irish. Some say it was the bush that spoke, but it must have been an enchanted voice in it, and it gave him the knowledge of all the things of the world. The bush withered up afterwards, and it is to be seen on the roadside now between this and Rahasine.' There is a poem of his about a bush, which I have never seen, and it may have come out of the cauldron of Fable in this shape.

A friend of mine met a man once who had been with him when he died, but the people say that he died alone, and one Maurteen Gillane told Dr. Hyde that all night long a light was seen streaming up to heaven from the roof of the house where he lay, and 'that was the angels who were with him'; and all night long there was a great light in the hovel, 'and that was the angels who were waking him. They gave that honour to him because he was so good a poet, and sang such religious songs.' It may be that in a few years Fable, who changes mortalities to immortalities in her cauldron, will have changed Mary Hynes and Raftery to perfect symbols of the sorrow of beauty and of the magnificence and penury of dreams.

[1900]

II

When I was in a northern town a while ago I had a long talk with a man who had lived in a neighbouring country district when he was a boy. He told me that when a very beautiful girl was born in a family that had not been noted for good looks, her beauty was thought to have come from the Sidhe, and to bring misfortune with it. He went over the names of several beautiful girls that he had known, and said that beauty had never brought happiness to anybody. It was a thing, he said, to be proud of and afraid of. I wish I had written out his words at the time, for they were more picturesque than my memory of them.

[1902]

SPEECH ON THE CHILD AND THE STATE

PERHAPS there are some here, one or two, who were present some thirty-six years ago at a meeting in my house, at which this society was first proposed. I think that meeting was the beginning of what is called the Irish Literary Movement. We and Dr. Hyde and his movement, which began three or four years later with the foundation of the Gaelic League, tried to be unpolitical, and yet all that we did was dominated by the political situation. Whether we wrote speeches, or wrote poems, or wrote romances or wrote books of history, we could not get out of our heads that we were somehow pleading for our country before a packed jury. And that meant a great deal of strain, a great deal of unreality, and even a little hysteria. Now there is no one to win over. Ireland has been put into our hands that we may shape it, and I find all about me in Ireland today a new overflowing life. To this overflowing life I attribute that our audiences at the Abbey Theatre have doubled, that the interest in music is so great that the Royal Dublin Society, which a few years ago was content with a hall that held seven hundred people, finds its new hall that holds some fifteen hundred so much too small, that every afternoon concert has to be repeated in the evening. Nor is it only appreciation that has grown, for where there is the right guidance and the right discipline, young men are ready for the hardest work. Colonel Brase does not find it hard to get his young men to practise many hours a day, his difficulty is sometimes to get them to cease work.

I know no case where the best teaching has been brought to Ireland in vain, and to-day there is a greater desire than ever before for expression, I think I may also say for discipline. The whole nation is plastic and receptive, but it is held back, and will be held back for some time to come by its lack of education, education in the most common and necessary subjects.

For that reason I put so much reliance in your patriotism and your patience that I am going to talk to you about education in the Primary Schools. Perhaps, indeed, I but speak of it because it is so running in my head that I would speak badly of anything else. I have been going round schools listening at a school attendance committee, talking to schoolmasters and inspectors. Many of you have influence in Ireland, influence through the Press, or through your friends, and I want to impress upon you that the schools in Ireland are not fit places for children. They are insanitary, they are out of repair, they are badly heated, and in Dublin and Cork they are far too small. The Government inherited this state of things, this old scandal; they want to put it right, but they will not be able to do so unless public opinion is with them, above all perhaps, unless just the kind of people who are here to-night are prepared to defend them and support them. The Government is introducing a Compulsory Education Bill, but we have all our individual responsibility, and we must see to it that compulsory education does not come into force — I do not say does not pass — until those schools are fitted for their work. And if the children are going to be forced to school you must not only see that those schools are warm and clean and sanitary, but you must do as other countries are doing more and more, and see that children during school hours are neither half-naked nor starved.

You cannot do this by money alone, you must create some body of men with knowledge, that can give enough attention to see that all does not go to ruin again. Many of us think that you can only accomplish this by having a county rate struck,

and by having county committees to supervise the spending
of the money. No one proposes to interfere with the present
manager's right to appoint and dismiss teachers. That right is
cherished by the clergy of all denominations but the ablest
managers would, I believe, welcome popular control if confined to heating, housing, clothing, cleaning, etc. The old system has broken down, and all know that it has.

Only when the schools have been made habitable will the
question arise that most interests us — what are you going to
teach there? Whether Gaelic be compulsory or voluntary, a
great deal of it will be taught. At present Gaelic scholars assure
me that there is nothing to read in modern Irish except for
very young children who love fairy-tales. You must translate,
you must modernise. A Committee of the Senate, of which I
was chairman, has made a recommendation to the Government asking it to endow research into old, middle and
modern Irish. Nothing is decided, but I think the Government will make this grant. Probably most of the books so
produced will be in middle or ancient Irish, and in any case
unsuitable for young children. They will, however, supply the
material from which in some degree a vivid modern literature
may be created. I think the Government should appoint some
committee of publication and so make possible a modern
Gaelic literature. Let us say, Dr. Douglas Hyde, Mr. James
Stephens, who is always working at his Irish, and Mr. Robin
Flower, who is a great scholar and a fine critic. They would
not have time to do much of the great work themselves, but
they could put others to it. Up to, say, ten years old, a child is
content with a wild old tale, but from ten years on you must
give it something with more of the problems of life in it. I
would like to see the great classics, especially of the Catholic
Latin nations, translated into Gaelic.

The tendency of the most modern education, that in Italy,

let us say, is to begin geography with your native fields, arithmetic by counting the school chairs and measuring the walls, history with local monuments, religion with the local saints, and then to pass on from that to the nation itself. That is but carrying into education principles a group of artists, my father among them, advocated in art teaching. These artists have said: 'Do not put scholars to draw from Greek or Roman casts until they have first drawn from life; only when they have drawn from life can they understand the cast.' That which the child sees — the school — the district — and to a lesser degree the nation — is like the living body: distant countries and everything the child can only read of is like the cold Roman or Greek cast. If your education therefore is efficient in the modern sense, it will be more national than the dreams of politicians. If your education is to be effective you must see to it that your English teaching also begins with what is near and familiar. I suggest therefore another commission or committee to find writers who can create English reading books and history books, which speak of Ireland in simple vivid language. Very few such books exist, indeed I can only think of Mr. Standish O'Grady's *Bog of Stars*, published at the suggestion of this Society many years ago. That book is a fine piece of writing, and the books I think of should be fine pieces of writing, written by men of letters, chosen by men of letters; yet I do not think that I would exclude from the children's books any simple masterpiece of English literature. Let them begin with their own, and then pass to the world and the classics of the world.

There are two great classics of the eighteenth century which have deeply influenced modern thought, great Irish classics too difficult to be taught to children of any age, but some day those among us who think that all things should begin with the nation and with the genius of the nation, may press them upon the attention of the State. It is impossible to consider any modern philosophical or political question without being influenced knowingly or unknowingly by movements of thought that originated with Berkeley, who founded the Trinity College Philosophical Society, or with Burke, who founded the Historical. It would be but natural if they and those movements were studied in Irish colleges, perhaps especially in those colleges where our teachers themselves are trained. The Italian Minister of Education has advised his teachers continually to study the great classics, and he adds that those great classics will be as difficult to them as is the lesson to the child, and will therefore help them to understand the mind of a child.

In Gaelic literature we have something that the English-speaking countries have never possessed — a great folk literature. We have in Berkeley and in Burke a philosophy on which it is possible to base the whole life of a nation. That, too, is something which England, great as she is in modern scientific thought and every kind of literature, has not, I think. The modern Irish intellect was born more than two hundred years ago when Berkeley defined in three or four sentences the mechanical philosophy of Newton, Locke and Hobbes, the philosophy of England in his day, and I think of England up to our day, and wrote after each 'We Irish do not hold with this,' or some like sentence.

Feed the immature imagination upon that old folk life, and the mature intellect upon Berkeley and the great modern idealist philosophy created by his influence, upon Burke who restored to political thought its sense of history, and Ireland is reborn, potent, armed and wise. Berkeley proved that the world was a vision, and Burke that the State was a tree, no mechanism to be pulled in pieces and put up again, but an oak tree that had grown through centuries.

Teacher after teacher in Ireland has said to me that the young people are anarchic and violent, and that we have to show them what the State is and what they owe to it. All over the world during the Great War the young people became anarchic and violent, but in Ireland it is worse than elsewhere, for we have in a sense been at war for generations, and of late that war has taken the form of burning and destruction under the eyes of the children. They respect nothing, one teacher said to me. 'I cannot take them through Stephen's Green because they would pull up the plants.' Go anywhere in Ireland and you will hear the same complaint. The children, everybody will tell you, are individually intelligent and friendly, yet have so little sense of their duty to community and neighbour that if they meet an empty house in a lonely place they will smash all the windows. Some of the teachers want lessons on 'Civic Duty', but there is much experience to show that such lessons, being of necessity dry and abstract, are turned to mockery. The proper remedy is to teach religion, civic duty and history as all but inseparable. Indeed, the whole curriculum of a school should be as it were one lesson and not a mass of unrelated topics. I recommend Irish teachers to study the attempt now being made in Italy, under the influence of their Minister of Education, the philosopher Gentile, the most profound disciple of our own Berkeley, to so correlate all subjects of study. I would have each religion, Catholic or Protestant, so taught that it permeate the whole school life, and that it may do so, that it may be good education as well as good religion, I would have it taught upon a plan signed, as it is in Italy, by the representative of the Government as well as by the religious authority. For instance, the Italian teachers are directed by the Minister to teach 'no servile fear'. Up to three years ago in Ireland religion could not be taught in school hours, and even now, though that regulation is no longer binding, it is often nothing but a daily lesson in the Catechism. In Italy it takes four forms, that it may not be abstract, and that it may be a part of history and of life itself, a part, as it were, of the foliage of Burke's tree. First, praying, the learning and saying of simple prayers; second, singing, the learning and singing of famous religious songs; third, narration, the reading, or perhaps among the younger children the hearing, and writing out in the child's own words of stories out of the Bible, and stories of the great religious personages of their own country; fourth, contemplation, by which I mean that dogmatic teaching which stirs the mind to religious thought. The prayers and songs for an Irish school exist in abundance. There are, for instance, many religious songs in Gaelic with their traditional music, and they are already published in little books.

Every child in growing from infancy to maturity should pass in imagination through the history of its own race and through something of the history of the world, and the most powerful part in that history is played by religion. Let the child go its own way when maturity comes, but it is our business that it has something of that whole inheritance, and not as a mere thought, an abstract thing like those Graeco-Roman casts upon the shelves in the art-schools, but as part of its emotional life.

One never knows where one's words carry, and I, in speaking, though I speak to you all, am thinking perhaps of some one young man or some one young girl who may hear my words and bear them in mind years hence. Even he and she may do nothing with my thought, but they may carry it, or some other among you may carry it, as a bird will carry a seed clinging to its claws. I am thinking of an Egyptian poem, where there are birds flying from Arabia with spice in their claws. I do not think any of you are millionaires, and yet permit me to dream that my words may reach one that is. If the

Government were to do all that I suggest, if after the schools are put in good repair it were to get together the right editors and they find the right authors, if all the textbooks necessary to create a religious and secular culture in Irish and English were published, there would still be much that no Government, certainly no Government of a poor country, can accomplish. England has had great educational endowments for centuries, everyone knows with what lavish generosity the rich men of America have endowed education. Large sums of money have been sent to Ireland for political ends, and rich Irish-Americans have largely contributed, and we all hope, I think, that there is no further need for that money. If societies like this interest themselves in Irish education and spread that interest among the Irish educated classes everywhere, money may be sent to us to cheapen the price of school-books for the poor, or to clothe the poorer children, or to make the school buildings pleasanter to a child's eyes, or in some other way to prepare for an Ireland that will be healthy, vigorous, orderly, and above all, happy.

[1925]

SPEECH ON COPYRIGHT PROTECTION

Amendment 247, Section 154 of the *Industrial and Commercial Property (Protection) Bill*.

(1) Subject to the provisions of this Act, copyright shall subsist in Saorstat Eireann for the term hereinafter mentioned in every original literary, dramatic, musical, and artistic work, if —

    (a) in the case of a published work, the work was first published within Saorstat Eireann or a part of the British dominions to which the benefit of this Part of this Act extends; and . . .

(2) . . .

    (a) to produce, reproduce, perform, or publish any translation of the work; . . .

MR. CUMMINS: The object of the amendment primarily is to make Dublin what it once was — a great centre of printing, one of the leading centres, perhaps, in the British Isles, when it turned out a quality of work equal to any of its kind. . . . That is one of the objects of the amendment — to promote and encourage the printing trade in Dublin. Another object, of course, is that incidentally you give employment to a very large number of the members of the trade, who are at present largely unemployed.

DR. YEATS: I think I may, perhaps, allay some of the feelings of the Senators by demonstrating, as I shall, that the proposal of Senator Cummins is entirely absurd and unworkable. Last Monday evening a very distinguished scholar came to see me.

He has devoted his life to editing texts in Middle and Old Irish. He told me that scholars and members of learned societies were alarmed. He began by pointing out to me that much has been done lately in phonetics in the vernacular, that is to say, taking down Irish dialects. It is very important work, and is an attempt to record the pronunciation of the various dialects of Ireland. They are not taken down in any alphabet of any country, but in a special set of symbols. No Irish publisher possesses those symbols. The result is that those books, recording the Irish dialect, are printed in Copenhagen and Germany. He pointed out to me that if this were passed certain scholars who have done this work, who are not citizens of the Saorstat, would possess the copyright of their work. Those who are citizens of the Saorstat would possess it in every country except their own. He then went on to point out to me that practically all works of learning are produced by certain Presses which are subvented from universities.

There is no publisher in Ireland who will accept or could accept such books. These books are brought to the University Press in Cambridge or the Clarendon Press in Oxford, or rather to the publishing houses which take their name from these Presses. These books pay the authors practically nothing at all. The learned man is satisfied merely that his scholarship should be given to the world. If you pass this law these men will have copyright in every country except their own. I should add further that in publishing a work of this kind it is not only necessary to find the publisher who will take your work and pay for the printing, but it is desirable to find the publisher who has that very expensive thing — a highly-trained 'reader to the press'. No Irish publisher possesses it, as I know to my cost, but it is of enormous importance when dealing with works of learning. It may be said that as these learned men cannot be published except by subventioned presses, no matter what law you pass, they will not be printed in Ireland; that they should be left out of the argument.

We are thinking of the future. This is an ill-educated country. We all hope that will change. You are dealing with works fifty years after the death of the author. Such copyright may be all he has to leave to his children; some of these books, years and years hence, may be of considerable value. There are other works of scholarship which are of immediate value. At the Cambridge University Press are published great universal histories. One, a modern history, is finished. The Ancient History and Medieval History are unfinished. These are the works of a great many different scholars. One scholar's work may run into 300 pages. The work of these texts is done by University scholars. Those are men who cannot change their citizenship. Those men who have done this work cannot set up British citizenship. At once on the publication of this great universal history an Irish publisher can take 300 pages out, perhaps, the research of a man's life, and publish it here. Probably when this many-volumed ancient history is completed it may contain a large section on Early Ireland, hundreds of pages that could be taken out immediately and published in this country.

It is quite obvious that no Irish author, no matter how patriotic, could persuade publishers of these universal histories to print in Ireland. They are always printed in certain University Presses which have a subvention from the university. I will give you another example. Many Irish scholars have done work on the Encyclopedia Britannica. They cannot very well persuade publishers of the Encyclopedia Britannica to print in Ireland.

MRS. WYSE-POWER: They are not publishers. They are only employed to do the work.

DR. YEATS: I do not understand the point of that. The

editors of the Encyclopedia will get their lives of O'Connell, of Burke, and of Parnell from Irish writers. Those authors will not succeed in inducing the great Encyclopedia Britannica Company to change their whole habits of printing and print in Ireland. The idea is absurd. The Irish publisher can extract these lives of O'Connell, Burke and Parnell, containing the latest information on their subjects, and can publish them here, and what is more there is at present no law whatever which can prevent him sending them to England. Anyone can write from England, as they write at present to an Irish bookseller, and ask for such a book. At present there is no machinery to stop these books from going to England. What will happen is, Irish scholars will not be employed because they have only an impaired copyright to offer. I am sure no one in this House wishes to do this great injury to Irish scholars. That, I think, we are agreed to.

I dare say, however, when they come to considering a creative writer they are in a different sphere. There is the idea that a creative writer is making a great deal of money. They have in their imagination that he is. A few are singularly wealthy men — Mr. George Bernard Shaw, Mr. Arnold Bennett, and Mr. H. G. Wells. These men are exceptional. No doubt they can dictate to their publishers and tell them where they are to print. If the publisher does not agree to print wherever they dictate they can say: 'I will go to another publisher.' Remember an old couplet of the eighteenth century. It is not far out when you go over in your own mind the lives of men whose work has become immortal. It is:

'Seven Grecian cities fought for Homer dead,
Through which the living Homer begged his bread.'

Very few authors win success before they reach forty years of age. Very few authors, no matter what their later careers, are

in a position to change their publishers or dictate to their publishers. One young Irish novelist of to-day has, I know, made
an agreement for a term of years. His publisher pays him so
much a year and he gives him all he produces. That man loses
his copyright unless he declares himself a British citizen. You
are compelling export of your authors. Perhaps I might be a
little personal. At the start I wish to say that I have had a very
smooth and easy career. I make no complaint whatever. I was
forty-five before I ever earned from my books or by serial
publication of their contents, as much as the £4 a week earned
by Irish printers. During the last four or five years of that
time I was able to enlarge my income by lecturing. I was not
in a position to change my publisher. My publisher was Mr.
A. H. Bullen. He had a rather famous Press — The Shakespeare Head Press. I cannot see myself going to Mr. A. H.
Bullen, who had given me beautifully printed books, and who
took me at a time another publisher refused me, and saying:
'I shall withdraw unless you change your printers.' Even much
more celebrated men than I am have had the same experience
even towards the end of their lives. Robert Browning told
Lady Gregory that he would have made more money at any
profession, even making matches. He was not in a position to
change his publisher. Do you think it is a dignified position
for a nation to say: 'You will not have copyright in Ireland
unless you can cajole your publisher; speak smooth to him?'
Cajole! that is what you want authors to do. You are passing a
law of cajolery.

I notice another result to which I wish to draw your attention. No Irish author can serialise his work in the English Press
or newspaper and keep his copyright. No author, I think,
however successful, who is dependent on his work for a living
can afford to give up serialising his work in the English Press.
Just as you have no Irish publishers prepared to take Irish

authors' work, you have no Irish magazines or Irish newspapers prepared at their own expense to undertake the serialising of authors' work, and give anything like adequate pay for it; if they could pay for it at all. One Irish author — I will not mention names — a very celebrated woman, has at this moment ready for publication an autobiography covering many years and dealing with many things and personalities important in Irish history. It deals also with many great English, social and political questions. That autobiography will be serialised in the English Press. If this law is passed it will be immediately pirated by the Irish Press, which will not pay a penny to the author. It will also be pirated in book form. You cannot compel an English newspaper or review to print in Ireland for the sake of one contribution. It would be preposterous. So far as the copyright of books is concerned I do not suppose it personally will affect me. I have done the bulk of my work. Can I go to my publisher and say: 'I want you to print in Ireland'? If he says 'No,' what am I to do? He has all my works, my collected edition: I lose heavily if I detach my work from that uniform edition, and have broken faith with those who purchased that edition on the understanding that it is to be a genuine collected edition. Cajolery! This great State is going to pass a law by which people are to be cajoled to do what it wants. I will not leave this country because you appropriate my books, the few I have to write. If you made it impossible for me or any Irish author to serialise our work our income would suffer. I shall not leave this country, but shall move to the border, and I assure you I shall become exceedingly eloquent if I do.

There is no reason in the world why this town should not become a centre of printing and publishing. I am not speaking in entire ignorance. I have some little experience. Some twenty-five years ago at the establishment of the Abbey

Theatre I became editor of the Cuala Press. It is a hand press which employs several Irish printers all the year round. Nearly all my first editions have been printed by that Press. The first editions of a great many writers were printed there. As it is now the longest-established hand press in these islands, I have a right to say we have succeeded. There is no reason why what we have done in a small way cannot be done by this country on a large scale. If you are to do it on a large scale you must do the work as well and as cheaply as it is done elsewhere. There is a misunderstanding about printing. The artisan prints well. He seldom does bad work. The bad work that prevents your publishers and printers succeeding is done because they have not men of taste to select type, arrange proper proportions, margins, binding and the other necessaries of well-turned-out books. You can make a great centre of publishing and printing here, because Ireland has a good literary prestige in the world now. But, if you got all the Irish authors in the world to publish here they would not be, in themselves, sufficient in number to make it a great publishing centre. If you are going to make it even a paying centre for printing and publishing, apart from making it a great centre, you must keep the good-will of the publishers of the world, and you must keep the goodwill of the men of letters of the world. You will certainly not do so by what will be considered all over Europe as pirating. The educated opinion of Europe sees no difference between the property in a book and the property in an article of manufacture. You would not think of confiscating Jacob's biscuits because the tin in which they are put up was not made in Ireland. That is the educated opinion of Europe.

I have here a document to which I would like to draw the attention of those interested in Irish publishing. Some time ago a book by an Irish author was printed in America. I have a protest signed by 150 men, whose names are those of men of great eminence all over Europe. I will mention some of these names. They are from all countries.

Germany is represented by that man often described as the greatest mathematician and man of science of our day — Einstein. There are appended the names of other celebrated German authors. Russia is represented by the president of the famous Russian academy of letters. Spain is represented by the President of the Spanish Academy, Azarin; the most celebrated of her dramatists, Benavente, and the great Catholic philosopher, Miguel de Unamuno. Italy is represented by her Minister of Education, Giovanni Gentile, who is also a very great philosopher, and who, it may be of interest to some Senators to know, has organised the entire education of Italy in a way of far greater perfection than any educational system of Europe. It may be also well to know that he has restored religious education to the schools. Austria is represented by Hofmannsthal, a very great dramatist and poet. Belgium is represented by the dramatist, Maurice Maeterlinck, and France is represented by various members of the French Academy of great eminence. England is represented by a great many names, such as John Galsworthy and Bertrand Russell.

That appeal is not merely an appeal to American opinion to condemn piracy; it is an appeal to advertisers to withdraw advertisements from the publisher who has committed this act of piracy. Do you think Irish publishing houses will flourish if they carry on piracy of that kind? No, decidedly not. The world has become sensitive in recent years on the question of literary copyright, because it involves the prestige of men of letters in all countries. You can only make a successful publishing or printing house here if you keep the goodwill of publishers and the goodwill of men of letters.

[11 March 1927]

*   *   *

INTRODUCTION TO *THE WORDS UPON THE WINDOW-PANE*

I

SOMEBODY said the other night that Dublin was full of clubs — he himself knew four — that met in Cellars and Garrets and had for their object our general improvement. He was scornful, said that they had all begun by drawing up a programme and passing a resolution against the censorship and would never do anything else. When I began my public life Dublin was full of such clubs that passed resolutions and drew up programmes, and though the majority did nothing else some helped to find an audience for a school of writers. The fall of Parnell had freed imagination from practical politics, from agrarian grievance and political enmity, and turned it to imaginative nationalism, to Gaelic, to the ancient stories, and at last to lyrical poetry and to drama. Political failure and political success have had the same result except that to-day imagination is turning full of uncertainty to something it thinks European, and whether that something will be 'arty' and provincial, or a form of life, is as yet undiscoverable. Hitherto we have walked the road, but now we have shut the door and turned up the lamp. What shall occupy our imagination? We must, I think, decide among these three ideas of national life: that of Swift; that of a great Italian of his day; that of modern England. If the Garrets and the Cellars listen I may throw light upon the matter, and I hope if all the time I seem thinking of something else I shall be forgiven. I must speak of things that come out of the common consciousness, where every thought is like a bell with many echoes.

My little play *The Words upon the Window-pane* came to me amidst considerations such as these, as a reward, as a moment of excitement. John O'Leary read, during an illness, the poems of Thomas Davis, and though he never thought them good poetry they shaped his future life, gave him the moral simplicity that made him so attractive to young men in his old age, but we can no longer permit life to be shaped by a personified ideal; we must serve with all our faculties some actual thing. The old service was moral, at times lyrical; we discussed perpetually the character of public men and never asked were they able and well-informed, but what would they sacrifice? How many times did I hear on the lips of J. F. Taylor these words: 'Holy, delicate white hands'? His patriotism was a religion, never a philosophy. More extreme in such things than Taylor and O'Leary, who often seemed to live in the eighteenth century, to acknowledge its canons alone in literature and in the arts, I turned from Goldsmith and from Burke because they had come to seem a part of the English system, from Swift because I acknowledged, being a romantic, no verse between Cowley and Smart's *Song to David*, no prose between Sir Thomas Browne and the *Conversations* of Landor. But now I read Swift for months together, Burke and Berkeley less often but always with excitement, and Goldsmith lures and waits. I collect materials for my thought and work, for some identification of my beliefs with the nation itself, I seek an image of the modern mind's discovery of itself, of its own permanent form, in that one Irish century that escaped from darkness and confusion. I would that our fifteenth, sixteenth, or even our seventeenth century had been the clear mirror, but fate decided against us.

Swift haunts me; he is always just round the next corner.

Sometimes it is a thought of my great-great-grandmother, a friend of that Archbishop King who sent him to England about the 'First Fruits', sometimes it is Saint Patrick's, where I have gone to wander and meditate, that brings him to mind, sometimes I remember something hard or harsh in O'Leary or in Taylor, or in the public speech of our statesmen, that reminds me by its style of his verse or prose. Did he not speak, perhaps, with just such an intonation? This instinct for what is near and yet hidden is in reality a return to the sources of our power, and therefore a claim made upon the future. Thought seems more true, emotion more deep, spoken by someone who touches my pride, who seems to claim me of his kindred, who seems to make me a part of some national mythology, nor is mythology mere ostentation, mere vanity if it draws me onward to the unknown; another turn of the gyre and myth is wisdom, pride, discipline. I remember the shudder in my spine when Mrs. Patrick Campbell said, speaking words Hofmannsthal put into the mouth of Electra, 'I too am of that ancient race':

> Swift has sailed into his rest:
> Savage indignation there
> Cannot lacerate his breast.
> Imitate him if you dare,
> World-besotted-traveller; he
> Served human liberty.

'In Swift's day men of intellect reached the height of their power, the greatest position they ever attained in society and the State. . . . His ideal order was the Roman Senate, his ideal men Brutus and Cato; such an order and such men had seemed possible once more.' The Cambridge undergraduate into whose mouth I have put these words may have read similar words in F. S. Oliver, 'the last brilliant addition to English historians', for young men such as he read the newest authorities; probably Oliver and he thought of the influence at Court and in public life of Swift and of Leibniz, of the spread of science and of scholarship over Europe, its examination of documents, its destruction of fables, a science and a scholarship modern for the first time, of certain great minds that were mediaeval in their scope but modern in their freedom. I must, however, add certain thoughts of my own that affected me as I wrote. I thought about a passage in the Grammont *Memoirs* where some great man is commended for his noble manner, as we commend a woman for her beauty or her charm; a famous passage in the *Appeal from the New to the Old Whigs* commending the old Whig aristocracy for their intellect and power and because their doors stood open to like-minded men; the palace of Blenheim, its pride of domination that expected a thousand years, something Asiatic in its carved intricacy of stone.

'Everything great in Ireland and in our character, in what remains of our architecture, comes from that day . . . we have kept its seal longer than England.' The overstatement of an enthusiastic Cambridge student, and yet with its measure of truth. The battle of the Boyne overwhelmed a civilisation full of religion and myth, and brought in its place intelligible laws planned out upon a great blackboard, a capacity for horizontal lines, for rigid shapes, for buildings, for attitudes of mind that could be multiplied like an expanding bookcase: the modern world, and something that appeared and perished in its dawn, an instinct for Roman rhetoric, Roman elegance. It established a Protestant aristocracy, some of whom neither called themselves English[1] nor looked with contempt or dread upon con-

---

[1] Nor were they English: the newest arrivals soon inter-married with an older stock, and that older stock had inter-married again and again with Gaelic Ireland. All my childhood the Coopers of Markree, County Sligo, represented such rank and fashion as the County knew, and I had

quered Ireland. Indeed the battle was scarcely over when
Molyneux, speaking in their name, affirmed the sovereignty
of the Irish Parliament.[1] No one had the right to make our
laws but the King, Lords and Commons of Ireland; the battle
had been fought to change not an English but an Irish Crown;
and our Parliament was almost as ancient as that of England.
It was this doctrine[2] that Swift uttered in the fourth *Drapier
Letter* with such astringent eloquence that it passed from the
talk of study and parlour to that of road and market, and
created the political nationality of Ireland. Swift found his
nationality through the *Drapier Letters*, his convictions came
from action and passion, but Berkeley, a much younger man,
could find it through contemplation. He and his fellow-
students but knew the war through the talk of the older men.
As a boy of eighteen or nineteen he called the Irish people

it from my friend the late Bryan Cooper that his supposed Cromwellian
ancestor being childless adopted an O'Brien; while local tradition thinks
that an O'Brien, promised the return of her confiscated estate if she
married a Cromwellian soldier, married a Cooper and murdered him
three days after. Not, however, before he had founded a family. The
family of Yeats, never more than small gentry, arrived, if I can trust the
only man among us who may have seen the family tree before it was
burnt by Canadian Indians, 'about the time of Henry VII'. Ireland,
divided in religion and politics, is as much one race as any modern
country.

[1] 'Until 1691 Roman Catholics were admitted by law into both
Houses of Legislature in Ireland' (MacNeill's *Constitutional and Parliamentary History of Ireland*, p. 10).

[2] A few weeks ago the hierarchy of the Irish Church addressed without any mandate from Protestant Ireland, not the Irish people as they
had every right to, even in the defence of folly, but the Imperial Conference, and begged that the Irish Courts might remain subservient to
the Privy Council. Terrified into intrigue where none threatened, they
turned from Swift and Molyneux. I remind them that when the barons
of the Irish Court of Exchequer obeyed the English Privy Council in
1719 our ancestors clapped them into gaol. (1931.)

'natives' as though he were in some foreign land, but two or three years later, perhaps while still an undergraduate, defined the English materialism of his day in three profound sentences, and wrote after each that 'we Irishmen' think otherwise —'I publish . . . to know whether other men have the same ideas as we Irishmen' — and before he was twenty-five had fought the Salamis of the Irish intellect. The Irish landed aristocracy, who knew more of the siege of Derry and the battle of the Boyne delineated on vast tapestries for their House of Lords by Dublin Huguenots than of philosophy, found themselves masters of a country demoralised by generations of war and famine and shared in its demoralisation. In 1730 Swift said from the pulpit that their houses were in ruins and no new building anywhere, that the houses of their rack-ridden tenants were no better than English pigsties, that the bulk of the people trod barefoot and in rags. He exaggerated, for already the Speaker, Connolly, had built that great house at Celbridge where slate, stone, and furniture were Irish, even the silver from Irish mines; the new Parliament House had perhaps been planned; and there was a general stir of life. The old age of Berkeley passed amid art and music, and men had begun to boast that in these no country had made such progress; and some dozen years after Berkeley's death Arthur Young found everywhere in stately Georgian houses scientific agriculturalists, benefactors of their countryside, though for the half-educated, drunken, fire-eating, impoverished lesser men he had nothing but detestation. Goldsmith might have found likeable qualities, a capacity for mimicry[1] perhaps, among these lesser men, and Sir Jonah Barrington made them his theme, but, detestable or not, they were out of fashion. Miss Edgeworth described her *Castle Rackrent* upon the title-

---

[1] He wrote that he had never laughed so much at Garrick's acting as at somebody in an Irish tavern mimicking a Quaker sermon.

page of its first edition as 'the habits of the Irish squirearchy before 1782'. A few years more and the country people would have forgotten that the Irish aristocracy was founded like all aristocracies upon conquest, or rather, would have remembered, and boasted in the words of a mediaeval Gaelic poet, 'We are a sword people and we go with the sword.' Unhappily the lesson first taught by Molyneux and Swift had been but half learnt when the test came — country gentlemen are poor politicians — and Ireland's 'dark insipid period' began. During the entire eighteenth century the greatest landowning family in the neighbourhood I best knew in childhood sent not a single man into the English army and navy, but during the nineteenth century one or more in every generation; a new absenteeism, foreseen by Miss Edgeworth, began; those that lived upon their estates bought no more fine editions of the classics; separated from public life and ambition they sank, as I have heard Lecky complain, 'into grass farmers'. Yet their genius did not die out; they sent everywhere administrators and military leaders, and now that their ruin has come — what resolute nation permits a strong alien class within its borders? — I would, remembering obscure ancestors that preached in their churches or fought beside their younger sons over half the world, and despite a famous passage of O'Grady's, gladly sing their song.

'He foresaw the ruin to come, Democracy, Rousseau, the French Revolution; that is why he hated the common run of men ——, "I hate lawyers, I hate doctors," he said, "though I love Dr. So-and-so and Judge So-and-so," — that is why he wrote *Gulliver*, that is why he wore out his brain, that is why he felt *saeva indignatio*, that is why he sleeps under the greatest epitaph in history.' The *Discourse of the Contests and Dissensions between the Nobles and the Commons in Athens and Rome*, published in 1703 to warn the Tory Opposition of the day against the impeachment of Ministers, is Swift's one philosophical work. All States depend for their health upon a right balance between the One, the Few, and the Many. The One is the executive, which may in fact be more than one — the Roman republic had two Consuls — but must for the sake of rapid decision be as few as possible; the Few are those who through the possession of hereditary wealth, or great personal gifts, have come to identify their lives with the life of the State, whereas the lives and ambitions of the Many are private. The Many do their day's work well, and so far from copying even the wisest of their neighbours, affect 'a singularity' in action and in thought; but set them to the work of the State and every man Jack is 'listed in a party', becomes the fanatical follower of men of whose characters he knows next to nothing, and from that day on puts nothing into his mouth that some other man has not already chewed and digested. And furthermore, from the moment of enlistment thinks himself above other men and struggles for power until all is in confusion. I divine an Irish hatred of abstraction likewise expressed by that fable of Gulliver among the inventors and men of science, by Berkeley in his *Commonplace Book*, by Goldsmith in the satire of *The Good-Natured Man*, in the picturesque, minute observation of *The Deserted Village*, and by Burke in his attack upon mathematical democracy. Swift enforced his moral by proving that Rome and Greece were destroyed by the war of the Many upon the Few; in Rome, where the Few had kept their class organisation, it was a war of classes, in Greece, where they had not, war upon character and genius. Miltiades, Aristides, Themistocles, Pericles, Alcibiades, Phocion, 'impeached for high crimes and misdemeanours . . . were honoured and lamented by their country as the preservers of it, and have had the veneration of all ages since paid justly to their memories.' In Rome parties so developed that men born and bred among the Few were compelled to join one party or the other and to flatter and bribe. All civilisations must end in some such way, for the Many obsessed by emotion create a multitude of religious sects but give themselves at last to some one master of bribes and flatteries and sink into the ignoble tranquillity of servitude. He defines a tyranny as the predominance of the One, the Few, or the Many, but thinks that of the Many the immediate threat. All States at their outset possess a ruling power seated in the whole body as that of the soul in the human body, a perfect balance of the three estates, the king some sort of chief magistrate, and then comes 'a tyranny: first either of the Few or the Many; but at last infallibly of a single person'. He thinks the English balance most perfect in the time of Queen Elizabeth, but that in the next age a tyranny of the Many produced that of Cromwell, and that, though recovery followed, 'all forms of government must be mortal like their authors', and he quotes from Polybius, 'those abuses and corruptions, which in time destroy a government, are sown along with the very seeds of it' and destroy it 'as rust eats away iron, and worms devour wood'. Whether the final tyranny is created by the Many — in his eyes all Caesars were tyrants — or imposed by foreign power, the result is the same. At the fall of liberty came 'a dark insipid period through all Greece' — had he Ireland in his mind also? — and the people became, in the words of Polybius, 'great reverencers of crowned heads'.

Twenty-two years later Giambattista Vico published that *Scienza Nuova* which Mr. James Joyce is expounding or symbolising in the strange fragments of his *Work in Progress*. He was the opposite of Swift in everything, an humble, peaceful man, son of a Neapolitan bookseller and without political opinions; he wrote panegyrics upon men of rank, seemed to admire all that they did, took their gratuities and yet kept his dignity. He thought civilisation passed through the phases Swift has described, but that it was harsh and terrible until the Many prevailed, and its joints cracked and loosened, happiest when some one man, surrounded by able subordinates, dismissed the Many to their private business, that its happiness lasted some generations until, sense of the common welfare lost, it grew malicious and treacherous, fell into 'the barbarism of reflection', and after that into an honest, plain barbarism accepted with relief by all, and started upon its round again. Rome had conquered surrounding nations because those nations were nearer than it to humanity and happiness; was not Carthage already almost a democratic state when destruction came? Swift seemed to shape his narrative upon some clairvoyant vision of his own life, for he saw civilisation pass from comparative happiness and youthful vigour to an old age of violence and self-contempt, whereas Vico saw it begin in penury like himself and end as he himself would end in a long inactive peace. But there was a greater difference: Swift, a practical politician in everything he wrote, ascribed its rise and fall to virtues and vices all could understand, whereas the philosophical Vico ascribed them to 'the rhythm of the elemental forms of the mind', a new idea that would dominate philosophy. Outside Anglo-Saxon nations where progress, impelled by moral enthusiasm and the Patent Office, seems a perpetual straight line, this 'circular movement', as Swift's master, Polybius, called it, has long been the friend and enemy of public order. Both Sorel and Marx, their eyes more Swift's than Vico's, have preached a return to a primeval state, a beating of all down into a single class that a new civilisation may arise with its Few, its Many, and its One. Students of contemporary Italy, where Vico's thought is current through its influence upon Croce and Gentile, think it created, or in part created, the present government of one man surrounded by just such able assistants as Vico foresaw. Some philosopher has added this further thought: the classes rise out of the matrix, create all mental and bodily riches, sink back, as Vico saw civilisation rise and sink, and government is there to keep the ring and see to it that combat never ends. These thoughts in the next few generations, as elaborated by Oswald Spengler, who has followed Vico without essential change, by Flinders Petrie, by the German traveller Frobenius, by Henry Adams, and perhaps by my friend Gerald Heard, may affect the masses. They have already deepened our sense of tragedy and somewhat checked the naïver among those creeds and parties who push their way to power by flattering our moral hopes. Pascal thought there was evidence for and against the existence of God, but that if a man kept his mind in suspense about it he could not live a rich and active life, and I suggest to the Cellars and Garrets that though history is too short to change either the idea of progress or the eternal circuit into scientific fact, the eternal circuit may best suit our preoccupation with the soul's salvation, our individualism, our solitude. Besides we love antiquity, and that other idea — progress — the sole religious myth of modern man, is only two hundred years old.

Swift's pamphlet had little effect in its day; it did not prevent the impeachment and banishment a few years later of his own friends; and although he was in all probability the first — if there was another 'my small reading cannot trace it' — to describe in terms of modern politics the discord of parties that compelled revolutionary France, as it has compelled half a dozen nations since the war, to accept the 'tyranny' of a 'single person', it was soon forgotten; but for the understanding of Swift it is essential. It shows that the defence of liberty boasted upon his tombstone did not come from political disappointment (when he wrote it he had suffered none), and what he meant by liberty. Gulliver, in those travels written twenty years later, calls up from the dead 'a sextumvirate to which all the ages of the world cannot add a seventh': Epaminondas and Socrates, who suffered at the hands of the Many; Brutus, Junius Brutus, Cato the Younger, Thomas More, who fought the tyranny of the One; Brutus with Caesar still his inseparable friend, for a man may be a tyrant without personal guilt.

Liberty depended upon a balance within the State, like that of the 'humours' in a human body, or like that 'unity of being' Dante compared to a perfectly proportioned human body, and for its sake Swift was prepared to sacrifice what seems to the modern man liberty itself. The odds were a hundred to one, he wrote, that 'violent zeal for the truth' came out of 'petulancy, ambition, or pride'. He himself might prefer a republic to a monarchy, but did he open his mouth upon the subject would be deservedly hanged. Had he religious doubts he was not to blame so long as he kept them to himself, for God had given him reason. It was the attitude of many a modern Catholic who thinks, though upon different grounds, that our civilisation may sink into a decadence like that of Rome. But sometimes belief itself must be hidden. He was devout; had the Communion Service by heart; read the Fathers and prayed much, yet would not press the mysteries of his faith upon any unwilling man. Had not the early Christians kept silent about the divinity of Christ; should not the missionaries to China 'soften' it? He preached as law commanded; a man could save his soul doubtless in any religion which taught submission to the Will of God, but only one State could protect his body; and how could it protect his body if rent apart by those cranks and sectaries mocked in his *Tale of a Tub*? Had not French Huguenots and English Dissenters alike sinned against the State? Except at those moments of great public disturbance, when a man must choose his creed or his king, let him think his own thoughts in silence.

What was this liberty bought with so much silence, and served through all his life with so much eloquence? 'I should think,' he wrote in the *Discourse*, 'that the saying, *vox populi, vox dei* ought to be understood of the universal bent and current of a people, not of the bare majority of a few representatives, which is often procured by little arts, and great industry and application; wherein those who engage in the pursuits of malice and revenge are much more sedulous than such as would prevent them.' That *vox populi* or 'bent and current', or what we even more vaguely call national spirit, was the sole theme of his *Drapier Letters*; its right to express itself as it would through such men as had won or inherited general consent. I doubt if a mind so contemptuous of average men thought, as Vico did, that it found expression also through all individual lives, or asked more for those lives than protection from the most obvious evils. I remember J. F. Taylor, a great student of Swift, saying 'Individual liberty is of no importance, what matters is national liberty.'

The will of the State, whether it build a cage for a dead bird or remain in the bird itself, must always, whether interpreted by Burke or Marx, find expression through some governing class or company identified with that 'bent and current', with those 'elemental forms', whether by interest or training. The men of Swift's day would have added that class or company must be placed by wealth above fear and toil, though Swift thought every properly conducted State must limit the amount of wealth the individual could possess. But the old saying that there is no wisdom without leisure has somewhat lost its truth. When the physical world became rigid; when curiosity inherited from the Renaissance, and the soul's anxiety inherited from the Middle Ages, passed, man ceased to think;

his work thought in him. Spinoza, Leibniz, Swift, Berkeley, Goethe, the last typical figure of the epoch, recognised no compulsion but the 'bent and current' of their lives; the Speaker, Connolly, could still call out a posse of gentlemen to design the facade of his house, and though Berkeley thought their number too great, that work is still admired; Swift called himself a poor scholar in comparison with Lord Treasurer Harley. Unity of being was still possible though somewhat over-rationalised and abstract, more diagram than body; whereas the best modern philosophers are professors, their pupils compile notebooks that they may be professors some day; politicians stick to their last or leave it to plague us with platitudes; we poets and artists may be called, so small our share in life, 'separated spirits', words applied by the old philosophers to the dead. When Swift sank into imbecility or madness his epoch had finished in the British Isles, those 'elemental forms' had passed beyond him; more than the 'great Ministers' had gone. I can see in a sort of nightmare vision the 'primary qualities' torn from the side of Locke, Johnson's ponderous body bent above the letter to Lord Chesterfield, some obscure person somewhere inventing the spinning-jenny, upon his face that look of benevolence kept by painters and engravers, from the middle of the eighteenth century to the time of the Prince Consort, for such as he, or, to simplify the tale —

> Locke sank into a swoon;
> The Garden died;
> God took the spinning-jenny
> Out of his side.

'That arrogant intellect free at last from superstition': the young man's overstatement full of the unexamined suppositions of common speech. I saw Asia in the carved stones of

Blenheim, not in the pride of great abstract masses, but in that humility of flower-like intricacy — the particular blades of the grass; nor can chance have thrown into contiguous generations Spinoza and Swift, an absorption of the whole intellect in God, a fakir-like contempt for all human desire; 'take from her', Swift prayed for Stella in sickness, 'all violent desire whether of life or death'; the elaboration and spread of Masonic symbolism, its God made in the image of a Christopher Wren; Berkeley's declaration, modified later, that physical pleasure is the *Summum Bonum*, Heaven's sole reality, his counter-truth to that of Spinoza.

In judging any moment of past time we should leave out what has since happened; we should not call the Swift of the *Drapier Letters* nearer truth because of their influence upon history than the Swift who attacked in *Gulliver* the inventors and logicians; we should see certain men and women as if at the edge of a cliff, time broken away from their feet. Spinoza and the Masons, Berkeley and Swift, speculative and practical intellect, stood there free at last from all prepossessions and touched the extremes of thought; the Gymnosophists of Strabo close at hand, could they but ignore what was harsh and logical in themselves, or the China of the Dutch cabinet-makers, of the *Citizen of the World*: the long-settled rule of powerful men, no great dogmatic structure, few great crowded streets, scattered unprogressive communities, much handiwork, wisdom wound into the roots of the grass.

'I have something in my blood that no child must inherit.' There have been several theories to account for Swift's celibacy. Sir Walter Scott suggested a 'physical defect', but that seems incredible. A man so outspoken would have told Vanessa the truth and stopped a tragic persecution, a man so charitable have given Stella the protection of his name. The refusal to see Stella when there was no third person present suggests a man that dreaded temptation; nor is it compatible with those stories still current among our country people of Swift sending his servant out to fetch a woman, and dismissing that servant when he woke to find a black woman at his side. Lecky suggested dread of madness — the theory of my play — of madness already present in constant eccentricity; though, with a vagueness born from distaste of the theme, he saw nothing incompatible between Scott's theory and his own. Had Swift dreaded transmitting madness he might well have been driven to consorting with the nameless barren women of the streets. Somebody else suggests syphilis contracted doubtless between 1699 when he was engaged to Varina and some date soon after Stella's arrival in Ireland. Mr. Shane Leslie thinks that Swift's relation to Vanessa was not platonic,[1] and that whenever his letters speak of a cup of coffee they mean the sexual act; whether the letters seem to bear him out I do not know, for those letters bore me; but whether they seem to or not he must, if he is to get a hearing, account for Swift's relation to Stella. It seems certain that Swift loved her though he called it by some other name, and she him, and that it was platonic love.

> Thou, Stella, wert no longer young,
> When first for thee my harp was strung,
> Without one word of Cupid's darts,
> Of killing eyes or bleeding hearts;
> With friendship and esteem possest,
> I ne'er admitted Love a guest.
> In all the habitudes of life,
> The friend, the mistress, and the wife,
> Variety we still pursue,
> In pleasure seek for something new;

[1] Rossi and Hone take the same view, though uncertain about the coffee. When I wrote, their book had not appeared.

Or else comparing with the rest,
Take comfort that our own is best;
The best we value by the worst,
As tradesmen show their trash at first;
But his pursuits are at an end,
Whom Stella chooses for a friend.

If the relation between Swift and Vanessa was not platonic
there must have been some bar that affected Stella as well as
Swift. Dr. Delaney is said to have believed that Swift married
Stella in 1716 and found in some exchange of confidences that
they were brother and sister, but Sir William Temple was not
in Ireland during the year that preceded Swift's birth, and so
far as we know Swift's mother was not in England.

There is no satisfactory solution. Swift, though he lived in
great publicity, and wrote and received many letters, hid two
things which constituted perhaps all that he had of private life:
his loves and his religious beliefs.

'Was Swift mad? Or was it the intellect itself that was
mad?' The other day a scholar in whose imagination Swift has
a pre-eminence scarcely possible outside Ireland said: 'I sometimes feel that there is a black cloud about to overwhelm me,
and then comes a great jet of life; Swift had that black cloud
and no jet. He was terrified.' I said, 'Terrified perhaps of
everything but death,' and reminded him of a story of Dr.
Johnson's.[1] There was a reward of £500 for the identification
of the author of the *Drapier Letters*. Swift's butler, who had
carried the manuscript to the printer, stayed away from work.
When he returned Swift said, 'I know that my life is in your
hands, but I will not bear, out of fear, either your insolence or
negligence.' He dismissed the butler, and when the danger had
passed he restored him to his post, rewarded him, and said to

[1] Sheridan has a different version, but as I have used it merely to
illustrate an argument I leave it as Dr. Johnson told it.

the other servants, 'No more Barclay, henceforth Mr. Barclay.' 'Yes,' said my friend, 'he was not afraid of death but of life, of what might happen next; that is what made him so defiant in public and in private and demand for the State the obedience a Connacht priest demands for the Church.' I have put a cognate thought into the mind of John Corbet. He imagines, though but for a moment, that the intellect of Swift's age, persuaded that the mechanicians mocked by Gulliver would prevail, that its moment of freedom could not last, so dreaded the historic process that it became in the half-mad mind of Swift a dread of parentage: 'Am I to add another to the healthy rascaldom and knavery of the world?' Did not Rousseau within five years of the death of Swift publish his *Discourse upon Arts and Sciences* and discover instinctive harmony not in heroic effort, not in Cato and Brutus, not among impossible animals — I think of that noble horse Blake drew for Hayley — but among savages, and thereby beget the *sans-culottes* of Marat? After the arrogance of power the humility of a servant.

II

When I went into the theatre café after the performance a woman asked a question and I replied with some spiritualistic anecdote. 'Did that happen with the medium we have seen to-night?' she said: and yet May Craig who played the part had never seen a séance. I had, however, assisted her by self-denial. No character upon the stage spoke my thoughts. All were people I had met or might have met in just such a séance. Taken as a whole, the man who expected to find whippet-racing beyond the grave, not less than the old man who was half a Swedenborgian, expresses an attitude of mind of millions who have substituted the séance-room for the church. At most séances there is somebody who finds symbol where his neighbour finds fact, but the average man or woman thinks that the dead have houses, that they eat and sleep, hear lectures, or occasionally talk with Christ as though He were a living man; and certainly the voices are at times so natural, the forms so solid, that the plain man can scarce think otherwise.

If I had not denied myself, if I had allowed some character to speak my thoughts, what would he have said? It seems to me that after reading many books and meeting many phenomena, some in my own house, some when alone in my room, I can see clearly at last. I consider it certain that every voice that speaks, every form that appears, whether to the medium's eyes and ears alone or to some one or two others or to all present, whether it remains a sight or sound or affects the sense of touch, whether it is confined to the room or can make itself apparent at some distant place, whether it can or cannot alter the position of material objects, is first of all a secondary personality or dramatisation created by, in, or through the medium. Perhaps May Craig, when alone in her room after the play, went, without knowing what she was doing, through some detail of her performance. I once saw an Abbey actor going up the stairs to his dressing-room after playing the part of a lame man and saw that he was still limping. I see no difference except one of degree between such unconscious movements and the strange powerful grotesque faces imprinted by the controls of Eusapia Palladino upon paraffin wax. The Polish psychologist Ochorowicz, vexed by the mischievous character of his medium's habitual control, created by suggestion a docile and patient substitute that left a photograph of its hand and arm upon an unopened coil of film in a sealed bottle. But at most séances the suggestions come from sub-conscious or unspoken thought. I found the preacher who wanted Moody's help at a séance where the mind of an old doting general turned all into delirium. We sat in the dark and voices came about us in the air; crowned head after crowned head spoke until Cromwell intervened and was abused by one of the sitters for cutting off the head of 'Charles the Second', while the preacher kept repeating, 'He is monopolising the séance, I want Mr. Moody, it is most important I should get Mr. Moody.' Then came a voice, 'King George is here.' I asked which of the Georges, and the sitter who hated Cromwell said, 'King George, our George; we should all stand up,' but the general thought it would be enough if we sang 'God save the King.' We sang, and then there was silence, and in the silence from somewhere close to the ceiling the clear song of a bird. Because mediumship is dramatisation: even honest mediums cheat at times either deliberately or because some part of the body has freed itself from the control of the waking will, and almost always truth and lies are mixed together. But what shall we say of their knowledge of events, their assumption of forms and names beyond the medium's knowledge or ours? What of the arm photographed in the bottle?

The Indian ascetic passing into his death-like trance knows that if his mind is not pure, if there is anything there but the symbol of his God, some passion, ambition, desire, or phantasy will confer upon him its shape or purpose, for he is entering upon a state where thought and existence are the same. One remembers those witches described by Glanvil who course the field in the likeness of hares while their bodies lie at home, and certain mediumistic phenomena. The ascetic would say, did we question him, that the unpurified dead are subject to transformations that would be similar were it not that in their case no physical body remains in cave or bed or chair, all is transformed. They examine their past if undisturbed by our importunity, tracing events to their source, and as they take the form their thought suggests, seem to live backward through time; or if incapable of such examination, creatures not of thought but of feeling, renew as shades certain detached events of their past lives, taking the greater excitements first. When Achilles came to the edge of the blood-pool (an ancient substitute for the medium) he was such a shade. Tradition affirms that, deprived of the living present by death, they can create nothing, or, in the Indian phrase, can originate no new Karma. Their aim, like that of the ascetic in meditation, is to enter at last into their own archetype, or into all being: into that which is there always. They are not, however, the personalities which haunt the séance-room: these when they speak from, or imply, supernormal knowledge, when they are more than transformations of the medium, are, as it were, new beings begotten by spirit upon medium to live short but veritable lives, whereas the secondary personalities resemble those eggs brought forth without the assistance of the male bird. They, within their narrow limits, create; they speak truth when they repeat some message suggested by the past lives of the spirit, remembered like some pre-natal memory, or when, though such instances must be few, begotten by some spirit obedient to its source, or, as we might say, blessed; but when they neither repeat such message nor were so begotten they may justify passages in Swedenborg that denounce them as the newspapers denounce cheating mediums, seeing that they find but little check in their fragmentary knowledge or vague conscience.

Let images of basalt, black, immovable,
Chiselled in Egypt, or ovoids of bright steel
Hammered and polished by Brancusi's hand,
Represent spirits. If spirits seem to stand
Before the bodily eyes, speak into the bodily ears,
They are not present but their messengers.

Of double nature these, one nature is
Compounded of accidental phantasies.
We question; it but answers what we would
Or as phantasy directs — because they have drunk the blood.

I have not heard of spirits in a European séance-room re-
enacting their past lives; our séances take their characteristics
from the desire of those present to speak to, or perhaps obtain
the counsel of, their dead; yet under the conditions described
in my play such re-enacting might occur, indeed most haunt-
ings are of that nature. Here, however, is a French traveller's
account of a séance in Madagascar, quoted by César de
Vesme:

> ... One, Taimandebakaka, of the Bara race, and re-
> nowned in the valley of the Menamaty as a great sorcerer,
> evoked one day in my presence in his village the souls of
> Captain Flayelle and of Lieutenant Montagnole, both killed
> at Vohingheso in a fight with the Baras four years before.
> Those present — myself and some privileged natives — saw
> nothing when Taimandebakaka claimed to see the two per-
> sons in question; but we could hear the voices of officers
> issuing orders to their soldiers, and these voices were
> European voices which could not be imitated by natives.
> Similarly, at a distance we could hear the echoes of firing
> and the cries of the wounded and the lowing of frightened
> cattle — oxen of the Fahavalos.

III

It is fitting that Plotinus should have been the first philosopher to meet his daimon face to face, though the boy atten-
dant out of jealousy or in convulsive terror strangled the

doves, for he was the first to establish as sole source the timeless individuality or daimon instead of the Platonic Idea, to prefer Socrates to his thought. This timeless individuality contains archetypes of all possible existences whether of man or brute, and as it traverses its circle of allotted lives, now one, now another, prevails. We may fail to express an archetype or alter it by reason, but all done from nature is its unfolding into time. Some other existence may take the place of Socrates, yet Socrates can never cease to exist. Once a friend of mine was digging in a long-neglected garden and suddenly out of the air came a voice thanking her, an old owner of the garden, she was told later, long since reborn, yet still in the garden. Plotinus said that we should not 'baulk at this limitlessness of the intellectual; it is an infinitude having nothing to do with number or part' (*Ennead V*. 7. I.); yet it seems that it can at will re-enter number and part and thereby make itself apparent to our minds. If we accept this idea many strange or beautiful things become credible. The Indian pilgrim has not deceived us; he did hear the bed where the sage of his devotion slept a thousand years ago creak as though someone turned over in it, and he did see — he himself and the old shrine-keeper — the blankets all tossed about at dawn as if someone had just risen; the Irish country-woman did see the ruined castle lit up, the bridge across the river dropping; those two Oxford ladies did find themselves in the garden of the Petit Trianon with Marie Antoinette and her courtiers, see that garden as those saw it; the gamekeeper did hear those footsteps the other night that sounded like the footsteps of a stag where stag has not passed these hundred years. All about us there seems to start up a precise inexplicable teeming life, and the earth becomes once more, not in rhetorical metaphor, but in reality, sacred.

[1931]

FROM *A VISION*

INTRODUCTION

'This way of publishing introductions to books, that are God knows when to come out, is either wholly new, or so long in practice that my small reading cannot trace it'. — SWIFT.

I

THE other day Lady Gregory said to me: 'You are a much better educated man than you were ten years ago and much more powerful in argument.' And I put *The Tower* and *The Winding Stair* into evidence to show that my poetry has gained in self-possession and power. I owe this change to an incredible experience.

II

On the afternoon of October 24th, 1917, four days after my marriage, my wife surprised me by attempting automatic writing. What came in disjointed sentences, in almost illegible writing, was so exciting, sometimes so profound, that I persuaded her to give an hour or two day after day to the unknown writer, and after some half-dozen such hours offered to spend what remained of life explaining and piecing together those scattered sentences. 'No,' was the answer, 'we have come to give you metaphors for poetry.' The unknown writer took his theme at first from my just published *Per Amica Silentia Lunae*. I had made a distinction between the perfection that is from a man's combat with himself and that which is from a combat with circumstance, and upon this simple distinction he built up an elaborate classification of men according

to their more or less complete expression of one type or
the other. He supported his classification by a series of geometrical symbols and put these symbols in an order that
answered the question in my essay as to whether some prophet
could not prick upon the calendar the birth of a Napoleon or a
Christ. A system of symbolism, strange to my wife and to
myself, certainly awaited expression, and when I asked how
long that would take I was told years. Sometimes when my
mind strays back to those first days I remember that Browning's Paracelsus did not obtain the secret until he had written
his spiritual history at the bidding of his Byzantine teacher,
that before initiation Wilhelm Meister read his own history
written by another, and I compare my *Per Amica* to those
histories.

*   *   *

V

For the same reason they asked me not to read philosophy
until their exposition was complete, and this increased my
difficulties. Apart from two or three of the principal Platonic
Dialogues I knew no philosophy. Arguments with my father,
whose convictions had been formed by John Stuart Mill's attack upon Sir William Hamilton, had destroyed my confidence
and driven me from speculation to the direct experience of the
Mystics. I had once known Blake as thoroughly as his unfinished confused Prophetic Books permitted, and I had read
Swedenborg and Boehme, and my initiation into the 'Hermetic Students' had filled my head with Cabbalistic imagery,
but there was nothing in Blake, Swedenborg, Boehme or the
Cabbala to help me now. They encouraged me, however, to
read history in relation to their historical logic, and biography
in relation to their twenty-eight typical incarnations, that I

might give concrete expression to their abstract thought. I read with an excitement I had not known since I was a boy with all knowledge before me, and made continual discoveries, and if my mind returned too soon to their unmixed abstraction they would say, 'We are starved.'

*   *   *

XIII

Some, perhaps all, of those readers I most value, those who have read me many years, will be repelled by what must seem an arbitrary, harsh, difficult symbolism. Yet such has almost always accompanied expression that unites the sleeping and waking mind. One remembers the six wings of Daniel's angels, the Pythagorean numbers, a venerated book of the Cabbala where the beard of God winds in and out among the stars, its hairs all numbered, those complicated mathematical tables that Kelly saw in Dr. Dee's black scrying-stone, the diagrams in Law's *Boehme*, where one lifts a flap of paper to discover both the human entrails and the starry heavens. William Blake thought those diagrams worthy of Michael Angelo, but remains himself almost unintelligible because he never drew the like. We can (those hard symbolic bones under the skin) substitute for a treatise on logic the *Divine Comedy*, or some little song about a rose, or be content to live our thought.

*   *   *

XV

Some will ask whether I believe in the actual existence of my circuits of sun and moon. Those that include, now all recorded time in one circuit, now what Blake called 'the pulsation of an artery', are plainly symbolical, but what of those that fixed, like a butterfly upon a pin, to our central date, the first day of our Era, divide actual history into periods of equal length? To such a question I can but answer that if sometimes, overwhelmed by miracle as all men must be when in the midst of it, I have taken such periods literally, my reason has soon recovered; and now that the system stands out clearly in my imagination I regard them as stylistic arrangements of experience comparable to the cubes in the drawing of Wyndham Lewis and to the ovoids in the sculpture of Brancusi. They have helped me to hold in a single thought reality and justice.

[23 November 1928, and later]

BOOK V: DOVE OR SWAN

*   *   *

IV

A.D. I to A.D. 1050

GOD is now conceived of as something outside man and man's handiwork, and it follows that it must be idolatry to worship that which Phidias and Scopas made, and seeing that He is a Father in Heaven, that Heaven will be found presently in the Thebaid, where the world is changed into a featureless dust and can be run through the fingers; and these things are testified to from books that are outside human genius, being miraculous, and by a miraculous Church, and this Church, as the gyre sweeps wider, will make man also featureless as clay or dust. Night will fall upon man's wisdom now that man has been taught that he is nothing. He had discovered, or half-discovered, that the world is round and one of many like it, but now he must believe that the sky is but a tent spread above a level floor, and that he may be stirred into a frenzy of anxiety and so to moral transformation, blot out the knowledge or half-knowledge that he has lived many times, and think that all eternity depends upon a moment's decision. Heaven itself, transformation finished, must appear so vague and motionless that it seems but a concession to human weakness. It is even essential to this faith to declare that God's messengers, those beings who show His will in dreams or announce it in visionary speech, were never men. The Greeks thought them great

495

men of the past, but now that concession to mankind is forbidden. All must be narrowed into the sun's image cast out of a burning-glass and man be ignorant of all but the image.

The mind that brought the change, if considered as man only, is a climax of whatever Greek and Roman thought was most a contradiction to its age; but considered as more than man He controlled what Neo-Pythagorean and Stoic could not — irrational force. He could announce the new age, all that had not been thought of, or touched, or seen, because He could substitute for reason, miracle.

We say of Him because His sacrifice was voluntary that He was love itself, and yet that part of Him which made Christendom was not love but pity, and not pity for intellectual despair, though the man in Him, being *antithetical* like His age, knew in it the Garden, but *primary* pity, that for the common lot, man's death, seeing that He raised Lazarus, sickness, seeing that He healed many, sin, seeing that He died.

Love is created and preserved by intellectual analysis, for we love only that which is unique, and it belongs to contemplation, not to action, for we would not change that which we love. A lover will admit a greater beauty than that of his mistress but not its like, and surrenders his days to a delighted laborious study of all her ways and looks, and he pities only if something threatens that which has never been before and can never be again. Fragment delights in fragment and seeks possession, not service; whereas the Good Samaritan discovers himself in the likeness of another, covered with sores and abandoned by thieves upon the roadside, and in that other serves himself. The opposites are gone; he does not need his Lazarus; they do not each die the other's life, live the other's death.

It is impossible to do more than select an arbitrary general date for the beginning of Roman decay (Phases 2 to 7, A.D. 1

to A.D. 250). Roman sculpture — sculpture made under Roman influence whatever the sculptor's blood — did not, for instance, reach its full vigour, if we consider what it had of Roman as distinct from Greek, until the Christian Era. It even made a discovery which affected all sculpture to come. The Greeks painted the eyes of marble statues and made out of enamel or glass or precious stones those of their bronze statues, but the Roman was the first to drill a round hole to represent the pupil, and because, as I think, of a preoccupation with the glance characteristic of a civilisation in its final phase. The colours must have already faded from the marbles of the great period, and a shadow and a spot of light, especially where there is much sunlight, are more vivid than paint, enamel, coloured glass or precious stone. They could now express in stone a perfect composure. The administrative mind, alert attention had driven out rhythm, exaltation of the body, uncommitted energy. May it not have been precisely a talent for this alert attention that had enabled Rome and not Greece to express those final *primary* phases? One sees on the pediments troops of marble Senators, officials serene and watchful as befits men who know that all the power of the world moves before their eyes, and needs, that it may not dash itself to pieces, their unhurried, unanxious, never-ceasing care. Those riders upon the Parthenon had all the world's power in their moving bodies, and in a movement that seemed, so were the hearts of man and beast set upon it, that of a dance; but presently all would change and measurement succeed to pleasure, the dancing-master outlive the dance. What need had those young lads for careful eyes? But in Rome of the first and second centuries, where the dancing-master himself has died, the delineation of character as shown in face and head, as with us of recent years, is all in all, and sculptors, seeking the custom of occupied officials, stock in their workshops toga'd

marble bodies upon which can be screwed with the least possible delay heads modelled from the sitters with the most
scrupulous realism. When I think of Rome I see always those
heads with their world-considering eyes, and those bodies as
conventional as the metaphors in a leading article, and compare in my imagination vague Grecian eyes gazing at nothing,
Byzantine eyes of drilled ivory staring upon a vision, and
those eyelids of China and of India, those veiled or half-veiled
eyes weary of world and vision alike.

Meanwhile the irrational force that would create confusion
and uproar as with the cry 'The Babe, the Babe is born' — the
women speaking unknown tongues, the barbers and weavers
expounding Divine revelation with all the vulgarity of their
servitude, the tables that move or resound with raps — but
creates a negligible sect.

All about it is an *antithetical* aristocratic civilisation in its
completed form, every detail of life hierarchical, every great
man's door crowded at dawn by petitioners, great wealth
everywhere in few men's hands, all dependent upon a few, up
to the Emperor himself who is a God dependent upon a
greater God, and everywhere in Court, in the family, an in-
equality made law, and, floating over all, the Romanised Gods
of Greece in their physical superiority. All is rigid and station-
ary, men fight for centuries with the same sword and spear,
and though in naval warfare there is some change of tactics to
avoid those single combats of ship with ship that needed the
seamanship of a more skilful age, the speed of a sailing ship
remains unchanged from the time of Pericles to that of Constantine. Though sculpture grows more and more realistic and
so renews its vigour, this realism is without curiosity. The
athlete becomes the boxer that he may show lips and nose
beaten out of shape, the individual hairs show at the navel of
the bronze centaur, but the theme has not changed. Philosophy

alone, where in contact with irrational force — holding to Egyptian thaumaturgy and the Judean miracle but at arm's length — can startle and create. Yet Plotinus is as *primary*, as much a contradiction of all that created Roman civilisation, as St. Peter, and his thought has its roots almost as deep among the *primary* masses. The founder of his school was Ammonius Sacca, an Alexandrine porter. His thought and that of Origen, which I skimmed in my youth, seem to me to express the abstract synthesis of a quality like that of race, and so to display a character which must always precede Phase 8. Origen, because the Judean miracle has a stronger hold upon the masses than Alexandrian thaumaturgy, triumphs when Constantine (Phase 8) puts the Cross upon the shields of his soldiers and makes the bit of his war-horse from a nail of the True Cross, an act equivalent to man's cry for strength amid the animal chaos at the close of the first lunar quarter. Seeing that Constantine was not converted till upon his deathbed, I see him as half statesman, half thaumaturgist, accepting in blind obedience to a dream the new fashionable talisman, two sticks nailed together. The Christians were but six millions of the sixty or seventy of the Roman Empire, but, spending nothing upon pleasure, exceedingly rich like some Nonconformist sect of the eighteenth century. The world became Christian, 'that fabulous formless darkness', as it seemed to a philosopher of the fourth century, blotted out 'every beautiful thing', not through the conversion of crowds or general change of opinion, or through any pressure from below, for civilisation was antithetical still, but by an act of power.

I have not the knowledge (it may be that no man has the knowledge) to trace the rise of the Byzantine State through Phases 9, 10 and 11. My diagram tells me that a hundred and sixty years brought that State to its 15th Phase, but I that know nothing but the arts and of these little, cannot revise the series of dates 'approximately correct' but given, it may be, for suggestion only. With a desire for simplicity of statement I would have preferred to find in the middle, not at the end, of the fifth century Phase 12, for that was, so far as the known evidence carries us, the moment when Byzantium became Byzantine and substituted for formal Roman magnificence, with its glorification of physical power, an architecture that suggests the Sacred City in the Apocalypse of St. John. I think if I could be given a month of Antiquity and leave to spend it where I chose, I would spend it in Byzantium a little before Justinian opened St. Sophia and closed the Academy of Plato. I think I could find in some little wine-shop some philosophical worker in mosaic who could answer all my questions, the supernatural descending nearer to him than to Plotinus even, for the pride of his delicate skill would make what was an instrument of power to princes and clerics, a murderous madness in the mob, show as a lovely flexible presence like that of a perfect human body.

I think that in early Byzantium, maybe never before or since in recorded history, religious, aesthetic and practical life were one, that architect and artificers — though not, it may be, poets, for language had been the instrument of controversy and must have grown abstract — spoke to the multitude and the few alike. The painter, the mosaic worker, the worker in gold and silver, the illuminator of sacred books, were almost impersonal, almost perhaps without the consciousness of individual design, absorbed in their subject-matter and that the vision of a whole people. They could copy out of Gospel books those pictures that seemed as sacred as the text, and yet weave all into a vast design, the work of many that seemed the work of one, that made building, picture, pattern, metalwork of rail and lamp, seem but a single image; and this vision, this proclamation of their invisible master, had the

Greek nobility, Satan always the still half-divine Serpent, never the horned scarecrow of the didactic Middle Ages.

The ascetic, called in Alexandria 'God's Athlete', has taken the place of those Greek athletes whose statues have been melted or broken up or stand deserted in the midst of corn-fields, but all about him is an incredible splendour like that which we see pass under our closed eyelids as we lie between sleep and waking, no representation of a living world but the dream of a somnambulist. Even the drilled pupil of the eye, when the drill is in the hand of some Byzantine worker in ivory, undergoes a somnambulistic change, for its deep shadow among the faint lines of the tablet, its mechanical circle, where all else is rhythmical and flowing, give to Saint or Angel a look of some great bird at miracle. Could any visionary of those days, passing through the Church named with so un-theo-logical a grace 'The Holy Wisdom', can even a visionary of to-day wandering among the mosaics at Ravenna or in Sicily, failed to recognise some one image seen under his closed eye-lids? To me it seems that He, who among the first Christian communities was little but a ghostly exorcist, had in His assent to a full Divinity made possible this sinking-in upon a super-natural splendour, these walls with their little glimmering cubes of blue and green and gold.

I think that I might discover an oscillation, a revolution of the horizontal gyre like that between Doric and Ionic art, be-tween the two principal characters of Byzantine art. Recent criticism distinguishes between Graeco-Roman figures, their stern faces suggesting Greek wall-painting at Palmyra, Graeco-Egyptian painting upon the cases of mummies, where character delineations are exaggerated as in much work of our time, and that decoration which seems to undermine our self-control, and is, it seems, of Persian origin, and has for its appropriate symbol a vine whose tendrils climb everywhere and display among their leaves all those strange images of bird and beast, those forms that represent no creature eye has ever seen, yet are begotten one upon the other as if they were themselves living creatures. May I consider the domination of the first *antithetical* and that of the second *primary*, and see in their alternation the work of the horizontal gyre? Strzygowski thinks that the church decorations where there are visible representations of holy persons were especially dear to those who believed in Christ's double nature, and that wherever Christ is represented by a bare Cross and all the rest is bird and beast and tree, we may discover an Asiatic art dear to those who thought Christ contained nothing human.

If I were left to myself I would make Phase 15 coincide with Justinian's reign, that great age of building in which one may conclude Byzantine art was perfected; but the meaning of the diagram may be that a building like St. Sophia, where all, to judge by the contemporary description, pictured ecstasy, must unlike the declamatory St. Peter's precede the moment of climax. Of the moment of climax itself I can say nothing, and of what followed from Phase 17 to Phase 21 almost nothing, for I have no knowledge of the time; and no analogy from the age after Phidias, or after our own Renaissance, can help. We and the Greeks moved towards intellect, but Byzantium and the Western Europe of that day moved from it. If Strzygowski is right we may see in the destruction of images but a destruction of what was Greek in decoration accompanied perhaps by a renewed splendour in all that came down from the ancient Persian Paradise, an episode in some attempt to make theology more ascetic, spiritual and abstract. Destruction was apparently suggested to the first iconoclastic Emperor by followers of a Monophysite Bishop, Xenaias, who had his see in that part of the Empire where Persian influence had been strongest. The return of the images may, as I see things, have been the failure of synthesis (Phase 22) and the first sinking-in and dying-down of Christendom into the heterogeneous loam. Did Europe grow animal and literal? Did the strength of the victorious party come from zealots as ready as their opponents to destroy an image if permitted to grind it into powder, mix it with some liquid and swallow it as a medicine? Did mankind for a season do, not what it would, or should, but what it could, accept the past and the current belief because they prevented thought? In Western Europe I think I may see in Johannes Scotus Erigena the last intellectual synthesis before the death of philosophy, but I know little of him except that he is founded upon a Greek book of the sixth century, put into circulation by a last iconoclastic Emperor, though its Angelic Orders gave a theme to the image-makers. I notice too that my diagram makes Phase 22 coincide with the break-up of Charlemagne's Empire and so clearly likens him to Alexander, but I do not want to concern myself, except where I must, with political events.

Then follows, as always must in the last quarter, heterogeneous art; hesitation amid architectural forms, some book tells me; and interest in Greek and Roman literature; much copying out and gathering together; yet outside a few Courts and monasteries, another book tells me, an Asiatic and anarchic Europe. The intellectual cone has so narrowed that secular intellect has gone, and the strong man rules with the aid of local custom; everywhere the supernatural is sudden, violent, and as dark to the intellect as a stroke or St. Vitus' dance. Men under the Caesars, my own documents tell me, were physically one but intellectually many, but that is now reversed, for there is one common thought or doctrine, town is shut off from town, village from village, clan from clan. The spiritual life is alone overflowing, its cone expanded, and yet this life — secular intellect extinguished — has little effect upon men's conduct, is perhaps a dream which passes beyond the reach of conscious mind but for some rare miracle or vision. I think of it as like that profound reverie of the somnambulist which may be accompanied by a sensuous dream — a Romanesque stream perhaps of bird and beast images — and yet neither affect the dream nor be affected by it.

*   *   *

Written at Capri, February 1925

WHAT WE DID OR TRIED TO DO

I

As the most famous and beautiful coins are the coins of the Greek Colonies, especially of those in Sicily, we decided to send photographs of some of these, and one coin of Carthage, to our selected artists, and to ask them, as far as possible, to take them as a model. But the Greek coins had two advantages that ours could not have, one side need not balance the other, and either could be stamped in high relief, whereas ours must pitch and spin to please the gambler, and pack into rolls to please the banker.

II

We asked advice as to symbols, and were recommended by the public: round towers, wolf hounds, shamrocks, single or in wreaths, and the Treaty Stone of Limerick; and advised by the Society of Antiquaries to avoid patriotic emblems altogether, for even the shamrock emblem was not a hundred years old. We would have avoided them in any case, for we had to choose such forms as permit an artist to display all his capacity for design and expression, and as Ireland is the first modern State to design an entire coinage, not one coin now and another years later, as old dies wear out or the public changes its taste, it seemed best to give the coins some relation to one another.

The most beautiful Greek coins are those that represent

some god or goddess, as a boy or girl, or those that represent
animals or some simple object like a wheat-ear. Those beautiful forms, when they are re-named Hibernia or Liberty,
would grow empty and academic, and the wheat-ear had been
adopted by several modern nations. If we decided upon birds
and beasts, the artist, the experience of centuries has shown,
might achieve a masterpiece, and might, or so it seemed to us,
please those that would look longer at each coin than anybody
else, artists and children. Besides, what better symbols could
we find for this horse-riding, salmon-fishing, cattle-raising
country?

III

We might have chosen figures from the history of Ireland,
saints or national leaders, but a decision of the Executive
Council excluded modern men, and no portraits have come
down to us of St. Brigid or King Brian. The artist, to escape
academical convention, would have invented a characteristic
but unrecognisable head. I have before me a Swedish silver
coin and a Swedish bronze medal, both masterly, that display
the head of their mediaeval King, Gustavus Vasa. But those
marked features were as familiar to the people as the incidents
of his life, the theme of two famous plays. But even had we
such a figure a modern artist might prefer not to suggest some
existing knowledge, but to create new beauty by an arrangement of lines.

IV

But how should the Government choose its artists? What
advice should we give? It should reject a competition open to
everybody. No good artist would spend day after day design-
ing, and perhaps get nothing by it. There should be but a few

competitors, and whether a man's work were chosen or not he should be paid something, and he should know, that he might have some guarantee of our intelligence, against whom he competed. We thought seven would be enough, and that of these three should be Irish. We had hoped to persuade Charles Shannon, a master of design, whose impressive caps and robes the Benchers of the King's Inn had rejected in favour of wig and gown, to make one of these, but he refused, and that left us two Dublin sculptors of repute, Albert Power and Oliver Sheppard, and Jerome Connor arrived lately from New York. Before choosing the other four we collected examples of modern coinage with the help of various Embassies or of our friends. When we found anything to admire — the Italian coin with the wheat-ear or that with the Fascist emblem; the silver Swedish coin with the head of Gustavus Vasa; the American bison coin — we found out the artist's name and asked for other specimens of his work, if we did not know it already. We also examined the work of various medallists, and, much as we admired the silver Gustavus Vasa, we preferred a bronze Gustavus Vasa by the great Swedish sculptor Carl Milles.

Carl Milles and Ivan Mestrovic, sculptor and medallist, have expressed in their work a violent rhythmical energy unknown to past ages, and seem to many the foremost sculptors of our day. We wrote to both these and to James E. Fraser, designer of the bison and of some beautiful architectural sculpture, and to Publio Morbiducci, designer of the coin with the Fascist emblem, but Fraser refused, and Mestrovic did not reply until it was too late.[1] We substituted for Fraser the

[1] We had written to a wrong address and our letter took some time reaching him. He made one magnificent design and, on discovering that the date had passed, gave it to the Irish Free State with great generosity.

American sculptor Manship, the creator of a Diana and her
dogs, stylised and noble. But as yet we had no Englishman,
and could think of no one among the well-known names that
we admired both as sculptor and medallist. After some hesitation, for Charles Ricketts had recommended S. W. Carline,
designer of a powerful Zeebrugge medal, and of a charming
medal struck to the honour of Flinders Petrie, we selected, on
the recommendation of the Secretary of the British School at
Rome, Percy Metcalfe, a young sculptor as yet but little
known.

V

Because when an artist takes up a task for the first time he
must sometimes experiment before he has mastered the new
technique, we advised that the artist himself should make
every alteration necessary, and that, if he had to go to London or elsewhere for the purpose, his expenses should be paid.
An Irish artist had made an excellent design for the seal of the
Dublin National Gallery, and that design, founded upon the
seal of an Irish abbey, had been altered by the Mint, round
academic contours substituted for the planes and straight lines
of a mediaeval design. One remembers the rage of Blake
when his designs came smooth and lifeless from the hands of
an engraver whose work had been substituted for his. The
Deputy Master of the Mint has commended and recommended to other nations a precaution which protects the
artist, set to a new task and not as yet a craftsman, from the
craftsman who can never be an artist.

VI

We refused to see the designs until we saw them all together. The name of each artist, if the model had been signed,

was covered with stamp paper. The models were laid upon tables, with the exception of one set, fastened to a board, which stood upright on the mantelpiece. We had expected to recognise the work of the different artists by its style, but we recognised only the powerful handling of Milles on the board over the mantelpiece. One set of designs seemed far to exceed the others as decorations filling each its circular space, and this set, the work of Percy Metcalfe, had so marked a style, and was so excellent throughout, that it seemed undesirable to mix its designs with those of any other artist. Though we voted coin by coin, I think we were all convinced of this. I was distressed by my conviction. I had been certain that we could mix the work of three or four different artists, and that this would make our coinage more interesting, and had written to Milles, or to some friend of his, that it was unthinkable that we should not take at least one coin from so great an artist. Nobody could lay aside without a pang so much fine work, and our Government, had it invited designs, without competition, from either Morbiducci or Manship, would have been lucky to get such work as theirs. Manship's Ram and Morbiducci's Bull are magnificent; Manship's an entirely new creation, Morbiducci's a re-creation of the Bull on the Greek coin we had sent him as an example. That I may understand the energy and imagination of the designs of Milles I tell myself that they have been dug out of Sicilian earth, that they passed to and fro in the Mediterranean traffic two thousand years and more ago, and thereupon I discover that his strange bull, his two horses, that angry woodcock, have a supernatural energy. But all are cut in high relief, all suggest more primitive dies than we use to-day, and turned into coins would neither pitch nor pack.

What can I say of the Irish artists who had all done well in some department of their craft — Sheppard's 'O'Leary' at the

Municipal Gallery, and Power's 'Kettle' at the Dublin
National Gallery, are known, and Connor's 'Emmet' may
become known — except that had some powerful master of
design been brought to Dublin years ago, and set to teach
there, Dublin would have made a better show? Sir William
Orpen affected Dublin painting, not merely because he gave
it technical knowledge, but because he brought into a Dublin
Art School the contagion of his vigour. The work of Metcalfe, Milles, Morbiducci, Manship, displays the vigour of
their minds, and the forms of their designs symbolise that
vigour, and our own is renewed at the spectacle.

VII

As certain of the beasts represent our most important industry, they were submitted to the Minister for Agriculture
and his experts, and we awaited the results with alarm. I have
not been to Chartres Cathedral for years, but remember
somewhere outside the great door figures of angels or saints,
whose spiritual dignity and architectural effect depend upon
bodies much longer in proportion to the length of their heads
than a man's body ever was. The artist who must fill a given
space and suggest some spiritual quality or rhythmical movement finds it necessary to suppress or exaggerate. Art, as some
French critic has said, is appropriate exaggeration. The expert
on horse-flesh, or bull-flesh, or swine-flesh, on the other hand,
is bound to see his subject inanimate and isolated. The coins
have suffered less than we feared. The horse, as first drawn,
was more alive than the later version, for when the hind legs
were brought more under the body and the head lowered, in
obedience to technical opinion, it lost muscular tension; we
passed from the open country to the show-ground. But, on
the other hand, it is something to know that we have upon

our half-crown a representation of an Irish hunter, perfect in all its points, and can add the horseman's pleasure to that of the children and the artists. The first bull had to go, though one of the finest of all the designs, because it might have upset, considered as an ideal, the eugenics of the farmyard, but the new bull is as fine, in a different way. I sigh, however, over the pig, though I admit that the state of the market for pig's cheeks made the old design impossible. A design is like a musical composition, alter some detail and all has to be altered. With the round cheeks of the pig went the lifted head, the look of insolence and of wisdom, and the comfortable round bodies of the little pigs. We have instead querulous and harassed animals, better merchandise but less living.

VIII

I have given here my own opinions and impressions, and I have no doubt my Committee differs from some, but I know no other way of writing. We had all our points of view, though I can only remember one decision that was not unanimous. A member had to be out-voted because he wanted to substitute a harrier for a wolf-hound on the ground that on the only occasion known to him when hare and wolf-hound met the wolf-hound ran away. I am sorry that our meetings have come to an end, for we learned to like each other well.

What remains to be said is said in the name of the whole Committee. Our work could not have been done so quickly nor so well had not the Department of Finance chosen Mr. McCauley for our Secretary. Courteous, able and patient he has a sense of order that fills me with wonder.

[928]

FROM *ON THE BOILER*

PRELIMINARIES

I

LAST year the Lord Mayor sent out an intelligent Christmas card, an eighteenth-century print of some Dublin street; but this year his card had a drawing of the Mansion House as it is to-day. It is clear that architecture interests him. Let him threaten to resign if the Corporation will not tell the City Architect to scrape off the stucco, pull down the cast-iron porch, lift out the plate glass, and get the Mansion House into its eighteenth-century state. It would only cost a few hundred pounds, for the side walls and their windows are as they should be, and Dublin would have one more dignified ancestral building. All Catholic Ireland, as it was before the National University and a victory in the field had swept the penal laws out of its bones, swells out in that pretentious front. Old historic bricks and window-panes obliterated or destroyed, its porch invented when England was elaborating the architecture and interior decoration of the gin-palace, its sole fitting inhabitant that cringing firbolg Tom Moore cast by some ironmonger — bronze costs money — now standing on the other side of Trinity College near the urinal.

This has not occurred to the Lord Mayor, a good, amiable, clever man, I am told, because he thinks, like English royalty, that his duty is to make himself popular among the common people, and architectural taste is at present articulate only in the few. His time is taken up opening crèches, talking everything but politics, presiding at dinners, going sober to bed.

The whole State should be so constructed that the people should think it their duty to grow popular with King and Lord Mayor instead of King and Lord Mayor growing popular with them; yet, as it is even, I have known some two or three men and women who never, apart from the day's natural kindness, gave the people a thought, or who despised them with that old Shakespearean contempt and were worshipped after their death or even while they lived. Try to be popular and you think another man's thought, sink into that slow, slothful, inanimate, semi-hypocritical thinking Dante symbolised by hoods and cloaks of lead.

II

I read in the *Irish Times* of October 20, 1937, that the Galway Library Committee is indignant and has written to a firm of publishers to protest. John Eglinton said in his memoir of AE that a mob had broken into a public library, taken out the books of certain eminent authors and burnt them in the street. The Committee did not require, it seems, the dictation of a mob to do its duty. They had some years ago discussed whether 'the works of Mr. Bernard Shaw were works which should be kept in a public library, and on a division it was decided that the books of Shaw be not kept. It was suggested at the time that any book which was offensive should be burned. There was no other way of getting rid of them.' I do not mention this incident because of its importance — there have been similar burnings elsewhere in Ireland — but that I may stand between these men and their critics. They are probably clever, far-seeing men when ploughing their fields, selling porter, or, if they make their living by teaching class, when they have shut the school doors behind them; but show them a book and they buzz like a bee in a bottle. I know nothing of them except those few printed words, but it seems probable that many men in Irish public life should not have been taught to read and write, and would not have been in any country before the middle of the nineteenth century. Some of the Galway Committee may have a family tradition of some grandfather, or grandfather's cousin or nephew, who set out to seek learning supported by the contributions of relations and friends, and found at the journey's end, if he had reasonable luck, not a government-appointed dunce, but a man who loved his book and taught something of great people and great literature. Thackeray heard two ragged boys leaning over the Liffey parapet discussing 'wan of the Ptolemies'. Forcing reading and writing on those who wanted neither was a worst part of the violence which for two centuries has been creating that hell wherein we suffer, unless indeed the spoilt priest in *John Bull's Other Island* was right and the world itself is Hell. I once travelled up from Limerick with an old priest and a girl of thirteen or fourteen. He had written an essay on Gladstone and it lay upon his knees. He began talking to the girl about it. 'Who was Gladstone?' 'I don't know, Father.' 'Was he at the Siege of Limerick?' 'Yes, Father,' this with a sudden brightening. When he asked about Parnell and the Land Bill and found that she had heard of neither he turned to me with 'Sir, if you ever meet anyone of importance please tell them that this kind of ignorance is spreading everywhere from the schools.'

Perhaps now they learn these names by rote, but I see nowhere evidence that ignorance has abated. Our representative system has given Ireland to the incompetent. There are no districts in County Galway of any size without a Catholic curate, a young shopkeeper, a land-owner, a sawyer, with enough general knowledge to make a good library committee. I remember the volunteers who policed the country, dealt out justice, and had all men's respect.

III

When I was first a member of the Irish Senate I discovered
to my surprise that one learned in three months more about
every Senator's character and capacity than could have been
learned from years of ordinary life. I came to know the
Ministers more slowly, for each attended only when his own
department was concerned. The thirty men nominated by
President Cosgrave were plainly the most able and the most
educated. I attached myself to a small group led by an old
friend of my father's, Andrew Jameson, for I knew that he
would leave me free to speak my mind. The few able men
among the elected Senators had been nominated for election
by Ministers. As the nominated element began to die out —
almost all were old men — the Senate declined in ability and
prestige. In its early days some old banker or lawyer would
dominate the House, leaning upon the back of the chair in
front, always speaking with undisturbed self-possession as at
some table in a board-room. My imagination sets up against
him some typical elected man, emotional as a youthful chim-
panzee, hot and vague, always disturbed, always hating something or other.

The Ministers had not been elected. They had destroyed a
system of election and established another, made terrible de-
cisions, the ablest had signed the death-warrant of his dearest
friend. They seemed men of skill and mother-wit, men who
had survived hatred. But their minds knew no play that my
mind could play at; I felt that I could never know them. One
of the most notable said he had long wanted to meet me. We
met, but my conversation shocked and embarrassed him. No,
neither Gogarty nor I, with our habit of outrageous conversation, could get near those men. Yet their descendants, if they
grow rich enough for the travel and leisure that make a

finished man, will constitute our ruling class, and date their origin from the Post Office as American families date theirs from the *Mayflower*. They have already intermarried, able stocks have begun to appear, and recent statistics have shown that men of talent everywhere are much linked through marriage and descent. The Far East has dynasties of painters, dancers, politicians, merchants, but with us the dancer may be the politician's mother, though I cannot think of any example; the painter his rebellious son.

I was six years in the Irish Senate; I am not ignorant of politics elsewhere, and on other grounds I have some right to speak. I say to those that shall rule here: 'If ever Ireland again seems molten wax, reverse the process of revolution. Do not try to pour Ireland into any political system. Think first how many able men with public minds the country has, how many it can hope to have in the near future, and mould your system upon those men. It does not matter how you get them, but get them. Republics, Kingdoms, Soviets, Corporate States, Parliaments, are trash, as Hugo said of something else, "not worth one blade of grass that God gives for the nest of the linnet." These men, whether six or six thousand, are the core of Ireland, are Ireland itself.'

IV

As I write these words the Abbey Players are finishing a successful American tour. These tours, and Irish songs and novels, when they come from a deeper life than their nineteenth-century predecessors, are taking the place of political speakers, political organisations, in holding together the twenty scattered millions conscious of their Irish blood. The attitude towards life of Irish writers and dramatists at this moment will have historical importance. The success of the Abbey Theatre has grown out of a single conviction of its founders: I was the spokesman because I was born arrogant and had learnt an artist's arrogance — 'Not what you want but what we want' — and we were the first modern theatre that said it. I did not speak for John Synge, Augusta Gregory, and myself alone, but for all the dramatists of the theatre. Again and again somebody speaking for our audience, for an influential newspaper or political organisation, has demanded more of this kind of play, or less or none of that. They have not understood that we cannot, and if we could would not comply; the moment any dramatist has some dramatic sense and applies it to our Irish theme he is played. We may help him with his technique or to clear his mind of the second-hand or the second-rate in their cruder forms, but beyond that we can do nothing. He must find himself and mould his dramatic form to his nature after his own fashion, and that is why we have produced some of the best plays of modern times, and a far greater number of the worst. And what I have said of the dramatists is true of the actors, though there the bad comedians do not reach our principal company. I have seen English producers turn their players into mimics; but all our producers do for theirs, or so it was in my day and I suppose it is still the same, is to help them to understand the play and their own natures.

Yet the theatre has not, apart from this one quality, gone my way or in any way I wanted it to go, and often, looking back, I have wondered if I did right in giving so much of my life to the expression of other men's genius. According to the Indians a man may do much good yet lose his own soul. Then I say to myself, I have had greater luck than any other modern English-speaking dramatist; I have aimed at tragic ecstasy, and here and there in my own work and in the work of my friends I have seen it greatly played. What does it matter that it belongs to a dead art and to a time when a man spoke out of an experience and a culture that were not of his time alone, but held his time, as it were, at arm's length, that he might be a spectator of the ages? I am haunted by certain moments: Miss O'Neill in the last act of Synge's *Deirdre*, 'Draw a little back with the squabbling of fools'; Kerrigan and Miss O'Neill playing in a private house that scene in Augusta Gregory's *Full Moon* where the young mad people in their helpless joy sing *The Boys of Queen Anne*; Frank Fay's entrance in the last act of *The Well of the Saints*; William Fay at the end of *On Baile's Strand*; Mrs. Patrick Campbell in my *Deirdre*, passionate and solitary; and in later years that great artist Ninette de Valois in *Fighting the Waves*. These things will, it may be, haunt me on my death-bed; what matter if the people prefer another art, I have had my fill.

[1939]

NOTES TO *SELECTED CRITICISM*

THE IRISH NATIONAL LITERARY SOCIETY

p. 18 Duffy's Library a series of Irish books selected by Sir
Charles Gavan Duffy (1816–1903), Irish journalist, founded the Young
Ireland party, became Premier of Victoria, returned to Europe in
1880, president of the Irish Literary Society.
Thomas of Erceldoune known also as Thomas the Rymer (*fl.* 1220–
97), Scottish seer and poet.
p. 19 Mr John O'Leary (1830–1907) influenced by the Young
Ireland movement as a student, leader of the Fenian movement,
imprisoned in 1865, released in 1870 on condition he left Ireland for
fifteen years. He spent his exile in Paris. On O'Leary's return to
Dublin in 1885, he exerted a strong influence on Yeats.
Dr Douglas Hyde (1860–1949), founder of the Gaelic League, first
President of Ireland; poet, scholar, translator. **Dr Sigerson** Dr George
Sigerson (1838–1923), translator, scientist and Senator of the Irish
Free State. **Count Plunkett** Count George Noble Plunkett (1851–
1948), Irish poet and art critic. **Miss Katharine Tynan** (1859–1931),
Irish novelist and poet, married H. A. Hinkson in 1893. **Miss Maude
Gonne** (1866–1953), Irish revolutionary with whom Yeats fell in
love in 1889. Despite repeated proposals from Yeats she married
John MacBride in 1903, separated from him in 1905. He was shot in
1916 for his part in the Rising. **Mr Richard Ashe King** (1839–1932),
Irish clergyman and later man of letters. **Mr Standish O'Grady**
(1846–1928) Irish historian, novelist and journalist, author of *History of
Ireland: The Heroic Period* (1878), important influence on the literary
renaissance. **Strongbow** Richard FitzGilbert de Clare, Earl of
Pembroke (d. 1176), landed in Ireland in 1170, having married Eva,
daughter of Dermot, King of Leinster, whom he succeeded in 1171.

FROM **WILLIAM BLAKE AND HIS ILLUSTRATIONS TO THE DIVINE COMEDY**

p. 26. Correggio Antonio Allegri da Correggio (1494–1534), Italian
painter. **Bartolozzi** Francesco Bartolozzi (1727–1815), Italian engraver.

Stothard Thomas Stothard (1755–1834), English illustrator and painter.

p. 29 Young's 'Night Thoughts' a didactic poem by Edward Young (1683–1765).

p. 30 Blair's 'Grave' *The Grave*, written by Robert Blair (1699–1746), is similar in character to *Night Thoughts*. **Schiavonetti's** possibly Andrea Schiavone (1522?–82) Italian painter whose poems included 'The Adoration of the Magi'. **Thornton's Virgil** Robert John Thornton (1768?–1837), edited Virgil in a school edition (1812); the 3rd edition in 2 volumes was published in 1821. **Woollett** William Woollett (1735–1835), English draughtsman and engraver.

Strange Sir Robert Strange (1721–92), Scottish line engraver. **Marc Antonio** Marc Antonio Raimondi (*c.* 1480–1530), Italian engraver. **Linnell** John Linnell (1792–1882), English portrait and landscape painter, friend of Blake.

p. 32 Orcagno a Florentine architect whose real name was Andrea di Crone (1308?–68?). **Giotto** (1266–1336), Italian painter.

A SYMBOLIC ARTIST AND THE COMING OF SYMBOLIC ART

p. 33 AE (George Russell, 1867–1935), poet, essayist and mystic, an active member of the Irish literary renaissance and Home Rule Movement, and a founder of the Abbey Theatre. He edited the *Irish Statesman*. **Miss Althea Gyles** Althea Gyles (1868–1949), symbolic painter, member of the Order of the Golden Dawn, whom Yeats met in theosophical circles in Dublin in the late 1880s.

p. 34 Mr Whistler James Abbott McNeill Whistler (1834–1903), American painter and etcher who settled in Chelsea in 1863. **Mr Beardsley** Aubrey Vincent Beardsley (1872–98), black and white artist and editor of the *Yellow Book*. **Sir Edward Burne-Jones** (1833–98), romantic painter and designer, friend of D. G. Rossetti and William Morris. **Mr Ricketts** Charles Ricketts (1866–1931), painter, sculptor, art critic, stage-set designer. Co-editor of *The Dial* (1889–97). **Degas** Hilaire Germaine Edgar Degas (1834–1917), French painter.

p. 35 Villiers de l'Isle-Adam Comte Villiers de l'Isle-Adam (1838–89), French writer and pioneer of the symbolist movement. **Miss Macleod** Fiona Macleod (William Sharp, 1855–1905), Scottish novelist, essayist and biographer.

THE AUTUMN OF THE BODY

p. 38 'The Temptation of St Anthony' *La Tentation de Saint Antoine* (1874), a play by Gustave Flaubert. **Axel** Symbolist drama by Comte Villiers de l'Isle-Adam. See note above. **Maeterlinck** Maurice Maeterlinck (1862–1949), Belgian symbolist poet and dramatist, author of *L'Oiseau Bleu* and *La Mort*. **Flaubert** Gustave Flaubert (1821–80), French novelist, author of *Madame Bovary*.

p. 39 Mr Lang Andrew Lang (1844–1912), Greek scholar, anthropologist, poet and man of letters, author of *Custom and Myth*, co-translator of the *Odyssey* and *Iliad*. **Mr Gosse** Sir Edmund Gosse (1849–1928), civil servant, conversationalist, man of letters, author of *Father and Son* (autobiography), poems and various biographies and critical studies. **Mr Dobson** Henry Austin Dobson (1840–1921), poet and biographer.

p. 39 Mr Bridges Robert Bridges (1844–1930), appointed Poet Laureate in 1913, critic and anthologist, author of *The Testament of Beauty* (1929).

p. 40 An Irish poet AE, George William Russell. See note above. **'Kalevala'** ('Land of Heroes'), national epic poem of Finland.

p. 41 Mr Symons Arthur Symons (1865–1945), poet and critic who described symbolism to English readers, friend of Yeats with whom he shared rooms in 1896. **Mallarmé's** Etienne Mallarmé (1842–98), French symbolist poet, author of *L'Après-midi d'un faune*.

THE SYMBOLISM OF POETRY

p. 43 Mr Arthur Symons see note above.

p. 44 Giovanni Bardi Conte del Vernio (1534?–1612), Italian nobleman, scholar and inventor of opera. **the Pléiade** a group of late 16th-century French poets.

p. 46 Nash (or Nashe), Thomas Nash (1567–1601), poet, dramatist, pamphleteer and author of *The Unfortunate Traveller, or the Life of Jacke Wilton*, a romantic tale of adventure.

p. 47 Arthur O'Shaughnessy (1844–81), poet and playwright; author of *Epic of Women* (1870), *Lays of France* (1872), *Music and Moonlight* (1874) and *Songs of a Worker* (1881).

p. 51 Demeter Greek goddess of corn-growing, earth and agriculture, mother of Persephone, who was carried off by Pluto to

Hades. So great was Demeter's grief that Jupiter allowed Persephone to spend part of the year with her mother. **Gérard de Nerval** properly Gérard Labrunie (1808–55), French writer. **Maeterlinck** see note, p. 521. **Villiers de l'Isle-Adam** see note, p. 521.

THE PHILOSOPHY OF SHELLEY'S POETRY

p. 53 a group The Dublin Hermetic Society which met in York Street. **Godwin's 'Political Justice'** William Godwin (1756–1836), philosopher and novelist. His best novels are *Caleb Williams* (1794) and *St Leon* (1799). He had a great influence on Wordsworth, Coleridge and Shelley.

p. 61 the Sidhe the gods of ancient Ireland, the people of the fairy hills.

p. 64 the Echtge hills a range of hills east of Gort, Lady Gregory's home in Co. Galway. **Slieve ná nog** Mountain of the Young.

p. 67 Plato's cave a reference to Plato's *Republic*, Book 7. **Porphyry** (AD *c.* 233–304), Neoplatonist. His chief writings include lives of Plotinus and Pythagoras, *Sententiae*, *De Abstinentia*, and the *Epistola ad Marcellam*, addressed to his wife.

p. 68 Taylor's translation Thomas Taylor (1758–1835), known as 'The Platonist'; he translated Plato, Aristotle, Neoplatonists and Pythagoreans. **Mr Lang's translation** see note, p. 521. **Zoroaster's** Zoroaster was the founder of the Magian religion, probably a Persian living in the sixth century BC. Zoroastrianism has two spirits, one of light and good, the other of darkness and evil.

p. 72 Maeterlinck see note, p. 521.

p. 74 Oisin . . . in the Gaelic poem probably Michael Comyn's 'The Lay of Oisin in the Land of Youth', on Brian O'Looney's translation of which Yeats partially founded his own poem, *The Wanderings of Oisin* (1889).

p. 77 Proclus (*c.* 412–85), Neoplatonist, born in Constantinople. **Emilia Viviani** an Italian girl admired by Shelley and the subject of his poem *Epipsychidion*.

FROM MAGIC

p. 81 Bulwer Lytton's Edward Robert Bulwer Lytton, first Earl of Lytton (1831–91), poet and statesman, Viceroy of India. Many of his writings appeared under the pseudonym of Owen Meredith.

geomancy divination by means of figures or lines, particularly by observing points and lines on the earth or on paper, or by means of figures formed by pebbles or particles of earth thrown down at random. **p. 81 chiromancy** the art of predicting events or telling fortunes by examining the hand. **cabbalistic symbolism** the Cabbala or Kabbala are medieval Jewish writings preserved by occultists. They blend cosmogony and explanations of Biblical material.

p. 84 'Frankenstein' or *The Modern Prometheus*, a tale of terror by Mary Shelley, in which Frankenstein creates a monster which murders Frankenstein's brother and bride and finally Frankenstein himself.

p. 89 'Carmina Gaedelica' *Ortha nan Gaidheal, Carmina Gadelica* (1900), hymns and incantations with illustrative notes . . . collected in the Highlands and Islands of Scotland and translated into English by Alexander Carmichael. **Finn mac Cumhal** legendary hero of the Fenian cycle of tales. **'Paracelsus'** Paracelsus (1493–1541), magician, alchemist, astrologer, sometimes regarded as the founder of modern chemistry. He once held a Chair of Physic and Surgery in Basle.

FROM AT STRATFORD-ON-AVON

p. 96 Mr Gordon Craig Edward Gordon Craig (1872–1966), English actor and stage designer, son of Ellen Terry. His aim of simplifying the scene and emphasizing the actors was acclaimed in Germany, Italy and Russia. In 1905 he travelled through Europe with Isadora Duncan; settled in Italy in 1906 and founded a theatrical art school in Florence in 1913.

p. 97 Mr Benson Sir Frank Benson (1858–1939), actor-manager. **Balzac** Honoré de Balzac (1799–1850), French novelist, author of *La Comédie Humaine*, a collection of depictions of French life.

p. 99 Professor Dowden Edward Dowden (1843–1913), first Professor of English Literature at Trinity College, Dublin. A friend of J. B. Yeats, he did not support the Irish literary revival, and was a Unionist in politics. He wrote a *Life of Shelley; Shakespeare, his Mind and Art; Puritan and Anglican*, and other critical studies.

p. 100 Verlaine Paul Verlaine (1844–96), French symbolist poet. **p. 101 Gervinus** Georg Gottfried Gervinus (1805–71), critic who became Professor of History at Göttingen. His commentaries on Shakespeare were translated into English in 1862. **Bentham** Jeremy Bentham (1748–1832), English writer on law, whose writings affected legislation and the administration of the law.

FROM EDMUND SPENSER

p. 107 Lollards 14th-century heretics, followers of Wycliffe and others of similar views. **Langland** William Langland (1330?–1400?), poet, author of *The Vision Concerning Piers the Plowman*. **the other great English allegory** *The Pilgrim's Progress*, by John Bunyan (1628–88).

p. 110 Emerson Ralph Waldo Emerson (1803–82), American transcendental philosopher, poet and lecturer. **Thomas à Kempis's** Thomas Hammerlein (1380–1471), who became a monk and wrote *De Imitatione Christi*.

p. 111 William Morris (1834–96), poet, translator, artist, decorator, printer, manufacturer and socialist, author of *The Life and Death of Jason*, *The Earthly Paradise* and *Sigurd the Volsung*. He founded the Kelmscott press.

p. 113 Hugo Victor Hugo (1802–85), French poet and novelist, author of *Notre Dame de Paris* and *Les Misérables*. He entered politics in 1848, was exiled 1851–70. **Rabelais** François Rabelais (1494?–1553), French humanist, physician and satirical author of *Pantagruel* and *Gargantua* as well as the *Third Book* and *Fourth Book*. Urquhart translated the first three books into English. **Theocritus** Greek poet of the third century BC, author of the *Idylls*, pastoral poems.

p. 115 the Four Masters Conary and Cucogry O'Clery and Ferfesa O'Mulcrony, who compiled the *Annals of the Four Masters* (also called *Annals of Donegal*) during 1633–6 in the Franciscan monastery of Donegal.

p. 116 The Great Demagogue Oliver Cromwell (1599–1658), Lord Protector. He arrived in Ireland in 1649, sacked Drogheda and Wexford, and was responsible for the Act of Settlement by which Irish gentry were transplanted to Clare and Connacht and their lands handed over to Army officers and men, nine counties being confiscated. **Cairbry Cat-Head** Cairbry Cat-Head led the lower classes in an anti-monarchical revolution, *c.* AD 90, but the Irish, still liking monarchy, called him their king. See Thurneysen, *Zeitschrift für Celtische Philologie*, XI, 56, and T. F. O'Rahilly 'Cairbre Cattchenn' in Feil Sgribhinn Eóin Mhin Néill (1940), pp. 101–10. I owe this information to Mr Brendan Kennelly.

p. 117 Claude's Claude Lorrain (1600–1682), French landscape painter.

p. 118 Smart Christopher Smart (1722–71), English poet.

p. 120 Matthew Roydon (1580–1622), English poet.

FROM **THE HAPPIEST OF THE POETS**

p. 122 an old turreted house Sandymount Castle, Dublin.

p. 123 Habundia's Kin probably a reference to Domina Abundia, a beneficent fairy whose name occurs in poems of the Middle Ages, who brought plenty to those whom she visited.

p. 124 Mr Mackail John William Mackail (1859–1945), British classical scholar; Professor of Poetry at Oxford (1906–11); awarded the OM in 1935.

THE GALWAY PLAINS

p. 127 Lady Gregory Lady Isabella Augusta Gregory (1852–1932), translator and dramatist, daughter of Dudley Persse, a rich landowner, and widow of Sir William Gregory. After meeting Yeats she became interested in the Irish renaissance and was a co-founder of the Abbey Theatre.

p. 128 Raftery Anthony Raftery (1784–1834), blind Irish Gaelic poet.

FIRST PRINCIPLES

p. 130 Pascal Blaise Pascal (1623–62), French mathematician and religious philosopher. **Montaigne** Michel Eyqyem de Montaigne (1533–92), French essayist. **Emerson** see note, p. 524.

p. 131 J. F. Taylor John Francis Taylor (1850?–1902), Irish orator (QC 1892) and journalist.

p. 132 'The Rising of the Moon' a play by Lady Gregory included in *Seven Short Plays* (1909). **Fenians** originally a semi-mythical, semi-historical military body said to have been raised for the defence of Ireland against Norse raids; later an association for promoting the overthrow of English government in Ireland.

p. 133 Lollard preacher Sir John Oldcastle (d. 1417).

p. 136 Cervantes Saavedra Miguel de Cervantes (1547–1616), Spanish novelist, dramatist and poet.

p. 137 the Fianna see note above on Fenians.

p. 138 Virgil the reference is to *Eclogue IV*, ll. 31–6, where Virgil prophesies a second Argo and a second Troy. See Yeats's poem 'Two Songs from a Play', *Collected Poems*, p. 239. **Dr Hyde** see note, p. 519. **Father Peter O'Leary** (b. 1839), Gaelic scholar.

p. 139 Ariosto Ludovico Ariosto (1474–1533), author of *Orlando Furioso*, an Italian romantic epic.

p. 143 Columbanus (or Columban), St Columbanus (543–615), born in Leinster, founded monasteries in Gaul and died at Bobbio in the Apennines where he had founded a monastery in 612. **Beckford** William Beckford (1759–1844), traveller and novelist; his 'one memorable book', *Vathek*, is an oriental tale. **Prof. Dowden's** see note, p. 523. **Lowell** James Lowell (1819–91), American poet and critic.

p. 144 The Well of English Undefiled Geoffrey Chaucer (*c.* 1345–*c.* 1400).

p. 144 Sir Charles Gavan Duffy see note, p. 519 . **Professor York Powell** (1850–1904), don at Christ Church and Regius Professor of History at Oxford, who wrote poetry and was a friend of J. B. Yeats.

p. 145 Campbell Thomas Campbell (1777–1844), Scottish poet, chiefly remembered for his war songs and patriotic poems.

p. 146 Mr John Eglinton (b. 1868), pen-name of W. K. Magee, Irish essayist and poet who was at school with Yeats in Dublin. **Flaubert** see note, p. 521. **Björnson** Björnstjerne Björnson (1832–1910), Norwegian novelist and playwright.

p. 149 Villon François Villon (1431–80[9]), French poet, whose chief works are 'Petit Testament' and 'Grand Testament'; his 'Ballade des Dames du Temps Jadis' was translated by Rossetti.

FROM **DISCOVERIES**

p. 151 'Little Eyolf' (1894), play by Henrik Ibsen (1828–1906).

p. 152 the hangings of '98 the Irish rebellion of 1798 was savagely suppressed.

p. 153 Villon see note above.

p. 154 Tintoretto's Tintoretto, actually named Jacopo Robusti, was born in Venice where there are many specimens of his art, which includes 'St George and the Dragon', 'The Last Supper', 'The Crucifixion', 'The Resurrection' etc.

p. 155 'The Knight of the Burning Pestle' (1613), a comedy by Beaumont and Fletcher. **'The Silent Woman'** alternative title of *Epicœne*, a comedy by Ben Jonson.

p. 157 a Herr Nordau Max Simon Nordau (1849–1923) was born in Budapest, became a physician, wrote some novels and travel books, but is best known for *The Conventional Lies of Society, Paradoxes* and *Degeneration*.

p. 159 Balzac see note, p. 523.

FROM POETRY AND TRADITION

p. 161 Charles V (1337–80), called Charles the Wise, was born at Vincennes and reigned from 1364 to 1380; he was a patron of art and literature and collected a large library at the Louvre. **Duke Guidobaldo** Guidobaldo de Montefeltro, Duke of Urbino (1472–1508), who built the magnificent palace at Urbino, which Yeats visited in 1907, and about which he read in Castiglione's *The Book of The Courtier*. **Duke Frederick** Frederico de Montefeltro, Duke of Urbino (1410–82) father of Guidobaldo.

p. 164 Castiglione Baldassare Castiglione (1478–1529), Italian humanist, author of *Il Cortegiano* (*The Courtier*).

ANIMA HOMINIS

p. 166 Boehme Jacob Boehme (1575–1624), German theosophist and mystic. **one close friend** Lady Gregory. **Maeterlinck** see note, p. 521. **Burne-Jones** Sir Edward Burne-Jones (1833–98), English painter, friend of Rossetti and William Morris.

p. 168 Savage Landor Walter Savage Landor (1775–1864), poet and author of *Imaginary Conversations* (prose). **Beckford** see note above. **Leigh Hunt** (1784–1859), essayist and poet. **Simeon Solomon** (1840–1905), English painter and draughtsman.

p. 169 Shadwell Charles Lancelot Shadwell (1840–1919), sometime Provost of Oriel College, Oxford, translated Dante's *Purgatorio* (Pt I, 1892; Pt II, 1899) and his *Paradiso* (1915). **Guido Cavalcanti** (*c.* 1230–1300), Italian poet. **Gino da Pistoia** (1270–1336), Italian jurist and poet, friend of Dante.

p. 170 Giovanni Guirino It is possible that Yeats may be referring here to *Guerino il Meschino* (the Wretched) an Italian romance by Andrea of Florence (a contemporary of Dante), first printed in Padua in 1473. Miss Audrey Stead has suggested that Yeats may have come across this romance in reading John F. Hogan, *Life and Works of Dante Alighieri* (1899) pp. 336–8, who says Dante may have gained his knowledge of Irish legend through this romance.

p. 170 Johnson Lionel Johnson (1867–1902), poet and critic. **Dowson** Ernest Dowson (1867–1900), English poet who spent much of his youth and later life in France.

p. 171 an old artist probably John Butler Yeats, Yeats's father.

p. 172 Saint Francis St Francis of Assisi, Giovanni Francesco Bernardone (1181?–1226), founder of the Franciscan Order, devoted himself to the relief of the poor and sick. **Caesar Borgia** (1476–1507), Italian general and administrator.

p. 173 Dodona in Epirus, seat of the oldest oracle (of Zeus) in Greece.

p. 174 Plutarch's precepts Plutarch (c. 46–120) was a Greek biographer. **'Wilhelm Meister'** *Wilhelm Meisters Wanderjahre* (1821) by Goethe (1749–1832). **Heraclitus** (c. 400–440 BC), Greek philosopher. His *Concerning Nature* (c. 513 BC) contains his view that all things were in a state of flux.

p. 176 Edwin Ellis (1848–1916), minor critic and poet; he and Yeats edited Blake, the edition appearing in 1893.

p. 178 a woman of incredible beauty see Yeats's note in *Autobiographies* (1956) p. 576 for a full account of this vision or dream. **Balzac's** see note, p. 523. **Christian Cabbala** see note, p. 523.

p. 180 Ariosto see note, p. 526.

A PEOPLE'S THEATRE

p. 181 Romain Rolland (1866–1944), French novelist, dramatist and critic.

p. 182 Swedenborg Emanuel Swedenborg (1688–1772), Swedish philosopher, scientist and mystic.

p. 184 Nietzsche Friedrich Wilhelm Nietzsche (1844–1900), born in Röcken, studied at Bonn and Leipzig. He won distinction for his treatises on tragedy.

p. 187 Henley William Ernest Henley (1849–1903), poet, critic and editor.

p. 190 Mr Dulac Edmund Dulac (1882–1953), English painter and designer, born in France. **Mr Rummell** Walter Rummell (b. 1887), son of Franz Rummel; Anglo-German pianist and composer.

p. 191 Chaliapin Fedor Ivanovich Chaliapin (1873–1938), Russian opera singer.

p. 192 the Wild Geese description of Irishmen who left Ireland to fight abroad in continental armies. **D'Annunzio** Gabrielle

D'Annunzio (1863–1938), Italian poet, novelist, dramatist and journalist.
p. 193 A certain friend of mine Yeats himself, who had not yet
published these poems under his own name.

THE IRISH DRAMATIC MOVEMENT

p. 195 Parnell Charles Stewart Parnell (1846–91), an Irish landowner,
leader of the Irish parliamentary party, repudiated by Gladstone, by
the Irish hierarchy and by the Irish party when his relationship with
Mrs O'Shea became public.
p. 196 Lady Gregory see note, p. 525. **a little old tower** Ballylee
Castle which Yeats bought in 1917 and named Thoor Ballylee.
p. 197 Raftery see note, p. 525.
p. 198 Mr Edward Martyn (1859–1923), Irish dramatist, co-founder
of the Irish Literary Theatre, interested in church music, lived in Tulira
Castle, Galway.
p. 199 Miss Allgood Sara Allgood (1883–1950), Irish actress and sister
of Maire O'Neill. **Miss Maire O'Neill** Molly Allgood (d. 1952), Irish
actress who was engaged to Synge, later married T. H. Mair, drama
critic of the *Manchester Guardian*.
p. 201 Dublin Castle centre of British administration in Ireland.
Cardinal Logue His Eminence Michael Logue (1840–1924),
cardinal archbishop of Armagh. **Miss Horniman** Annie Elizabeth
Frederika Horniman (1860–1937), English theatrical director.
p. 205 Mr Lennox Robinson's Lennox Robinson (1886–1958), Irish
playwright and manager of the Abbey Theatre from 1910, author of
The White-headed Boy and *Drama at Irish*.

INTRODUCTION TO 'FIGHTING THE WAVES'

p. 207 Hildo van Krop Hildo van Krop (b. 1884), Dutch sculptor.
George Antheil George Antheil (b. 1901), American composer of
Polish descent, born in New Jersey, studied under Bloch and spent some
years in Europe as a professional pianist.
p. 208 Standish O'Grady see note, p. 519. **Parnell** see note above.
Padraic Colum's Padraic Colum (1881–1972), poet and playwright.
p. 209 Balzac see note, p. 523.
p. 210 Sir William Crookes (1832–1919), English chemist and
physicist.

p. 211 Mr Sacheverell Sitwell's Sacheverell Sitwell (b. 1897), English critic and poet. **Dr Gogarty's** Oliver St John Gogarty (1878–1957), Irish poet, doctor and Senator of the Irish Free State, friend of Yeats. **D'Annunzio** see note, pp. 528–9. **'Sigurd the Volsung'** (1876), epic by William Morris.

p. 212 'Tuatha de Danaan' the tribes of the goddess Dana, gods of ancient Ireland.

p. 213 Professor Richet Charles Robert Richet (1850–1935), French physiologist awarded the Nobel Prize in 1913.

p. 214 Gemistus Plethon (c. 1355–1450), Greek scholar; counsellor in the Peloponnesus to Manuel and Theodore Palaeologus and went to the Council of Florence in 1439.

ON D. H. LAWRENCE

p. 216 Twenty Years a-growing autobiographical account of childhood and youth in the Blasket Islands by Maurice O'Sullivan. It was originally written in Gaelic and then translated by Moya Davies and George Thomson.

FROM THE INTRODUCTION TO 'THE OXFORD BOOK OF MODERN VERSE'

p. 217 Verlaine see note, p. 523. **William Watson** (1858–1935), poet whose *Collected Poems* appeared in 1906.

p. 218 Campbell Joseph Campbell (1879–1944), poet and playwright, took part in the Ulster theatre movement. **Colum** see note, p. 529. **The Shropshire Lad** *A Shropshire Lad* (1896), a collection of poems by A. E. Housman (1859–1936).

p. 219 James Stephens (1882–1950), Irish poet, novelist and broadcaster, author of *The Crock of Gold*. **Frank O'Connor** (pen-name of Michael O'Donovan, b. 1903), Irish novelist, short-story writer, critic and translator. **O'Rahilly** Egan O'Rahilly (*fl.* 1690–1726), Gaelic poet. **Lady Gregory** see note, p. 525.

p. 220 Davies William Herbert Davies (1871–1940), poet and author of *The Autobiography of a Super-tramp*. **Binyon** Laurence Binyon (1869–1943), poet, authority on Chinese art. **Sturge Moore** Thomas Sturge Moore (1870–1944), poet, artist and art critic, friend of Yeats. **'Michael Field'** pseudonym of Katharine Bradley (1846–1914) and

Edith Cooper (1862–1913), English collaborating authors of lyric poetry and poetic dramas. **Sacheverell Sitwell** see note, p. 530. **Robert Bridges** see note, p. 521.

p. 122 Aubrey Beardsley's Aubrey Vincent Beardsley (1872–98), black and white artist, art editor of the *Yellow Book*. **Elinor Wylie** (1885–1928), American poetess and novelist.

p. 223 Poincaré Raymond Poincaré (1860–1934), French statesman.

p. 224 Manet Edouard Manet (1832–83), French painter. **Rousseau** Douanier Rousseau (1844–1910), French painter. **Courbet** Gustave Courbet (1819–77), French painter. **John Gray** John Miller Gray (1850–94), Scottish art critic.

p. 225 Francis Thompson (1859–1907), poet, rescued from poverty by the Meynells, author of *The Hound of Heaven*. **Lionel Johnson** see note, p. 527.

p. 228 Smart's see note, p. 524. **Stendhal** pseudonym of Henri Beyle (1783–1842), French novelist, author of *Le Rouge et le Noir* and *La Chartreuse de Parme*. **Huysmans's** Joris Karl Huysmans (1848–1907), French novelist.

p. 229 Turner Walter James Redfern Turner (1889–1946), Australian-born poet, novelist and music critic; friend of Yeats.

p. 230 Pater's Walter Horatio Pater (1839–94), Oxford don and author of *Studies in the History of the Renaissance, Marius the Epicurean, Appreciations* etc.

p. 231 Herbert Read Sir Herbert Read (1893–1968), English poet, critic, publisher and anarchist. **Berkeley** George Berkeley (1685–1753), Irish bishop and philosopher, author of *Essay towards a New Theory of Vision, Principles of Human Knowledge* etc. **Grosseteste** Robert Grosseteste (d. 1253), bishop, poet, philosopher, theologian and author of *Compendium Scientiarum*.

p. 232 Dorothy Wellesley Lady Dorothy Wellesley (1889–1956), English poetess. **William Morris** see note, p. 524.

p. 233 Nicholas of Cusa (1401–64), son of a poor fisherman who became Archdeacon of Liège and later Bishop of Brixen. **Ernest Dowson's** see note, p. 527.

p. 234 Florence Farr (Mrs Emery), member of a group of students of the occult, friend of Yeats, died in Ceylon in 1917.

p. 235 Heraclitus see note, p. 528. **Madge** Charles Madge (b. 1912), English poet and sociologist; Professor of Sociology at the University of Birmingham since 1950.

p. 235 Henley see note, p. 528.

p. 236 Spinoza Benedict Spinoza (1632–77), Jewish philosopher born in Amsterdam, author of posthumous *Ethics* (1677). **Twelfth of July** anniversary of the Battle of Boyne, 1689, celebrated in Ulster.

MODERN POETRY: A BROADCAST

p. 238 Ernest Dowson see note, p. 528. **Lionel Johnson** see note, p. 528.

p. 241 Inigo Jones (1573–1652), architect, designer of masques. **Verlaine** see note, p. 523.

p. 242 Charles Ricketts (1866–1931), See note, p. 520. **Delacroix** Ferdinand Victor Eugène Delacroix (1798–1863), French painter. **Sturge Moore** see note above. **Edith Cooper** see note on Michael Field, p. 530.

p. 243 Miss Bradley see note on Michael Field, p. 530. **Landor's** see note, p. 527.

p. 244 'A Shropshire Lad' see note, p. 530. **York Powell** see note, p. 526. **Paul Fort** (b. 1872), French writer of ballads and prose poems.

p. 249 Turner's see note, p. 531. **Dorothy Wellesley's** see note, p. 531. **Herbert Read's** see note, p. 531. **Nicholas of Cusa** see note, p. 531.

p. 253 James Stephens see note above. **Senator Gogarty's** see note, p. 530.

A GENERAL INTRODUCTION FOR MY WORK

p. 256 John O'Leary see note, p. 519. **Thomas Davis** (1814–45), poet, educated at Trinity College, Dublin; called to the Irish Bar in 1838. One of the founders of the *Nation* and of the Young Ireland party.

p. 257 Standish O'Grady see note, p. 519. **O'Curry** Eugene O'Curry (1796–1862), Gaelic scholar, author of *Manners and Customs of Irish People*. **Mitchel** John Mitchel (1815–75), Irish revolutionary, founded the *United Irishman*, transported and escaped to America, returned to Ireland in 1872, became MP; author of *Jail Journal*. **O'Donovan** John O'Donovan (1809–61), Gaelic scholar, edited *The Annals of the Four Masters* (1848–51).

p. 258 Hayes O'Grady Standish Hayes O'Grady (1832–1915), Irish scholar who lived 30 years in California as civil engineer before compiling *Catalogue of Irish MSS in British Museum* (completed by

Robin Flower); his best work was *Silva Gadelica*, 2 vols, (1892). **Lady Gregory** see note, p. 525. **Lady Charlotte Guest's 'Mabinogion'** Lady Charlotte Guest (1812–95), translated the *Mabinogion* (1838–49). **Rosses Point** district in Sligo where Yeats spent holidays as a child. **Queen Maeve** legendary Queen of Connaught, reputedly buried on Knocknarea, Sligo.

p. 259 Professor Burkitt Francis Crawford Burkitt (1864–1935), English theologian.

p. 260 'tetragrammaton agla' the four-lettered name for the Hebrew God, pronunciation of which was forbidden. The Cabbalists claimed they knew the name and could, through this knowledge, perform miracles. **Doneraile** market town in County Cork. **James Stephens** see note, p. 530. **George Russell** see note, p. 520. **Pearse** Patrick Henry Pearse (1879–1916), Irish poet and orator, shot for his part in the 1916 Rising, when he was president of the provisional government. **the Red Branch** a cycle of Gaelic legends dealing with the Red Branch heroes. **Cuchulain** the 'Hound of Ulster', hero of Red Branch legends. **Jesse** a genealogical tree representing the genealogy of Christ from 'the root of Jesse', used in the Middle Ages as a decoration for walls and windows. **MacDonagh** Thomas MacDonagh (1878–1916), Irish poet and critic, shot for his part in the 1916 Rising.

p. 261 Mr Arnold Toynbee (b. 1889), English historian.

p. 262 Parnell see note, p. 529. **Lord Edward** Lord Edward Fitzgerald (1763–98), Irish leader, president of the military committee of the United Irishmen in 1796, wounded and died in prison after leading an abortive rising. **Swedenborg** see note, p. 528. **Shri Purohit Swāmi** an Indian monk with whom Yeats worked on a translation of the *Upanishads* in 1935–6, for whose books he wrote forewords.

p. 262 Lecky William Edward Hartpole Lecky (1838–1903), Irish historian, author of *History of Rationalism*, *History of England* and other works.

p. 264 François Dominique Toussaint Toussaint L'Ouverture (*c.* 1746–1803), commander of forces in San Domingo in 1796, liberated the island and became its president, but was captured by the French and died in prison in France.

p. 265 Thomson James Thomson (1700–1748), poet, author of *The Seasons* and *The Castle of Indolence*. **Cowper** William Cowper (1731–1800), poet and letter-writer.

p. 266 Turner see note, p. 531. **Lawrence** D. H. Lawrence

(1885–1930), novelist and poet. **Sir Thomas Browne** (1605–82),
graduated in Leyden as a doctor; author of *Religio Medici* (1643), *Urn
Burial* and *Garden of Cyrus* (1658). **George Moore** (1852–1933), Irish
novelist and playwright who wrote maliciously of Yeats in *Hail and
Farewell*, an account of Dublin life. **Milton's or Shelley's Platonist**
the references are to *Il Penseroso* I and *Laon and Cythna* II, frag. II.

p. 266 that tower Palmer drew an illustration by Samuel Palmer
(1805–81), watercolour landscape painter and etcher, in an edition of
Milton's *Minor Poems* (1889).

p. 267 Deirdre heroine of the tale of 'The Sons of Usna', one of
'Three Sorrowful Stories of Erin'; she was to marry King Conchubar
but ran away with Naoise to Scotland; they returned to Ireland under
a safe conduct but Conchubar had Naoise killed on their return. In one
version of the legend Deirdre then kills herself. **Paul Fort's** see note,
p. 532. **Robert Bridges** see note, p. 521.

p. 269 Mallarmé see note, p. 521. **Leonardo** Leonardo da Vinci.
O'Connell Bridge chief bridge over the River Liffey in Dublin.

NOTES TO *SELECTED PROSE*

AUTOBIOGRAPHICAL WRITINGS

REVERIES OVER CHILDHOOD AND YOUTH

p. 275 My father John Butler Yeats (1839–1922), studied law before
becoming an artist; lived in London, 1867–80, Dublin, 1880–87,
moved to Bedford Park, London, in 1887, and to New York in 1909.
My grandmother Elizabeth Pollexfen (*née* Middleton, her mother
being also a Pollexfen, from Jersey).

p. 276 my brothers and sisters Robert (d. 1873), John Butler (Jack,
the artist), Elizabeth (Lolly) and Susan Mary (Lily).

p. 278 [my] mother Susan Pollexfen, whom J. B. Yeats married in
1863. **Our house . . . a house overlooking the harbour** houses on
the peninsula of Howth, which forms the northern arm of Dublin Bay.

p. 281 Manfred the hero of a drama by Byron. **Prince Athanase . . .
Alastor . . . 'The Revolt of Islam'** works by Shelley.

p. 282 Irving's Sir Henry Irving (1838–1905), actor; knighted in 1895.
Managed the Lyceum 1879–99. Buried in Westminster Abbey.
Benson's Sir Frank Robert Benson (1858–1939), Shakespearian
actor-manager; knighted in Drury Lane Theatre in 1916.

p. 283 a Wordsworthian scholar probably the Rev. Stopford
Augustus Brooke (1832–1916), poet, preacher and critic, editor of
The Treasury of Irish Poetry and President of the Irish Literary Society
the younger Ampère Jean Jacques Antrine Ampère (1800–1864),
son of André Marie Ampère, lectured on the history of literature at
Marseilles and became Professor in the Collège de France in 1830.

p. 284 George Pollexfen (d. 1910), Yeats's maternal uncle, lived in
Sligo, a hypochondriac, interested in youth and horsemanship, as
well as in magic and astrology. **William Middleton** (d. 1832), the
poet's great-grandfather, who married Elizabeth Pollexfen of Jersey.

p. 285 My brother John Butler (Jack) Yeats (1871–1957), artist and
author. **Avena House** a Middleton property at Ballisodare, near
Sligo.

p. 287 raths Irish forts. **Knocknarea** a mountain overlooking Sligo.
Darwin Sir Charles Robert Darwin (1809–82), naturalist,
originated the theory of evolution; author of *On the Origin of
Species by means of Natural Selection* (1859). **Huxley** Thomas Henry
Huxley (1825–95), philosopher and scientist, coined the word
'agnostic' to describe his own attitude, supported Darwin; author of
Man's Place in Nature (1863) and *Ethics and Evolution* (1893).

p. 290 Edwin Ellis see note, p. 528. **Nettleship** J. T. Nettleship
(1841–1902), Pre-Raphaelite painter and friend of J. B. Yeats, whose
symbolic paintings were admired by W. B. Yeats. Augustus John
married his daughter.

p. 291 my late headmaster William Wilkins (1852–1912), poet,
brother of George Wilkins, who was also a poet, headmaster of the High
School, Dublin (1879–1908). **So-and-so** Charles Johnston, son of the
MP for Ballykilbeg, schoolfriend of Yeats at the High School, married a
niece of Madame Blavatsky.

p. 292 Reichenbach Karl, Baron von Reichenbach (1788–1869), born
in Stuttgart and made a fortune as a manufacturer in Moravia.
Discoverer of paraffin and creosote. **'Esoteric Buddhism'** by A. P.
Sinnett (1840–1921), of which the second edition was published in
London in 1883.

p. 293 Brahmin philosopher Mohini Chatterjee, visited Dublin in

1885, referred to in two poems by Yeats, 'An Indian upon God' and
'Mohini Chatterjee'. **Oldham** Charles Hubert (d. 1926), Professor of
Commerce, University College, Dublin.

p. 294 O'Leary's see note, p. 519.

p. 295 Callanan Jeremiah John Callanan (1795–1829), Irish poet,
ballad collector, translator, died in Portugal.

p. 296 a Catholic friend possibly Katharine Tynan (1859–1931), Irish
poet and novelist, married H. A. Hinkson in 1893.

I BECAME AN AUTHOR

p. 300 my English and Irish schools the Godolphin School,
Hammersmith, and the High School, Dublin, founded by Erasmus
Smith in 1870. **Charles Johnston** see note, p. 535.

p. 302 Bury John Bagenal Bury (1861–1927), held chairs of Modern
History at Trinity College, Dublin, and Cambridge, author of
History of the Later Roman Empire, *History of Greece* and other works.

p. 303 Lord Acton Sir John, first Baron Acton (1834–1902), Regius
Professor of Modern History, Cambridge, author of *Lectures
on Modern History*. **Standish O'Grady** see note, p. 519. **Isadora
Duncan** (1878–1927), American dancer; travelled widely in Europe
demonstrating her new style of dancing, based on the figures in
Greek vase painting, and influenced the development of ballet.
Founded schools in Berlin, Salzburg and Vienna.

FOUR YEARS: 1887–91

p. 305 Carolus Duran (1838–1917), French painter, best known for
his portraits of Emile Girardin, Mlle Croizette etc. **Bastien-Lepage**
Jules Bastien-Lepage (1848–84), French realist painter.

p. 306 Huxley see note, p. 535. **Tyndall** John Tyndall (1820–93), Irish
physicist; elected FRS in 1852 and Professor at the Royal Institute in
1852. Died from accidental poisoning with chloral. **Titian's 'Ariosto'**
Tiziano Vecelli (1477–1576) painted portraits as well as sacred and
mythological subjects. Ludovico Ariosto (1474–1533) was the author of
Orlando Furioso, a romantic epic.

p. 307 Miss Maud Gonne see note, p. 519. **Florence Farr** (d. 1917),
Mrs Emery, actress, occultist, friend of Yeats. She died of cancer
while teaching in Ceylon.

p. 308 W. E. Henley see note, p. 528. **Rothenstein** Sir William
Rothenstein (1872–1945), Bradford-born artist; studied at the Slade
and in Paris, won fame as a portrait painter and was Principal of the
Royal College of Art from 1920 to 1935.

p. 309 Salvini Tommaso Salvini (1830–1915), Italian actor, born in
Milan. Immensely popular in London in Shakespearian roles,
especially as Othello and Hamlet. Played in comedy, but won fame
as tragedian. The part he played in fighting in the revolutionary war
of 1848 added to his popularity. **Cosimo de Medici** (1389–1464),
surnamed 'Pater Patriae', member of the family that ruled Florence
from 1434 and were Dukes of Tuscany from 1569 to 1737; patron of
art, architecture and literature.

p. 311 Turner Joseph Mallord Turner (1775–1851), landscape painter.
Charles Whibley (1859–1930), English scholar, critic and
journalist. **Kenneth Grahame** (1859–1932), author of *The Golden
Age, The Wind in the Willows* and other works. **Barry Pain**
(1864–1928), novelist. **R. A. M. Stevenson** (1847–1900), Scottish
printer and art critic. **Stepniak** Stepnyak, 'Son of the Steppe',
nom de guerre of Sergius Mikhailovich Kravchinsky (1852–95), Russian
revolutionary.

p. 313 Whistler James Abbott McNeill Whistler (1834–1903),
American painter and etcher who settled in Chelsea in 1863.

p. 314 Schopenhauer Arthur Schopenhauer (1788–1860), passionistic
philosopher who believed that will is the only reality; author of
The World as Will and Representation (1829).

p. 315 William Morris's (1834–96), poet, translator, decorator,
manufacturer, printer, socialist; author of *The Life and Death of Jason,
The Earthly Paradise, Sigurd the Volsung* and other works. **Walter
Crane** (1845–1915), English painter, poet and socialist, born in
Liverpool, son of portrait painter Thomas Crane. Well known as an
illustrator of children's books. Principal of the Royal College of Art
from 1898 to 1899. **Cobden-Sanderson** Thomas James Cobden-
Sanderson (1840–1922), English printer and bookbinder, born in
Alnwick. Leader of the 19th-century revival of artistic typography.
Worked with William Morris and founded Doves Press in 1900,
which issued Doves Bible in 1903. The press closed in 1916 and he threw
the type into the Thames. **Cockerell** Sir Sydney Cockerell (1867–
1962), secretary to William Morris and the Kelmscott Press (1892–8).
Hyndman Henry Mayers Hyndman (1842–1921), English

socialist. **Prince Kropotkin** Prince Peter Alexeivitch Kropotkin
(1842–1921), Russian geographer, savant and revolutionary. **Parnell**
see note, p. 529. **Michael Davitt** (1846–1906), Irish politician and
author, served nine years of a fifteen-year sentence for acting as
Secretary of the Irish Republican Brotherhood; founded the Land
League, became MP. **Burne-Jones** Sir Edward Coley Burne-Jones
(1833–98), romantic painter, friend of Rossetti and Morris, edited
Punch.

p. 317 Watts George Frederick Watts (1817–1904), painter, first
attracted attention by his cartoon of Caractacus (1843), later known
for portraits of notabilities; married Ellen Terry in 1864, but parted
from her after a year. Declined a baronetcy, awarded the OM in 1902.

p. 319 Thoreau Henry David Thoreau (1817–62), friend of Emerson,
revolutionary ascetic, whose *Walden* describes natural phenomena
observed during his solitary stay for two and a half years in a hut on the
shore of the Walden pond. **Lough Gill** a lake in Sligo.

p. 320 Poggio's Gian Francesco Poggio Bracciolini (1380–1459),
Italian humanist. **Poliphili** this was Francesco Colonna's
Hypnerotomachia Poliphili. See W. B. Yeats's *Letters to Katharine Tynan*,
ed. Roger McHugh, 1953, p. 172.

p. 321 Ernest Rhys (1859–1946), Anglo-Welsh editor and poet, born
in London, but spent much of his youth in Carmarthen. Became a
mining engineer, but abandoned this for writing in 1886. Edited the
Camelot Classics series for Walter Scott's publishing house; best known
as editor of Everyman's Library. **Lionel Johnson** (1867–1902), minor
poet and critic. **Ernest Dowson** (1867–1900), minor poet of the
nineties. **Victor Plarr** (1863–1929), minor poet, edited Dowson's
Autobiography, joint author of the *Books of the Rhymers' Club* and of the
Garland (1898). **Ernest Radford** (*fl.* 1882–1920), minor poet, member
of the Rhymers' Club. **John Davidson** (1851–1909), poet and
playwright. **Richard Le Gallienne** (1866–1947), English writer, born
in Liverpool. Became a journalist in London, 1891; later lived in New
York. Published many volumes of prose and verse. **T. W. Rolleston**
(1857–1920), Irish writer, German scholar and editor. **Selwyn Image**
(1849–1930), English artist. **Edwin Ellis** see note, p. 528. **John
Todhunter** (1839–1916), Irish physician, author and patron. **Arthur
Symons** see note, p. 521. **Herbert Horne** (1864–1916), architect and
writer on art; member of the Rhymers' Club. **William Watson**
(1858–1935), poet; his *Collected Poems* appeared in 1906. **Francis**

Thompson (1859–1907), poet, rescued from poverty by the Meynells, author of *The Hound of Heaven*. **Olive Schreiner** (Mrs S. C. Cronwright, 1862–1920), South African novelist and writer.

p. 324 Simeon Solomon (1840–1905), English painter and draughtsman. **another Solomon** Joseph Solomon (1860–1927), English portrait and mural painter; elected RA in 1906 and PRBA in 1918. Born in London, served in the First World War and initiated use of camouflage in the British Army.

p. 325 Inigo Jones (1573–1652), architect, designer of scenery for many masques. **Charles Ricketts** see note, p. 520. **Charles Shannon** (1886–1937), English painter and lithographer, a friend of Ricketts.

p. 326 Thomas Davis (1814–45), Irish poet and journalist, leader of the Young Ireland party, founded the *Nation* (1842). **Alcibiades** (*c.* 450–404 BC), Athenian statesman and general, pupil of Socrates, kinsman of Pericles. Proposed Sicilian expedition, recalled, escaped, returned to Athens in 407, finally murdered in Phrygia.

p. 329 Madame Blavatsky Helena Petrovna Blavatsky (1831–91), born in Russia, married General Blavatsky, founded the Theosophical Society with Colonel Olcott in 1875 and wrote several books about theosophy. **MacGregor Mathers** Samuel Liddell (MacGregor) Mathers (1854–1918), a student of magic and Rosicrucianism, lived in Paris from 1891.

p. 331 Eliphas Levi a Frenchman who visited England in the 1860s. **Henri Bergson** (1859–1941), French philosopher, author of *L'Évolution Créatrice* (1907) and other works.

IRELAND AFTER PARNELL

p. 335 Mr George Russell (AE) see note, p. 520.

p. 336 John Eglinton see note, p. 526.

p. 338 Gustave Moreau (1826–1902), French painter.

p. 339 Swedenborg Emanuel Swedenborg (1688–1772), Swedish mystic, philosopher and scientist, saw visions and devoted his life after 1745 to explaining the scriptures.

p. 340 Emerson Ralph Waldo Emerson (1803–82), American transcendental philosopher, poet and essayist.

p. 342 Chapman George Chapman (1559?–1634?), scholar, poet, dramatist and translator of Homer. His works include *Bussy D'Ambois* and *The Gentleman Usher*. **George Herbert** (1593–1633), metaphysical

poet and clergyman, author of 'The Temple'. **Francis Thompson**
see note, p. 531.

HODOS CHAMELIONTOS

p. 345 Hyde Douglas Hyde (1860–1949), founder of the Gaelic League,
first President of Ireland, poet, scholar and translator, author of *Love-
Songs of Connacht*. **Swedenborg** see note above. **Boehme** Jacob
Boehme (1575–1624), German peasant mystic.

THE STIRRING OF THE BONES

p. 349 Mr Dillon John Dillon (1851–1927), Irish politician, succeeded
Justin McCarthy as leader of the anti-Parnellite party, and John
Redmond as leader of the Nationalist Party, 1918. **Mr Redmond**
John Edward Redmond (1856–1918), Irish politician, supported
Parnell, leader of the reunited Irish party in 1900, supported England
in the First World War.
p. 350 Mr Birrell's Augustine Birrell (1850–1933), Chief Secretary for
Ireland, 1907–16, critic, and author of *Obiter Dicta* (1884–7).
p. 352 James Connolly (1870–1916), revolutionary, organized the
Citizen Army, shot as a leader of the 1916 Rising. **Patrick Pearse**
(1879–1916), revolutionary, shot as a leader of the 1916 Rising, poet and
orator, founded St Enda's School. **Lord Edward Fitzgerald** (1763–98),
Irish leader, President of the United Irishmen, wounded when leading
an abortive rising, died in prison.

DRAMATIS PERSONAE

p. 355 Arthur Symons: see note, p. 521. **Lady Gregory** see note,
p. 525.
p. 356 Lady Gregory's husband Sir William Gregory (1817–92),
politician, later Governor of Ceylon, Irish landowner. **Stubbs** George
Stubbs (1724–1806), English anatomist, engraver and painter on enamels.
Painter of animals. **Canaletto** properly Antonio Canale (1697–1768),
Venetian painter. **Guardi** Giovanni Antonio Guardi (1699–1760),
Venetian painter of religious subjects. **Zurbarán** Francisco Zurbarán
(1598–1662), Spanish religious painter. His masterpiece, an altar-piece,
is in the museum at Seville. He came to be known as the 'Spanish
Caravaggio'. **Augustus John** (1878–1962), British painter; elected RA

in 1928 (resigned in 1938 and reelected in 1940). Awarded the OM in 1942.

p. 357 Sir Richard Burton (1821–90), Indian army officer, travelled adventurously, wrote travel books, translated the *Arabian Nights* and Camoens's *Lusiads*. **Edward Martyn's** see note, p. 529. **Mrs Jopling** (formerly Mrs Louise Romer), landscape and portrait painter, exhibited at the Royal Academy from 1870 on.

p. 358 Lord Clanricarde (1832–1916), Irish landowner. **Sir Hugh Lane** (1874–1915), Lady Gregory's nephew, a connoisseur, offered a collection of French Impressionist paintings to Dublin on condition that they were properly housed. The offer was refused. He later added a pencilled unwitnessed codicil to his will, leaving the pictures to Dublin, before going down on the *Lusitania*. But the British Government refused to give the pictures to Ireland until a compromise agreement was reached in 1959. **John Shawe-Taylor** nephew of Lady Gregory.

p. 359 Sir Jonah Barrington (1760–1834), Irish judge and historian, author of *Personal Sketches* and *Historic Memoirs*.

p. 360 My great-grandmother Corbet Jane Grace Corbet was married by Rev. W. B. Yeats (1806–62); her mother was Grace Armstrong before her marriage into the Corbet family. **her son** Robert Corbet, a former Governor of Penang, owner of Sandymount Castle, Dublin, who committed suicide. **Ruskin's Rose** Rose La Touche, with whom Ruskin fell in love at the age of forty; she was then ten. Seven years later he proposed to her, and this in the words of Professor Quentin Bell, *Ruskin* (1963), p. 60, 'marked the beginnings of a long series of separations, short reunions, quarrels, reconciliations and *démarches* which lasted for ten miserable years'.

p. 361 George Moore (1852–1933), novelist, lived in Paris and London, joined in the Irish literary movement, wrote *Hail and Farewell* about his Dublin experiences, returned to London.

p. 364 Manet's Edouard Manet (1832–83), French painter; helped to form the group out of which the Impressionist movement arose. **Zola** Émile Zola (1840–1902), French naturalistic novelist. **Karl Marx** (1818–83), radical editor in Cologne, collaborated in political philosophy with Engels in Paris, returned to Cologne, expelled again, settled in London and wrote *Das Kapital*, a theory of political economy critical of the capitalist system, advocating abolition of private property by class war, and distribution of work and sustenance to individuals by the community.

ESTRANGEMENT

p. 371 A— C— Lady Gregory.

THE BOUNTY OF SWEDEN

p. 376 Nobel Prize winners Yeats won the Nobel Prize in 1923.
'The Prisoner of Zenda' (1894), a popular romantic novel by
Anthony Hope (1863–1933).
p. 377 Gobelins a French family of dyers, probably of Reims, who, in
about 1450, founded a factory near Paris which became famous for its
tapestry. Especially well known was Jean Gobelin (alias Giles, d. 1476),
dyer and inventor. **Watteau** Jean Antoine Watteau (1684–
1721), French genre painter of *fêtes champêtres*, shepherds and
shepherdesses. **Fragonard** Jean Honoré Fragonard (1732–1806),
painter, born in Grasse. His works 'La Chemise Enlevée' and
'Bacchante Endormie' are in the Louvre. **Castiglione's** see note, p. 527.
p. 378 Urbino town in north-east Italy, seat of the Montefeltre family,
much admired by Yeats for its patronage of the arts. **Bembo's** Pietro
Bembo (1470–1547), Italian writer and ecclesiastic who became a
cardinal in 1539.

PAGES FROM A DIARY

p. 381 the system *A Vision*, privately published in 1926 and in an
altered version by Macmillan in 1937. **Burke** Edmund Burke (1729–97),
Irish politician, lawyer, philosopher and orator, fought for the
emancipation in the House of Commons from George III of American
colonies, Irish trade, Irish parliament, Irish Catholics, of India from the
East India Company's rule; he opposed the Jacobinism of the French
Revolution. Author of *A Philosophical Enquiry into the Sublime and
Beautiful*.
p. 382 my Huguenot grandmother Grace Corbet, wife of the Rev.
William Butler Yeats. **Bishop King** William King, Archbishop of
Dublin (1650–1729). **Berkeley** George Berkeley (1685–1753), Bishop
of Cloyne, philosopher. Author of *Principles of Human Knowledge*
(1710) and other works.
p. 383 Renvyle Oliver Gogarty's family house in Connemara, burnt
down in the troubles and when rebuilt used as a hotel. **Michael's**
Michael Butler Yeats, the poet's son, born in 1921 and educated at
St Columba's College, Dublin.

p. 384 Hone's Joseph M. Hone (1882–1959), Irish biographer and critic. He and M. M. Rossi wrote a life of Berkeley, 1931, with an introduction by Yeats. **M. M. Rossi** Italian philosopher, now Professor of Italian at the University of Edinburgh.

p. 385 T. C. D. Trinity College, Dublin, founded by Queen Elizabeth in 1591.

p. 386 Descartes René Descartes (1596–1650), French mathematician, physicist and philosopher, had great influence on the development of science and philosophy through his *Le Discours de la Méthode* (1637).

LETTERS

TO KATHARINE TYNAN

p. 388 'Oisin' Yeats's poem 'The Wanderings of Oisin' (1889). **Kegan Paul** now the publishing firm of Routledge and Kegan Paul, formerly Kegan Paul, Trench Trübner and Company. **Nutt** Alfred Trübner Nutt (1856–1910), English publisher and folklorist; Celtic scholar. **York Powell** Frederick York Powell (1850–1904), Regius Professor of History at Oxford, who wrote poetry and was a friend of J. B. Yeats. **Renan** Ernest Renan (1823–92), a learned French writer, historian and philologist. **Russell** see note, p. 520.

p. 391 Uncle George Pollexfen see note, p. 535.

p. 392 Charley Johnston see note, p. 535. **Madame Blavatsky's** see note, p. 539.

p. 393 Miss O'Leary Ellen O'Leary, sister of John O'Leary, see note, p. 519. **Sladen** Douglas Brooke Wheelton Sladen (1856–1947), English writer, lived seven years in Australia, where he was first Professor of History at Sydney, before returning to England to become a man of letters in 1886.

p. 394 Ashe King Richard Ashe King (1839–1932), Irish clergyman who became a man of letters in London.

TO LADY GREGORY

Miss Gonne see note, p. 519.

p. 395 Lady Mayo wife of the Earl of Mayo, 1822–72, who was Viceroy of India, educated at Trinity College, Dublin; he was Chief Secretary for Ireland in 1852, 1858 and 1866.

TO JOHN QUINN, 4TH OCTOBER 1907

p. 396 Quinn John Quinn, Irish-American lawyer, patron of Yeats
from 1902; arranged his American lecture tours and helped the Irish
literary movement. **Fitzmaurice** George Fitzmaurice (b. *c.* 1875)
wrote several plays for the Abbey Theatre. See L. Miller, 'George
Fitzmaurice: a Bibliographical Sketch', *Irish Writing*, 1951; J. D. Riley,
'The Plays of George Fitzmaurice', *Dublin Magazine*, xxxi, 1955.
'The Playboy' Synge's *The Playboy of the Western World*. **Boyle**
William Boyle (1853–1922), civil servant, Irish dramatist.
p. 397 McManus possibly Seumas MacManus (1869–1960) poet,
novelist and playwright.
p. 398 Robert Robert Gregory (1881–1918), Lady Gregory's son,
painter, shot down in error over Italy, subject of four poems by Yeats:
'Shepherd and Goatherd', 'In Memory of Major Robert Gregory',
'An Irish Airman Foresees his Death' and 'Reprisals'.

TO JOHN QUINN, 7TH JANUARY 1908

Shannon see note, p. 538.
p. 399 Mancini Antonio Mancini (1852–1930), Italian painter; painted
Yeats and Lady Gregory.

TO J. B. YEATS, 29TH NOVEMBER 1909

Mrs Campbell Mrs Patrick Campbell (1865–1950), actress, became
famous in *The Second Mrs Tanqueray*. Played Eliza Doolittle in
Pygmalion and formed a long friendship with Shaw.
p. 401 the Prime Minister Herbert Henry Asquith, first Earl of
Oxford and Asquith, British Liberal statesman who became Prime
Minister in 1908. His regime was notable, among other things, for the
upholding of Irish Home Rule. **Edmund Gosse** (1849–1928), civil
servant, conversationalist, man of letters, author of critical studies,
biographies and *Father and Son*. **Lord Cromer** Evelyn Baring Cromer
(1841–1917), Earl (1901), Secretary to his cousin Lord Northbrook
when Viceroy of India.
p. 402 General Ian Hamilton (1853–1947), born of Scottish family in
Corfu; served with distinction in Afghanistan (1878) and the Boer wars
(1881, 1889–1901) and led the Gallipoli Expedition (1915). Lieutenant
of the Tower, 1918–20. **'Blanco'** Shaw's play *The Shewing-Up of
Blanco Posnet*.

TO J. B. YEATS, 21ST NOVEMBER 1912

p. 403 Sandymount Robert Corbet's home was in Sandymount near Dublin, and here J. B. Yeats lived when he was an undergraduate. **Isaac Butt** (1813–79), Irish barrister, politician and author; founded *Dublin University Magazine* and *Protestant Guardian*. J. B. Yeats devilled for him before becoming an artist. **Potter** Frank Huddlestone Potter (1845–87), member of the Royal Society of British Artists, studied in London and Antwerp. **Nettleship** see note, p. 535. **Wilson** George M. Wilson (1848–90), painter, friend of Nettleship and J. B. Yeats.

TO J. B. YEATS, 14TH MARCH [1916]

p. 404 Wyndham Lewis's Percy Wyndham Lewis (1884–1957), artist, novelist and essayist.

TO OLIVIA SHAKESPEAR, 22ND MARCH [1923]

p. 406 Olivia Shakespear (d. 1938), novelist and close friend of Yeats, who first met her in 1894; he kept up a close friendship with her until her death. **Michael Collins** (1890–1922), fought in the 1916 Rising, commander in the Irish Free State Army, killed by Republicans in the Civil War.

p. 407 George Mrs W. B. Yeats (*née* Georgie Hyde Lees). **Pound** Ezra Pound (1885–1972), American poet and critic who acted as Yeats's secretary in 1913. He married Mrs Shakespear's daughter. **Binyon's 'Blake'** Laurence Binyon (1869–1943), poet, keeper of prints and drawings at British Museum, authority on Chinese art and author of works on Blake.

TO OLIVIA SHAKESPEAR, 25TH MAY [1926]

MacKenna's 'Plotinus' Stephen MacKenna (1888–1934), Irish classical scholar who translated Plotinus.

TO OLIVIA SHAKESPEAR, 2ND MARCH [1929]

p. 410 Auntille George Antheil (b. 1901), American composer of Polish descent, born in New Jersey. Studied under Ernest Bloch and spent some years in Europe as a professional pianist.

TO OLIVIA SHAKESPEAR, 27TH FEBRUARY [1934]

the Swāmi'[s] book Shri Purohit Swami was an Indian monk
whom Yeats helped in the thirties; he wrote prefaces to his translations
of the Upanishads. **old Budge's interview** Sir Ernest A. Wallis Budge
was a well-known egyptologist. The interview appeared in the *Daily
Express*, 17 January 1934. **'blue shirts'** Irish fascist organization led by
Eoin O'Duffy (1892–1944).

ESSAYS AND MYTHOLOGIES

A VISIONARY

p. 423 A Visionary this is a description of George Russell (AE), see
note, p. 520.

p. 424 Thomas of Erceldoune (*c.* 1220–97), seer and poet, traditional
source of many oracles.

RED HANRAHAN

p. 426 Hanrahan a character invented by Yeats; see 'The Tower',
Collected Poems, p. 220. **Samhain Eve** November Night,
November 1.

p. 427 Mary Lavelle a character invented by Yeats.

p. 432 Slieve Echtge Sliab Aughty, a hill near Lady Gregory's home,
Gort, Co. Galway.

THE DEATH OF HANRAHAN THE RED

p. 437 the Shee the Sidhe, gods of ancient Ireland.

p. 439 Castle Dargan a (ruined) castle in Sligo.

'DUST HATH CLOSED HELEN'S EYE'

p. 445 Raftery Anthony Raftery (1784–1834), blind Gaelic poet.

THE CHILD AND THE STATE

p. 452 Colonel Brase Colonel Fritz Brase (born in Germany, d. 1940) served German Army (1914–18), Director Irish Army School of Music (1923–40).

p. 454 Mr James Stephens see note, p. 530. **Mr Robin Flower** (1861–1946), English librarian and Celtic scholar, author of *The Irish Tradition*.

p. 455 Mr Standish O'Grady's see note, p. 519.

p. 457 Gentile Giovanni Gentile (1875–1944), Italian idealist philosopher.

SPEECH ON COPYRIGHT PROTECTION

p. 463 O'Connell Daniel O'Connell (1775–1847), Irish politician and orator.

p. 467 Azarin presumably Azorin, pen name of Spanish novelist and critic, José Martinez Ruiz (1874–1967). **Benavente** Jacinto Benavente y Martinez (1866–1954), Spanish dramatist, awarded the Nobel Prize in 1922. **Miguel de Unamuno** (1864–1936), Spanish philosopher and writer. **Hofmannsthal** Hugo von Hofmannsthal (1874–1929), German poet and dramatist, wrote librettos for Richard Strauss. **Maurice Maeterlinck** (1862–1949), Belgian poet and dramatist, author of *L'Oiseau Bleu* etc.

INTRODUCTION TO 'THE WORDS UPON THE WINDOW-PANE'

p. 469 Thomas Davis see note, p. 532. **J. F. Taylor** (*c.* 1850–1902) Irish orator and journalist. **Cowley** Abraham Cowley (1618–67), poet and essayist. **Smart's** Christopher Smart (1722–71), poet, author of 'Song to David'.

p. 470 Archbishop King see note, p. 542. **F. S. Oliver** (1864–1934), historian, author of *Endless Adventure* (1931).

p. 471 Leibniz Gottfried Wilhelm Leibniz (1646–1717), German philosopher and mathematician, discovered infinitesimal calculus at approximately the same period as Newton by a different method. **Grammont 'Memoirs': Memoires de la Vie du Comte de Gramont**, an anonymous work (1713), written by Anthony Hamilton, the Count's brother-in-law, edited by Walpole and later by Scott. They give information about the French and English courts of the time.

p. 472 Molyneux William Molyneux (1656–98), Irish MP, author of *The Case of Ireland Stated* (1698), the first declaration of the Irish case for independence.

p. 473 Arthur Young (1741–1820), unsuccessful farmer and agricultural theorist, author of *Tour in Ireland* and *Travels in France*. **Sir Jonah Barrington** see note, p. 541.

p. 474 Miss Edgeworth Maria Edgeworth (1767–1849), Irish regional novelist, author of *Castle Rackrent, The Absentee* etc.

p. 475 Miltiades (*c.* 550–489 BC), Athenian general, defeated the Persians at Marathon. **Aristides** (b. *c.* 520 BC), Athenian statesman, arranged quotas of Greek states and Confederacy of Delos, nicknamed 'The Just'. **Themistocles** (*c.* 528–462 BC), Athenian statesman, reputedly responsible for the victory against the Persians at Salamis. Later responsible for the naval policy which was the basis of the power of Athens. **Pericles** (495–429 BC), Athenian general and statesman, responsible for founding many colonies; in charge during the Peloponnesian war until death through plague. **Alcibiades** see note, p. 539. **Phocion** (fourth century BC), Athenian general and statesman, preserved peace with Philip and Alexander, condemned to death when democracy was restored in 318.

p. 476 Polybius (*c.* 205–*c.* 123 BC), Greek historian. **Giambattista Vico** Giovanni Battista Vico (1668–1744), Neopolitan philosopher and jurist.

p. 477 Sorel probably Georges Sorel (1847–1922), French syndicalist philosopher, a road engineer who, in middle age, turned to politics and became champion of Dreyfus. **Croce** Benedetto Croce (1866–1952), Italian philosopher and critic, author of *Filosofia dello Spirito*. **Gentile** see note, p. 547.

p. 478 Oswald Spengler (1880–1936), German philosopher, author of *The Decline of the West*. **Flinders Petrie** Sir William Matthews Flinders Petrie (1853–1942), English egyptologist; occupied the Chair of Egyptology at University College, London, 1892–1933. **Frobenius** Joannes Frobenius (1460–1527), German printer. **Henry Adams** (1838–1918), American man of letters, autobiographer. **Gerald Heard** (b. 1889), English writer, author of *The Ascent of Humanity*, *A New Hypothesis of Evolution* etc., and literary editor of the *Realist* (1929).

p. 479 Epaminondas (*c.* 418–362 BC), defeated Spartan supremacy by attacking at Leuctra with the deep left wing of the army in 371 BC; defeated them again at Mantineia but was fatally wounded in this battle. **Brutus** Marcus Junius Brutus (85–43 BC), joined Pompey in the Civil War, pardoned by Caesar, joined the conspiracy against him; he and Cassius were defeated at Philippi by Octavian and Antony, and he committed suicide. **Junius Brutus** Lucius Jun i us Brutus (d. 508 BC), legendary first consul of Rome, expelled the Tarquins. **Cato the Younger** Marcus Porcius Cato (95–46 BC), Stoic politician with a reputation for fairness. **Thomas More** Sir Thomas More (1478–1535), Lord Chancellor, 1529–32, executed in 1535; scholar, patron of art, author of *Utopia*, *History of Richard III* etc.

p. 481 Spinoza Benedict Spinoza (1632–77), Jewish philosopher, author of *Ethics* (1677); he denied personal immortality and the transcendental distinction between good and evil. **Lord Treasurer Harley** Robert Harley, first Earl of Oxford (1661–1724), British statesman who, in 1710, became Chancellor of the Exchequer. Dismissed from office in 1714 and sent to the Tower in 1715, but was acquitted by peers after two years. **imbecility or madness** Swift suffered from Ménière's disease. For an account of his medical history see T. G. Wilson, 'Swift's Personality and Death Masks', *Review of English Literature*, July 1962. **Lord Chesterfield** (1694–1773), statesman and diplomat.

p. 482 Stella Swift's name for Esther Johnson (d. 1728) whom he met in Sir William Temple's house when he was secretary there; they remained close friends until her death, and he was buried by her side in St Patrick's Cathedral. **Strabo** (*c.* 63 BC–?) author of a history which continues that of Polybius, and of a historical geography of the Roman Empire. **Vanessa** Swift's name for Esther Vanhomrigh (1690–1723), whom he met in London in 1708; she fell in love with him and Swift's poem *Cadenus and Vanessa* records their unhappy relationship.

p. 483 Lecky William Edward Hartpole Lecky (1838–1903), Irish historian, author of *History of Rationalism*, *History of England* etc. **Varina** Swift's name for Jane Waring. **Mr Shane Leslie** (b. 1885), Irish critic and man of letters.

p. 484 Dr Delaney Dr Patrick Delaney (1684–1768), Dean of Down, friend and executor of Swift, on whom he wrote a book. **Sheridan** Rev. Thomas Sheridan (1687–1738), Irish schoolmaster, scholar and friend of Swift.

p. 485 John Corbet character in Yeats's play. **Hayley** William Hayley (1745–1820), poet, biographer and autobiographer, friend of Cowper and Blake. **Marat** Jean Paul Marat (1743–93), French revolutionary politician. **May Craig** Irish actress.

p. 486 Eusapia Palladino Laurence Benedict Palladino (1837–1927), Italian–American Roman Catholic missionary. **Ochorowicz** Julijan Ochorowicz (d. 1917). **Moody's** Dwight Lyman Moody (1837–99), American evangelist, part compiler of *Sacred Songs and Solos* with Ira David Sankey.

p. 487 Glanvil Joseph Glanvil (1636–80), clergyman and savant, attacked scholasticism in *The Vanity of Dogmatizing* (1661).

p. 488 Brancusi Constantin Brancusi (1876–1957), Romanian sculptor.

p. 489 César de Vesme editor of the *Annals of Psychical Sense*. His book *Storia dello Spiritismo* (1896) was published in an English translation as *A History of Experimental Spiritualism* in 1931.

p. 490 those two Oxford ladies Charlotte Anne Elizabeth Moberly (1846–1937), Principal of St Hugh's College, Oxford (1886–1915) and Eleanor Frances Jourdain (d. 1924), Principal of St Hugh's College (1915–24).

INTRODUCTION TO 'A VISION'

p. 491 'Per Amica Silentia Lunae' title of a volume of essays by Yeats, published in 1918.

p. 492 John Stuart Mill's (1806–73), the utilitarian philosopher, logician and political economist. **Sir William Hamilton** (1805–65), Irish mathematician. **Cabbalistic imagery** the Cabbalah or Kabbala, Hebrew writings preserved by occultists since the Middle Ages; they blend cosmogony and explanations of Biblical material.

p. 493 the Pythagorean numbers Pythagoras, Greek philosopher, who lived in the sixth century BC. He assigned a mathematical basis to the universe and musical principles were prominent in his system. **Kelly** possibly Hugh Kelly (1739–77), an Irishman who wrote three comedies including *The School for Wives* (1773). **Dr Dee's** John Dee (1527–1608), English alchemist. His works deal with logic, mathematics, astrology, alchemy, geography and the calendar. **Law's Boehme** William Law (1686–1761), mystic, author of treatises on practical Christian morality, became influenced by Boehme, whose work he translated. **'the pulsation of an artery'** probably a reference to Blake's poem 'Time' which uses the phrase 'pulsation of the artery' referred to by Yeats and Ellis in their edition of Blake's *Works* (1893), I, 278.

p. 494 Brancusi see note above.

AD 1 TO AD 1050

p. 495 the Thebaid district of Egypt, known for Christian monks and hermits.

p. 498 Constantine Constantine the Great (306–37), Roman Emperor, converted to Christianity, transferred the capital of the Empire to Byzantium and renamed it Constantinople.

p. 499 Ammonius Sacca (*c.* 175–242), Greek philosopher, founder of Neoplatonic philosophy and teacher of Plotinus. **Origen** (*c.* 185–253), followed Clement as second thinker of the Alexandrian school; his theories on reincarnation were rejected by the Church.

p. 500 Justinian Justinian I (483–565), Emperor of Constantinople (527–65), built St Sophia, drew up a code of Roman law and was successful in war.

p. 502 Strzygowski Josef Strzygowski (1862–1941), Austrian historian and art critic. **Xenaias** also known as Philoxenus, a Syrian theologian, appointed Bishop of Hierapolis by Zeno in 485, exiled to Cappadocia by Justinian I and later put to death there. He translated the Gospels into Syrian.

p. 503 Johannes Scotus Erigena (*c.* 1265–1308?), realistic philosopher, whose followers dominated scholasticism until the 16th century.

WHAT WE DID OR TRIED TO DO

p. 505 the Treaty Stone of Limerick the Treaty of Limerick (1691), signed between Sarsfield and William's commander Ginkle after the second siege of Limerick.

p. 506 King Brian Brian Boramha (926–1014), King of Leinster, killed by the Danes in the Battle of Clontarf, which checked their inroads. **Gustavus Vasa** Gustavus I of Sweden (1496–1560).

p. 507 Charles Shannon see note, p. 539. **Albert Power** (1883–1945), Irish sculptor. **Oliver Sheppard** (d. 1941), Irish sculptor. **Jerome Connor** (b. 1875), Irish sculptor. **Carl Milles** (1875–1955), Swedish sculptor, especially renowned as a designer of fountains. **Ivan Mestrovic** (1883–1962), Yugoslav sculptor; a shepherd boy who was taught woodcarving by his father and eventually studied in Vienna and Paris. Designed the National Temple at Kossovo; lived in England during the First World War and designed many war memorials.

James E. Fraser (1876–1953), American sculptor. **Publio Morbiducci** (1889–1937), Italian sculptor.

p. 508 S. W. Carline Sydney William Carline (1888–1929), English landscape and portrait painter. **Percy Metcalfe** (b. 1895), English sculptor who designed Irish coinage.

p. 509 Sheppard's 'O'Leary' see note, p. 519.

p. 510 Power's 'Kettle' statue of Thomas Kettle (1880–1916), Irish author and politician, killed in action in France. **Connor's 'Emmet'** statue of Robert Emmet (1778–1803), Irish patriot executed for leading rebellion.

PRELIMINARIES

p. 512 the Lord Mayor Alderman Alfred Byrne (1882–1956), Senator of the Irish Free State (1928–31) Lord Mayor of Dublin (1930–39; 1954–5).

p. 514 'John Bull's Other Island' play by Shaw.

p. 515 President Cosgrave William T. Cosgrave (1880–1965), President of Executive Council, Irish Free State (1922–32). **Andrew Jameson** (1855–1941), Irish banker and industrialist, High Sheriff of Co. Dublin 1902; Senator of Irish Free State (1922–6). **Gogarty** Oliver St John Gogarty (1878–1959), Irish doctor, Senator, poet and wit.

p. 518 Miss O'Neill Maire O'Neill (d. 1952), Irish actress (sister of Sara Allgood) Synge's fiancée. She married G. H. Mair. **Kerrigan** J. M. Kerrigan, an Abbey actor who played in the theatre in the 1920s and left the company in the 1930s in the United States. **Frank Fay . . . William Fay** two brothers who played an important role in the history of the Abbey Theatre. **Ninette de Valois** (b. 1898), stage name of Edris Stannus, British ballerina, born in Ireland; Director of Ballet at the Abbey Theatre, later at Sadler's Wells.

SELECT BIBLIOGRAPHY

Yeats's criticism occurs in various places in his prose writings, and can be found in his reviews, articles, essays and letters, as well as in *A Vision*, and his Senate speeches. The introductions and notes to editions of his own work and to anthologies and selections or editions of the work of other writers also contain his views on life and literature. For fuller details the reader is advised to consult Allan Wade, *A Bibliography of the Writings of W. B. Yeats* (3rd ed., 1968).

WORKS CONTAINING CRITICISM

The Collected Works in Verse and Prose of William Butler Yeats (8 vols, 1908)

Letters to the New Island (ed. Horace Reynolds, 1934)

A Vision (1937)

On the Boiler (1939)

Letters on Poetry from W. B. Yeats to Dorothy Wellesley (1940; 1964)

Letters to Katharine Tynan (ed. Roger McHugh, 1953)

W. B. Yeats and T. Sturge Moore. Their Correspondence (ed. Ursula Bridge, 1953)

Letters (ed. Allan Wade, 1954)

Autobiographies (1956)

The Variorum Edition of the Poems of W. B. Yeats (ed. Peter Allt and Russell K. Alspach, 1957). Contains introductions and notes to volumes of Yeats's poetry.

Mythologies (1959)

The Senate Speeches of W. B. Yeats (ed. Donald R. Pearce, 1960)

Essays and Introductions (1961)

Explorations (1962)

The Variorum Edition of the Plays of W. B. Yeats (ed. Russell K. Alspach, 1966). Contains introductions and notes to Yeats's volumes of plays.

Uncollected Prose by W. B. Yeats (vol. 1, ed. John P. Frayne, 1970). This contains Yeats's first reviews and articles from 1886 to 1896, and will be followed by a further volume of similar material.

BIOGRAPHICAL AND CRITICAL STUDIES OF YEATS

Joseph Hone, *W. B. Yeats 1865–1939* (1943; rev. ed., 1963)

A. Norman Jeffares, *Yeats: Man and Poet* (1949; rev. ed., 1962)

Birgit Bjersby, *The Interpretation of the Cuchulain Legend in the Works of W. B. Yeats* (1950)

T. R. Henn, *The Lonely Tower* (1950; rev. ed., 1965)

G. B. Saul, *Prolegomena to the Plays of W. B. Yeats* (1958)

F. A. C. Wilson, *W. B. Yeats and Tradition* (1958)

F. A. C. Wilson, *Yeats's Iconography* (1960)

A. G. Stock, *W. B. Yeats. His Poetry and Thought* (1961; rev. ed., 1964)

A. Norman Jeffares (ed.), *A Review of English Literature* [Yeats number] (July 1963)

Peter Ure, *Yeats* [in Writers and Critics Series] (1963)

Peter Ure, *Yeats the Playwright* (1963)

Helen Vendler, *Yeats's Vision and the Later Plays* (1963)

Denis Donoghue (ed.), *The Integrity of Yeats* (1964)

Edward Engelberg, *The Vast Design* (1964)

M. C. Bradbrook, *English Dramatic Form: A History of its Development* (1965)

Curtis Bradford, *Yeats at Work* (1965)

S. B. Bushrui, *Yeats's Verse-Plays: The Revisions 1900–1910* (1965)

Denis Donoghue and J. R. Mulryne (eds.), *An Honoured Guest: New Essays on W. B. Yeats* (1965)

A. Norman Jeffares and K. G. W. Cross (eds.), *In Excited Reverie* (1965)

D. E. S. Maxwell and S. B. Bushrui (eds.), *W. B. Yeats 1865–1965: Centenary Essays* (1965)

Shotaro Oshima, *W. B. Yeats and Japan* (1965)

B. Rajan, *W. B. Yeats: A Critical Introduction* (1956)

Corinna Salvadori, *Yeats and Castiglione: Poet and Courtier* (1965)

Robin Skelton and Ann Saddlemyer (eds.), *The World of W. B. Yeats* (1965)

Alex Zwerdling, *Yeats and the Heroic Ideal* (1965)

Donald T. Torchiana, *W. B. Yeats and Georgian Ireland* (1966)

A. Norman Jeffares, *A Commentary on the Collected Poems of W. B. Yeats* (1968)

Joseph Ronsley, *Yeats's Autobiography. Life as Symbolic Pattern* (1968)

Austin Clarke, *The Celtic Twilight and the Nineties* (1969)